A History of DUMFRIES and GALLOWAY

Sir Herbert Maxwell,
BART., M.P.

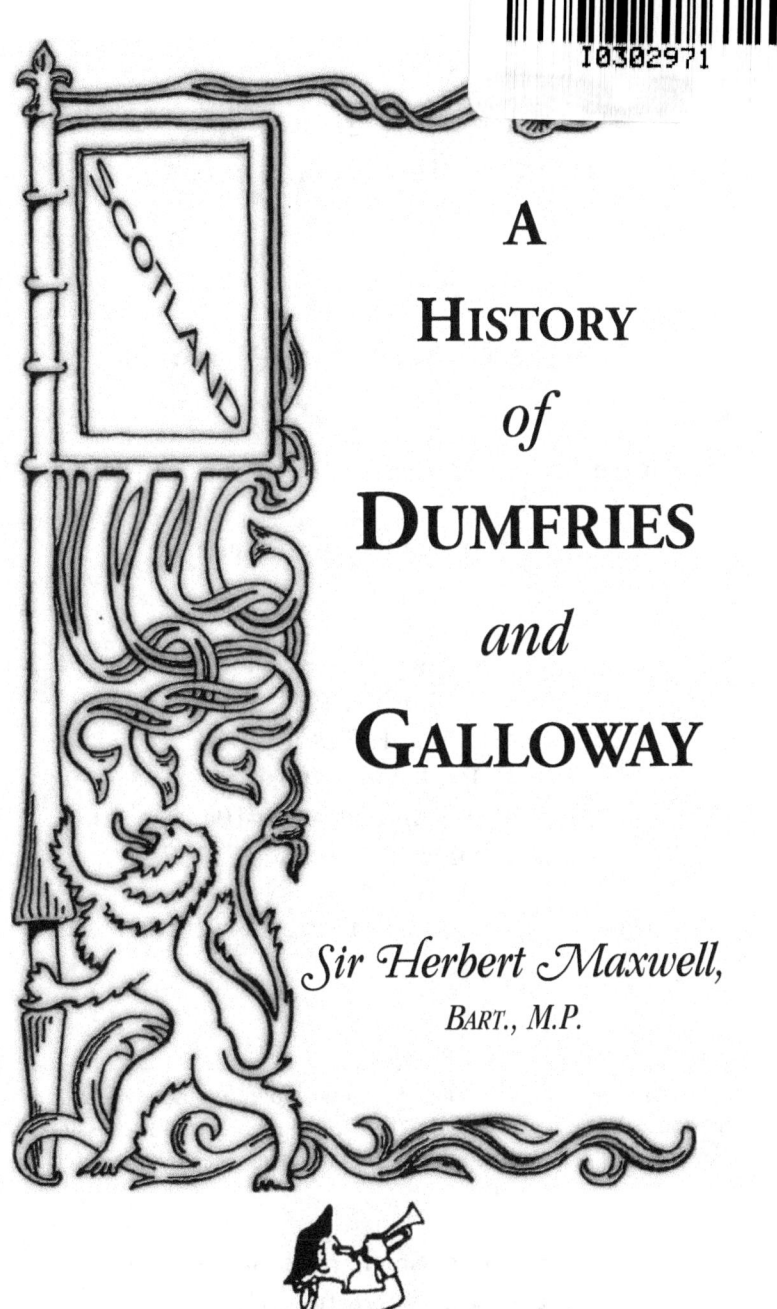

HERITAGE BOOKS
2011

HERITAGE BOOKS
AN IMPRINT OF HERITAGE BOOKS, INC.

Books, CDs, and more—Worldwide

For our listing of thousands of titles see our website
at
www.HeritageBooks.com

A Facsimile Reprint
Published 2011 by
HERITAGE BOOKS, INC.
Publishing Division
100 Railroad Ave. #104
Westminster, Maryland 21157

Copyright © 1896 Sir Herbert Maxwell, Bart., M.P.

— Publisher's Notice —
In reprints such as this, it is often not possible to remove blemishes from the original. We feel the contents of this book warrant its reissue despite these blemishes and hope you will agree and read it with pleasure.

International Standard Book Numbers
Paperbound: 978-0-7884-0756-7
Clothbound: 978-0-7884-8851-1

A HISTORY

OF

DUMFRIES AND GALLOWAY

BY

SIR HERBERT MAXWELL, Bart., M.P.

AUTHOR OF 'THE TOPOGRAPHY OF GALLOWAY,' ETC.

WILLIAM BLACKWOOD AND SONS
EDINBURGH AND LONDON
MDCCCXCVI

THIS VOLUME IS DEDICATED

to

JOHN HAMILTON DALRYMPLE,

TENTH

EARL OF STAIR, K.T., LL.D.,

Lord Lieutenant of Ayrshire and Wigtownshire, who, by his personal qualities, has added to the hereditary honours of his house the affectionate respect of all who know him.

INTRODUCTION.

So many writers have already dealt with the history of the district forming the subject of the following chapters, that some justification must be attempted for going over the ground again.

One of two different objects, it seems to me, ought to be kept in view in compiling a summary of the history of any province. On the one hand, a writer may devote himself to collecting and repeating the traditions lingering among the people, and transcribing events from the narratives of former chroniclers, without making too searching inquiry into the evidence on which they rest. On the other hand, he may venture to reject such local lore as will not endure critical analysis, and, working in the light of the research which during the last two centuries has been so patiently and fruitfully directed on the records of the past, apply himself to sift what is authentic from what rests only on hearsay, and confine himself to preparing what shall be a concise and trustworthy, even though it may be a dry, narrative of such events as are capable of historic proof.

It is the latter of these objects that I have set before me. Recent and abler writers have yielded to the fascination of romantic legend and shadowy tradition, and if, as is not unlikely, disappointment be encountered by those who shall search these pages in vain for such charming incidents as that of Bruce and the Spider, or such blood-curdling episodes as the execution of Maclellan of Bomby by the Black Douglas, my excuse lies in the absence of satisfactory evidence to the alleged facts. The bias of early historians may be traced in the contradictory accounts they give of the same incidents, and the dawn of literature in our land was too feeble to allow fables, errors, or falsehoods to be "nailed to the counter" at once. Indeed it is not the nature of these myths to spring into existence full-feathered. They are the product of slow incubation and gradual fledging. The wild stories told by Blind Harry about Wallace, and by Boece and Buchanan about Bruce, have no place in the earlier chronicles. Statements in the chronicles themselves must often be taken with great reserve; with how much greater reserve must those stores be accepted which have passed from lip to lip of generations, without even the frail check upon human prejudice and passion which is provided by the printing-press and editor's desk.

But the time is not unfitting for an impartial and dispassionate review of the course of events and social change in Dumfriesshire and Galloway, concise enough to be within reach of those connected with the south-west, conscientious enough to be relied on as a textbook for easy reference, and leaving undisturbed, save where necessity arises for dispelling fallacy, the accumulations of fable and tradition which have gathered over the past.

The ballad literature of the south-west is so profuse and picturesque, and so closely woven into the true story of our country, that I have found it difficult to refrain from quoting it at greater length than I have done. But to have indulged in wide excursions in the field so thoroughly worked by Allan Cunningham, Sir Walter Scott, and the late Professor Veitch, would have swelled the present work far beyond its prescribed scope and size.

The narrative has not been brought beyond the close of the eighteenth century, because no one requiring information about events since that time need be at any loss for authoritative records. The changes during the present century have, indeed, been sweeping and rapid, but they have not been violent, and to trace their course would take a great part of the space which I have thought it better economy to devote to those centuries where the light is less full and more conflicting. But in spite of the alteration brought about in the outward aspect of the country by improved agriculture and the development of railways, and in the social condition of its inhabitants by education and by a franchise repeatedly extended, the southwestern counties of Scotland have not lost all traces of earlier ages. Witness to the continuity of its ethnology is borne by the prevalence among the population of the old Gaelic or Pictish nomenclature, mixed with a strong leaven of Anglo-Saxon and some traces of Scandinavian names.

Were I to name all the writers, living and departed, to whom I have been indebted for much of the information presented in these pages, the list would be a very long one. It must not be supposed that I am insensible to the advantage derived from their labours because I have not mentioned all of them by name. But the labours of three students in particular have brought to light such a mass of documentary evidence bearing on the course of events from the thirteenth to the end of the sixteenth century, that I cannot refrain from acknowledging the extent to which I have availed myself of their compilations. These are Sir Francis Palgrave, whose volume on 'Documents and Records illustrating the History of Scotland' was published by the Commissioners of Public Records in 1837; Mr Joseph Bain, who edited the four volumes of the 'Calendar of Documents relating to Scotland,' 1881-88; and the Rev. Joseph Stevenson, whose two volumes of 'Historical Documents relating to Scotland' appeared in 1870.[1]

Mr J. H. Starke of Troqueer Holm, Dumfries, has been at the pains to go over the proofs. Much assistance was rendered by the late Mr Allardyce in revising the earlier chapters. In his death, which took place while the work was in the press, we have

[1] These works are referred to in the text under the names of Palgrave, Bain, and Stevenson respectively.

to lament the loss of one who had acquired an extraordinary store of knowledge of the history of his country. In compiling the bibliography valuable help was rendered by Mr Starke, Mr M. M. Harper of Castle Douglas, and Mr Alexander Waugh of Newton-Stewart.

CONTENTS.

CHAPTER I.

FROM THE INVASION OF AGRICOLA, A.D. 79, TO THE BUILDING OF THE WALL OF ANTONINE, A.D. 140 . . . 1

CHAPTER II.

FROM THE BUILDING OF THE WALL OF ANTONINE, A.D. 140, TO THE CLOSE OF THE NORSE DOMINION . . 22

NOTE A. MAGNUM MONASTERIUM 46

CHAPTER III.

FROM THE DEATH OF MALCOLM CANMORE IN 1092 TO THE INTRODUCTION OF THE FEUDAL SYSTEM IN 1234 . 47

CHAPTER IV.

FROM THE DEATH OF ALAN OF GALLOWAY IN 1234 TO THE CORONATION OF ROBERT DE BRUS IN 1306 . . 62

NOTE B. THE CASTLE OF DUMFRIES . . . 101
NOTE C. THE BRUCE PEDIGREE 102
NOTE D. THE MACDOUALLS 103

CHAPTER V.

FROM THE BATTLE OF BANNOCKBURN IN 1314 TO THE FALL OF THE HOUSE OF DOUGLAS IN 1452 . . . 106

   NOTE E. THE LOCHMABEN STONE 132

CHAPTER VI.

FROM THE FALL OF THE HOUSE OF DOUGLAS IN 1452 TO THE BATTLE OF FLODDEN IN 1513 136

CHAPTER VII.

FROM THE BATTLE OF FLODDEN IN 1513 TO THE TREATY OF NORHAM IN 1550 158

   NOTE F. THE CLANS ON THE WEST MARCHES . . 183
   NOTE G. MONITION OF CURSING AGAINST THE BORDER CLANS 186

CHAPTER VIII.

FROM THE REFORMATION IN 1560 TO 1598 . . . 190

CHAPTER IX.

FEUD BETWEEN THE MAXWELLS AND THE JOHNSTONES, FROM 1572 TO 1620 204

CHAPTER X.

FROM 1598 TO THE BATTLE OF PHILIPHAUGH IN 1645 . . 227

   NOTE H. BLAEU'S GEOGRAPHY 253

CHAPTER XI.

FROM THE SURRENDER OF CHARLES I. IN 1646 TO THE DEATH OF CHARLES II. IN 1685 255

   NOTE I. ECCLESIASTICAL DISCIPLINE . . . 289

CHAPTER XII.

FROM THE REVOLUTION IN 1688 TO THE STUART RISING IN 1715   291

    NOTE K. CONDITION OF THE SOUTH-WESTERN COUNTIES IN THE SEVENTEENTH CENTURY 313

CHAPTER XIII.

FROM THE JACOBITE COLLAPSE IN 1715 TO THE CLOSE OF THE CENTURY 318

    NOTE L. THE JACOBITE RISING OF 1745 . . . 360

LIST OF BOOKS RELATING TO, OR PUBLISHED IN, DUMFRIES-SHIRE AND GALLOWAY 363
PRINCIPAL MAPS OF DUMFRIESSHIRE AND GALLOWAY . . 400
INDEX 403

LIST OF MAPS.

ANANDALE, EUSDALE OR ESKDALE, AND LIDDESDALE . *p.* 320
From Moll's Atlas, 1725.

DUMFRIES OR NITHISDALE . . . . *p.* 324
From Moll's Atlas, 1725.

WIGTOWN, KIRKCUDBRIGHT, AND DUMFRIES { *In pocket at end of volume.*
From the Ordnance Survey.

DUMFRIESSHIRE AND GALLOWAY.

CHAPTER I.

FROM THE INVASION OF AGRICOLA, A.D. 79, TO THE BUILDING OF THE WALL OF ANTONINE, A.D. 140.

WHEN that excellent soldier Julius Agricola arrived during the summer of A.D. 78 to take command of the Roman forces in Great Britain, he found the whole of what are now the southern and midland English counties, as well as South Wales, included in the Roman province. It is uncertain where the northern frontier had been drawn, and how far the powerful tribe of Brigantes had been driven out of their possessions in Lancashire and Yorkshire. War had been carried on with the Brigantes, the principal opponents of the Roman advance in the north, since Publius Ostorius, governor of Britain, first came in contact with them about A.D. 50. Students of history have put greatly varying interpretations on the description given by Tacitus of the operations of Agricola; but they all agree that, immediately on his arrival, he marched against the Ordovices in the west, and conquered North Wales and Anglesea before going into winter quarters.

It was probably during the summer of 79 (though here again interpreters greatly differ) that operations were directed against the Selgovæ, a branch of the Brigantes dwelling on the north shore of the Solway as far as the Nith, occupying what is now Dumfriesshire; and beyond them to the west of that river, which Ptolemy called the Novios, against the Novantæ.

The name Selgovæ or Elgovæ has been compared with the Gaelic *sealg* (shallug), in its aspirated form *shealg* (hallug), the chase, suggesting that this tribe was known as "the Hunters." No more reliance may be placed on this than is due to a plausible guess. It is possible, however, that in Ptolemy's Selgovæ exists a form of the name now written Solway, formerly Sulwe. But the only Gaelic name for this estuary preserved to us is that found in the Irish Life of Adamnan, where an account is given of Adamnan's mission to Saxonland in 687 to recover some Irish captives. "Adamnan went to demand the prisoners, and put in at *Tracht Romra*. The strand is long, and the flood rapid—so rapid, that if the best steed in Saxonland, ridden by the best horseman, were to start from the edge of the tide when it begins to flow, he could only bring his rider ashore by swimming, so extensive is the strand and so impetuous is the tide." *Tracht* is the Gaelic *tragh*, a strand, but the meaning of *Romra* is lost. The Solway corresponds with Ptolemy's Ituna Æstusis, estuary of the Ituna or Eden (?).

As for the name Novantæ, it is evidently formed from the river Novios, just as Bæda, six centuries later, wrote of this western tribe as Niduarii—people of the Nid or Nith.

Agricola seems, then, to have subdued the Selgovæ and Novantæ, and introduced them to some of the customs of civilisation, before carrying his arms in the following season of

80 against a different race;[1] although some historians have interpreted a passage in Tacitus to mean that the Selgovæ and Novantæ were not dealt with until Agricola's fifth season's campaign. The statement of Tacitus is as follows: "In the fifth year of Agricola's expeditions, having first embarked on board ship, he subdued in many successful encounters tribes unknown before that time, and that part of Britain which looks towards Ireland." Now this could only refer to one of two parts of the coast of North Britain—namely, the Rhinns of Galloway and the promontory of Cantyre—the only parts of Scotland from which Ireland is plainly visible. When it is considered that Agricola's operations in his fourth campaign were chiefly confined to strengthening by a line of forts[2] the northern frontier of the territory annexed to the province in the campaign of the third summer, a frontier which was drawn from the Forth near Borrowstounness to Old Kilpatrick on the Clyde, it is much more likely that, as Skene believed, he crossed the Firth of Clyde in his fifth summer, and, marching through Cowal and Cantyre, viewed Ireland from the shores of the Atlantic, than that he so long delayed the conquest of Galloway.[3] He was far too skilful a master of strategy to have left the warlike Selgovæ and Novantæ to threaten his line of communication. Besides, Tacitus uses an expression in describing the advance in the second summer which implies that it lay along the sea-coast rather than through the heart of the country,—*æstuaria ac silvas ipse prætentare*— to feel his way in person among the estuaries and forests —exactly describing progress along the Solway towards the Irish Sea.

On the whole, therefore, the most probable interpretation

---

[1] "Novas gentes aperuit."—Tacitus.
[2] "Quod tum præsidiis firmabatur."—Tacitus.
[3] Celtic Scotland, vol. i. p. 47.

of the chronology of Tacitus indicates the subjugation of Dumfriesshire and Galloway as the work of Agricola's second season in Britain.

Over the ethnography of Selgovæ and Novantæ much controversy has taken place. It is probable that on the shores of Solway, as in the rest of the British Isles, there was at one time an aboriginal race, small and dark-haired, which early Greek writers describe as being replaced by the larger-limbed, fairer-skinned Celts. The early Irish historical legends contain numerous allusions to this people, generally known as Firbolg. But as it cannot be affirmed that any trace of these has been identified, either in the traditions or sepulchral remains of this particular district, further speculation about them is for the present futile. The fairest inference from the majority of place-names in Novantia—now Galloway—as well as from the oldest recorded personal names, is that it was long inhabited by people of the Goidelic or Gaelic branch of Celts, speaking the same language, no doubt with some dialectic variation, as the natives of Ireland and the rest of what is now Scotland.[4] The Cymric or Welsh speech, which was afterwards diffused among the Britons of Dumfriesshire and Strathclyde, did not prevail to dislodge innumerable place-names in the Goidelic language which still remain within the territory of the Strathclyde Britons. That the people who dwelt longest in Galloway spoke neither the Welsh form of Celtic nor the Pictish dialect of Gaelic, may be inferred from the absence of any certain traces of either of these languages among their names of places. Yet, as will be shown hereafter, they bore the name of Picts long after it had

[4] Reginald of Durham, writing in the twelfth century, has preserved one word of Galloway Pictish. He says that certain clerics of Kirkcudbright were called *scollofthes* in the language of the Picts. This is a rendering of the Latin *scolasticus*, differing not greatly from the Erse and Gaelic *scolog*, more widely from the Welsh *yscolheic*.

fallen into disuse in other parts of Scotland. They were Picts, yet not the same as northern Picts dwelling beyond the Mounth, nor as the southern Picts dwelling between the Mounth and the Forth; Gaels, yet not of one brotherhood with other Gaels — a distinction emphasised by the name given to them of *Gallgaidhel* or stranger Gaels. This term became in the Welsh speech *Gallwyddel* (*dd* sounds like *th* in " this "), whence the name of Galloway, which still denotes the Stewartry of Kirkcudbright and the shire or county of Wigtown.

Not much light is thrown on the early ethnography of this part of Scotland by the geography of Claudius Ptolemæus, who surveyed the country at the beginning of the second century, and probably derived much of his information from those who served under Agricola and his successors in command; nevertheless a large proportion of the place-names given by him are obviously Latinised or Hellenised versions of Celtic. Thus, of the four towns assigned by Ptolemy to the Selgovæ, Trimontium, corresponding in position to Birrenswark, where remains of both native and Roman earthworks may be traced, has been commonly applied to the Eildon Hills, from the irresistible suggestion of *tres montes*, triple peak. But the prefix is far more likely to be the common Gaelic *treamh*, or Welsh *tre* or *tref*, and the name was probably in Welsh *tre mynydd*, or in Gaelic *treamh monaidh*, signifying " hill village."[5] Uxellon, near the mouth of the Nith, was probably Wardlaw Hill,[6] and is a Greek rendering of the Welsh *uchel*, high, which remains in such names as Ochiltree,[7]

---

[5] The same prefix occurs in Troqueer, Traquair, Terregles (formerly Travereaglis), and many other names in this district.

[6] Wardlaw, the watch-hill: in later years the rallying-place of the Maxwells, wardens of the Western Marches, whose slogan was " Bide Wardlaw ! "

[7] *Uchel tre*, high village or farm.

the Ochils, &c. Corda appears to have been Sanquhar, and to retain as a prefix the same syllable *caer*, which the modern name bears as a suffix.[8] Carbantorigon, assigned by Ptolemy to a position between the Nith and the Dee, also contains the syllable *caer* or *cathair* (caher), and may possibly be the notable earthwork now known as the Moat of Urr, or, locally, as the King's Mount.

Unluckily for our knowledge of the ancient topography of Galloway, the distribution of the tribes bordering on the Solway, and the situation of the chief strongholds, Ptolemy's survey was dislocated by an extraordinary blunder, affecting the south-west of Scotland more severely than any other part of the British Isles. All that part of the island of Britain lying north of the Tweed is canted at right angles to the rest towards the east; *Novantum chersonesus*, now the Rhinns of Galloway, is made to lie towards the north-east instead of south by west, and the extremity of it, *Novantum promontorium*, now the Mull of Galloway, is made to appear the northernmost point of Caledonia instead of the southernmost. It is as though maps of South and North Britain had been drawn on separate sheets and afterwards pasted together, the sheet of North Britain being laid sidewise instead of endwise. To put this right, the geographer has exaggerated the length of the Solway Firth from 70 to nearly 200 miles.[9]

Making due allowance for this derangement of distances and inversion of the points of the compass, it is still possible to recognise some of the chief features, natural and artificial. To the north, as Ptolemy put it, but really to the west, of Novius or the Nith, is Deva or the Kirkcudbright Dee. Then

---

[8] Sanquhar=Gaelic, *sean cathair* (caher), old fortress, a name which indicates its antiquity, even in Gaelic times, as a place of defence.

[9] See "Analysis of the Ptolemaic Geography of Scotland," by the late Captain F. W. L. Thomas, R.N., in the Proceedings of the Society of Antiquaries of Scotland, vols. xi. and xii.

comes Ienæ Æstuarium, as it is written in later editions, corresponding with Wigtown Bay; but, as Skene has pointed out,[1] this is rendered Fines Æstus by the earlier copyists, and may possibly denote the limit or *finis* of Agricola's advance in his second campaign. It is noteworthy that the river forming this estuary and dividing the county of Wigtown from the Stewartry of Kirkcudbright is called at this day the Cree, written Creth in the thirteenth century, a name which seems to be formed of the Gaelic *crioch* (creegh), a boundary. The next river mentioned is named Abravannus, corresponding with the Luce, flowing into Abravannus Sinus or Luce Bay. This is obviously a Latinised form of the Gaelic *aber amhuinn* (avun), mouth of the river. The last inlet within the confines of Galloway is Rerigonius Sinus, of which name, Rerigon, a contracted form, survives in Loch Ryan.[2]

Besides Carbantorigon, which seems to have been actually within the territory of the Novantæ, though assigned by Ptolemy to the Selgovæ, two other towns (πόλεις or *oppida*) are given by him as belonging to the first-named tribe—Λουκοπιβία or Lucopibia, on the eastern promontory of Wigtownshire, and Rhetigonium, obviously intended for Rerigonium, standing on the shore of Rerigonius Sinus or Loch Ryan. Camden identified Lucopibia with Whithorn—and perhaps he was right, for within a mile of that town is a well-preserved Roman camp, the only one remaining in Wigtownshire; but he is led far astray when he goes on to account for the modern name, Whithorn, the Anglo-Saxon *hwit ærn*, as arising out of Lucopibia.[3] That was conferred two hundred

---

[1] Celtic Scotland, vol. i. p. 66, note.
[2] The lake or ford of Reon, in the early Welsh poems.
[3] "Neirunto this (Vigtoune) Ptolemee placed the city Leucophibia, therafter the episcopall seat of St Ninian, wich Beda calleth Candida Casa, and wee now in this same sense Whithorne. What say you then if Ptolemee, after his maner, translated that name in Greeke λευκα οικιδια,

ROMAN REMAINS.

and fifty years later than Ptolemy's day, when Ninian built his church of St Martin, which Ailred said was the first building of stone and lime in Britain. Of course this could only be said truly of that particular part of Britain, where it is likely enough that the novel structure would earn the title of White House or Candida Casa, from its contrast with the dark native dwellings of mud and wattle.

Too much reliance, however, must not be placed on the exact localities indicated by Ptolemy, because, besides the exaggeration of distances in the Solway district, which makes it necessary to divide every measurement by three, the unit of his notation was usually ten miles, so that there is uncertainty in the exact position of every town to the extent of nineteen miles.

Skene observes that "the remains of the numerous Roman camps and stations which are still to be seen in this district, comprising the counties of Dumfries, Kirkcudbright, and Wigtown, attest the extent to which Agricola had penetrated through that country and garrisoned it with Roman troops."[4] Herein this usually cautious writer has been betrayed into a statement which will not bear investigation. In Dumfriesshire there are, indeed, several remains of Roman work, but in Galloway those which can with certainty be assigned to that nation are few and far between. The rectangular intrenchments at Dunrod, Carse Moat, and Carminnow, in the Stewartry of Kirkcudbright, seem to be Roman work, but they are very small, and could only accommodate detached companies; and the camp at Rispain, near Whithorn, was probably not constructed for more than 300 or 400 legionaries,

that is, Whitt-houses (instead whereof the transcribers have thrust upone us Leucophibia), wich the picts termed Candida Casa." — Camden's Britannia.

[4] Celtic Scotland, vol. i. p. 43.

with auxiliaries, or 1000 men in all. No Roman road, such as invariably marked permanent occupation, has been traced west of the Nith, nor is there any evidence to justify the name of Roman attached to a fine bridge thrown across the Minnock near Minniwick. No road or trace of pavement is visible on either side of it, where the unbroken heath stretches for miles, and the most that can be said is that the bold arch and solid masonry recall the character of undoubted Roman work elsewhere. The intractable nature of the native stone of Galloway, hard Silurian greywacke and granite, might account for the absence of Roman inscriptions; nothing of Roman manufacture has yet turned up within the province save portable objects of metal or pottery, such as might be stolen or taken in barter by the natives.

On the whole, therefore, there is negative evidence to weigh against the prolonged occupation of Galloway by the Romans, though, as will be seen, it was nominally part of the province until their final departure from Britain, and troops were sent on service there from time to time. The infrequency of Roman remains in Galloway is all the more significant in the presence of abundant traces of native habitations and strongholds. In no part of Britain are there greater numbers of hill-forts, mote-hills, earthworks, burial cairns, hut-circles, and lake-dwellings. Implements of stone, bronze, and iron, ornaments of gold, bronze, and earthenware, have been recovered in great numbers from almost every parish; but the objects of Roman manufacture hitherto discovered in Galloway have been out of all proportion to native productions. Everything points to the presence of a numerous native population for a prolonged period; and although much uncertainty must always prevail as to the approximate dates of dwellings and manufactured objects surviving from the time before Scotland became united under one crown, diligent antiquaries have of late years recovered unmistakable evidence of the mode of life among the natives during the Roman occupation.

But if the Romans have left few traces of permanent occupation in the country of the Novantæ or Atecott Picts, evidence of their former presence is more abundant in that of the Selgovæ. There are, indeed, no remains of the importance of those underlying the neighbouring city of Luguvallium (Carlisle), and lying along the course of Hadrian's great wall, but the earthworks on Birrens attest the former presence of a large body of imperial troops for a prolonged period.[5]

On the Ordnance Survey maps of Dumfriesshire various fragments of ancient highways are marked as Roman. These

---

[5] While these pages were being written in the summer of 1895, a systematic exploration of the Roman camp at Birrens was being conducted by the Society of Scottish Antiquaries, under the direction of Dr Christison and Dr Macdonald. A full report on the important discoveries made last year, as well as those of previous years, will appear in the volume of the Society's 'Proceedings' to be published in 1897. Meanwhile mention may be made of a tablet of singular interest bearing the following inscription :—

```
IMP CAES · T  A . . . . ADR
AN . . . . NINO · AVG · . . . . NT ·
MAX . . . TR POT · XVI · COS IIII
   COH · II . . . . R · MIL · EQ · C · L ·
SVB · IVI . . . . . . LEG · AVG · PR · PR ·
```

The tablet was found in fragments at the bottom of the well in the camp, but it is not difficult to supply most of the missing letters, and Dr Macdonald has interpreted the inscription as follows: "In the reign of the Emperor Cæsar Titus Ælius Hadrianus Antoninus Augustus [Pius], Father of his Country, Chief Pontiff, invested with the tribunitial power sixteen times, four times consul, the Second Cohort of Tungrians, a thousand strong, of which a due proportion is cavalry, and in possession of the privilege of Latin citizenship, (erected this) under Jul . . . . Legate of the Emperor as Governor (of Britain)."

Unfortunately the missing letters after IVI in the last line deprive us of an opportunity of supplying a blank in the list of Roman governors of Britain after Lollius Urbicus. Antoninus Pius became tribune for the six-

have lately been the subject of critical examination at the hands of Dr Macdonald.[6] He divides them into four sections :—

1. *The Lower Annandale road*, of which four parts are shown in the Ordnance map—"one in Kirkpatrick-Fleming, about three-quarters of a mile long; another in Hoddam, upwards of a mile; a third partly in Hoddam and partly in Tundergarth, nearly two miles; and a fourth in Dryfesdale, about a quarter of a mile."[7] These fragments mark the most natural route from the western border to the valley of the Clyde, leading close past the great camp of Birrens.[8]

2. *The Upper Annandale road*, running from Gallaberry Hill along the east bank of Annan through Applegarth into Wamphray, across the Evan into Lanarkshire. Dr Macdonald cut several sections across this road in the summer of 1893; but though it was found to be covered with a layer of small stones above a layer of larger ones, the nearest ap-

teenth time in A.D. 153; in other words, that was the sixteenth year of his reign, and presumably the date of the inscription.

A beautifully decorated altar found in the same place bore the following inscription :—

DISCIP·
AVG·
COH·II·
TVNGR·
ML·EQ·CL·

which reads as follows: "To the Discipline of the Emperor, the Second Cohort of Tungrians, a thousand strong, with a due proportion of cavalry, and in possession of the privilege of Latin citizenship, (erected this)."

Among other inscriptions is one by the celebrated Sixth Legion, "Victrix, Pia, Fidelis," which formed part of the garrison of Britain for so long.

[6] Proceedings of the Society of Antiquaries of Scotland, vol. xxiii., session 1893-94, p. 298. [7] Ibid., p. 299.

[8] At Birrens were discovered in 1731 a statue of the goddess Brigantia, an altar dedicated to Mercury, and the inscribed pedestal of a statue of Mercury (Clerk's 'Memoirs of My Life,' pp. 138-140 and 222). These are now in the National Museum of Antiquities, where also may be seen a small bronze statuette of Mercury, found some years ago on the farm of Blairbuy, parish of Glasserton, Wigtownshire.

proach to a pavement consisted in large flat stones placed for a breadth of 6 or 7 feet along the west side of the road, and a single row of large stones along the east side.

3. *The Nithsdale road* is marked on the map a little to the north-west of Lochmaben, and again in Tinwald parish not far from Lochmaben. It reappears as the Well Path in the north of Durisdeer parish.

4. *The Cairn valley road* is an isolated fragment on high ground "overlooking the sources of the Ken, the Skarr, the Shinnel, and the Dalwhat;"[9] but its connection with a Roman origin is extremely slender. The conclusion is that, although the first three of these roads correspond with the lines which would naturally be chosen in the formation of highways by Agricola and his successors, there is very little, if anything, in their structural remains to identify them with Roman work.

Domitian, jealous of Agricola's success in subduing North Britain, recalled him to Rome in the year 87. In effect, the whole fruits of eight years' hard fighting were thrown away. Lucullus, who succeeded to Agricola's command, was put to death by order of Domitian: the native tribes re-entered the territory whence they had been driven, or resumed possession where they had been kept in subjection, and the Roman province of Britain shrank behind the northern boundary beyond which Agricola had first penetrated.

Nothing is known of events in North Britain in general, or Dumfriesshire and Galloway in particular, until the year 117, when Hadrian became emperor. It is supposed that the tribes north of the Forth had broken through the line of forts erected by Agricola, and overrun much of the land secured by him, and that the Brigantes had been pressing upon the

[9] Proceedings of the Society of Antiquaries of Scotland, vol. xxiii., session 1893-94, p. 317.

Roman outposts in attempts to regain the territory from which they had been driven in the reigns of Claudius and Vespasian. At all events there was disturbance enough to cause Hadrian to visit Britain in person in the year 120, when he built the celebrated wall which bears his name, marking off the northern limit of the province on a line between Solway and the mouth of the Tyne.

But though this great rampart was undoubtedly intended to be permanent, the necessity for constantly annexing new territory was forced upon the Roman colonists as irresistibly as the British Government find to be the case at the present day in South Africa. Those restless exiles, the Brigantes, broke out again in insurrection in the year 139, and Lollius Urbicus was sent by the Emperor Antonine to subdue them. Once more the frontier of the province was extended northwards, to the line chosen by Agricola between the Firths of Forth and Clyde, and the forts constructed by that general were connected by an earthen barrier now known as the wall of Antonine.

Considerable difference of interpretation has been put on the scanty records of this period. Skene, founding on the discovery of an inscription to the goddess Brigantia, discovered at Middlebie, within the territory of the Selgovæ of Dumfriesshire, assumes affinity, or at least permanent alliance, between the Brigantes and the Selgovæ, if not also the Novantæ of Galloway.[1] Professor Rhys, on the other hand, interprets the Greek author, Pausanias, who wrote the chronicle of this war, in a different sense.[2] Pausanias states that the Romans attacked the Brigantes because they had invaded a people tributary to Rome which he calls $\dot{\eta}$ $\Gamma\epsilon\nu o\nu\nu\acute{\iota}a$ $\mu o\hat{\iota}\rho a$, the Genunian sept. This name is curiously like one

---

[1] Celtic Scotland, vol. i. p. 71.
[2] Celtic Britain. By Professor J. Rhys. London, 1882.

applied by Adamnan, six centuries later, to a people of the West Highlands opposite Skye—namely, *Geona cohors*, the Geonian sept; but, of course, as the Brigantes never were in the Highlands, an explanation must be sought elsewhere. Professor Rhys detects in the Brigantes a people of Brythonic or Welsh stock, the progenitors of the Britons of Strathclyde, and suggests that the Genunians were none other than the Novantæ of Galloway, tributary to Rome and hereditary enemies of the Brythonic branch of Celts. After all, the evidence is very slender on either side, and it has to be confessed that the student is here reduced to something like pure conjecture.

There is, indeed, this to be said for Professor Rhys's view: during many centuries later than this time the Galloway Picts were at deadly enmity with the inhabitants of Strathclyde, evidence of which remains to this day in a remarkable rampart known as the Deil's Dyke. Train, the correspondent of Sir Walter Scott, and the chief source of that writer's acquaintance with Galloway lore and topography, accomplished a minute survey of this work, and his report on it was printed in the appendix to Mackenzie's 'History of Galloway.'[3] It is valuable because of the great changes effected by agriculture during the course of the present century, and enough of the Dyke still remains to satisfy us as to the fidélity with which Train described those parts which have disappeared since he wrote. The Deil's Dyke begins, says Train, on the east shore of Loch Ryan, on the farm of Beoch, thence by Braid Fell, Cairnzerran, Kilfeather, across Derry,[4] by the north end of Loch Maberry, Kirkcalla, Ochiltree, and Glenvernoch.[5]

---

[3] The History of Galloway. By the Rev. W. Mackenzie. 2 vols. Kirkcudbright, 1841.

[4] *Doire* (dirry), a wood, especially of oaks; a waste.

[5] *Gleann bhearnach* (varnagh), the gapped glen.

Between Ochiltree and Glenvernoch, Train notes, the Dyke "runs from the east side of the loch to the summit of the hill, where there are the remains of a watch-tower made of very large stones." This has since been used as a quarry for building field walls, and has disappeared, and so has a circular fort, 192 yards in diameter, which Train describes, immediately above Glendochart. On the farm of Knockvill[6] he traced the Dyke into the Cree, on the eastern bank of which it enters the Stewartry of Kirkcudbright, runs through the Camberwood, Terregan, across the moor of Drannandow,[7] between the standing-stones called the Thieves and the Nappers. "As it passes from Terregan to Drannandow, it runs through a bog, and is only perceptible by the heather growing long and close on the top of it; whereas on each side of it the soil only produces rushes and moss. Near the centre of the bog I caused the peat to be cleared away close to the dyke, and thereby found the foundations to be several feet below the surface." The course from the Craw Stane of Drannandow is noted along the south side of the hill of Garlick, through Auchinleck,[8] over the south flank of Dregmorn, crossing the Palnure[9] to Talnotrie, up Craignelder,[1] and so to Craigencallie.[2] "It is very entire in the Garrary, Clanry,[3] Duckieston, Largrave, and Knockreoch." Thence it may be traced by the Bridge of Deuch, through Muncaig,[4] Auchenshinnoch,[5] Glencairn,[6] Tynron, and so to the farm of

---

[6] *Cnoc bhile* (villy), hill of the great or old tree.
[7] *Draighnean dubh*, dark blackthorns.
[8] *Achadh na leac*, field of flat stones.
[9] *Pol n' iubhar* (ure), water of the yew-trees.
[1] *Creag n' eilte*, crag of the hinds (?).
[2] *Creag na cailleaich*, the old wife's crag.
[3] *Claenreach*, sloping ground.
[4] *Moine cathag* (caag), jackdaw hill (?).
[5] *Achadh na' sionach* (shinnagh), field of foxes.
[6] *Gleann carn*, glen of the cairns.

Southmains on the river Nith—in all, a course of more than fifty miles. It will be observed that it follows a line which lies slightly to the south of the present boundary between Galloway and the adjacent counties of Ayr and Lanark. Train states that Dr Clapperton of Annan traced the Dyke through part of Annandale; but he left no note of his survey, and no remains are visible at this day east of the Nith. Train describes the bank as being invariably 8 feet broad at the base, which corresponds pretty nearly with a fragment of the rampart which I have examined on the farm of Derry in Penninghame parish; but most of it has now disappeared and been used for building fences. The fosse is on the northern side, showing that the work was constructed by dwellers in Galloway against the people in Ayrshire and Lanarkshire—*i.e.*, Strathclyde. No doubt the bank would be strengthened with palisades, and, fortified at intervals by watch-towers and intrenched camps, would be a formidable obstacle to a force invading from the north.[7]

Such is, or rather was, the Deil's Dyke; and it may well be that the Novantæ or Niduarian Picts threw it up as a defence against the Brigantes of Strathclyde. If Hadrian's visit was in truth brought about by the attacks of the Brigantes on the Novantæ of Galloway, tributaries to Rome, then it suggests the idea that when that emperor originated the device of wall-building as a defence, and shut out his tributary Novantæ from the province by building the great wall from Solway to Tyne, he may at the same time have encouraged them to protect themselves by a rampart of their own. The

---

[7] The two extremities of the Deil's Dyke are mentioned in the 'Book of Taliessin,' x. 50 :—
"Between Caer Rian and Caer Rywg."

Caer Rian is Cairn Ryan on Loch Ryan; Caer Rywg is Crawick on the Nith. Taliessin's poems are attributed to the seventh century.

most, however, that can be said is, that this speculation is as likely to be right as any other.

Our knowledge of the mode of life pursued and the degree of civilisation attained by the primitive inhabitants of south-western Scotland would be extremely meagre if it rested on the evidence of such terrestrial remains as have survived the operations of agriculture and the successive replacement of ancient structures by new dwellings occupying the old sites. But during the last thirty years attention has been directed to a class of habitations which have been so well preserved by reason of the sites occupied as to remain in much the same condition as when their inhabitants deserted them. The presence, moreover, of articles of Roman manufacture indicate that these dwellings were contemporary with the Roman occupation. Antiquaries knew very little about crannogs or lake-dwellings in Scotland, until the exploration in 1862 of a group of them exposed by the drainage of Dowalton Loch in the parishes of Kirkinner, Sorby, and Glasserton. These have yielded fragments of Roman ware of the kind usually called Samian, and in one instance a large bronze vessel, ornamented with the head of Medusa, and bearing on the handle a Roman maker's name.[8] More than a hundred years before the time of Agricola, Julius Cæsar had described the natives of Britain making use of wooden piles and marshes in their intrenchments. Dr Munro declares his belief that this was a universal practice among the Celts, who brought their knowledge of it in their migration from Central and Southern Europe.[9] Be this as it may, the interest aroused by the discoveries at Dowalton, following on those in the Swiss lakes, has resulted in finding crannogs prevalent all over Scot-

[8] Found on a crannog in Dowalton in 1863. Now in the National Museum of Antiquities, Edinburgh.

[9] Lake-Dwellings of Europe. By R. Munro, M.D. London, 1890. P. 491.

land, except in those lakes where natural islets provided ready-made refuge; and it may be safely assumed that they were in universal use among the Selgovæ and Novantæ at the time of Agricola's invasion.

Certain conclusions may be drawn from their structure as to the aspect of the country, and, from the objects found on them, as to the degree of civilisation attained by the inhabitants, their food, and even their clothing.

In the first place, the immense amount of material required to build a crannog, which was a framework of massive oak logs mortised together, filled with huge bundles of brushwood secured by innumerable piles of oak, Scots fir, or ash, and decked with solid oak planking, implies the presence of dense forest in a country subsequently wholly denuded of wood. It was estimated that in building a simple crannog which was exposed on the drainage of Barhapple Loch, a very small sheet of water near Glenluce, upwards of 3000 large trees had been employed, besides those used in the erection of dwellings on the island, and the construction of causeways to the shore, an invariable feature in lacustrine habitations. This crannog and the buildings on it had been destroyed by fire, as was shown by several large prepared beams partially burnt. Not only were trees abundant where now there are none, except in artificial plantations, but they were of great size. Canoes, hollowed out of solid oak-trunks, are commonly found near crannogs; for although the islands are connected with the shore by causeways, these are always interrupted at the end farthest from the shore, for purposes of defence. Five such canoes were found among the Dowalton group, varying in length from 25 to 21 feet. It might seem impossible to find at the present day in the whole of Wigtownshire living oaks of equal magnitude to these, unless one bears in mind the methods still employed by primitive boat-builders, who wedge out a tree-stem during the process of hollowing, so as to make the breadth of the boat considerably greater than the original diameter of the trunk.

The diet of the early inhabitants is revealed by the refuse-heaps in these islands. They contain bones of oxen (*Bos longifrons*), swine, goats (or long-horned sheep), red-deer, and roe-deer. The marrow bones are always split. Charred corn (resembling barley) has been found, and immense numbers of hazel-nut shells. Bruising or pounding stones for preparing food, and querns for grinding corn, are among the commonest objects discovered; but, unlike the earlier Swiss pile-dwellings, all the Scottish crannogs which have been examined up to this time have been inhabited by people who knew the use of bronze and iron. The presence of heavy oak beams in the very foundation of these structures, neatly morticed in a fashion that could not be accomplished except with metal instruments, proves that not only the later inhabitants, but the original builders, used iron, or, at least, bronze. The stone axes and cutting implements which abound on dry land must either have been made by an earlier race ousted by the Celts who built the islands, or these must have acquired the use of metal before the advent of the Romans. Lumps of iron, bronze slag, and crucibles found on some of the islands prove that the "gow" or smith was already an important individual in the community.

Of textile fabric the only recorded instance was a piece of coarse dark woollen stuff which the present writer himself took from under some stones on one of the Dowalton crannogs, shortly after the receding water had left it bare. Unfortunately this was afterwards mislaid and lost. A piece of a leather shoe, with stamped ornamental pattern, was found in one of the canoes at Dowalton, and is now in the Edinburgh Museum. Armlets of porcelain or vitreous paste and jet, and beads of the same materials and of glass, are of frequent occurrence, some of which may have been obtained by barter, while others, judging from refuse of vitreous slag, seem to have been made on the spot. A penannular brooch of bronze, possibly Roman, and a circular ornament of bronze, of Celtic design, and with depressed spaces for *champlevé* enamel (the well-known *opus Britannicum*), both found in the Dowalton crannogs, testify that the people who dwelt in these structures, which, after centuries of submersion, now look so squalid and miserable, practised and appreciated some of the arts of peace. Still more convincing of the advanced native art of the period (if indeed they may be assigned to this period) are an extraordinary bronze mask with horns, found in a morass at Torrs, in the parish of Kelton, now in the collection at Abbotsford, and an ornamental mirror of bronze found in draining a bog at Balmaclellan. The last-mentioned lay with several other articles, forming four parcels, each wrapped in coarse linen cloth, 3 feet below the surface. Both the mask and the mirror belong to a school of art classed as late Celtic, and they are mentioned here because, having been found in bogs, they probably belong to the crannog period, and because the design is of the same character as the above-mentioned circular bronze ornament found in Dowalton.

The contents of the crannogs have been dwelt on with greater detail than may be given to objects found on dry land, because, from having been found in association with Roman work, they afford indubitable evidence of the scale of culture attained by the primitive inhabitants of the southwest at the earliest period when they come into notice. No such exact evidence is at hand as to the time when the numerous land-dwellings — hill forts, hut-circles, and intrenched "kraals" — were inhabited. Such remains are often found within very short distances of the lake-dwellings, but we are reduced to bare speculation as to how far they were contemporary with each other. Did the whole population at one time inhabit lake-dwellings, relying on water as their defence against attack from human enemies and wolves? or did part of them, as is more probable, live in booths on land, protected by a rampart of stones or of earth strengthened by palisade? The fact that they possessed flocks and herds, as testified by the remains of food in their islands, implies that these people used terrestrial and lacustrine dwellings simultaneously; and some part of the land-dwellings and strongholds which can still be traced may, with tolerable certainty, be attributed to the Novantæ encountered by Agricola.

Massive gold ornaments have from time to time been turned up in the course of cultivating the land, but there is generally some doubt as to the exact localities and circumstances of such discoveries, owing to apprehension on the part of the finder of the effects of the law of Treasure Trove.[1] Consequently it has not yet been possible to assign such objects to an approximate date, through ignorance of other remains to which they were lying in juxtaposition.

[1] In Scotland the law of *Ultimus Hæres* stands in place of that of Treasure Trove in England. It is even more rigorous in its provisions, for under it every article of whatsoever material is claimed for the Crown as *ultimus hæres*, or ultimate heir, of any object of which the original owner is unknown. But it cannot be too widely understood that the Treasury has recently minuted that the finder of any object of archæological interest shall receive payment of the full intrinsic value thereof.

CHAPTER II.

FROM THE BUILDING OF THE WALL OF ANTONINE, A.D. 140, TO THE CLOSE OF THE NORSE DOMINION.

From 140, the date of the construction of Antonine's wall, for a period of more than two centuries, no allusion can be interpreted as referring to Galloway. While Dumfriesshire, in common with the whole of the rest of Scotland between the walls of Antonine and Hadrian, was under Roman government, the inference from events towards the close of the fourth century is that Galloway, though probably tributary, was left under the rule of its native chiefs.

In the year 360 those ancient enemies of Agricola, the northern Picts and the Picts of Manau, allied themselves with two other nations which now first appear on the scene,—the Scots from Ireland and the Saxons, who had probably obtained a footing on the north shores of the Forth.[1] They took possession of parts of the province between the walls, and after holding them for four years, were joined by a fourth people called by Ammianus the Atecotti, "bellicosa hominum natio"—a warlike race of men. Who these last were may be inferred by the manner in which Theodosius the elder, who was sent to expel the invaders in 369, disposed of them. The poet Claudian says that he drove the Saxons

---

[1] Ammianus Marcellinus, xxvi. 4, xxvij. 8, 9.

to Orkney, the Picts to Thule (*i.e.*, the north), and the Scots back to Ierne, Erin or Ireland.² But the Atecotts must have been a people living between the walls, and can hardly be other than the Novantæ or Niduarian Picts. These Theodosius enrolled and sent for service on the Continent. St Jerome mentions having seen them in Gaul, "a British people who fed on human flesh"; but this unpleasant comment can only have been made on hearsay, and is therefore untrustworthy evidence.

In entering upon the new chapter which at this date unfolds itself in the history of Galloway, it may be well to summarise the names under which it is believed the pagan natives of that part of Caledonia receive mention in history—

Novantæ . .	*Ptolemy*	A.D. 120.
Genonians . .	*Pausanias*	A.D. 140.
Atecotti . .	*Amm. Marcellinus* *St Jerome*	A.D. 364.

The records of North Britain down to within a few years of the close of the fourth century contain no allusion to the introduction of Christianity. Nevertheless, that a Christian Church existed within the Roman province of Britain from the beginning of the fourth century at latest, has been proved by the presence of two British bishops, Eborius of York and Restitutus of London, at the Council of Arles in 314.³ It is not, therefore, unreasonable to suppose that the worship of Christ had been brought into the district between the walls of Hadrian and Antonine during the Roman occupation. This is supported by the testimony of Ailred, who in

---

² "De tertio consulatu Honorii Augusti panegyris," lines 54-56.

³ History of the Catholic Church of Scotland. By A. Bellesheim. Translated by D. Oswald Hunter Blair. Four vols. Edinburgh, 1887. Vol. i. p. 4.

the twelfth century compiled the life of St Ninian, as he himself tells us, from "a book of his life and miracles written in the vulgar tongue." This Ninian he declares to have been the son of a king, a Christian, "in that region, it is supposed, in the western part of the Island of Britain where the ocean, stretching as an arm, and making, as it were, on either side two angles, divideth at this day [*i.e.*, *c.* 1150] the realms of the Scots and the Angles, which till these last times belonging to the Angles, is proved not only by historical record, but by actual memory of individuals, to have had a king of its own."[4] Ninian, therefore, was a native of the Solway shore, but whether of Cumberland, of Dumfriesshire, or of Galloway cannot now be determined. In the year 395, being then five-and-twenty, he was at Rome, where he had been for some years studying for the priesthood. In that year the Pope Siricius consecrated Ninian as Bishop, and he started on a mission to convert the Picts of Galloway. In this he probably received the assistance of the civil as well as the ecclesiastical authorities, for affairs had been going badly in North Britain since the expedition of Theodosius the elder. The revolt of Maximus and his proclamation as Emperor in Britain had taken place in 383. In 384 he repressed the Picts and Scots who assailed the province, but afterwards he took away all the forces he could collect, encountered and slew the Emperor Gratian in Gaul in 387, invaded Italy in 388, and lost his life at the battle of Aquileia. The Atecotts assailed the British subjects of Rome, till, in response to their appeal, Stilicho, the famous minister of Honorius, sent a legion to their assistance in 396. Having restored order, he followed the example of the elder Theodosius by enrolling the Atecotts

[4] Vita Niniani, c. i.

in the Roman army, giving them the title of Honoriani, after the Emperor Honorius. The 'Notitia Imperii,' compiled about this time, makes mention of the following corps stationed in Gaul, wherein the distinction between the first and second enlistment may be traced:—

> Atecotti.
> Atecotti juniores Gallicani.
> Atecotti Honoriani seniores.
> Atecotti Honoriani juniores.

But Stilicho had plenty to do with his legions on the Continent. The Western Empire, severed from the Eastern on the death of Theodosius the Great in 395, was rent with intrigue within and threatened by formidable foes without. Therefore he would cordially encourage any attempt to reduce these irrepressible Atecotts—the fierce tribes of Novantia — to peaceable habits. Christianity had already proved itself the surest engine of civilisation, and Ninian set out on his mission to make Christians of the Atecotts. He turned aside on his journey from Rome to sojourn with Martin, Bishop of Tours, one of the most celebrated evangelists of his time, and landed in Galloway in 396 at the place now known as the Isle of Whithorn. This is so accurately described in Ailred's Life that there can be little hesitation in rejecting the theory that Ninian built his first church at Whithorn, three miles inland from the isle, where the ruins of St Martin's Priory now stand. "He selected for himself a site in the place which is now termed Witerna, which, situated on the shore of the ocean, and extending far into the sea on the east, west, and south sides, is closed in by the sea itself, while only on the north is a way open to those who would enter." It would hardly be possible more minutely to describe in so few words the peninsula on which may now be seen a small ruined church, doubtless on the site of that erected by Ninian, of which it seems to be a thirteenth-century reconstruction. This must have been the original Candida Casa, the White House. Before the building was finished news was brought to Ninian of the death of Bishop Martin in 397, to whose memory he forthwith dedicated the church.

The Magnum Monasterium, or Monastery of Rosnat—Futerna of Irish writers—which within a century of Ninian's death became a famous seminary of secular and religious learning, probably occupied the ground on which the ruined priory now stands within the town of Whithorn.[5] But it would be vain to search here for traces of the original building. Extensive ruins do, indeed, remain, but the earliest part of them do not date further back than the twelfth century. A richly decorated doorway of late Norman work on the south side of the nave is still in fair preservation, though it has been sorely blemished by a groove having been ruthlessly cut through the mouldings to receive the roof of a porch when the building was used as a parish kirk after the Reformation.

Nevertheless, the persistence of tradition, often so delusive, has been the means within the last few years of revealing direct traces of the presence of Ninian. About three miles west of Whithorn, and the same distance north-west of the Isle of Whithorn, there is on the shore of Glasserton parish a certain cavern, which has ever been distinguished among many similar refts in the cliff by the name of St Ninian's Cave. It was said that Ninian used to retire here for prayer and meditation, but no remains of occupation were visible other than names of visitors scrawled on the rock. In 1871

---

[5] See Note A, Magnum Monasterium, p. 46.

the late Dean Stanley, collecting material for his 'Lectures on the History of the Church of Scotland,' visited the cave, and a lady who accompanied him discovered, by a curious and appropriate fortune, what may possibly be the oldest relic of that church. This was a small Latin cross, deeply punched out of the rock wall of the cave and thickly overgrown with lichen. Twelve years later the members of the Ayrshire and Galloway Archæological Association undertook the thorough exploration of the cave, with the result of completely verifying its repute as a place of religious resort. The opening and much of the interior were encumbered with rocks fallen from the roof: when these were removed by the labours of many days, a paved floor, a wall built across the cave mouth, and a stone stair leading down to the interior, were exposed. A stone basin or font lay under a rill at the door, and seventeen crosses, some of a Latin, others of a Celtic type, were found either carved on the cave walls or on detached stones. One of these crosses bore the fragment of a Runic inscription. Now it is not suggested that these remains date so far back as the fourth century; indeed the Runes and a stone in the pavement bearing the legend,

```
SANCT
NI  P
```

point to the cave having been a religious retreat in later centuries. But there can be little doubt that its original sanctity was derived from Bishop Ninian having resorted to it for devotional purposes.

We seem to come nearer the actual relics of Ninian's mission in some inscribed stones at Kirkmadrine, in the parish of Stoneykirk.[6] The first of these bears beneath the cross the legend—

>
> HIC IACENT
> SCI ET PRAE
> CIPVI SACER
> DOTES ID EST
> VIVENTIVS
> ET MAVORIVS.

That is, "Here lie holy and excellent priests, namely, Viventius and Mavorius." The other stone has been damaged, and all that remains of the inscription is—

>
> . . . . . S ET
> FLORENTIVS.

The third stone seems to have disappeared, but a drawing of it has been preserved, which shows that, like the others, it bore the cross with the peculiar monogram on the upper limb known as the *labarum* of Constantine.[7] This is common in Gaulish monuments and those of the catacombs, but it is remarkable that, so far, these stones at Kirkmadrine, and one at Whithorn bearing an inscription to St Peter, are the only instances where this classic form of cross has been found in North Britain.

Chalmers confused the suppressed parishes of Kirkmadrine (for there are two of the same name in Wigtownshire, the other being now included in Sorby) with Kirkmaiden (of which name there were also two parishes, one still remaining, the other united to Glasserton), and classed both of them as dedications to St Medan. Dr John Stuart pointed out this blunder, and suggested that the saint commemorated was

---

[6] Stoneykirk is a modern form of the older Steneker (1535) or Stevenskirk (1725)—*i.e.*, a dedication to St Stephen. The familiar "Steenie" has been confused with "Staney" and improved (?) into Stoney.

[7] See papers by Mr J. G. H. Starke, in 'Transactions of the Dumfriesshire and Galloway Antiquarian Society,' 1887-88 and 1889-90.

Mathurinus, of high repute in Gaul, and contemporary with St Martin and St Ninian. His name in Gaelic would be Madrin. But a still more probable explanation suggests itself in the name of Martin himself, of which the Gaelic form would be Matrainn, or, in the oblique case, Matrin. In the classical names Viventius, Mavorius, and Florentius, we seem to trace the personality of Gaulish clerics, trained under Bishop Martin, who either accompanied Ninian and his masons on their first landing, or joined him later when the work of proselytising had spread into the interior of Novantia.

For Ninian's mission was a complete success. Whatever may have been the national religion professed by the Novantæ,—whether, as is probable, it was a primitive form of Animism, modified by Druid magic on the one hand and the classical cult of Rome on the other,—they embraced Christianity for the time, and Ninian was able to go farther afield and preach the Gospel in Northern parts. But the new faith was not destined to endure long. The Roman Power was tottering, and though Stilicho repeatedly sent legions to maintain the province in its full extent to the Wall of Antonine, he had as often to withdraw them. The anarchy which ensued in North Britain is briefly but graphically described by Bede: "[The people] saved themselves from starvation by robbing and plundering one another, adding by their own domestic broils to the calamities occasioned by foreigners, till the whole country was left destitute of food, except such as could be procured by the chase."[8] Under these conditions the worship of the "White Christ" was almost swept away in Galloway, the bulk of its people relapsing into paganism. But apparently Ninian, who, it is supposed, died about the year 432, was spared the anguish of seeing the total wreck of his labours, for, says Ailred, "he was buried in the church of the blessed Martin,

[8] Ecclesiastical History, c. xii.

which he had built from the foundation." Nor is it certain that the church at Whithorn ever lacked a band of the faithful to carry on the services even in the darkest hour, for notices of it occur from time to time in the Irish Annals during the remainder of this century. In the 'Book of Ballymote' it is stated that Carnach, son of Sarran, king of the Britons, was abbot of the House of Martin. Carnach's brother, Leurig, succeeded Sarran as king, and turned the monastery into a fort. Thereupon Carnach got Murcertach, son of Erc, to dethrone and slay his brother. Carnach afterwards went to Ireland, and established monasticism there on the lines of Whithorn.[9]

It is perhaps to Whithorn, therefore, alone among the towns of Scotland, that honour is due for having maintained the worship of the Almighty uninterrupted for fifteen hundred years.

Hitherto, it will be observed, no mention has been made of ecclesiastical events in Dumfriesshire or in that part of Galloway now known as the Stewartry of Kirkcudbright. The narrative of Ninian, though embracing many parts of Scotland, is not directly connected with the country between the Cree and the Nith, and it is a singular fact that although in Wigtownshire Ninian is commemorated in many dedications,[1] his name is not attached to any place in the Stewartry.

The chronology of events leading up to the abandonment

---

[9] It is worthy of note that Carnach in old Erse means a pagan priest—*i.e.*, one who ministers at a cairn. The term would be easily transferred to one who ministered at an altar. Cairnie and Carnachan are still common surnames in Galloway.

[1] 1. Penninghame. "There is at present a bell in the Church of Penygham with this inscription in Saxon letters, *Campana Sancti Niniani de Penygham, M.*, dedicat, as it seems, to Saint Ninian, in the thousand year after the birth of Christ."—Symson's 'Large Description of Galloway,' 1692.

"Item (the xvij day of March), to ane man that bure Sanct Ninianes bell

of Britain bears so importantly on the district between the walls that it may be convenient to summarise the conclusions come to after comparing the various fragments of narrative :—

A.D.
383. Maximus revolts and is elected emperor.
387. He invades Gaul with the Roman legions stationed in Britain.
396. Valentia (*i.e.*, Scotland between the walls) invaded by Northern Picts and Scots from Erin. Britons inhabiting Valentia apply to Rome for succour. Stilicho sends a legion which drives out the invaders, repairs the Wall of Antonine, between Forth and Clyde, and re-establishes it as the northern frontier of the province.
397. Bishop Ninian begins his mission among the Atecott Picts.
402. All Roman troops again withdrawn from Britain.
403. Valentia again invaded by Picts and Scots. Britons again appeal to Rome.
406. Roman troops, once more in Britain, garrison the Wall of Hadrian, between Solway and Tyne.
407. Constantine finally withdraws Roman troops from Britain.
408. Picts overrun Valentia, break through Southern wall, and ravage Cumbria.
409. Provincials resist invaders, and having invited assistance of the Saxons, repel them. Honorius formally frees the British provinces.

On their departure from Britain in 407 the Roman Government probably calculated on re-establishing their authority at no distant day, and left certain officials of native birth to administer the government, which for a time they had been forced to relinquish. For some time previous to this Britain had been divided into five provinces, of which Valentia, the

(in Pennyghame), ix. s."—Lord Treasurer's accounts of expenses incurred by King James IV. in a pilgrimage to Whithorn, 1506-7.
  2. St Ninian's Chapel of the Cruives, in Penninghame parish.
  3. Ninian's Well, in Wigtown parish.
  4. Killantringan, in Port Patrick parish—*i.e.*, *cill sheant Ringain* (Gaelic *sh* silent), St Ringan's Chapel.
  5. Chipperdingan, a well in Kirkmaiden parish—*i.e.*, *tiobar Dingain*, Dingan's (Ninian's) Well.

northernmost, so named by Theodosius in honour of the Emperor Valentinian, was left under the rule of Cunedda or Kenneth, the son of Edarn or Æternus. Tradition says that his mother was a daughter of Coel Hen, British King of Strathclyde, whose name is preserved in that of the district of Kyle in Ayrshire, and in our nursery rhyme of Old King Cole.[2] Cunedda's official title as ruler of Valentia was Dux Britanniarum, or Duke of the Britains. He left eight sons, some of whom became, like their father, very powerful and distinguished. From one of these, Meireon, the county of Merioneth is named; from another, Keredig, the county of Cardigan.

Wales, or the country of the Cymri, at this time extended from the Severn to the Clyde, and comprised all modern Wales, Cheshire, Lancashire, part of Westmorland, Cumberland, Dumfriesshire, Ayrshire, Lanarkshire, and Renfrewshire. Novantia, however, remained Pictish — *i.e.*, Goidelic — in speech and race. Thus, whatever had been the affinity in earlier centuries between the Selgovæ of Dumfriesshire and the Novantæ or Atecotts of Galloway, it had been replaced in the sixth century by hereditary racial enmity. Galloway was peopled by Atecott Picts; Annandale, Nithsdale, and Strathclyde by Britons, Cymri, or Welshmen.

Bede, writing in the early part of the eighth century, fixes the first arrival of Saxons in Britain in A.D. 449, but it is certain that they were pretty numerously established before that. The Angles, it is true, did not settle in Northumbria under Ida till 547; but another Teutonic race — the Frisii, Frisones, or Frisians — had made important settlements at an earlier time. Prosper Aquitanus, writing in 455, states in his Chronicle, under the year 441, "Britain up to this time is brought widely under dominion of the Saxons by various

---

[2] Coel Hen signifies Old Coel.

conflicts and transactions." One of these settlements seems to have been fixed on the banks of the Nith, and in Dumfries is preserved the name given to it by the Celtic population—*dún Fris*, the Frisians' fort.³

In the sixth century, then, there were four races contending for what was formerly the Roman province of Valentia—(1) the Britons, Cymri, or Welsh, ancient subjects of Rome, who may be regarded as the legitimate inhabitants; (2) the Northern and Southern Picts, representing the older or Goidelic strain of Celts, with an admixture, perhaps, of aboriginal Ivernians, with whom may be associated the Atecott Picts west of the Nith; (3) the Scots from Erin, also Goidelic, but distinct from the Picts, not yet firmly settled in Lorn and Argyll under Aedan, the grandson of Fergus Mór Mac Eirc, but making descents wherever they could find a footing,⁴ and destined to give their name to Alban in later centuries as "Scotland"; and (4) the Teutonic colonists.

The Chronicle of Nennius is filled between the years 516 and 532 with the exploits of Arthur, the shadowy hero of Welsh song, whom he describes as a leader in alliance with the British chiefs fighting against the Saxons. He specifies the sites of Arthur's twelve great battles, and states that the Saxons were defeated in all of them.⁵ But these Germanic tribes were constantly reinforced from the Continent, until at

³ Among twenty-eight cities named in Britain by Nennius one is called Caer Bretain, the fortress of the Britons—Dunbarton; another Caer Pheris, the fortress of the Frisians—Dumfries, which should be written, more accurately, Dunfries.

⁴ "Scotti per diversa vagantes"—Scots wandering hither and thither—as Ammianus Marcellinus describes them in the fourth century. In Cormac's glossary the name is written *Scuit*, and *scuite* is translated "a wanderer."

⁵ All these battle-fields have been tentatively identified with places in Scotland, and the confusion which has led to their being assigned to the limits of modern Wales arises out of the ancient extent of Wales, from Severn to Clyde, having been overlooked.

length the Anglian kingdom of Bernicia was founded by Ida in 547. Ida died in 559, and was succeeded by Ella, who added to Bernicia the district of Deira, lying between the Humber and Tees, forming it into the Saxon kingdom of Northumbria, with which the province of Galloway was to be so intimately connected in later years.

We now arrive at something like historic certainty of events in the south-west. The Angles were pagans. The Picts of Novantia had generally relapsed from Christianity into their original cult, of which the traditions had been kept alive by the native bards, and a large part of the Welsh population in the valleys of Annan, Nith, and Clyde had followed them. The Welsh leader was Gwendolew, who claimed descent from Coel Hen—Old King Cole. But there was still a Roman party among these Northern Britons, led by Rydderch Hael —that is, Roderick the Liberal—who adhered to Christianity.

The great issue between the pagans and Christians was fought out on the borders of Dumfriesshire in 573, at a place called Ardderyd, now Arthuret, on the Scottish bank of the Esk.[6] Gwendolew's camp was about four miles north of this, and gave the name still borne by a stream called Carwhinelow —that is, *caer Gwendolew*, Gwendolew's camp.[7] The Christian champion Rydderch was completely victorious, and became ruler of the Strathclyde Britons, under the title of King of Alclut.

Light broadens on the page of Caledonian history with the dawn of the seventh century, and thenceforward we are able to trace something like a connected narrative of its rulers and their political relations. Nevertheless, the chronicles of the

---

[6] As in Welsh *dd* sounds *th*, this name has undergone little change in 1300 years.

[7] The parish of Carruthers in Dumfriesshire probably takes its name from *caer Rydderch*, Roderick's camp.

THE FOUR KINGDOMS. 35

period are so inextricably entangled with fable and so often irreconcilable with each other, that it would not be possible within the limits of this work to do more than repeat the chief conclusions to which the labours of Skene and his successors have brought them.

Alban, or, as we now call it, Scotland, had by this time resolved itself into four dominions, each under its separate line of kings. The Picts held the country north of the Forth, their chief town being near the mouth of the Ness; Argyle and Lorn formed the kingdom of Dalriada, populated by the Scottish (that is, Irish) descendants of the colony of Fergus Mór. The British kingdom of Alclut or Strathclyde was the northern portion of the Cymric territory, or old Wales, once extending from Cornwall to Dunbarton, but permanently severed, first, by the Saxon king Ceawlin, who in 577 took possession of the country round Bath and Gloucester; and second, by Edwin, King of Bernicia, at the great battle of Chester in 613. Strathclyde, then, comprised a tract extending from the Derwent in Cumberland to Loch Lomond, the capital being called in Welsh Alclut, or the cliff on the Clyde, but known to the Dalriadic and Pictish Gaels as *dún Bretann*, the fort of the Welshmen.

On the east the Saxon realm of Bernicia stretched from the Humber to the Forth under King Edwin, who has left his name in Edinburgh, the Saxon title of the town which the Gaels called Dunedin, but whose seat of rule was Bamborough. Just as the territory of the Atecott Picts was separated from Strathclyde by the rampart now known as the Deil's Dyke, so Bernicia was separated from Strathclyde by the Catrail, an earthwork crossing the upper part of Liddesdale.

Besides these four realms there was a debatable strip of country between the Lennox Hills and the Grampians, including the carse of Stirling and part of Linlithgowshire, chiefly inhabited by the Southern Picts or Picts of Manau; and, lastly, the old territory of the Niduarian or Atecott Picts, who had managed to retain autonomy under native princes, and a degree of independence, by means of powerful alliances.

At the beginning of the seventh century, then, Dumfriesshire was under the rule of the Welsh kings of Strathclyde, while Wigtownshire and Kirkcudbright, soon to acquire the name of Galloway, were under their native Pictish princes.

Chalmers, founding chiefly on the record of a victory gained by the men of Ulster over the Britons in 682 at a place called Maigiline, gives his readers to understand that Galloway was subdued and peopled by the Cruithne or Picts of Erin, and attributes the similarity of place-names in Ulster and Galloway to that cause. But in fact there is no evidence of such a conquest. Maigiline is to be identified—not, as Chalmers supposed, with Mauchline in Ayrshire, but—with Moylinny in Antrim, and the battle there was not an incident in an Irish invasion of Strathclyde, but in a British invasion of Ulster. The enmity between the Strathclyde Britons and the Ulstermen would tend to make the Galloway Picts throw in their lot with their congeners of Ulster, and no doubt intercourse between them was frequent and generally amicable, leading to intermarriage and relationship of blood. But there is not the least ground for believing that Galloway was overrun at this time in a hostile sense by the people from the opposite Irish coast.

But the Atecott Picts did undergo about this time a very important change in their foreign relations. The successors of Edwin, King of Bernicia, became, as the price of their alliance, *ard-righ* or overlords of Galloway, and under them the native chiefs ruled the people. Ceolwulf, who succeeded to the throne of Bernicia, or, as it had now become, Northumbria, in 729 erected Whithorn into a bishopric, "on account," says Bede, "of the increasing number of believers." Pecthelm was the first bishop, a suffragan of the diocese of York, and this relation between the two sees subsisted till the death of Bishop Michael in 1350.

Bede, bringing his history to a close in 731, represents North Britain at that time as enjoying an unusual state of peace. He describes the Picts as under treaty of amity with the Anglian rulers of Northumbria, the Scots quietly occupying their dominion in Argyle and Lorn, and the Britons (including, of course, Dumfriesshire), "though they, for the most part, through domestic hatred, are adverse to the nation of the Angles, and wrongfully, and from wicked custom, oppose the appointed Easter of the whole Catholic Church, yet . . . though in part they are their own masters, partly they are also brought under subjection to the Angles."

In 737 Ceolwulf, King of Northumbria and overlord of Galloway, became a monk, and was succeeded by his cousin Eadberct. This king went to war with the Northern Picts and Scots, but seems to have retained his hold on the Atecott Picts, who became involved in their overlord's quarrel.

In 740 Galloway was invaded by Alpin, the son of Echach, King of Scots, by a Pictish princess. Alpin had been alternately king of the Northern Picts (726) and of the Scots of Dalriada (*c.* 729), but having lost both sovereignties he landed a force in Galloway, of which district he possessed himself. But a native chief named Innrechtach defeated him somewhere near the Dee in 741, and he was forced to retreat to Loch Ryan. While riding through a ford in Glenapp he was killed by a man hidden in a wood, and his burial-place is marked to this day by a large stone called Laicht Alpin, Alpin's grave, which gives the name to the farm of Laicht on which it stands. An event of such moment is just the one to be fitly commemorated in place-names, hence Glenapp may be confidently interpreted as a contracted form of *gleann Alpin*.

Eadberct's forces arrived in time to reinforce Innrechtach in pursuing Alpin's defeated army. The result was that all Carrick and Kyle were added to the Northumbrian realm. This was the high-tide mark of Saxon dominion in the north. Its chronicles during the latter half of the eighth century show that the domestic difficulties of the Northumbrian overlords of Galloway had become so pressing as to divert them from all thought of further conquest. The time had arrived when the alliance which had endured between the Saxons of Northumbria and the Picts of Galloway for more than two centuries was to be broken off. For Northumbria, penetrated by civil feuds and weakened by the struggles of rival claimants to her throne,[8] had now to prepare for a death-struggle with a terrible foe from without, the Norsemen, who in 793 sacked the religious settlement at Lindisfarne, and effected descents upon various parts of the Anglian coast. The Saxons withdrew from Galloway, and the suzerainty was given up. The Niduarian Picts were once more thrown upon their own resources, and in order to maintain their nationality some new alliance had to be sought for.

Gradually the Viking pirates crept round the Caledonian shores; their black *kyuls* found as good shelter in the lochs of the west as in the fiords of Norway and the Baltic, whence they had sailed. Iona fared no better than Lindisfarne, and now it seemed as if the pagan torch must fire the sacred shrine of St Ninian at Whithorn. But to the warlike prowess of

---

[8] Osulf, succeeding Eadberct in 757, was killed by the usurper Ethelwold, who was dethroned by Alchred in 765. Alchred was overthrown by Ethelred, and he by Elfwold, Alchred's brother, in 778. Elfwold was murdered by his own soldiers in 789, to be succeeded by his nephew Osred; but the dethroned Ethelred reappeared in 790, killed his rivals, only to be himself assassinated in 794.

their Atecott ancestors these Picts of Galloway seem to have added the talent of far-seeing diplomacy, by means of which the Norsemen, instead of desolating their land like the rest with fire and sword, were induced to fraternise with them and make common cause. What were the terms paid by Christians for their alliance with pagans can never now be revealed. It is plain from the place-names of Norse origin scattered through the Stewartry and the shire, among those in Gaelic and Saxon speech, that there was a permanent Scandinavian settlement there, but we are left to imagine whether the relations between the two races were those of overlords and tributary, or whether they merely became fellow-pirates. At all events the connection cost the Galloway men the respect of other Celtic communities. The Irish chronicler MacFirbis declares that they renounced their baptism and had the customs of the Norsemen, and it is in the ninth century that they first appear mentioned as *Gallgaidhel* or foreign Gaels, taking with the Vikings part in plundering and devastation.[9] So it came to pass that their monastery of Candida Casa was spared. Somewhere about 875, Eadwulf, Bishop of Lindisfarne, and Eadred, Abbot of Carlisle, were fleeing to Ireland with the relics of St Cuthbert from these terrible Norsemen. Embarking on the Cumberland coast, they were driven by a storm into the Solway,[1] and found an asylum with

[9] *Gall*, a stranger or foreigner, especially in a hostile sense. The *Lochlannach* or Norsemen were classed by the Gaels as *Fingall*, white or fair strangers, the Norwegians, and *Dubhgall*, dark strangers, the Danes. If the Picts of Galloway had not already received the title of Gallgaidhel by reason of their alliance with Eadberct against the Picts and Scots, the origin of the name must be assigned to this period. As already said, *Gallgaidhel*, the stranger Gaels, was written in Welsh Galwyddel (pronounced *Galwythel*), and became in monkish Latin Galweithia, Galwedia, or Gallovidia, and in popular language Galloway.

[1] It was during this voyage that the miraculous preservation of St Cuthbert's book of the Gospels is said to have taken place. Washed overboard in the storm, it was thrown upon the beach uninjured.

the brethren at Whithorn. The existence of the monastery of Candida Casa proves that the Norsemen dealt otherwise with the monks of Galloway than with those they found on other parts of the coast.

Meanwhile Alpin, king of the Scots of Dalriada (not to be confused with him who had perished in Glenapp in 741), had been expelled from his kingdom by the Northern Picts. His son Kenneth (in Gaelic, *Cinaedh*), afterwards renowned as Kenneth MacAlpin, had taken refuge in Galloway. By the help of his relatives there, and the co-operation of the Norsemen, he was able to regain his kingdom of Dalriada and afterwards defeat the Northern Picts in the epoch-making battle of Fortrenn. The result of this great campaign was that he was crowned king at Scone in 844, and, thereafter subduing the country as far south as the Tweed, first united the realm of Alban, or, as we call it, Scotland,[2] under one crown. There fall, however, to be excepted from this settlement Sutherland, Caithness, the Orkneys and Shetland, some of the Western Isles, and Galloway, as being all subject to Norse dominion.

It has been plausibly suggested that the right which for many centuries afterwards was undoubtedly claimed by and conceded to the men of Galloway to march in the van of Scottish armies, was conferred on them by Kenneth MacAlpin in recognition of their services at this momentous time. The new king certainly gave proof of the value he set upon these services by giving his daughter in marriage to a Galloway chief called Olaf the White.[3]

---

[2] For a hundred years after this event Scotia was the literary name of Erin or Ireland, while Scotland was known in the vernacular as Alba, genitive Albann, and Scotsmen as Albannach. The title Duke of Albany signifies Duke of the Scots.

[3] It is not certain whether Olaf was a native Galwegian or a Norse leader settled in Galloway. His name written in Gaelic becomes Amhlaiph or

In the same year, 844, in which Kenneth was crowned King of Alban, the Gallgaidhel or Picts of Galloway assisted Olaf to seize the throne of Dublin. In 852 they invaded the territory of one of the innumerable so-called kings in Ireland — namely, Aedh, King of Ailech — but were defeated with much slaughter.[4] Olaf, supported by Imhair,[5] now appears as the enemy of the Gallgaidhel, who with the Norsemen, and assisted by Ketil Flatnose (Caittil Finn), King of the Sudreys or Western Isles, and father-in-law of Olaf, invaded Munster in 856.

These so-called invasions were doubtless purely piratical, but on the death of Kenneth MacAlpin in 860, Olaf made a determined attempt on the crown of Alban. Inheritance among the Picts was invariably through the female line. Olaf's wife, being daughter to Kenneth, gave him a better claim under Pictish law than Kenneth's son, Constantin. In company with Imhair, Olaf captured Dunbarton in 872, and held a great part of Alban, retreating with much booty and many captives to Galloway, whence the whole party sailed in two hundred ships to Dublin.[6]

A mighty devastation of Strathclyde and Galloway is recorded in 875 by Simeon of Durham, and this is corroborated in the 'Annals of Ulster,' where reference is made to a bloody defeat of the Picts by the Dubhgall or Danes. In 878 Eocha,

---

Amhalghadh (pronounced Owlhay), and remains in the modern patronymic Macaulay. Macherally and Terally in Kirkmaiden parish, corresponding to Magherawley and Tirawley in Ireland, signify the plain (*machair*) and the land (*tir*) of Olaf. Lefnoll on the shores of Loch Ryan, written of old Lefnollo, is *lethpheighinn Amhalghaidh* (leyfin owlhay), Olaf's halfpenny land; but of course the reference in these names cannot be assigned with greater certainty to this, the first-mentioned Olaf or Aulay, than to any of those who have borne the name since.

[4] Chronicles of Scots and Picts, p. 403.
[5] Imhair or Ivor, a Norse Galwegian chief.
[6] Annals of Ulster.

son of Run, King of Strathclyde, succeeded to the throne of Alba on the death of Aedh, the last of Kenneth's sons. This he did according to the Pictish law of descent, his grandmother having been sister of Constantin.

The next important personage to appear in Galloway history is Ronald the Dane, titular King of Northumbria, styled also Duke of the Galwegians,[7] in right of the ancient superiority of the Saxon kings over the Picts. With Olaf of the Brogues (Anlaf Cuaran), grandson of Olaf the White, as his lieutenant, he drove the Saxons before him as far south as Tamworth. This was in 937, but in 944 the tide of victory rolled north again. King Eadmund drove Ronald out of Northumbria to take refuge in Galloway.[8] Of this province he and his sons continued rulers till the close of the tenth century. But these were Dubhgalls or Danes, and they now fell to war with the Fingalls or Norse, who possessed themselves of the province. Galloway, on account of its central position between Ireland, Cumbria, and Strathclyde, and still more because of its numerous shallow bays and sandy inlets, so convenient for Viking galleys, was then in higher esteem than it has ever been since among maritime Powers.

Sigurd the Stout, Earl of Orkney, grandson of Thorfinn the Skull-cleaver, was lord of Galloway in 1008. His resident lieutenant was a native prince, Malcolm, whose name appears in the Sagas as Earl Melkoff. We know that Malcolm's headquarters were at Whithorn, for it is related in Nial's Saga how Sigurd's tax-gatherer, being on his way to join his master in Ireland, heard of his defeat and death at the

---

[7] "Reginaldus rex Northumbrorum ex natione Danorum et dux Galwalensium."—Flores' History.

[8] Craig Ronald, a rugged hill on the shores of Loch Grannoch, may possibly have been the fastness chosen by the fugitive king, or Loch Ronald, in Kirkcowan parish, in which there are two crannogs, one of great size.

battle of Clontarf, A.D. 1014, and bore up for Whithorn, where he spent the winter with Malcolm.

It is hardly possible that the tangled tale of Macbeth's murder of Duncan and his usurpation of the throne of Scotia will ever be clearly unravelled, but this much seems tolerably certain, that Macbeth ruled in concert with the powerful Norse Earl Thorfinn, who succeeded Earl Melkoff or Malcolm at Whithorn, and, according to the 'Chronicum Regum Manniæ,' "lived long at Gaddgeddli [Galloway], the place where England and Scotland meet." Thorfinn is said to have possessed nine earldoms, of which Galloway was probably one,—Buchan, Mar, Mearns, Angus, Sutherland, Ross, Moray, and Dale being the others. But his suzerainty over Galloway did not prevent the existence of a native king of Galloway,[9] for in 1034 the 'Annals of Ulster' take note of the death of *Suibhne mac Cinæda ri Gallgaidhel*—that is, Sweeny, the son of Kenneth, King of Galloway.[1] Suibhne was succeeded by Diarmid, who was slain in battle in 1072.[2]

In 1057 Malcolm Canmore, son of the murdered Duncan, attacked the usurper Macbeth, defeated and slew him, and became King Malcolm III. of Scotia. The great Earl Thorfinn having died in the same year, Malcolm most prudently married his widow Ingibiorg, of the Pictish race, thereby bringing under his rule the Norse districts of Scotland, including Galloway. Consolidation was now the order of the day. The Norse influence, undermined by the effects

---

[9] It is usual to translate the Gaelic *ri* or *righ* by "king," but in truth these native rulers were but chiefs, tributary to and supported by, first, the Saxons of Northumbria, then by the Norse earls.

[1] The connection between the old Atecott Picts and the Norsemen had endured so long that at this time the distinction between natives and foreigners must have become rather obscure. Suibhne is the Gaelic or Erse rendering of the Norse Swein, just as Anlaf or Amhalgaidh was of Olaf.

[2] Annals of Tighernach.

of the battle of Clontarf, was steadily on the wane. The island of Britain, soaked as it was with centuries of bloodshed, was resolving itself into the two main dominions of England and Scotland—a process which the Church, relieved from oppression by the pagan Norsemen, lent her influence to accelerate. The native rulers of Galloway showed some hesitation as to the realm into which they would seek admission. Tradition and custom tempted them to union with their old overlords the Saxon Earls of Northumbria; but the Saxon power was waning, as the Roman and the Norse had waned before. Geography as well as linguistic and racial affinity turned the scale, and the Galwegians became lieges of the Scottish king.

In this manner closed the dominion of the Norsemen over Galloway, and such parts along the Solway shore of Dumfriesshire as they had been able to hold by force. Their strength ever lay in their ships, but of their handiwork some traces probably remain in a peculiar kind of cliff tower, which may be seen at various parts of the coast, such as Castle Feather [3] and Carghidoun [4] near the Isle of Whithorn, and Port Castle on the shore of Glasserton parish.

Much less equivocal are the remains of Scandinavian occupation preserved in the place-names of the south-west. Many hills still bear the title "fell"—the Norse *fjall*—often pleonastically prefixed to the Gaelic *barr*, as in Fell o' Barhullion, in Glasserton parish, or disguised as a mere suffix, as in Criffel.[5] The well-known test-syllable *by*, a village, farm, or dwelling, so characteristic of Danish rather than of Norse occupation, takes the place in southern districts which *bólstaðr* holds in northern. Lockerby, the dwelling of Locard or Lock-

---

[3] *Caiseal Pheadhair* (?), Peter's castle.
[4] *Carrig a' duin*, crag of the fort.
[5] Formerly written Crafel, probably *kraka fjall*, the crow-hill.

hart, Canonbie, and Middlebie in Dumfriesshire — Busby, Sorby, and Corsbie in Wigtownshire—are instances in point. *Vík*, a creek or small bay, gives the name to Southwick parish and Senwick (*sand vík*, sandy bay); and *nés*, a cape, appears in Sinniness (*sunnr nés*, south point) and Borness (*borh nés*, burgh or fort point); but Auchness is in another language, being the Gaelic *each inis*, horse-pasture. Pastoral occupation is implied in Fairgirth (*fær garðr*, sheep-fold); but Cogarth, the cow-pen, is more probably Saxon than Scandinavian, for though in modern Danish "cow" is *ko*, in old Norse it was *kýr*. Tinwald, like Dingwall in the north, is *þinga völlr*, the assembly-field, and Mouswald, *mosi völlr*, the moss-field.

Queen Ingibiorg died in time to enable Malcolm to seek a still more important alliance than that by his first marriage, and in 1069 he married Margaret, daughter of the Anglo-Saxon king, Eadgar Aetheling. From this date may be traced the beginning of the long warfare which for so many centuries desolated the borderland of England and Scotland. Malcolm, claiming in name of Eadgar the right of rule over all Cumbria and part of Northumbria, overran all that country, which brought him into contact with William Rufus. This led to the invasion of Scotland by William, and ended in Malcolm doing homage to the English king for the territories of Lothian and Cumbria. Finally Malcolm, after a fruitful and powerful reign of thirty-five years, was slain by treachery in 1093 at Alnmouth in Northumberland; the southern part of Cumbria was annexed to England, and the border between England and Scotland fixed not very differently from what it is at the present day.

NOTE A.

MAGNUM MONASTERIUM.

PERSONS of both sexes were trained at Whithorn for a religious life. In the Irish life of St Modwenna, who founded a chapel in Galloway called Chill-ne-case, which cannot now be identified, there is preserved a hymn by the monk Mugentius, prefaced by an account of the incident which led to its composition, so vivid as to deserve transcription as an illustration of life and morals in the great Monastery of Rosnat or Whithorn in the sixth century :—

"Mugent made this hymn in Futerna [Whithorn].[1] The cause was this—Finnen of Magbhile [Moville] went to Mugent for instruction, and Rioc and Talmach and several others with him. Drust was king of Britain then, and had a daughter Drustice, and he gave her to Mugent to be taught to read, and she fell in love with Rioc, and she said to Finnen, 'I will give thee all the books which Mugent has if thou wilt give me Rioc to marriage.' And Finnen sent Talmach to her that night in the form of Rioc, and he knew her, and thence was conceived and born Lonan of Treoit. But Drustice supposed that Rioc had known her, and she said that Rioc was the father of her son. But this was false, because Rioc was a virgin. Then Mugent was wroth, and sent a certain youth into the church saying, 'Whosoever comes first unto thee this night into the church, smite him with an axe.' He said this because Finnen was in the habit of going first into the church; but, notwithstanding, on that night, by the providence of the Lord, Mugent himself went first to the church, and the youth smote him; as the prophet saith, 'For his travail shall come, and his wickedness shall fall on his own head.' And then Mugent said, *Parce*, because he thought the enemies would spoil the people, or (this was the cause that the hymn was made) that the sin thereof might not be visited on the people."

Then follows the hymn, which is of indifferent literary merit. It is printed in 'The Historians of Scotland,' vol. v. p. 292 (Edinburgh, 1874).

---

[1] Gaelic and Pictish speakers used *f* or *g* where Welsh and Saxon sounded *w*. Thus St Finan of Moville, who was a pupil of Mugent's, is commemorated at Kirkgunzeon in Pictish Galloway, and at Kilwinning in Cymric Ayrshire.

CHAPTER III.

FROM THE DEATH OF MALCOLM CANMORE IN 1092 TO THE INTRODUCTION OF THE FEUDAL SYSTEM IN 1234.

For thirty years after the death of Malcolm Canmore in 1092 Scotland was distracted by disputes about the succession, and it seemed as if the realm would be once more splintered into the old patchwork of rival regalities. Of Queen Margaret's four sons, Eadgar, the eldest, disregarding the successive coronation of Duncan, Malcolm's brother, and Donald, his son by Ingibiorg, established himself at Edinburgh as King of Scots. At his death in 1107 he left Scotland north of Forth and Clyde to his brother Alexander, and all the Lothians and Cumbria, including Dumfriesshire and Galloway, to David, his youngest brother. Alexander dying in 1124, Scotland was reunited under the sceptre of David, except the northern and western isles, over which the Norsemen still held sway.

Now David having been taken to England as a boy by his sister Matilda when she married Henry I., had been educated there and thoroughly imbued with the spirit of feudal chivalry, a fact which was to have no slight influence on the social state of Scotland. One of his companions at the English Court was one Fergus, of the line of Galloway princes or native rulers, who was destined to introduce the feudal system into the south-west. He married Elizabeth, natural daughter of

Henry I., and sister of Sibilla, who married Alexander I., brother of David.

On David succeeding Alexander in 1124, he made a proclamation to his subjects, addressed to "all good men of my whole kingdom—Scottish, English, Anglo-Norman, and Gallovidians." Thus the people of Galloway were still recognised as a distinct race, ruled by Fergus, whose chief seat was not at Whithorn, as heretofore had been customary with the "kings" of Galloway, but on an island still known as the Palace Isle, in the lake called after him Loch Fergus, near St Mary's Isle. He was an enlightened ruler, but his expenditure in church-building alone must have far exceeded any revenues he can have drawn from Galloway. Probably Elizabeth brought to him an ample dowry.

Of the first of the religious houses built by Fergus no trace now remains beyond the green mounds marking the foundations. It stood about three miles from Stranraer, and has long been popularly known as Saulseat, which has been erroneously glossed *Sedes animarum*, but was more correctly termed *Monasterium viridis stagni*, the monastery of the green lake, because of its position on the shores of a small lake in Inch parish, which takes a greenish tint from time to time, owing to the multitudinous development of spore-like vegetable bodies. This house he handed over to monks from Premontré in Picardy. His next foundation was also in favour of the Premonstratensian Order—the Priory of Whithorn. Some fragments of his original building remain there, including the beautiful south door of late Norman work; but the west tower, which Symson mentions as still standing in the seventeenth century, has disappeared, and the whole of the east end, choir, and transept, have been ruthlessly destroyed. All ancient buildings of any pretension which remain as ruins in Galloway west of the Dee have suffered grievously from the avidity with which they have been ransacked for freestone. The native stone is hard intractable Silurian, with occasional intrusive masses of granite. This served for the walls of Whithorn and other ecclesiastical structures, but the coigns, pillars, and carved work were wrought in imported freestone, and have afforded convenient quarries to all who chose to take them, whether masons erecting a farm-steading, or housewives wanting a bit of "free" to scrub a doorstep. When the bishopric of Candida Casa was restored in 1126, Gilla Aldan was sent to York for consecration, in signification of the renewal of the ancient Saxon see. Tungland, on the Dee, was the next great church built by Fergus; then followed S. Maria de Trayll, now St Mary's Isle; but the noblest structure of all was Dundrennan Abbey. Of this splendid building there remain but the transept and choir, a consummate example of Early Pointed work. This was a Cistercian house, having been colonised from Rievaux, of which Ailred, who wrote the life of Ninian, was abbot at the time.

Feudalism, of which the young King of Scots was so much enamoured, was not introduced into Scotland without exciting serious opposition among the native chiefs, who naturally preferred the system under which they had risen to importance. In 1130, Angus, Earl of Moray, raised an insurrection to resist foreign innovations. Fergus of Galloway joined him, or at least was so seriously implicated that, on the rebellion being suppressed and the insurgents dispersed, he had to take sanctuary in Holyrood Abbey. Thus it came to pass that when in 1138 King David declared war against Stephen of England, Fergus was still under a cloud. His Picts of Galloway, therefore, whom it was his proud privilege to lead as the vanguard of the Scottish host, were placed under command of the king's nephew, William

Fitz-Duncan, in whose veins ran the Pictish blood of his grandmother Ingibiorg. David led his forces as far south as Durham without much opposition, for Stephen was occupied in the south of England. The Galwegian Picts gave some trouble by their ardour for plunder, and at Durham insubordination rose to actual mutiny. King David having ordered the release of a lady whom they had taken captive, and finding his commands disregarded, went in person to the Pictish camp to enforce them; on which the Galwegians threatened to slay him and his courtiers.[1] William, however, succeeded in restoring discipline by spreading a false report that the English were at hand; after which the army separated into two forces, David marching to lay siege to Norham, and William leading his unruly troops to lay waste part of Lancashire.

It was his intention to seize Clitheroe, but here they found a well-equipped force of English cavalry drawn up under the walls of that town. The Galwegians were led to the attack without delay—a mere rabble, it seemed, against well-disciplined troops; but such was the fury of their onset that the English fell into confusion, and were routed with much slaughter. Many knights were taken prisoners, much booty was captured, and, having thus atoned for their misbehaviour at Durham, the Galwegians were marched back to rejoin the king's army at Northallerton.

The English host lay under Walter d'Espec on Culton Moor, where their standard, a ship's mast bearing the banners of St Peter of York, St John of Beverley, and St Wilfrid of Ripon, had been set up. There were those in the English camp, Anglo-Norman barons holding fiefs on Scottish as well as on English soil, whose interest it was to bring about mediation between the two monarchs. Among those who

[1] Richard of Hexham.

thus owed double allegiance was Robert de Brus, first Lord of Annandale, who, coming to audience with David, besought that he might be allowed to arrange terms. The king, it is said, was inclined to yield; but William Fitz-Duncan, incensed by a slight put on his Galloway men, to whom de Brus referred as "not men, but brute beasts, void of piety and humanity," interposed fiercely, charging de Brus with treachery, and prevailed on the king to refuse all negotiations. Thereupon de Brus, commenting bitterly on the king's sudden confidence in the Galwegians, withdrew, but, as is said, left his son to perform for David the military service which the father owed for his lands in Annandale.

David's army outnumbered that of Stephen, but he was weak in cavalry and archers. With these he proposed to lead the attack, upon which the Galloway division loudly claimed their right to form the van. In vain the king and his generals argued with them—they would fight there or nowhere; and at last, though against his judgment, David consented, for he could not afford to lose their services.

The English cavalry dismounted and stood like a wall of steel to receive the tumultuous onset of the Picts. "Albanaid! Albanaid!" cried the Galwegians. "Yry! Yry!" shouted back the English in derision;[2] yet the violence of the onslaught threw them into some confusion, which Prince Henry, charging with his cavalry, turned into a rout. It was the only support the Galwegians got that day. The word went abroad that the King of Scots was slain: an English soldier stood waving a head, which he declared was David's. It was false, as the king proved by his own presence; but whether from fear or from jealousy, the other Scottish divisions would not advance, but left the Galwegians unsupported. These had carried the

[2] "Yry!"—i.e., *Eire*, Irish. To this day "Eerish" is a term of contempt in Galloway.

English position; yet the battle of the Standard was lost to the Scottish cause, and with ranks sorely thinned the Pictish division retreated towards Galloway. At Carlisle they were overtaken by the Papal legate, Alberigo of Ostia, who persuaded them to release all the women they had carried off captive. There is a tradition that during the action the younger de Brus of Annandale, fighting in the Scottish ranks, was taken prisoner by his own father, who afterwards brought the boy before Stephen and asked where it was the royal will he should be imprisoned. "Take him to his nurse!" was the king's reply.

Fergus of Galloway had married his daughter Affric to Olaf, King of Man. Wymond, a monk of Furness, had been consecrated Bishop of Man, but, renouncing his vows, married the daughter of Somerled, King of the Isles, and a near relative of Olaf. On leaving the Church Wymond assumed the name of MacEth (Mackay or M'Kie), and claimed to be the son of Angus, Earl of Moray, who had been killed in the rebellion of 1130. Somewhere between the years 1141 and 1150 this man raised the standard of revolt, summoning to it all the Celtic chiefs, who resented the intrusion of so many Anglo-Norman lords. After some months' successful pillaging in the north, he landed a force on the coast of Galloway, calculating, no doubt, on the support of Queen Affric's people.[3] But the Galloway Picts proved faithful in their allegiance to King David. Fergus, their lord, was absent at the time, being, in truth, still in hiding because of his complicity with Moray's rising; but an able lieutenant was found in brave Bishop Gilla Aldan of Whithorn, who gathered all available force to resist MacEth.

---

[3] Knockeffrick, in Kirkinner parish, seems to preserve Queen Affric's name. It overlooks the estuary of the Cree.

A battle took place on the west shore of the estuary of the Cree: tradition states that there was a personal encounter between the brave bishop and the renegade, in which the latter was borne to the ground. At all events MacEth had to flee, making his escape with difficulty across the fords of Cree. His own men rose against him after his defeat, put out his eyes and made him a eunuch, after which he lived long as a prisoner in Roxburgh Castle.

The Wigtownshire railway now traverses the scene of this battle at a place called Causwayend, about midway between Wigtown and Newton-Stewart, and the stream over which the line runs is still called the Bishop's Burn.[4] Fergus crept back into King David's favour by an ingenious ruse. Alwyn, Abbot of Holyrood, suffered Fergus to assume the dress of a canon regular and to sit among the brethren assembled in chapter to receive the king. The Abbot then addressed the king, praying him "to pardon us and every one of us every fault committed against your Majesty, and in token of this gracious pardon to bestow upon every one of us the kiss of peace." Whereupon the King replied, "Dear brethren, I forgive you all; I commend myself to your prayers." After this involuntary reconciliation, the king received Fergus back into full confidence, and restored him to his former office, in gratitude for which the penitent lord built the Priory of Trayle (St Mary's Isle), and handed it over to the Abbey of Holyrood.

But now comes a sad chapter in the history of this great man, for Fergus has earned that title by the mark he has left on the history of his province. King David died in

---

[4] It is doubtful whether the name can be connected with this battle; it is more likely to have been taken from Clairy, a residence of the bishops of Whithorn in later times, which stood on the bank of this stream. Clairy is the Gaelic *clerech*, a clergyman.

1153, and was succeeded by Malcolm, a boy of ten years old. Somerled and other northern chiefs put forward Donald, a son of the pretender MacEth, as a claimant to the throne. Fergus, so far from supporting Donald, seized him when he sought sanctuary at Whithorn, and sent him to prison at Roxburgh, where the elder MacEth still lay. But Fergus's allegiance was not proof against the incapacity for rule shown by Malcolm IV. and his ministers. Henry II. first persuaded Malcolm to resign to him the Scottish territory south of the Tweed, and then took him to fight under his banner in France, a country with which Scotland was then at peace. The Scots nobles declared they would not have Henry as king over them,[5] and Malcolm was summoned home in haste to find disaffection far advanced, and the Galwegians in open revolt in support of William, great-grandson of their Lady Ingibiorg. Malcolm was besieged at Perth by six of his chief earls, but a reconciliation was effected by intervention of the clergy. Fergus, the last to rise, remained alone in rebellion. Twice Malcolm led an army against him, and twice his invasion of Galloway was repulsed. On his returning again with a stronger force, Fergus submitted on favourable terms, and retired once more to Holyrood Abbey, where he died as a monk in 1161.

Fergus was succeeded in the lordship of Galloway by his son Uchtred. His name is preserved appended to many charters, notably to one, a royal grant in favour of Robert de Brus, signed at Lochmaben in 1165. He built the beautiful Abbey of Lincluden, where a Benedictine nunnery was established. From the writings of Ailred, Abbot of Rievaux, we obtain a brief view of Galloway ecclesiastical life at this time. He was at Kirkcudbright[6] on the feast

---

[5] Fordun, Annals, iii.
[6] Formerly Kilcudbrit—*cil Cudbert*, the chapel of St Cuthbert.

of St Cuthbert, March 20, which was celebrated by solemn services, in the course of which a penitent was miraculously freed from an iron belt. Thereafter a bull, offered in oblation to St Cuthbert, was tied to a stake and baited by the students. Ailred was shocked at such unclerical barbarity and rebuked the young men, one of whom, telling the visitor to mind his own business, was straightway gored by the bull.

In 1173 William the Lion invaded England with an army composed, it is said, chiefly of Galwegians under Uchtred and his brother Gilbert. After a year of pillage in the lands north of Humber, the Scottish king was captured by Barnard de Balliol; whereupon bitter dissension ensued in the Scottish camp, Gilbert accusing his elder brother of treachery. Uchtred was forced to fly: returning to Galloway, he found his own castles closed against him, and, after wandering some time as a fugitive, was finally captured in a cave near Portpatrick which still bears his name—Cave Ouchtred. His brother Gilbert, having first torn out his eyes and brutally mutilated him,[7] put him to death. Then, to secure himself against the vengeance of the Scottish Government, he sent a secret embassy to Henry II., in the names of his murdered brother and himself, offering allegiance to the English Crown. Roger Hoveden and Robert de Val were sent to accept the homage of the two brothers, and to assure them of Henry's cousinly affection; but finding on arrival the true state of affairs—that not only had Uchtred been barbarously murdered, but that a number of Anglo-Normans, faithful subjects of King William, had also been put to death—they refused to have any dealings with the murderer of their king's relative.[8] William the Lion was

---

[7] "Abscessis testiculis et oculis evulsis."
[8] "Consanguineum Henrici regis."—Benedict, Abbas.

now restored to liberty, though as the vassal of Henry, and marched into Galloway to punish Gilbert; but once more the prowess of the Picts proved too strong for the royal arms, and the king had to content himself with the submission of his rebellious subject, who accompanied him to York. There King William and Lord Gilbert both did homage to King Henry; the latter paying £1000 indemnity for his crimes, and giving his son Duncan as hostage.[9]

On the death of the cruel Gilbert in 1185, Roland, son of Uchtred, claimed the lordship of Galloway, and, in a battle "sare, scharpe, and snell,"[1] defeated Gilpatrick, who championed the cause of Duncan, a hostage in England. Next he drove out a freebooter, Gilcolm, who had taken possession of part of Gilbert's dominions and established himself as Lord of Galloway, which, ever since the slaughter of King Alpin, the son of Echach, in 740, had been held to include Carrick.

But Henry II., espousing the cause of Duncan, prepared to invade Galloway, and marched with a strong force as far as Carlisle. There, by the intervention of King William, an agreement was entered into, by which Roland was confirmed Lord of Galloway, and Carrick was handed over to Duncan.

Mr Joseph Bain, in his able introduction to the first volume of the 'Calendar of Documents relating to Scotland,' has called attention to the close alliance which was long maintained between the English Court and the two branches of the House of Galloway, represented by Alan and Thomas, grandsons of the murdered Uchtred, and Duncan, Earl of Carrick, son of the murderer Gilbert. Large tracts of land in Ireland were given by King John to all three of them, and Roland, the father of Alan and Thomas, obtained extensive estates in the

---

[9] Calendar of Documents relating to Scotland, vol. i. p. 23 *et passim*.
[1] Wyntoun, b. vii. c. 8, l. 1.

shires of Northampton, Huntingdon, and Bedford, in right of his wife, Elena de Moreville.[2] The connection of the see of Whithorn with the Archbishopric of York formed another link between Galloway and the English monarchs. Thus in 1215 King John commands the "custos" of the archbishop to give the Bishop of Whithorn 20 marks for his expenses, until it be seen how much he ought to be allowed daily.[3]

In June of the same year Alan of Galloway sends King John a good hound in return for two geese which the king had given him at Windsor.[4] Sometimes, however, Alan had to be smartly reminded of his duty. In 1219 the Sheriff of Rutland was ordered to seize the Lord of Galloway's lands in that county until he (Alan) should do homage as he was bound to do. His lands in Ireland were also seized, but were restored to him in 1220, after he had done fealty.[5]

About this time there seems to have been some scarcity in Galloway, for there are numerous warrants granted by Henry III. to the Abbots of Glenluce, Dundrennan, and other religious houses, to enable them to buy corn in Ireland.[6] A similar licence was issued in 1237 to Erkin, merchant of Kirkcudbright.[7]

We are left to imagine how it fared with the commonalty among all the selfish contests between great lords, perplexed by their double allegiance to the English and Scottish kings. What degree of liberty, civil or personal, did they enjoy? to what grade of civilisation had they attained? Of one thing only we are assured, that they were ever ready to respond to the frequent summons to arms. One such summons came from their liege lord of England in 1186, when Roland was sent to quell an insurrection on the Welsh marches; another the following year from the King of Scotland, in obedience to

[2] Bain, vol. i. p. 47. [3] Ibid., p. 109. [4] Ibid., p. 111.
[5] Ibid., pp. 126, 136. [6] Ibid., *passim*. [7] Ibid., p. 251.

which he led his men to suppress a rebellion in the north, slew Donald Bane on the moor of Mongarvey, in Badenoch, and scattered his forces.

Roland founded the Abbey of Glenluce in 1190, and manned it with Cistercians from Melrose. Of this fine building little is now standing except the chapter-house and gate-house, which, however, are of a much later date than the twelfth century. Of the nave only the foundations remain. Thomas Hay of Park, who was appointed commendator after the Reformation, probably used the abbey church as a quarry in building the mansion-house of Park, which still remains entire.

In 1196 Roland became Constable of Scotland. Dying in 1199, he left two sons, Alan, who succeeded him as Lord of Galloway, and Thomas, who became Earl of Athole. Alan, styled by Buchanan " by far the most powerful of Scotsmen," married the daughter of the Earl of Huntingdon, brother of William the Lion.

> " This erle Dawy had douchters thre ;
> Margret the first of tha cald he ;
> This Margret wes a pleysand May,
> Hyr weddit Alayne off Gallway." [8]

Besides the lands of Galloway, he inherited from his father vast estates in the counties of Northampton and Leicester, for which he did homage to King John of England in a peculiar way. Though present himself at a meeting of the English and Scottish kings at Durham in 1212, he seems to have vested his English estates, for the occasion only, in Prince Alexander of Scotland, who performed obeisance for them. King John had before this, in 1207, infeft Alan in the lands of Antrim, in reward for services of a Galwegian fleet and army. It is an example how strangely the allegiance of the Scottish magnates was divided at this time, that Alan, though Constable of Scot-

---

[8] Wyntoun, b. viii. c. 6, l. 1249.

land, took a leading part with the English barons in their controversy with John, and was present at Runnymede at the signing of Magna Charta in 1215. Three years before, in 1212, he had sent his natural son Thomas with seventy-six ships to lay waste the coast of Derry;[9] and thirteen years later he waged war on behalf of Reginald, one of the rival kings of Man, whose daughter had married the above-mentioned Thomas. This embroiled him with Haco, King of Norway, who favoured the claims of Olaf to the throne of Man, and a furious exchange of challenges took place. Haco warned Alan of the consequences which would follow if he persisted in supporting Reginald: Alan replied that ships sailed as easily from Galloway to Norway as from Norway to Galloway.

Dying in 1234, Alan was buried at Dundrennan Abbey. He was the last of the Galloway lords to receive from the chroniclers the title of king.[1] He left but three legitimate children, all daughters, and all married to Norman lords: Helena to Roger de Quenci, Earl of Winchester; Devorguila to John de Balliol of Barnard; and Christian to William de Fortibus, Earl of Albemarle.

While Galloway remained up to this time mainly in possession of her native lords, the old Gallgaidhel, Dumfriesshire had passed much more largely into the hands of feudal Norman knights. Dunegal of Stranid,[2] whose chief seat was at Sanquhar, left several sons when he died about 1140, undoubtedly of the old Celtic stock. But his descendants cannot now be traced. Permanent surnames, in the modern sense, were unknown in these early days. Terri-

---

[9] Annals of Ulster, *ad ann.* 1212 and 1213.
[1] "1234. Ailin MacUchtraigh ri Galgaidel mortuus est" (Alan, the son of Uchtred, King of Galloway, died).—Annals of Ulster.
[2] Strath Nid—*i.e.*, Nithsdale.

torial lords, indeed, were designated by the titles of their lands in addition to their baptismal names; but members of the Celtic families had only a personal name, and a to-name, not hereditary, indicative either of their paternity or of some peculiarity of appearance, character, or occupation.[3] Even among the Norman lords, or Celtic lords adopting Norman style, there was much vagueness of designation. Thus Alanus *dapifer* or the Steward, progenitor of the royal house of Stuart, had a son Walter, who signed Walter Fitz Alan. Walter's son became Alan Fitzwalter, and so on. Sometimes, as in the case of Bruce, Douglas, and Maxwell, powerful lords acquired lands in Dumfriesshire and retained their territorial names derived from their possessions elsewhere. Bruce was "de Brus" in Normandy; Douglas was "of Douglas"—*dubh glas*, the dark stream, which gave the name to his lands in Lanarkshire; while Maxwell, a name often disguised as the Norman Maccusville, was in reality a salmon-pool on the Tweed, close to Kelso Bridge, still called Maxwheel. Maccus, the son of Unwin, a Saxon lord, obtained the fishery before 1150, which was then named Maccus's wiel or pool. The lands adjacent got the name, and the descendants of Maccus became known as Herbert, John, or Aymer "de Maccuswel," and became a powerful family in Dumfriesshire and Galloway. As time went on and regular surnames became a necessity among all classes, territorial surnames became diffused among the vassals and

---

[3] The change from the patronymic to the locative style of surname among the Celts is well illustrated by Camden: "In late times—in the time of King Henry VIII.—an ancient worshipful gentleman of Wales, being called at the pannell of a jury by the name of Thomas Ap William Ap Thomas Ap Richard Ap Hoel Ap Evan Vaghan, &c., was advised by the judge to leave that old manner; whereupon he afterwards called himself Moston (Mostyn), according to the name of his principal house, and left that surname to his posteritie."

serfs, who, under the clan system which prevailed as generally on the Borders as in the Highlands, often assumed the names of their chieftains or feudal superiors.[4] There was practical cause for this sometimes, as when, in a later day, the Earl of Menteith declared war against all men except the king and those of the name of Graham, a step which would attract considerable popularity to that surname in the district of the Lennox and Menteith.

[4] Some traces of primitive vagueness may still be detected in the matter of surnames in Galloway. A gamekeeper, formerly in my employment, was commonly known as Sandy Clanachan, but his official name on the pay-book was Saunders M'Lean, and all his sons call themselves M'Lean.

CHAPTER IV.

FROM THE DEATH OF ALAN OF GALLOWAY IN 1234 TO THE CORONATION OF ROBERT DE BRUS IN 1306.

FEUDALISM, which seems to have quietly established itself in Dumfriesshire, was not to obtain ascendancy in Galloway without a contest. On the death of Alan in 1234 the native gentry were by no means disposed to suffer the superiority of their ancient province to pass into the hands of his three alien sons-in-law. First they offered the lordship of the province to the king, and when this was declined they besought him to appoint Thomas, Alan's illegitimate son, to rule over them. This also was refused; so when Thomas, materially supported by his friends in Ulster, raised the standard of independence, the people of Galloway readily rallied round him. Alexander II. led an army against them, and, after being nearly overwhelmed in the forests and mosses, quelled the revolt and dispersed the rebels. Thomas fled to Ireland, but reappeared next year in the Rhinns with a force of Irish. This time he met with no encouragement, and surrendered to the king, who, with singular clemency, let him off with a short imprisonment. But punishment fell heavier on the people: the Irish kerns were put to the sword, two of their chiefs by the king's orders being taken to Edinburgh, there to be torn asunder by horses, and the lands and churches of Galloway were severely wasted by the royal troops. The prior and sacristan of Tungland were slain in their own church.[1]

With the establishment of feudalism the people of Galloway —that is to say, the Pictish population—practically lost their freedom. It may not have been a freedom fraught with many privileges: it was burdened with the condition of military service at the bidding of the chief, and the profits of agricultural enterprise were restricted to what could be made out of the wasteful runrig culture and common pasturage. The material condition of the rural population cannot have been deteriorated by the introduction of feudal customs, and may very likely have been actually improved. But they were free no longer. There was, indeed, a grade of *liberetentes*— of free tenants—holding farms from the barons or from the religious houses; but below them were the mass of bondmen and neyfs, and henceforward every charter of lands conveyed to the landlord, whether layman or cleric, power over the *bondi et nativi*[2] almost as absolute as over any other product of the soil or chattel on the estate. Almost, but not quite as absolute, for the law which held the serf *astrictus glebæ*— bound to the soil, he and his posterity for ever being forbidden to leave it—also protected him from capricious sale or removal by the lord of the soil.[3] It was their lot to cultivate the soil, receiving in return only enough food to keep themselves and their families, a kind of cattle of superior intelligence and value.

[1] Fordun, xliii.

[2] Charters of this period usually contained the expression *cum bondis et bondagiis* as well as *cum nativis* or *hominibus*. The distinction between the two is not clear. Probably the first meant bond-servants and their families, whether imported or purchased; and by the second is implied the remains of the native race, thus brought into perpetual servitude according to Norman custom.

[3] A succinct summary of the powers vested in feudal barons is given in 'Scottish Legal Antiquities,' by Cosmo Innes.

A trial, which took place in Dumfries Castle about the year 1259, is worth quoting in some detail, as showing the hereditary jealousy existing between the Saxon and Welsh population of Dumfriesshire and the old Picts of Galloway; and being, as well, a good illustration of the way surnames arose among the common people.

On Monday, after the feast of SS. Fabian and Sebastian, inquisition was made on Richard son of Robert son of Elsa (Elizabeth?) before the king's bailiffs. The witnesses were Adam Long, Adam Mille, Hugh Schereman, Roger Wytewelle, Richard Haket, Walter Faccinger, Thomas Scut, Robert Muner, Thomas calvus (the bald), Robert Boys, William Scut, William pellaparius (the skinner), Henry tinctor (the dyer), and others. They deponed that the prisoner Richard and Adam molendarius (the miller) met on Sunday next after the feast of St Michael at St Michael's church, whereupon Adam defamed Richard by calling him a thief—viz., "Galuvet" (a Gallovidian). It seems to have been quite well understood that "thief" and "Gallovidian" were convertible terms from a Dumfriesian point of view. Next Thursday, Adam, standing at a house door, was warned by a woman that Richard was coming down the street and advised to keep out of his way. "Not I!" said Adam; "I have a knife as sharp as he." He then drew a knife and attacked Richard, who defended himself with his sword, and, in doing so, killed Adam. "I have not killed thee," he said, as the other lay mortally wounded, "thou hast done it thyself." The verdict of the baron's jurors and the burgesses' jurors was unanimous, that "Richard is faithful, but Adam was a thief and a defamer."

In 1246 Christian, the third of Alan's daughters, died, and Galloway was divided between the other two brothers-in-law,

[1] Acts of Parliament of Scotland, vol. i. p. 87.

de Quenci, Earl of Winchester, and John de Balliol—the Cree being the boundary between the two territories. De Quenci held what is now Wigtownshire, de Balliol what is now the Stewartry of Kirkcudbright. But in 1251 a new dignitary appeared in Galloway. Alexander III. being then only ten years old, Comyn, Earl of Buchan, his brother Alexander, Earl of Menteith, and their nephew, the Lord of Badenoch, were at the head of affairs. The office of Justiciary of Galloway was created, to which John Comyn of Badenoch was appointed—a man, says Fordun, "prone to robbery and rashness." The Earl of Buchan married de Quenci's daughter Elizabeth, and on the death of de Quenci not only got himself installed High Constable of Scotland, but seized the sole lordship of Western Galloway, which ought by feudal right to have been divided among de Quenci's three daughters. Meanwhile, though the old Pictish gentry saw their lands passing rapidly into the hands of Norman lords, it was well for the people that de Balliol and de Quenci proved enlightened rulers. The prosperity which prevailed under them accounts for the affection afterwards shown to their memory, and for the course which the Gallovidians steered in the coming struggle.

De Quenci is generally believed to have made his chief residence at Cruggleton Castle, though this is disputed by the author of 'Lands and their Owners in Galloway,'[5] who stoutly maintains that the castle remained in the possession of Kerle, a native chief, from whom he claims descent. Be this as it may, nothing now remains of this ancient stronghold but a fragment of vaulting, perched high on a cliff overlooking Wigtown Bay. Distant about a quarter of a mile stands a ruined church, lately repaired by the Marquis of Bute, which, being built in the Norman style, must have been standing before and during the rule of de Quenci.

[5] Mr P. H. M'Kerlie.

De Balliol lived at Botel, now written Buittle,[6] where his wife Devorguila gave birth to John de Balliol, the future King of Scotland. Her husband died in 1269, but she survived him for twenty-one years, during which she proved a capable and considerate ruler.

> "A bettyr lady than scho wes nane
> In all the yle of Mare Bretane."[7]

Before the elder de Balliol's death a successor had been appointed to Comyn as Justiciar of Galloway, in the person of Aymer de Maxwell, Chamberlain of Scotland, who also held the office of Sheriff of Dumfries.

Devorguila inherited a full measure of the pious and constructive spirit of her ancestor Fergus. Chief among her ecclesiastical achievements must be reckoned the Abbey of Sweetheart (*Abbacia Dulcis Cordis* or Douxquer), now called New Abbey, erected to her husband's memory—best preserved of all the ruins in the south-west. De Balliol had been buried where he died, at Barnard Castle, but his widow caused his heart to be embalmed and placed in a "cophyne" of ebony and silver, which she kept constantly beside her. When she herself died in 1290 her husband's heart, from which the new abbey was named, was by her direction buried with her at Sweetheart.[8]

---

[6] From the Anglo-Saxon *botl*, a dwelling,—a word which yields such names as Bootle in Lancashire, Harbottle in Northumberland, Newbattle, Morebattle, &c. Of this once important building little now remains. It stood on the Urr, about a mile from Dalbeattie.

[7] Wyntoun, b. viii. c. 8, l. 1521. "Mare"—*i.e.*, more, greater; an early example of the phrase "Greater Britain."

[8] "Scho fowdyt in to Gallway
Off Cystews [Cistercians] ordyre ane Abbay;
Dulce-Cor scho gert thaim all,
That is Swet-Hart, that Abbay call:
And now the men off Gallway
Callys that sted the New Abbay."—Wyntoun, b. viii. c. 8, l. 1507.

The bulk of the people of Galloway at this time spoke Gaelic, though the religious houses doubtless spread Saxon speech in their immediate

Of Devorguila's foundations for Black Friars at Wigtown and for Grey Friars at Dumfries all traces have now been swept away, except what may be recognised in such names as Friars' Vennel, the oldest street in Dumfries, and at Wigtown the Monk Hill and its Gaelic equivalent, Drumanaghan.

Honoured as she is still in the south as the benefactress of Balliol College, Oxford,—which was founded by her husband, further endowed by provision in his will, and enriched by gifts and bequests of Devorguila herself,—her most enduring monument in the north is the stately bridge of nine arches, a miracle of engineering in its day, spanning the Nith at Dumfries, over which men still pass to and fro between Galloway and Dumfriesshire—emblematic, it might seem, of the bond which, after her demise, was to unite those hereditary foes, the Picts of Galloway and the Britons of Strathclyde. Yet before that union should be effected there was to come a period of strife more bitter, more famous, and more lasting in effect, than all the slayings and burnings that had yet befallen North Britain.

Scotland had been industrious and become rich under the long reigns of William the Lion and the second and third Alexanders. She was now about to take the plunge into that long period of civil strife and war with England which were to reduce her so low that she became a by-word for poverty among European nations,—a condition from which she was never to rise until the legislative union with England should be accomplished.

Dumfries figures prominently in the golden reign of Alexander III. as the place of assembly for the royal fleet, which the king brought together to subdue Magnus, King of Man.

neighbourhood. Close to Sweetheart Abbey is the mansion of Shambelly, apparently so named in contrast to New Abbey, for it means *sean* (shan) *baile*, the old homestead or farm.

The Norse king, Haco, having been crushed at the battle of Largs in 1263, Alexander undertook in the following year to put an end to the Norse dominion in the Isle of Man. There is some discrepancy in the meagre accounts preserved of how this was effected. Fordun says that Magnus met Alexander at Dumfries and made submission to him there, and there are traces in the Scottish Exchequer Rolls [9] of diplomatic transactions conducted by Aymer de Maxwell, Sheriff of Dumfries, and Alexander Comyn, Earl of Buchan, Sheriff of Wigtown, who received payment for various embassies sent to Man, and for the maintenance of Manx hostages.[1] But there was hard fighting too, for Alexander the Steward and John Comyn landed in Man in 1270, and slew Ivor, who had usurped the throne. Ade, the son of Neson, owner of Bardonan in Galloway, was killed in the king's service there; but, in the end, the kingdom of Man became tributary to the Scottish Crown.

Alexander III. was killed in March 1286 by a fall from his horse. All through his long reign he had maintained cordial relations with his brother-in-law Edward I. of England, and, though the independence of Scotland had been jealously guarded, the subjects of both kings had lived at peace with each other. There arose, of course, occasional disputes between the dwellers on the Marches; but these were settled in course of law, or, where unusual bitterness arose, by arbitration. There were no signs to foretell the centuries of devastating war that were to follow.

Immediately after the king's death six guardians were ap-

---

[9] Vol. i. pp. 16, 22.

[1] The Sheriff of Wigtown accounts in 1265 for the expenditure of forty merks on the Castle of Wigtown *propter adventum Norwagensium*. Of this castle nothing now remains above the foundations, but it was then one of the twenty-three royal fortresses maintained for the defence of the realm.

pointed to administer the realm in the name of Margaret, the Maid of Norway, on whom the succession now devolved. King Edward of England, with far-seeing sagacity, at once began negotiations for her betrothal to his son, Prince Edward, in the view of uniting the two crowns. King Eric of Norway, the father of the infant queen, entered heartily into the project —being, indeed, under considerable pecuniary obligations to Edward; and Otho de Grandison and William de Hothum were sent as envoys to Rome, to obtain a bull of dispensation for a contract of marriage. This was granted, and everything promised fair for the fulfilment of King Edward's felicitous design.

But, before matters had gone thus far, Dumfriesshire and Galloway had been dragged into civil war on behalf of Robert de Brus, Lord of Annandale, afterwards to become known as "the Competitor." On September 20, 1286, certain nobles assembled at Turnberry Castle, and entered on a bond of mutual defence in order to secure the royal succession "according to the ancient customs hitherto approved and observed in the realm of Scotland."[2] Not a word of the child Queen Margaret. It was virtually a confederacy to set Robert de Brus on the throne, and an attempt was immediately made to effect this. All Scottish writers of the fourteenth century are significantly silent on the subject of this outbreak, obviously from disinclination to record anything which it might be contrary to the wishes of the reigning house to remember—although Balliol made it part of his averment in pleading before Edward in 1291. He stated that "when the bishops and great men of Scotland had sworn to defend the kingdom for their lady, the daughter of the Queen of Norway, . . . Sir Robert Bruce and the Earl of Carrick, his son, attacked the Castle of Dumfries with fire and arms and banners dis-

[2] Stevenson, vol. i. p. 22.

played, and, against the peace, expelled the forces of the queen who held the same. Hence Sir Robert advanced to the Castle of Botil.³ He then caused a proclamation to be made by one Patrick M'Guffok within the bailiary of the said castle. . . . Furthermore, the Earl of Carrick, by the assent and power of his father, took the Lady of Scotland's Castle of Wigtown, and killed several of her people there."⁴

A few fragments of evidence in support of Balliol's allegation have been preserved to our day. The lands of Bardonan in Galloway, a royal ward, were reported by Sir William de St Clair, Sheriff of Dumfries, to have lain uncultivated for two years because of the war ensuing on King Alexander's death.⁵ A similar report was made of the Crown lands in Wigtownshire by the sheriff, John Comyn, Earl of Buchan, with the additional note that the war was raised by the Earl of Carrick.⁶ Further, thanks to the delightfully gossiping manner in which it was the fashion in those days to keep the public accounts, we are informed that the reason for increased expenditure on the castles of Dumfries,⁷ Edinburgh, Jedburgh, and Ayr at this time was owing to the breaking out of war.⁸

But indeed there were more substantial grounds for this

---

³ Now Buittle, Balliol's residence in Galloway.
⁴ Palgrave, p. lxxx.
⁵ Exchequer Rolls of Scotland, vol. i. p. 35.
⁶ Ibid., p. 39. The Earl of Carrick was the son of Robert de Brus, Lord of Annandale, and obtained this historic earldom by his marriage with Marjorie, daughter of Niall, Nigel, or Neil, Earl of Carrick and great-grandson of Fergus, Lord of Galloway. She was also the widow of Adam of Kilconquhar, and it is said that she met young Robert de Brus one day returning from hunting, invited or compelled him to return with her to her Castle of Turnberry, where after fifteen days' dalliance she married him. The offspring of this marriage became Robert I. of Scotland.
⁷ See Note B, The Castle of Dumfries, p. 101.
⁸ Exchequer Rolls of Scotland, vol. i. pp. 37, 38, 42, 44.

rising than Lord Hailes was willing to admit on the evidence then before him. It would lead us too far away from the immediate affairs of the south-west to examine the special claims advanced on the part of de Brus, but this at least may be mentioned, that in 1238 Alexander II., being then an old man and despairing of issue, did, in presence of the Great Council of the nation, and with the approval of the prelates and barons assembled in Parliament, designate Robert de Brus, Lord of Annandale, as his heir in the kingdom of Scotland, being his nearest of kin. Whereupon the lords present, on command of the king, did fealty and homage to de Brus. All which was plainly set forth in the Appeal of the Seven Earls to Edward I.[9]

Meanwhile Edward I., who was in France, was pushing forward the preparations for the betrothal of Prince Edward and Queen Margaret. Terms, alike satisfactory to the interests of Scotland and England, were fixed by the treaty of Salisbury, November 6, 1289, and ratified at the Parliament of Birgham on March 14 following. Among those present at Birgham especially representing the people of Dumfriesshire and Galloway were Henry, Bishop of Galloway, John Comyn, Earl of Buchan, Robert de Brus, Earl of Carrick; the abbots of Glenluce, Dundrennan, and Tungland; the Prior of Whithorn; and the following barons: Robert de Brus, Lord of Annandale, Ingram de Balliol, Herbert de Maxwell, William de St Clair, Sheriff of Dumfries, William de Douglas, and William de Soulis.

Within a month of the conference at Birgham a ship was despatched from Yarmouth to bring Queen Margaret to the land of her espousals. She embarked safely at Bergen, but died somewhere off the Orkney Islands, and the Crown of Scotland was left in dispute between no fewer than thirteen

[9] Palgrave, pp. viii-xlix and 14-23.

claimants. These were ultimately reduced to three, of whom one was a lord of Galloway, another of Dumfriesshire. John de Balliol, a baron of vast possessions in England and France, claimed the Crown in right of descent from Margaret, his maternal grandmother, wife of Alan, and mother of Devorguila. Margaret was the eldest daughter of David, Earl of Huntingdon, brother of William the Lion, and grandson of David I. Robert de Brus, Lord of Annandale,[1] asserted a nearer claim, inasmuch as his mother Isabel was the second daughter of the Earl of Huntingdon. With the third principal claimant, Hastings, son of Huntingdon's third daughter, we have here no concern. The dispute was referred to the arbitrament of the King of England, who was acknowledged *pro hâc vice* Lord Paramount of Scotland. He summoned a court composed of forty members chosen by Balliol, a like number by Bruce, and twenty-four nominated by himself, which assembled at Norham, June 3, 1291. Their judgment was given on October 14, 1292, to the effect that " in every heritable succession, the more remote by one degree, lineally descended from the eldest sister, was preferable to the nearer in degree issuing from the second sister." Edward gave his award conformably in favour of Balliol, whose claim was, indeed, incontestable according to the principles of modern law, though not without doubt according to feudal practice, so far as then established: on November 19, John de Balliol, Lord of Galloway, received sasine of the kingdom, and was crowned at Scone on the 30th, St Andrew's Day.

But the fatal admission of English suzerainty had been made, of which the effect, though unforeseen at the time by the Scottish king and nobles, was soon to appear. Cases were carried on appeal from the Scottish Court of Balliol to that of his superior, Edward, at Westminster, which could

[1] See Note C, The Bruce Pedigree, p. 102.

only have one result—the actual, as well as the nominal, subjection of Scotland to England. In 1295 Balliol, under pressure of his barons and fired with a momentary spirit, renounced his homage to Edward, having already made alliance with Philip, King of France, then at war with the English. In the following month of February 1296 Edward summoned an army to assemble at Newcastle-on-Tyne, intending a descent on Scotland. At the same time, in order to create a diversion in his own favour in Galloway, he produced Thomas, the bastard son of Alan, Lord of Galloway, who had been in obscurity in England, if not in prison, for more than fifty years. This Thomas, it will be remembered, had once been desired by the people of Galloway to rule over them rather than allow the province to be divided among the daughters of Alan. So on March 6 Edward issued a proclamation as Overlord of Scotland to the good men and whole community of Galloway, signifying that at the request of Thomas he had consented to grant all their liberties and customs, as they and their ancestors held these in the time of King David and Lord Alan, and that he would consider as to relaxation or remission of their rents, which they had asked by the said Thomas.[2] A most diplomatic document this, and one that was to bear useful fruit to the English cause for many a year.

Balliol was as prompt as Edward in the matter of invasion. On March 26, 1296, the Earl of Buchan led Balliol's army to the invasion of Cumberland. Repulsed at Carlisle on the 28th, he marched into Northumberland and burned Hexham and Corebridge. Simultaneously Edward swept across the eastern Border, stormed Berwick with frightful slaughter, seized Roxburgh, Jedburgh, Dunbar, and Edin-

[2] Bain, vol. ii. p. 168.

burgh, and was allowed to enter Stirling, Perth, and Scone almost without opposition. On July 10, 1296, Balliol abdicated in his favour, was carried captive to London, and appeared no more in public life.

On September 8 Henry de Percy was appointed Warden of Galloway and custodian of the castles of Ayr, Wigtown, Cruggleton, and Buittle. The last named, having been the chief seat of the Balliol family in Scotland, now became a royal fortress.

In the spring of 1297 began the brief and brilliant career of him whose memory is more dearly and proudly cherished by Scotsmen than that of any other. Unfortunately, although the scenes of some of Wallace's earliest exploits are said to have been in Dumfriesshire, there are no trustworthy authorities to rely on, Blind Harry, who lived two centuries later, being the only one who has compiled a consecutive narrative. His poem is full of stirring events; but as there are many points in which his accuracy has been easily disproved, he is of little account as an authority. At Knockwood, in the parish of Kirkmichael, are some large stones called the Six Corses, and here it is said that Wallace, with a small party of sixteen swords, put to flight a company under Sir Richard Morland, who perished there with five others. After this he surprised the Castle of Lochmaben, then occupied by an English garrison, while its lord, the father of Robert I., was acting as Edward's governor of Carlisle.[3] At the same time Sir William de Douglas is supposed to have captured the keep of Durisdeer in Nithsdale.[4]

The stronger fortress of Sanquhar [5] was not far up the valley.

[3] Bain, vol. ii. p. 166.

[4] No part of this castle remains standing. It stood on the farm of Castle Hill, about 500 yards from Durisdeer church.

[5] The importance of this position, as commanding the passes into Upper Nithsdale, was recognised from the earliest times. Its name, Sanquhar

To secure this we are told that Douglas had recourse to stratagem. One Anderson, who supplied the garrison with fuel, was bribed to lend his clothes to one of Douglas's men, Dickson, to whom, disguised as a woodman and leading a load of fagots, the gate was opened. Dickson stabbed the porter and blew his horn, whereupon Douglas and his men swarmed over the drawbridge and overpowered the garrison. Every man in the place, including the captain, was put to the sword.[6] Next, Lord Clifford, then stationed at Lochmaben, and John de St John, governor of Dumfries, beleaguered Douglas in the castle he had seized; but Wallace, hastening from the Lothians, raised the siege and drove the English before him to Dumfries, and thence to Cockpool on the Solway. That night Wallace rested at Caerlaverock, the house of Sir Herbert de Maxwell, who probably favoured the lost cause of Balliol—the representative of national independence—although with the great majority of Scottish barons he had sworn fealty to Edward and signed the Ragman Roll.

This was probably the last appearance of Wallace in Dumfriesshire.[7] The Lord of Annandale had resigned the earldom

(pron. Sanker), as already remarked, signifies in Gaelic *sean cathair* (shan caer), the old fort. It is probably the Caer Rywg of Taliessin's poem, a name preserved in the Crawick Water, which joins the Nith at Sanquhar. The same chief's name appears in Saxon at Roxburgh, of old Rokisburh, Rywg's fort.

[6] The ruins of Sanquhar Castle may be seen on the west side of the Glasgow and South-Western Railway, near the town.

[7] The only record of Wallace having entered Galloway is that contained in the rhymes of Blind Harry. He describes how with Stewyn (Stephen) of Ireland and Kerlé (whose name is preserved in the modern form M'Kerlie) he captured a palisaded stronghold in that province:—

> "A strength thar was on the wattir of Cre
> Within a rock, rycht stalwart wrocht of tre."

There is a place on the Cree in Minnigaff parish called Wallace's camp, but nothing remains to show how it got the name, and Blind Harry's unsupported authority cannot be accepted.

of Carrick to his son, who in 1297 was twenty-three years of age. This young lord, the future king, was summoned to Carlisle, of which his father was still governor, and there swore on the consecrated host and the sword of Becket that he would be faithful and vigilant in the service of King Edward. He proved his sincerity by making a raid on the lands of Sir William de Douglas, then in arms with Wallace, but, according to Hemingburgh, promptly repented of an oath which he said had been extorted by force, and joined the Scottish army.[8] But he was among those barons who capitulated to de Clifford and de Percy at Irvine on July 9, 1297, giving his daughter Marjory as hostage for his fidelity to the English king, entering the service and drawing the pay of Edward. He had, therefore, no part in Wallace's glorious victory over Surrey and Cressingham at Stirling bridge. Sir William Douglas also submitted with Bruce at Irvine, but, though he voluntarily surrendered to his parole at Berwick, did not produce his hostages on the appointed day, and was imprisoned in irons.[9] From Berwick he was removed to the Tower, where he languished till his death, some time before January 20, 1298-99, when the king restored to his widow the dower lands of her first husband, William de Ferrars.[1]

When Edward I. sailed on his expedition to Flanders in August 1297, he released many Scottish knights who had been taken at Dunbar, on condition of their serving with him. Among these were five Comyns, including John "the Red," younger of Badenoch, and Sir Richard de Siward, formerly governor of Dumfries Castle.

More horrible was the fate of eleven wretched men of Galloway, who were confined in Lochmaben Castle during Wallace's operations as pledges of the loyalty of their province.

[8] Hemingburgh, vol. i. p. 119.   [9] Stevenson, vol. ii. p. 205, note.
[1] Ibid., p. 269.

They entered the gates of that terrible fortress in September 1297: only one of them left it alive, for by September 8, 1300, all the rest had found relief from their sufferings in death. Yet they were not confined as criminals, but as hostages, to whom the custom of war prescribed hospitable treatment. Their names were Lachlan Maclachlan; Donald, son of Thomas Acarson; Martin, son of Yvo of Slotham; John MacWilliam " Brownbeard"; Gilpatrick Macbreck, son of MacRory; Niven MacThomas, son of MacRory; Andrew MacEwen MacGill Rory; Matthew Macmorris MacSalvi; Yvo filius Schephert de Killo Osbern (Closeburn); John, son of Duncan Makhou; and (the sole survivor) Robert MacMaster.[2]

After his crushing defeat at Falkirk in July 1298, Wallace resigned the title of Governor of Scotland. For some time after that the Earl of Carrick acted a very dubious part. Hemingburgh says that " when he heard of the king's coming [westward after Falkirk], he fled from his face and burnt the Castle of Ayr which he held." But the testimony of both English and Scottish chroniclers is of little value, for it was the object of both, with different motives, to make it appear that Bruce attached himself early to the national cause. There is extant a letter[3] written by Bruce from Turnberry Castle on July 3, apparently in this year, to Sir John de Langton, Chancellor of England, begging a renewal of the protection to three knights who were with him on the king's service in Galloway. Again, in another document,[4] undated, but apparently written in the late autumn of 1298, Bruce is commanded by King Edward to bring 1000 picked men of Galloway and Carrick

---

[2] Letters from the Northern Registers, p. 187.

[3] Calendar of Documents, vol. ii. p. 255. Carrick was then reckoned a part of Galloway.

[4] Stevenson, vol. ii. p. 268.

to join an expedition about to be made into Scotland. However, as there is some doubt about the date of these papers, Bruce's attitude during 1298 must be held to be uncertain. It is to be noted, however, that when Edward, on returning to England after his victory at Falkirk, made grants of land in Scotland to his followers, Annandale and Carrick, held by the elder [5] and younger Bruce, were not among the lands so disposed of. Nevertheless, the Bruces do not seem to have been in possession of Annandale at this time, for in 1299 Sir Alan Fitz Warin defended Lochmaben Castle against the Earl of Carrick from 1st to 25th August.[6] This was the immediate outcome of a notable arrangement come to during that summer, whereby the Earl of Carrick (whom, to avoid confusion, I may hereafter designate by his modern title of Bruce), William de Lamberton, Bishop of St Andrews, and John Comyn of Badenoch (the "Red Comyn") constituted themselves guardians of Scotland in the name of King John (de Balliol). Bruce, as the principal guardian, was to have custody of the castles, but he appears to have been still wavering, for we hear nothing definite of his movements till after the year 1300, when Edward led the flower of his chivalry to the invasion of Dumfries and Galloway.

The siege of Caerlaverock, the chief castle of Sir John de Maxwell,[7] has been made famous by the pen of a scribe who accompanied the host, and has left a metrical catalogue

---

[5] The Lord of Annandale, Robert de Brus "le viel," was removed by Edward from the governorship of Carlisle in October 1297 (Bain, vol. ii. p. 244). In June following his property in England was distrained for debts owing to the king amounting to £2254, 14s. (Stevenson, vol. ii. p. 285). It is interesting to note that Hatfield, now the property and residence of the Marquis of Salisbury, was at that time part of the de Brus estates.

[6] Bain, vol. ii. p. 283.

[7] It is still in the possession of this family, in the person of Lord Herries.

of all the knights who took part in it and their armorial bearings.[8]

Leaving the main body at Carlisle, early in June the king rode forward to Dumfries with a small force and remained some days the guest of the Minorite Friars. Returning to Carlisle, he led his army across the Border, June 24 and 26, laying waste Annandale. Early in July Edward laid siege to the Castle of Caerlaverock with 3000 men. Its lord,[9] Sir John de Maxwell, was absent, but bravely did his garrison do their duty. "The gleam of gold and silver," says the anonymous poet, "and the radiance of rich colours displayed by the embattled host, illuminated the valley which they occupied. . . . Those of the castle seeing us arrive, might, as I well believe, deem that they were in greater peril than they could ever before remember." Notwithstanding, they showed no signs of fear, and kept up such a constant shower of great stones upon the escalading parties that the gay coats of many of the English knights were sorely damaged, and some were killed. But the English king was too good a

---

[8] "Caerlaverock was so strong a castle that it did not fear a siege; therefore the king came himself, because it would not consent to surrender. But it was always furnished for its defence, whenever it was required, with men, engines, and provisions. . . . It had good walls and good ditches, filled to the edge with water, and I believe there never was seen a castle more beautifully situated, for at once could be seen the Irish Sea to the west, and to the north a fine country surrounded by an arm of the sea, so that no born creature could approach it on two sides without putting himself in danger of the sea. Towards the south it was not easy, because there were many dangerous defiles of wood, marsh, and ditches, . . . and therefore it was necessary for the host to approach from the east, where the hill slopes."—Siege of Caerlaverock, translated. Sir Walter Scott is said to have taken his description in 'Ivanhoe' of the siege of Front-de-Bœuf's castle from this chronicle.

[9] It is not certain whether the siege in 1300 took place in the lifetime of Sir Herbert, fifth lord of Maxwell and third of Caerlaverock, or after the succession of his son Sir John. The latter surrendered to Edward, with Comyn and other barons, at Strathord on February 9, 1303-4.

soldier to attempt to carry such a strong place without all the latest appliances. His siege-train, besides battering-rams, contained robinets and catapults, which threw such a weight of stones into the place night and day that at the end of the second day the besieged were fain to capitulate. A white flag was displayed from a loophole of the gate tower; an English arrow passed through the hand of him who held it and pinned it to his face. The garrison surrendered on July 12 to the king's mercy, and marched out, when, to the astonishment of the besiegers, it was found to consist of no more than sixty fighting men. One would like to know the fate of these gallant fellows. The poet says their lives were spared by the clemency of the king, but the Chronicle of Lanercost relates that many of them were hung from the trees near the castle—a proceeding too much in character with the grim realities of war in the thirteenth century.[1]

It has commonly been asserted and believed that the castle thus besieged and dismantled by Edward stood some hundred yards to the south of the present ruin, where there are remains of earthworks; but this is not the case. The poem above quoted describes the building as being in the figure of a shield with three sides, and a tower on each angle, one of these a jumellated or double one of such dimensions as to receive the gate and drawbridge. That is a precise description of the castle as it now remains, with numerous later additions; and the curtain walls connecting the towers are of a style earlier than the fourteenth century. Edward

[1] In the previous year, 1299, Robert de Felton informed King Edward that the garrison of Caerlaverock had been doing great damage to his garrison of Lochmaben and the country round, but that on the Sunday after Michaelmas the English had a great success against them, and that, at the moment of writing, the head of Robert de Conigham, constable of Caerlaverock Castle, was set on the great tower of Lochmaben.—Bain, vol. ii. p. 279.

contented himself here, as at Dirleton, by throwing down the towers; and the outer walls now standing are the very same which he battered with his catapults and robinets.

From Caerlaverock the king's army advanced to Dumfries, and, defiling across Devorguila's beautiful bridge, entered Galloway. "Mountains and valleys," writes the fluent bard, "seemed suddenly alive with sumpter-horses, waggons with provisions, tents, and pavilions. Afar off was heard the neighing of his horses, many a beautiful pennon fluttering over the lances, many a banner displayed; and the days being fine and long, he rode leisurely to Kirkcudbright." But the destructive policy he had pursued in Annandale, the country of the Bruce, was for some reason completely reversed in Galloway, probably because the king found the people well disposed towards himself as the patron of Thomas of Galloway. All supplies were scrupulously paid for, and the abundance in which these were forthcoming testifies to the prosperity attained by the province under the rule of Balliol and Buchan. Cargoes of wheat, more than the mills near Dumfries could grind, were exported to Cumberland and Ireland for manufacture into flour, to be reshipped thence for the supply of his garrisons and of an army in the north.[2] From Kirkcudbright the king advanced as far as Cally, where his sojourn is perhaps commemorated in the name of a field on Enrick, called Palace Yard. From this place he sent detachments into Wigtownshire, receiving submission from the powerful native clan of MacDoualls,[3]

---

[2] From the Wardrobe Accounts the following prices appear to have been current: a whole ox, 5s. to 6s. 8d.; fat pigs, 2s. 2d. to 3s. 9d.; barley-malt, 4s. 4d. the qr.; oat-malt, 2s. 9d.; wheat-flour, 7s.; beans, 5s.; peas, 2s. 9d.; strong ale, 12s., 16s., 18s. the butt; small-beer, 8s.; *vinum clarum* (claret), £1, 10s. the hogshead; *vinum expensabile* (*vin ordinaire*), 40 hogsheads for £3, 18s. 4d.—less than a penny a gallon.

[3] See Note D, The Macdoualls, p. 103.

and returned to Dumfriesshire, passing the night of August 24 at *Douzquer*—Sweetheart Abbey.

Wallace had made appeal for the intervention of Pope Boniface VIII. in order to save Scotland from passing permanently under English dominion, in consequence of which the Pope directed a bull to King Edward, claiming Scotland as the immemorial fief of the Holy See, and calling upon him to desist from his conquests in that land. This document was handed to the king at Caerlaverock, and, though it could not have been agreeable to him to be interfered with thus, he complied with it so far as to begin negotiations for a truce. He remained with his Court at Dumfries until the end of October. A truce having been signed on the 30th of that month until Whitsunday following, Edward withdrew with his army into England, but left garrisons in those fortresses which he held on Scottish soil. The truce of Dumfries was afterwards prolonged till the end of November 1302.

But this truce was little regarded by some of the champions of independence. Sir Robert de Tilliol, governor of Lochmaben Castle, wrote to King Edward in September 1301, beseeching him to send reinforcements to enable him to resist Sir John de Soulis, Sir Simon Fraser, the Earl of Buchan, and others whom he names. He undertakes to hold the king's castle if 100 horsemen are sent him.[4] This seems a modest request, considering the forces opposed to him; for later in the same month he reports that Sir John de Soulis and Sir Ingelram de Umfraville came with 240 men-at-arms and 7000 foot, "e nous ardyrent nostre vile et assalyrent nostre pele demyway prime dekes a houre de noune, e puis sen partirent de nous e halerent logere pres de Annand et ardyrent e preyerent le pays la entore" (burnt

[4] Stevenson, vol. ii. p. 431.

for us our town and assailed our peel from the middle of prime till the hour of nones, and then they left us and went to lodge near Annan, and burnt and pillaged the country round about). They returned to the attack on the morrow, when Sir David de Brechin and Sir John de Vaus (Vans) were wounded, and many of their men killed. In the evening they moved off towards Dalswinton, and so through Nithsdale to Galloway.[5]

The Prince of Wales, who, had fortune favoured King Edward's diplomacy, would have been long ere this the consort of the Queen of Scotland, visited Dumfries in 1301; and the following extracts from his household accounts show the stages in his journey:—

Annan, Monday, October 17	total	£31 15 7
Blacksauch, " 18	"	29 17 10
Dumfries, Wednesday 19 till November 1		{ The same daily average.
Caerlaverock, November 2	"	37 3 0½[6]

A curious incident connected with this journey is related in a letter from William de Dorem to King Edward. He says that a spy came to him at Peebles from Nithsdale, and warned him of a gathering of Galloway men about to take place at Glencairn. They had told the spy that they had heard it was the intention of the Prince of Wales to visit St Ninian's shrine at Whithorn, so they had removed the image of the saint to New Abbey, and on the next morning when they looked for it, lo! it had gone back to Whithorn.[7]

All this time Bruce, as one of the guardians of Scotland in the name of King John, was bound to hostility with

[5] Stevenson, vol. ii. p. 432.   [6] Bain, vol. ii. p. 299.
[7] Ibid., p. 311.

England. Nevertheless, on February 16, 1302, King Edward, being then at Roxburgh, granted pardon, at the instance of the Earl of Carrick, to one Hector Askeloc for the slaughter of Cuthbert of Galloway;[8] and before the end of April following Bruce and his Carrick tenants had been received to the king's peace.[9] It is not difficult to divine the reason for Bruce's latest change of front. His father, the old Lord of Annandale, was approaching his end, and resistance to Edward would certainly have interfered with Bruce's peaceable succession to the English estates. But it is not very pleasant to know that, at that very time (April 6, 1302), King Philip of France was writing a letter[1] to Bruce and the other guardians, acknowledging receipt of their envoys, letters, and messages, praising them for their constancy to King John, and urging them to persevere. Considering the risks of the road, he refrains from putting into writing his proposals for their assistance, but he has told all to the Bishop of St Andrews, for whom he asks full credence. The precaution was not superfluous. This letter fell into Edward's hands, probably some years later, when Bishop Lamberton was taken prisoner. Meanwhile Bruce was on the best of terms with Edward, which saved Dumfriesshire from suffering by the invasion of 1302. Thereafter Comyn and Bishop Lamberton continued to act as guardians without his assistance. Bruce received orders on May 12, 1303, to join King Edward at Roxburgh with all the men-at-arms he can muster and 1000 foot from Carrick and Galloway.[2] On July 14 he received an advance of wages from the king,[3] and during this year he was the king's Sheriff of Lanark[4] and governor of Ayr Castle.[5] Comyn, Sir John de Maxwell, James the Steward, and others, were still in arms in the north; but

---

[8] Bain, vol. ii. p. 328.   [9] Ibid., p. 331.   [1] Ibid., p. 330.
[2] Ibid., p. 348.   [3] Ibid., p. 355.   [4] Ibid., p. 372.   [5] Ibid., p. 377.

they surrendered on terms in February 1304, leaving Stirling Castle to its fate and Sir William Wallace to carry on an irregular warfare in Menteith and the Lennox. On March 3 King Edward wrote to Bruce, applauding his diligence in hunting the patriots, and urging him earnestly "as the cloak is well made, so also make the hood."[6]

The Earl of Carrick attended King Edward's parliament held at St Andrews in mid-Lent; but his father, the old Lord of Annandale, dying at this time, he went to London and Essex to collect his rents and secure his succession. On April 16 the king wrote thanking him for sending on engines for the siege of Stirling;[7] on June 14, having done fealty, he was served heir;[8] and on June 17 his debts to the king were respited.[9] The motives of Bruce's conduct appear only too clearly on a perusal of these documents. The lustre which afterwards gathered round his arms, and the gratitude of his countrymen for setting free their land from the English yoke, have caused every historian to cast about for excuses to palliate his vacillation at this time, his desertion of Wallace, whose cause was identical with what he afterwards made his own, and his assassination of the Red Comyn in the Greyfriars Church at Dumfries. It is not possible to accept without reserve Fordun's and Wyntoun's circumstantial story how it was Comyn who first proposed that Bruce should seize the Scottish throne, to which, after Balliol, he (Comyn) had the nearest claim; how Comyn afterwards betrayed the design to Edward; how Bruce, warned by his kinsman the Earl of Gloucester, who sent him the significant present of a pair of spurs, rode from London to Lochmaben in seven days; and how he intercepted a messenger carrying despatches from Comyn to Edward, which, being read, re-

---

[6] Bain, vol. ii. p. 383. [7] Stevenson, vol. ii. p. 482.
[8] Bain, vol. ii. p. 403. [9] Ibid.

vealed to him the duplicity of his pretended ally. As David Macpherson, the eighteenth-century editor of Wyntoun, has shrewdly observed, all this has the air of a fable contrived to find justification of Bruce's murder of Comyn. The common object of Barbour, Fordun, and Wyntoun, as Scottish writers, was to make Bruce a hero and Edward a monster of iniquity. One writer after another has adopted and improved on this story, but it forms a significant comment on its veracity that later writers give it far more circumstantially than the earlier.

The most likely explanation is that Bruce, being of Norman descent, and holding extensive lands in England, was inclined by self-interest to support his English liege lord in making one realm of Scotland and England. This he did, openly or secretly, for seven years after the capitulation of Irvine. But when in 1304 his father died, and Bruce became himself the representative of the claim of his line to the throne, a broader horizon opened before him. By espousing the national Scottish cause he would, if successful, himself become a king, and it was with this in view that he entered in the same year into a secret treaty with William of Lamberton, Bishop of St Andrews. Notwithstanding this, he appeared at Westminster on September 16, 1305, three weeks after the execution of Wallace, as one of the nine Commissioners from Scotland summoned by Edward to settle the future government of that kingdom.[1] Not only so, but we have the actual terms of the oath which Bruce and the other Commissioners swore on our Lord's body, the holy relics,

---

[1] King Edward's nephew, John de Bretaigne, was appointed Lieutenant and Warden of Scotland. Four pairs of justiciaries were gazetted to preside respectively over Lothian, Galloway, the district between the Forth and the Mounth, and that beyond the Mounth. Those for Galloway were Sir Roger de Kirkpatrick and Sir Walter de Burghdon. Sheriffs were appointed for all the counties, Sir Richard de Siward being made Sheriff of Dumfries, and Thomas M'Culloch (Makhulagh) Sheriff of Wigtown (Bain, vol. ii. p. 458).

and the holy Gospels to give good advice for maintaining the peace of the king's dominions, especially in Scotland; to reveal loyally any hindrance they might know to the good government of Scotland; and, among other things, neither for hatred, affinity or other matter, oath or alliance heretofore made, to withhold counsel to their utmost knowledge and power. Nothing is more startling in the records of these times than the readiness of great men to perjure themselves, except, perhaps, the importance which statesmen continued to attach to the security of oaths.

Information of Bruce's secret treaty with Lamberton seems to have come, whether by Comyn or another, to the ears of Edward, whereupon Bruce beat a hasty retreat from London and ensconced himself in his Castle of Lochmaben.

The version of what followed given by Sir Thomas Gray in his 'Scalacronica' has not received the attention it deserves, coming from so high an authority. Writing as a prisoner of war in Edinburgh Castle in 1355, Gray, whose father, also Sir Thomas Gray, was one of Edward's bravest officers, declares that Bruce sent his two brothers, Thomas and Nigel, from Lochmaben to Dalswinton, to invite John Comyn to meet him in Dumfries, and give him an interview in the Church of Greyfriars. He directed his brothers to ride with Comyn, attack him and put him to death. They, however, were so hospitably and courteously entertained by their intended victim, that they could not bring themselves to hurt him, but brought him unharmed to Dumfries. "Leave him to me!" said Bruce, on hearing their story, and went to find Comyn in the church. Then Bruce proposed to Comyn that either he should support Comyn in his claim to the throne and receive Comyn's lands in consideration for his help, or that Comyn should support Bruce and receive the Bruce estates. "I will never be false to my fealty to King

Edward," replied Comyn. "Is that so?" cried Bruce; "I had different hopes of you, from what you and yours have told me. Since living thou wilt not do my will—take thy guerdon!" and stabbed him to the heart.

Now, whether it was by accident, as Fordun declares, or by agreement, as Gray affirms, that Bruce met John Comyn of Badenoch in the Greyfriars Church at Dumfries, or whether, as Wyntoun asserts, Bruce rode in from Lochmaben on purpose to confront Comyn and charge him with treachery, the fact alone is certain that they did meet there on February 10, 1306, that Bruce stabbed Comyn, and then fled from the church. Outside he met Sir Roger de Kirkpatrick of Closeburn[2] and Sir John de Lindsay, to whom he said, "I must be gone, for I doubt I have slain Comyn." These two then hastened into the church and found the wounded man, whom the friars had carried behind the altar. Comyn, in reply to the inquiry if he thought he was mortally wounded, said that he was not. "Then," exclaimed Kirkpatrick, "I'll mak siccar [sure]!" and plunged a dagger in his heart. Old Sir Robert Comyn, uncle to John, coming to his rescue, was also slain.[3]

It requires all our admiration for the subsequent gallantry of Bruce, and all our enthusiasm for the cause which he led, to enable us to forget this deed of blood, which, if, as there is too much reason to suppose, it was committed "under

---

[2] Hailes says it was Gospatric de Kirkpatrick, but the general belief is that it was Kirkpatrick of Closeburn, the newly appointed justiciary. The Lyon King-of-Arms of Scotland has indorsed the popular belief by conferring on the Kirkpatricks of Closeburn, as their crest, a hand holding a dagger, distilling drops of blood, and the motto "I make sure."

[3] Mr William M'Dowall, writing his 'History of the Burgh of Dumfries,' 1867, says that a fragment of old Greyfriars' Church still remained at that time incorporated in the kitchen of the "Kicking Horse" public-house, in Friars' Vennel. This tavern has since been pulled down, and the only trace left of this historic building exists in the name of the street.

tryst," was in the last degree heinous, even according to the lenient judgment of those times. Its immediate effect upon Bruce was to give him what he never had before—a single purpose. He had forfeited the favour of his English sovereign, often imperilled as it had been already: he had established a blood-feud with the powerful family of Comyn: henceforth he must secure his own safety by throwing himself with all his might into the national cause. Within six weeks of the murder he was crowned King of Scotland at Scone, March 27.[4] Two days later the ceremony was repeated, owing to an unexpected occurrence. Isabel, wife of John Comyn, Earl of Buchan, claimed her right, as the daughter of the Macduff, to place the crown on the new king's brow. Her brother, the Earl of Fife, was in the English interest, and her husband was so furious against her as to demand her execution; but King Edward interposed on her behalf, and she was sentenced to be confined in a cage at Berwick, in which she remained captive for seven years. Bruce's wife, Elizabeth de Burgh, his daughter Marjory, and his sister Christine, were taken in sanctuary at Tain, and sent prisoners to England. Another of his sisters, Mary, was placed in a cage at Roxburgh.[5] Nigel, his youngest brother, was hanged and be-

[4] In March 1306-7 King Edward pardoned Geoffrey de Coigners, at the request of his Queen Margaret, for concealing a certain coronet of gold with which Robert de Brus had caused himself to be crowned (Fœdera, i. 1012).

[5] It was ordained that three of these ladies should be confined in "kages," but these were not such barbarous structures as might be imagined from the name. It was directed that the Countess of Buchan's cage was to be constructed within a turret of Berwick Castle, made of lattice-work strengthened with iron. The countess was never to be allowed to leave it, nor to speak to any Scots man or woman; but she was to have two women to wait on her, and the cage was to be furnished like a comfortable chamber ("q̃ la kage soit ensi faite q̃ la Contesse y eit eesement de chambre cortoise"). The Princess Marjory was not so rigorously treated, for in the following March the Prior of Wattone had custody of her, and

headed at Berwick, and Christopher Seton, his brother-in-law, at Dumfries.⁶ Thomas and Alexander, two other brothers, landing in Loch Ryan, were taken by Dougal MacDouall and sent to Carlisle, where they were promptly executed. MacDouall's son was rewarded by King Edward with the gift in marriage of the heiress of Hugh de Champaigne.

Besides these victims there was terrible vengeance wreaked upon those taken in arms against King Edward. Sir John de Seton, who after Bruce's flight from Dumfries held the new Castle of Tibbers,⁷ built by Sir Richard de Siward in 1298, was summarily drawn and hanged at Newcastle-on-Tyne, together with fifteen knights and others taken with him.

Dumfries Castle was taken from Bruce's men on March 3 by some men of Galloway under Gilbert, son of the Lord Dovenald.⁸

Bruce, luckily, had not taken refuge at Tibbers or Dumfries, but he was now a fugitive, and sought shelter in the Highlands. Before his coronation, however, he had received absolution from his old ally Bishop Wishart of Glasgow, who admitted afterwards that he communicated the mass to him on the

was directed to allow her 3d. a-day for sustenance and one mark a-year for clothing!—Palgrave, 356-359.

⁶ Seton's widow afterwards founded and built a chapel of the Holy Rood on the spot where he had suffered, a hill on the north-east of the town. King Robert in 1323 endowed it with 100 shillings sterling, payable from the rent of Caerlaverock, to celebrate mass for ever for the soul of Sir Christopher. The site of the chapel is now occupied by St Mary's Church.

⁷ Little remains of this once important castle, situated on the Mar Burn in Drumlanrig park. I was gravely informed by a local authority that the name Tibbers was given to it because it had been built by the Emperor Tiberius! The real meaning of the name is apparent on examining the ruins. There is within them a very deep perennial well, which would be called in Gaelic *tiobar*. This word enters into many place-names in the south-west—*e.g.*, Auchentibbert (the well-field), Chipperdingan (St Ninian's well), Chippermore (the great well), &c.

⁸ Bain, vol. iv. p. 289.

Palm Sunday following the murder of the Red Comyn. MacDouall, Lord of Lorn, kinsman of those of the same name in Galloway who were so hostile to Bruce, owing to their relationship to Comyn, endeavoured to take him, but he escaped to Rachrin Island, where he lay hidden all winter. Coming thence to Arran, he landed in his own earldom of Carrick, surprising the English garrison of Turnberry Castle some time early in the spring of 1307. King Edward, already lying in what proved to be his last illness, had delegated the command of the forces in Scotland to Aymer de Valence, Earl of Pembroke. Bruce met with but a cold reception in Carrick, the people being overawed by the presence of the English. He could not muster more than 200 armed men, all told. Even these began to melt away, and he was fain to seek concealment in the Forest of Buchan, a wild and mountainous district between Loch Doon and Loch Trool, which at that time was clothed with dense woods.[9]

Of all districts in Scotland, except Lorn, Bruce's cause was held in greatest detestation in Galloway, the land of Comyn and Balliol, and his choice of the Galloway hills as a hiding-place in this his extremity can only be accounted for by their proximity to his own Carrick, where, if anywhere, he might count on support. Dougal MacDouall and other native Galloway chiefs were in the pay of King Edward, who had granted them special rewards for the capture of Sir Rainald de Crauford and other of Bruce's few supporters.[1]

[9] The trees have wellnigh disappeared now, but this tract is still called the Forest of Buchan, named, probably, after Bruce's bitterest foe, the Earl of Buchan, joint Lord of Galloway. It was in after times the favourite hunting-ground of the Kennedys, Earls of Cassilis, for the red-deer were plentiful and of great size. References to the chase are plentiful among the place-names of this region, such as the Shalloch of Minnock, from the Gaelic *sealg* (shallug), the chase, and Mulwharker, a hill in the forest, *meall adhairce* (aharky), hill of the hunting-horn, close to which is Hunt Ha'.   [1] Bain, vol. ii. p. 511.

The cause of Bruce was never so desperate as when he was hiding in these southern uplands. He had not an acre of ground he could call his own; three of his brothers and many of his devoted adherents had perished on the gibbet; his wife, daughter, and sisters were in captivity: how few remained whom he could trust! On every side his pursuers were closing round his refuge in Glen Trool. Edward's most famous generals were in hot pursuit. Aymer de Valence, the viceroy, smarting under the king's repeated reproaches for want of success and apparent inaction,[2] was on the borders of Ayrshire with 700 archers; Sir John de Botetourte, the warden, watched the passes of Nithsdale with 70 horse and 200 archers; Sir Robert de Clifford, with Sir John de Wigtown, guarded the fords of Cree; a special force of 300 Tynedale bowmen under Sir Geoffrey de Moubray and three captains were sent to search Glen Trool;[3] while, most dangerous of all, John of Lorn was hastening through Ayrshire with 22 men-at-arms and 800 active Highlanders. In mentioning the last-named force, Barbour, on whose narrative reliance must be chiefly placed in following the episodes of these critical weeks, gives remarkable evidence of veracity. Refusing to yield to the ordinary chronicler's tendency to exaggeration in dealing with numbers, he speaks of

> "Johne of Lorne and all his micht,
> That had of worthy men and wicht
> With him aucht hundreth men and ma."

This estimate is precisely corroborated by de Valence's warrant to pay John of Lorn for 22 men-at-arms and 800 men.[4] With this evidence before him, the reader will scarcely hesitate to prefer Barbour's statement that Bruce, while hiding in the forest, had with him a body fluctuating between 150 and 300 men, to Hemingburgh's, who asserts that his following amounted

[2] Bain, vol. ii. p. 504.   [3] Ibid., p. 510.   [4] Ibid., p. 250.

to 10,000! The good monk never saw the Galloway hill country, or he might have been puzzled to explain how such a force could be fed there.

But weakness in numbers was not all that troubled Bruce. It was essential that he should collect some troops, whether for offensive or simply defensive operations, and no doubt all the ruffians and broken men in the country would come readily enough. Among these there must have been plenty ready to earn a handsome reward by assassinating the Bruce. Such a one, it seems, Sir Ingelram de Umfraville scrupled not to hire—a one-eyed rogue of Carrick, who, having won the confidence of the King of Scots, waylaid him one morning, having with him his two sons. Bruce was alone, save for a single page; but he managed to kill them all, without receiving any hurt.

But the narrowest escape the King of Scots had was from John of Lorn. Douglas, fresh from the raid on his own lands which is well known in Border lore as "the Douglas Larder," had just rejoined his master in Glen Trool when de Valence advanced from the north into the hills. Bruce, watching his progress from the heights and slowly falling back before him, was unaware that Lorn had made a wide circuit to take him in rear. He very nearly fell into the trap. Having but 300 men with him, it would have been madness to show fight between two forces, each of which was greatly superior in numbers to his own. So he divided his company into three bands, ordering each to take a different way of escape through the forest. Lorn had brought with him a famous bloodhound, once the property of, and greatly attached to, Bruce. He relied on the dog fastening on the trail of his old master, and he was not disappointed. The hound settled on the scent of that band which remained with the king. The pursuit became so hot that Bruce, retaining with him only his foster-brother, made his followers scatter and seek safety in the crags, each for himself. Still the faithful bloodhound followed his track. Lorn, feeling sure he had the right quarry before him, now told off five fleet-footed Highlanders to run forward. These fellows soon overtook the king and his companion. Three of them attacked Bruce, while the two others engaged his attendant. Bruce slew one of his assailants, and, on the other two drawing off, turned to help his man. He killed one of these fresh foes; only three remained now out of five. Back came the two Highlanders who had first attacked the king, and made at him again. He slew them both, and his foster-brother vanquished the fifth.

But the peril was not past. Lorn's men were drawing near, with the sleuth-hound in leash. Bruce was so greatly exhausted that, descending into a wood, he declared he could go no farther. His attendant, however, implored him to make another effort, otherwise their fates were sealed. A stream ran through the wood; the fugitives dropped into it, and by travelling along the channel for some distance, threw the bloodhound off the trail, and thus made good their escape.

The natives also hunted the king with sleuth-hounds, but even among the people of this inhospitable place he made some friends. From the desolate shores of Loch Dee rises a hill called Craigencallie, the crag of the *cailleach*, or old woman, commemorating a venerable dame who sheltered the landless king in her cabin when his fortunes were at the lowest. Tradition runs that she was a widow with three sons, each by a different husband. Barbour mentions only two, but local lore is positive that there were three, and that their names were Murdoch, M'Kie, and M'Lurg. King Robert, before separating from his followers when hotly pursued by John of Lorn, had appointed the widow's hut as a rendezvous. His foster-brother, whom alone he had suffered to remain with him in his flight, had perished by the hands of three ruffians who attacked them in a hut on the moors, where they had sought shelter for the night. At the widow's cabin, therefore, the king arrived alone at the appointed time. He asked for food, of which he stood sorely in need. The widow told him that all wayfarers were welcome for the sake of one. The king asked who that one might be. "I'll tell thee," quoth the goodwife, "it is just good King Robert the Bruce, rightful lord of all this land. His foes are pressing him sorely now, but the day is coming when he shall have his own."

On hearing this Bruce made himself known; she welcomed him into the house, and set him down to a good meal. While he was refreshing himself the three sons returned. Their mother made them do obeisance straightway, and they offered to become the king's men. Bruce desired to see their skill with the bow. Murdoch, the eldest, let fly at two ravens perched on a crag, and transfixed them both with the same arrow. M'Kie then performed a more difficult feat, shooting a raven flying overhead; but M'Lurg missed his mark. After the widow's words had been fulfilled, and the king had come to his own, he asked her, so 'tis said, how he could reward her for her timely aid.

"Just give me," said she, "the wee bit hassock o' land between Palnure and Penkill." [5]

The request was granted. The "bit hassock," being about five miles long and three broad, was divided between the three sons. Hence the origin of the families of M'Kie of Larg, Murdoch of Cumloden, and M'Lurg of Kirouchtie. The feat of Murdoch is commemorated in the arms borne

---

[5] Penkill, formerly Polkill (Pont's map)—*i.e.*, *pol cill*, the church stream. It joins the Cree at Minigaff church.

by his descendants, enrolled in the Lyon Register as "*argent*, two ravens hanging paleways, *sable*, with an arrow through both their heads fessways, *proper*."[6]

Douglas and Edward de Brus, the king's brother, met Bruce at Craigencallie as agreed on, and about 150 followers turned up also. Douglas brought word that a large body of English were carelessly encamped in Raploch Moss near Loch Dee, and advised they should be attacked at once. Falling on the sleeping soldiers before dawn, Bruce and his men took them completely by surprise, slew many of them, and dispersed the rest.

But the romantic Glen of Trool was the scene of Bruce's earliest important success. King Edward, till the hour of his death, kept sending troops into Galloway in pursuit of the Scottish king, and repeatedly urged his commanders to extraordinary diligence in order to secure him. Aymer de Valence himself led his men-at-arms to the entrance of Glen Trool, till he found the country impassable for cavalry. Then, as tradition has it, he left his horses at the Borgan farm close to the junction of the Cree and Minnick Water, and pressed into the defile on foot, having with him a large force of archers.[7] As they pushed farther inland, the hills rose higher on either hand, till, on entering Glen Trool, they found them-

---

[6] The descendants of Murdoch retained possession of Cumloden till near the close of the eighteenth century.

[7] Full details of the composition of part of this force may be found in a pay warrant dated February 12–May 3, 1307 (Bain, vol. ii. p. 510), from which it appears that payment was made for one knight-banneret at 4s. a-day, 31 knights at 2s., 51 esquires at 12d., 24 sergeants-at-arms at 12d., 14 captains at 12d., 1419 archers at 2d., besides "hobelars," troopers, and others. All these seem to have been reinforcements sent to Sir Aymer, in addition to the troops for whose pay he was personally accountable. Barbour gives the number of the attacking party in Glen Trool as 1500 —a wonderfully moderate, and therefore probably an accurate, estimate for a partisan writer.

selves in such a narrow defile that it was scarcely possible to proceed except in single file. At a place called the Steps of Trool, where the hillside is almost precipitous, the Englishmen were attacked by a party posted in ambush above the track, who, by rolling down rocks and pouring flights of arrows and crossbow bolts, stopped their advance and drove them back with heavy loss. Between the dark mountains and the darker waters at the north-east end of Loch Trool lies a strip of green meadow, called of old in the Gaelic tongue Ringielawn (*roinn na' leamhan*, point of elms), but known now as the Soldiers' Holm, in memory of de Valence's men, who, it is said, were buried there. It is in solitudes such as this, where life has changed little in its outward aspect from remote antiquity, that tradition lingers longest and is least likely to be deceptive.

Nothing succeeds like success. The raid of Glen Trool probably took place about the end of April 1307, and on May 15 a letter was written from Forfar in Norman French to some high official in Edward's Court. The writer (whose name has not been preserved) says that Sir Robert de Brus never before had so much goodwill among his own followers, still less among the people at large, as he had now secured. It now seems, runs the letter, that he has the right, and God is openly for him, as he has destroyed all the king's power both among the English and Scots, and the English force is in full retreat. He warns his correspondent that if Bruce is allowed to escape from Galloway, all the country both north and south of the Forth will rise for him, and he implores the king to send more men-at-arms, or all will be lost. This remarkable letter[8] ends with a curious bit of lore. The king's enemies, says the writer, have published a prophecy of Merlin to the effect that after the death of "le Roi Coueytous" the

[8] Bain, vol. ii. p. 513.

Scottish people and the Bretons shall league together and get the mastery. The fierce old king, we may feel assured, needed no supernatural incentive to quicken his measures. He was on his way with a powerful army to enforce his authority and exact vengeance, when he died, the greatest of the Plantagenets, at Burgh-on-Sands on July 7, 1307. With his mighty spirit was removed the chief obstacle to Robert the Bruce's ambition. From all parts of Scotland the people began to rally freely to Bruce, who took the field with success against the English in Ayrshire, and thence pressed on to the central and eastern districts.

The death of Edward Longshanks made no difference in the energy of de Valence as king's lieutenant. The records teem with his despatches to his officers in the south-west, ordering garrisons, reinforcement and commissariat details. "Let a tonel of the king's wine," he writes from the Glenkens on July 24, 1307, to Sir James de Alilee or his lieutenant at Dumfries, "be given to Sir Ingelram de Umfraville and Sir Alexander de Balliol, that they may better do the king's business on the enemy."

But the tide in Scottish affairs had turned. The young King of England led the army which his father, a man of far different mould, had assembled, through Nithsdale to Cumnock. Halting at Tinwald on August 30, 1307, he signed a commission appointing Aymer de Valence Viceroy of Scotland. From Cumnock the king retreated again to Carlisle. Bruce sent his brother Edward to settle some old scores in Galloway and reduce that country to his allegiance. The chief objects of this chastisement would no doubt be the clan of MacDouall, whose chief had delivered Bruce's two brothers to execution at Carlisle in the spring.[9] Dougal MacDouall, "and

---

[9] On September 25, 1307, Edward II. directed that the men of Galloway who had fled before Bruce should be allowed to pasture their flocks and herds in Englewood forest.—Bain, vol. iii. p. 3.

others of the greater men" in those parts, appealed to King Edward for assistance, who accordingly commanded the Earl of Richmond, successor to Aymer de Valence in the Scottish lieutenancy, to collect a force and advance to their relief.

Edward Bruce, says Barbour—

> "Was of his handes ane nobill knicht,
> And in blithnes swet and joly,
> Bot he was outrageous hardy,
> . . . He discumfit comonly
> Many with quhene."[1]

He was victor in several sharp affairs, notably one near the Dee, where many men of local note perished, among them a Galwegian leader named Roland. But the decisive encounter took place near the Cree, probably on the plain below Kirouchtrie, where Sir Aymer de St John was encamped. Barbour had the account of the battle from the mouth of Sir Alan de Cathcart, one of Edward de Brus's officers. Edward de Brus, with a following of fifty men-at-arms, surprised the English under cover of a thick fog, and utterly routed them. A few of the chief men of Galloway now came into submission to King Robert; but some of the chief strongholds in the south-west were held for King Edward for several years after this. Barbour's dates, and those given by Lord Hailes in following him, are not exactly correct. Dumfries Castle was surrendered to King Robert in person on February 7, 1313, by Sir Dougal MacDouall,[2] who had probably been starved out, as there had been frequent complaints from him that stores were not delivered to him regularly. The Balliol's Castle of Buittle, the Comyn's Castle of Dalswinton, and Bruce's own Castle of Lochmaben, also were taken about this time, and Sir Eustace de Maxwell yielded up Caer-

---

[1] *Quhene*, wheen, few.

[2] Bain, vol. iii. p. 60. The date of the surrender is noted by the English receiver of stores at Carlisle on the margin of his account.

laverock, for the custody of which he had been receiving £22 a-year from the English Exchequer.

The ascendancy of Bruce of course brought about a complete reversal of the fortunes of his opponents and supporters.

In Dumfriesshire, Walter, third son of Sir John the Steward of Bonkill, who fell at Falkirk with Wallace, received the lands of Dalswinton; the king's paternal lordship of Annandale was bestowed on his gallant nephew, Thomas Randolph, Earl of Moray; the Kirkpatricks obtained substantial recognition for the bloody service rendered in Greyfriars Church, in the shape of the lands of Torthorwald, Pennersaughs, Bridburgh, and others. Sir Eustace Maxwell, having, it is supposed, atoned for his tardy allegiance to King Robert by good service in the Bannockburn campaign, was infeft anew in his lands of Caerlaverock.

In Galloway, Sir James Douglas, besides being reinstated in Douglasdale, received Percy's barony of Urr. Buchan's lands went to Lord de Soulis, and Fergus de Mandeville obtained MacDouall's lands of Stranraer.

It had been well for Scotland in general, and for Galloway in particular, if Edward de Brus, heir-presumptive to the throne, had contented himself with administering the affairs of the lordship of Galloway and the earldom of Carrick which the king conferred on him; instead of which, as is well known, he lost his life at the battle of Fagher, near Dundalk, after having been crowned nominal King of Ireland. He was succeeded in the lordship of Galloway by his illegitimate son, Alexander.

NOTE B.

THE CASTLE OF DUMFRIES.

ALL traces of this once important Border stronghold have now so completely disappeared, that the very site where it stood is a matter of uncertainty. Probably the original building stood on what is now called the Moat, overlooking the river, which, having been dismantled in 1570 by Lord Scrope, was replaced by the New Wark, erected to the north of where the Queensberry monument now stands, or, as some say, on the present site of Greyfriars' Church. The older building dated from very early times, being referred to as *vetus castellum* in a charter of William the Lion about the year 1180. It was one of the twenty-three castles maintained by the Government of Scotland in the thirteenth century for the protection of the realm, the others being Roxburgh, Jedburgh, Berwick, Edinburgh, Stirling, Dunbarton, Ayr, Wigtown, Kirkcudbright, Dundee, Cluny, Aboyne, Forfar, Kincardine, Aberdeen, Cromarty, Dingwall, Inverness, Nairn, Forres, Elgin, and Banff.[1] In 1291 these were given over by the Guardians of Scotland into the hands of Edward I. as Lord Paramount, and were handed over by him to John Balliol in the following year.

William de Boyville received a salary of 1 merk a-day as Edward's governor of Dumfries, Wigtown, and Kirkcudbright castles in 1290,[2] and was succeeded by Henry de Boyville, who, on March 12, 1292, acknowledges payment of 17 merks due for the custody of these castles, and, "forasmuch as his seal is not known in those parts," appends to the receipt the seal of William de St Clair, Sheriff of Dumfries.[3] Sir Richard de Siward and Walter de Curry also appeared as governors in this year, and in 1300, on Siward, *vel alium fidelem et idoneum*, being made Warden of Nithsdale, John de Dolyne was placed in charge of Dumfries Castle *cum pertinentibus*.[4] This de Siward, having taken part in Balliol's invasion of Northumberland in 1296, was made prisoner at Dunbar. In 1298 he was in the prison of Bristol, and King Edward ordered the rigour of his imprisonment to be relaxed,

---

[1] Rotuli Scotiæ, vol. i. pp. 11, 12.   [2] Stevenson, vol. i. p. 206.
[3] Ibid., p. 285.   [4] Patent Rolls, 27 Edward I., m. 28.

his fetters struck off, and his dungeon exchanged for a better chamber, because of the good service rendered by his father in Flanders.[5] In 1301, Sir Arnald Guillim de Podio being constable of Dumfries Castle, we have a note of the garrison left by Edward for its defence—viz., 4 carpenters, 1 smith and his assistant, a bow-maker, a baker, a cook, a janitor, a chaplain, a clerk, 2 watchmen, a washerwoman, 4 labourers, 1 constable, 2 men-at-arms, 12 grooms of the men-at-arms, and 17 crossbowmen; total 55.[6]

NOTE C.

THE BRUCE PEDIGREE.

The Bruce pedigree, a notable example of uninterrupted descent from father to son, is so confusing from the frequent recurrence of the name Robert, that it is here given in a condensed form.

1. Robert de Brus, died *c.* 1094, a Norman lord — one of *les sires de Breaux*—who brought 200 men to swell the Conqueror's invading army, received as his reward 40,000 acres of land in Yorkshire, comprising 43 manors in the East and West Ridings and 51 in the North Riding. He took his territorial name from the Castle of Bruis, near Cherbourg, the foundations of which may still be traced.

2. Robert de Brus, son of No. 1, became a friend of David I. at the Court of Henry I. of England, and subsequently received from David a grant of Annandale (Estrahannent), bordering on Niths-dale (Stranid), the territory of Dunegal. (Charter, *c.* 1124.) At the battle of the Standard, 1138, he renounced his Scottish fief of Annandale, perhaps in favour of his son, and, having vainly tried to dissuade King David from fighting, joined the forces of Stephen. He died in 1141.

3. Robert de Brus, second son of No. 2, named le Meschin (the cadet or stripling). He is said to have fought on the Scottish side at the battle of the Standard against his father, who took him prisoner. He held Annandale under David I., Malcolm IV., and William the Lion for the service of 100 knights. Died *c.* 1189.

4. Robert de Brus, third Lord of Annandale (if indeed he sur-vived his father). Married Isabel, daughter of William the Lion,

---

[5] Stevenson, vol. ii. p. 55.   [6] Bain, vol. ii. p. 320.

and must have died before 1191, in which year his widow married Robert de Ros.

5. William de Brus, fourth Lord of Annandale, younger son of No. 3. Died 1215.

6. Robert de Brus, fifth Lord of Annandale, son of No. 5. Married Isabel, niece of William the Lion and second daughter of David, Earl of Huntingdon, whence arose the subsequent claim of his son to the throne. Died 1245.

7. Robert de Brus, sixth Lord of Annandale; "the Competitor"; son of No. 6. He inherited ten knights' fees in England, being his mother's share of the earldom of Huntingdon, and married Isabel de Clare, daughter of the Earl of Gloucester. In 1238 Alexander II., with the consent of his great council, acknowledged this lord as his heir and caused the barons to do fealty to him, but the birth of Alexander III. in 1241 extinguished the claim. De Brus acquiesced in the award of Edward I., and, being stricken in years, resigned all his rights to his son the Earl of Carrick. He died in 1295.

8. Robert de Brus, seventh Lord of Annandale and (in right of his wife) Earl of Carrick. Married Marjory, daughter and heiress of Nigel or Niall, Earl of Carrick, who was the grandson of Gilbert, the son of Fergus, Lord of Galloway. She was a royal ward, and it is possible that the legend of her falling in love with de Brus, and carrying him off to her Castle of Turnberry, was invented to palliate his offence in marrying her without the king's leave. De Brus took King Edward's side against Balliol in 1296, in revenge for which Balliol seized Annandale and placed John Comyn in the lordship. He died in 1394.

9. Robert de Brus, eighth Lord of Annandale and Earl of Carrick, son of No. 8; became King of Scotland. Married 1, Isabella of Mar; 2, Elizabeth de Burgh.

NOTE D.

THE MACDOUALLS.

The claim of the Macdowalls of Garthland, MacDoualls of Logan, and M'Dowalls or M'Dougals of Freugh, all in Wigtownshire, to be descended from the Lords of Galloway of the line of Fergus, has been hotly disputed. Of the great antiquity of these families in the shire there can be no question. The MacDoualls of Logan still own the lands which have been in their possession from time immemorial; the Macdowalls of Garthland parted with their lands of that name in Wigtownshire in 1803, but purchased others near Lochwinnoch, in Renfrewshire, which they named Garthland; while of the M'Dowalls or M'Dougalls of Freugh, Patrick succeeded to the earldom of Dumfries in 1768, on the death of his uncle, fourth Earl of Dumfries. His daughter and heiress married John, Lord Mountstuart, eldest son of the Marquis of Bute. The present Marquis of Bute still owns part of the old M'Dowall lands in Kirkcowan parish.

Logan and Garthland were owned together in 1414 by Fergus MacDouall, as shown by a charter conveying them to his son Thomas. The claim of this family to represent the old lords of Galloway is a very ancient one, and has received recognition by heralds from the earliest times. The cognisance of Fergus, Lord of Galloway, is said to have been a white lion rampant on an azure field: Camden states that Henry I. of England granted to him the privilege of crowning the lion in consideration of special services. In the great seal of King John de Balliol the royal arms of Scotland are flanked by two smaller shields, one bearing the *orle* of de Balliol, the other the lion of the Lords of Galloway. All the branches of the MacDouall family have subsequently been confirmed in bearing the same arms. Garthland displays the lion crowned, Logan the lion gorged, with an open crown; while Freugh's lion was both gorged and crowned. M'Douall of Lorn, now merged in the Argyll Campbells, used to display the lion without the crown, the original bearing of Fergus.

Sir W. Dugdale (who died in 1686) mentions in his 'Monasticon' that Glenluce Abbey was founded by *Rolandus Macdoual princeps Gallovidiæ*, so the tradition was current in his day that the family of Fergus were known as MacDouall. But, previous to the thirteenth century, fixed surnames were absolutely unknown in Scotland. Fergus and his descendants may have been of the sept or clan MacDouall, and yet, from their conspicuous position, have never found it necessary to use the name as a distinction. It is at a time when surnames began to become general, at the close of the thirteenth century, that the name of Macdouall first appears prominently in Wigtownshire history. Among the signatures to the Ragman Roll *del counte de Wyggeton* (1292-96) appear Fergus MakDowylt and Dougal MacDowyl, besides Andreu de Logan.

The lands of Dowalton in Glasserton and Kirkinner parishes are traditionally connected with the old lords of Galloway, who are said to have resided in the castle which may still be seen in ruins on an island in Dowalton Loch (now drained). The adjacent farm, named Boreland, proves that the mansion was of sufficient importance to have a " bord-land," or home-farm, attached to it.

Connection between the line of Fergus and the MacDoualls may be traced in the recurrence among the latter of the names Fergus, Uchtred (or Uthred), Alan, and Gilbert. On weighing the whole evidence, it seems reasonable to suppose that the collaterals of Fergus formed the clan MacDouall, and that the patronymic emerged as a surname when necessity for one arose.

There is yet another suggestion in the name, to wit, that Douall, or Dougal, represents Dubh Gall, a Dane. Dougal, Lord of the Isles, was of the same blood as the MacDoualls of Galloway, Douall representing the aspirated form of Dougal, which becomes Doyle in Irish. MacCoull, in the West Highlands, has been interpreted as a form of MacDouall with the *d* aspirated into silence; but this name is also explained as a contraction of MacComghal. The Dubh Gall, or Danes, settled both in Galloway and Lorn. MacDugaill, the Dane's son, may be the true origin of a name written indifferently Macdougal and Macdowall. The present heads of the houses of Logan and Garthland both happen to have that complexion and hair which the Gael calls *dubh*, dark.

The MacDoualls, both those of Galloway and Lorn, were among the most inveterate enemies of Robert the Bruce, owing to their relationship with the Comyns.

CHAPTER V.

FROM THE BATTLE OF BANNOCKBURN IN 1314 TO THE FALL OF THE HOUSE OF DOUGLAS IN 1452.

ROBERT the First of Scotland was now on his throne, a hazardous seat for a man of less force of character than himself. To say that Scotland during the rest of his reign enjoyed a nearer approach to tranquillity than it had known since the death of Alexander III. may be true enough, but it is not saying much. It only means that Scottish raids into England were more incessant than English raids into Scotland. The gallant personality of the king had, indeed, won him popularity and respect on a national scale, and Bannockburn had decided many waverers among the barons; but a long and lamentable time of Border warfare between Scots and English began with the unsuccessful siege of Carlisle by King Robert, which lasted from July 22 to August 1, 1315. Its gallant defender, Sir Andrew de Harcla, afterwards fell into the hands of Sir John Soulis of Eskdale, who with only 50 men took prisoner Sir Andrew with 300, "horsyt jolily," and held him to ransom.[1] Barbour, unfortunately, forbears to tell the story of this exploit, observing—

> "I will nocht reherss the maner;
> For quha sa likis, thai may her [hear]
> Young wemen, quhen thai will plaie,
> Syng it amang thaim ilk day."

[1] Bain, vol. iii. p. 98.

Sir Andrew tantalises the modern reader in the same way, for in his petition to King Edward for ransom he says that his valet who bears the letter will explain how he was taken.

During the absence of King Robert in Ireland in 1316-17 the Border was left in the good keeping of Sir James Douglas, who, with Walter the Steward, was lieutenant of the realm.

It would be wearisome to recount all the raids on either side; suffice it to say that no part of Scotland suffered more grievously than Dumfriesshire in the international strife now beginning. Naturally more fertile than the neighbouring land of Galloway, the resources of Dumfriesshire could never, until the Union, be developed to the same degree as those of the old lordship of Fergus and his descendants. Witness to this is borne by the ecclesiastical remains of Dumfriesshire, which are meagre indeed compared with the stately structures west of the Nith. In the whole of her borders Dumfriesshire cannot show a single church approaching the proportions or beauty of Jedburgh, Kelso, Melrose, or Dryburgh beyond her eastern border, or Lincluden, Sweetheart, Dundrennan, Whithorn, or Glenluce beyond her western. On the other hand, the fortresses of Dumfriesshire are on a scale far exceeding anything possessed by Galloway, which, with the solitary exception of the Thrieve on the Dee, has no feudal remains rivalling the mighty piles of Caerlaverock, Morton, and Lochmaben. Cruggleton, indeed, the former stronghold of de Quenci and Comyn, must have been an important building, to judge from a water-colour drawing accompanying a report drawn up by an English official between 1563 and 1566, but no more than a mere fragment of it now remains.[2]

---

[2] British Museum, Cottonian MSS., Titus, c. xii. f. 76 to f. 87. The drawing of Cruggleton has been reproduced in facsimile in Mr Armstrong's 'History of Liddesdale, Eskdale, &c.' (Edinburgh, 1883), p. cvi, but it appears there under the erroneous title of Cardiness Tower.

On January 3, 1323, a very important conference took place at Lochmaben between the King of Scots and Sir Andrew de Harcla (who had been made Earl of Carlisle in reward for his gallant defence of that town). Lord Hailes and other writers have held that Lord Carlisle was guilty of treason to his king in this negotiation, but the truth seems to have been that he was in despair on account of Edward's unfitness for rule and the distracted state of the English Court, and saw nothing but disaster to his country in the prolongation of hostilities. King Robert, too, was in failing health, and it is not difficult to see in this transaction, as shown by Mr Bain in the light of his recent investigation,[3] an honest endeavour to settle the international quarrel on satisfactory and lasting terms.

There can be little doubt that, though Lord Carlisle was technically guilty of treason in conferring with one whom the law of England had proscribed as a rebel, both he and the King of Scots were sincerely desirous of securing peace for the poor farmers and common people of both realms. The union of the Crowns ever presented itself to wise politicians, both before and after this date, as the true solution of the quarrel between England and Scotland, and provision is made for this in the agreement drawn up between King Robert and Lord Carlisle.

But the proceedings came to naught. Carlisle was arrested and attainted a traitor, and affairs went along their old evil course. A truce, however, was concluded in 1323 to last for thirteen years.

Edward II. abdicated in 1326, and although his successor Edward III. ratified the existing truce on March 6, England was invaded by an army under Randolph and Douglas before June 15, who wasted the counties of Durham and Northum-

[3] Bain, vol. iii. p. xxxi.

berland. King Robert was not present with this expedition, according to the 'Chronicle of Lanercost,' because he was ill with leprosy, but really because he was at the head of an expedition to Ireland at the time.[4] A truce was patched up between England and Scotland in consequence of the success of Randolph; a treaty of peace was signed at Northampton in April 1328, and in July Prince David of Scotland married Princess Johanna, sister of Edward III., at Berwick.

We may pause here in following the course of events in order to consider what sort of troops were those Border men on which King Robert relied in his constant warfare with England. Froissart has left us a very minute description of the appearance and equipment of those which marched into Weardale with Douglas and Moray in 1327:—

"The Scots are bold, hardy, and much inured to war. When they make their invasions into England they march from twenty to four-and-twenty miles without halting, as well by night as day—for they are all on horseback, except the camp-followers, who are on foot.[5] The knights and squires are well mounted on large bay horses, the common people on little Galloways. They bring no carriages with them, on account of the mountains they have to pass in Northumberland; neither do they carry with them any provision of bread or wine, for their habits of sobriety are such in time of war that they will live a long time on flesh half sodden, without bread, and drink the river water without wine. They have, therefore, no occasion for pots and pans, for they dress the flesh of their cattle in the skins after they have taken them off; and being sure to find plenty of cattle in the country

---

[4] Bain, vol. iii. p. 167.

[5] This refers, of course, to the Border riders only, for the army that won Bannockburn was largely composed of foot-pikemen.

which they invade, they carry none with them. Under the flap of the saddle each man carries a broad plate of metal; behind the saddle a little bag of oatmeal. When they have eaten too much of the sodden flesh, and their stomachs appear weak and empty, they place this plate over the fire, mix water with their oatmeal, and when the plate is heated, they put a little of the paste upon it, and make a thin cake like a biscuit, which they eat to warm their stomachs. It is, therefore, no wonder that they perform a longer day's march than other soldiers. . . . Their little hackneys are never tied up or dressed, but turned immediately after the day's march to pasture on the heath or in the fields."

Holinshed has left an equally vivid picture of the English troops whom the Scots defeated in this campaign at Biland. They were all clothed in coats and hoods embroidered with flowers and branches very seemly, and they paid much attention to their beards. He quotes a rhyme composed by some wag in derision of their foppery :—

> "Long beardes, hartelesse,
> Paynted hoodes, wytlesse,
> Gaye coates, gracelesse,
> Make Englande thriftlesse." [6]

Robert I., "the restorer of Scottish monarchy," as Lord Hailes justly calls him, died at Cardross in 1329. So long as Randolph Earl of Moray's strong hand remained at the helm all went steadily; but he too died in 1332, and Edward Balliol, son of "the Competitor," profited by the weakness of the new Regent, Mar, to set up his standard. There were plenty of disinherited barons to support him—*les querrelleurs*, as the chroniclers call them. Edward Balliol, having defeated Mar at Dupplin, was crowned at Scone, September 24, 1332. The people of Galloway, faithful to their original

[6] Holinshed's Chronicle, vol. ii. p. 890.

allegiance, declared for his cause, and, strange to say, their lord, Alexander, natural son of Edward de Brus, was one of the first to lend support to the hereditary rival of his house. Sir Eustace de Maxwell, too, whose fidelity to King Robert had not always been above suspicion,[7] played a dubious part at this time. His lands in the counties of Dumfries and Roxburgh constantly lay open to English invasion, and he had ever a keen eye to keep on good terms with the English Government. He took up arms for Edward Balliol, assisted him to raise the siege of Perth, and was present at his coronation.[8]

The whole realm was now in confusion. It is believed, though this has been called in question, that the Earl of March and Archibald Douglas, fearing for the security of their own lands, concluded a truce with Balliol which was to last till February 2, 1333. This notwithstanding, Douglas, being with the Earl of Moray and Simon Fraser in Moffat on Christmas Eve, contrived an expedition to surprise Balliol, who lay at Annan. Whether reliance had been placed on the truce, or whether Yule-tide libations had prevailed to relax the vigilance of the garrison, Balliol's party were taken completely by surprise. Edward de Balliol and his brother Henry had gone to bed. Henry de Balliol and Walter Comyn were slain, and Edward galloped off to Carlisle in his night-shirt—

"On a barme horse with legys bare."[9]

---

[7] He was tried at Perth in 1320 on a charge of conspiracy against the crown and life of King Robert. Maxwell and four others were acquitted, but William de Soulis and the Countess of Strathern were convicted and sentenced to imprisonment for life, while Sir David de Brechin and three others were executed as traitors.

[8] February 1, 1335, Edward III. grants a manor of £40 a-year to Sir Eustace Maxwell (Privy Seals [Tower], 9 Edw. III., file 2).

[9] Wyntoun, bk. viii. c. 26, l. 3725. In reward for this exploit Douglas was appointed Regent of Scotland.

But if Balliol left his kingdom by the western Border in this unseemly disarray, he soon returned by the eastern, properly appointed, at the head of an English army, and won the battle of Halidon Hill near Berwick, July 19, 1333. Here were slain Archibald Douglas (the new Regent) and Alexander de Brus, Lord of Galloway, who had once more changed sides. But Balliol had to pay a heavy price for this triumph—no less than the surrender to Edward III. of the counties of Edinburgh, Roxburgh, Peebles, Dumfries, and Kirkcudbright, to remain for ever appanages of the English Crown. By a special act of grace Balliol received a fief of his paternal estates in Galloway, and resumed residence at Buittle. However humiliating it must have been to him who had been crowned King of Scotland to be the vassal of England for his private estates within the realm, it satisfied the people of Galloway, ever warmly attached to the house of Balliol. Moreover, they anticipated a return to what had contributed so largely to their prosperity in the past—peaceable intercourse with English markets. Duncan MacDouall and another native Galwegian chief, MacUlach,[1] were largely subsidised by the King of England. Sir Eustace de Maxwell, also, was in the service of the English Government, by whom he was appointed Sheriff of Dumfries. He was a faithless servant. When Edward III. invaded France in 1338, Maxwell, notwithstanding that he had just received money and munitions for Caerlaverock from the English exchequer, raised the men of Eastern Galloway in arms against the English Government. But in 1339 he returned again to his allegiance and received pardon. He died in 1342, an inglorious example of a baron who used his great power solely with a view to his own advancement.

[1] Head of the powerful family of M'Culloch. Probably the son of Thomas who was appointed Sheriff of Wigtown in 1305 by Edward I.

Edward III., upon whom had descended a large measure of the spirit of his grandfather, *malleus Scotorum*, again invaded Scotland in 1335, this time by the Western Marches. In July of that year he was encamped in the forest of Dalswinton,[2] and thence advanced to join forces with Balliol at Glasgow.

King David's dominions were now but a fraction of the realm held by his father. Dumfries and Kirkcudbright were, as we have seen, part of England, but Wigtownshire was still Scottish territory. In 1342 Sir Malcolm Fleming, Earl of Wigtown, was appointed sheriff of that county, with power to hold it against the other half of Galloway.

Who shall blame young King David for rashness in his ill-starred attempt to regain his rightful possessions? This attempt was made in 1346, when, marching through Dumfriesshire, he took the peel of Liddel.[3] Thence pushing on to Durham, with 2000 men-at-arms and a strong force of "hobelars" (light horse) and pikemen, he was taken prisoner at the battle of Neville's Cross, and with him many barons, including the Earl of Wigtown and Sir John Maxwell of Caerlaverock.[4] This might well be deemed a crushing blow to the house of Bruce; and so, no doubt, it would have been but for the incompetency of Edward Balliol, who was quite unequal to maintaining authority over his barons. The King of Eng-

---

[2] Bain, vol. iii. p. 211.

[3] According to Sir Thomas Gray and the 'Chronicle of Lanercost,' the governor, Sir Walter Selby, was beheaded. In an inquisition of 31 Edward III., Selby is referred to simply as having been slain.—Bain, vol. iii. p. 308.

[4] Sir John de Maxwell was imprisoned in the Tower of London, and died shortly afterwards. Balliol followed the shattered Scots army across the Border, wasted Nithsdale, Galloway, and Carrick, and possessed himself of Maxwell's Castle of Caerlaverock, which he garrisoned with Galwegians and made his principal residence for some time. John Maxwell's son, Herbert, received back Caerlaverock on making submission to King Edward in 1347.

land was absent on the campaign of Creci, and Sir Thomas Gray left in his 'Scalacronica' an authentic account of the progress of events as he witnessed them. Unluckily his chronicle, written in Norman-French, has been mutilated, and the part relating to these years has been lost. But Leland, who prepared a condensed translation of the original, gives the following passage:—

"In the meane whyle that King Davy was prisoner, the lords of Scotland, by a litle and a litle, wan al that they had lost at the bataille of Duresme [Neville's Cross]; and there was much envy emong them who might be hyest; for every one rulid yn hys owne cuntery; and King Eduarde was so distressid with his afferes beyound the se, that he toke litle regard to the Scottische matiers."

From some motive difficult to understand, whether from contempt for Balliol or because he thought it desirable that Scotland should be weakened by the presence of two kings, King Edward entered into negotiations with the Bruce party for the release of David. Balliol deputed three Galloway knights, Patrick MacUlach, William de Aldeburgh,[5] and John de Wigginton (Wigtown), to appear before Edward and protest against the infringement of his rights as King of Scotland. In 1353, while Balliol was absent at the English Court, William, Lord of Douglas, invaded Galloway in such force as to overawe the barons into taking the oath of fealty to David. Sir Dougal MacDouall, the leader of them and a most ardent champion of the cause of Balliol, submitted in the church of Cumnock, and thereafter remained faithful to the house of Bruce.[6]

[5] Now Auldbreck, near Sorbie, in Wigtownshire, a name which seems to perpetuate that of the Norman family of Vipont, or de Vetere Ponte, who owned these lands.

[6] Fordun gives the date of MacDouall's submission as 1356, and Lord Hailes as 1353 on the authority of Rymer. But Sir Dougal and his eldest

The negotiations for the release of David still dragged on, till Balliol, in despair at the desertion of his supporters in Galloway and weary of incessant fighting, finally resigned all claim to the Scottish Crown in favour of Edward III. Neither he nor any of his family were to appear again in the page of history.

King Edward, intent on securing the realm thus vacated for him, invaded Scotland, and penetrated as far as Haddington, but William, Lord of Douglas, had devastated the country before him so completely that he had to withdraw in order to save his army from starvation. In revenge he burnt every abbey, church, and town on his line of retreat, whence this invasion came to be known among all others as the "burnt Candlemas."

The Scots hung upon Edward's rear and inflicted such heavy losses upon his troops that he seems to have made up his mind that Scotland was further than ever from submitting to his rule. Negotiations for peace were resumed, until at last, in October 1357, King David was set free after a captivity of eleven years, the Scots undertaking to pay a ransom of 100,000 merks sterling. Perhaps the most striking clause in the treaty was that by which peace was agreed on for a thousand years!

A ghastly incident is recorded in this year, bringing to a fitting close the tragedy in Greyfriars Church fifty-one years before. Sir Roger de Kirkpatrick, son of one of Bruce's accomplices in the slaughter of the Comyns, had taken Caerlaverock from the English in 1356, and remained in it as keeper. To him came as guest in the month of June Sir James de Lindsay, son of the other accomplice. They seemed

---

son were already prisoners in England in 1346, before the battle of Neville's Cross (Bain, vol. iii. p. 266). Perhaps they changed sides oftener than once.

on the best of terms—both had been ever staunch adherents of the same cause, and fought side by side on many a field; but it is supposed that they had been rivals for the hand of her who was now Lady Kirkpatrick. Nothing is known of the circumstances which followed, save that Kirkpatrick was slain in the night, and that Lindsay mounted in haste, and galloped off into the darkness. However, he lost his way, and was taken in the morning not three miles from the scene of the murder. Lindsay's powerful relatives made intercession for him in vain; the circumstances of the crime were too atrocious, even according to fourteenth-century standard, to be excused on account of Lindsay's rank and past services. Lady Kirkpatrick having herself appeared before the king to demand justice on the assassin, he travelled to Dumfries, and held a court there for the trial of Lindsay, who was forthwith executed on the heading hill.

David II. was now king over all Scotland. Wholesale forfeiture of land and bestowal of new grants took place as usual on such revolutions of power. The lion's share fell to the family of Douglas. Of Balliol's three commissioners, John of Wigtown's lands fell to Fleming, Earl of Wigtown; William of Auldbreck made way for Sir Gilbert Kennedy, a Celtic chief in Carrick; while M'Culloch, with the other native landowners, Macdowalls, Maclellans, and Ahannays, must have felt grateful for the submission exacted from them in 1353 by William, Lord of Douglas, now created an earl.

David II. died in 1371, and was succeeded by his nephew, Robert II., first of the Stuart line, who conferred the lordship of Galloway on Archibald, natural son of the Good Sir James Douglas, "becaus," says Sir Richard Maitland, "he tuke grit trawell to purge the country of Englis blude."[7] He is well

[7] MS. History of the Douglases, by Sir Richard Maitland of Lethington, 1560.

remembered in Galloway as Archibald the Grim—not because of any special ferocity such as characterised some of his descendants, for he was a just and considerate ruler, but, as Maitland explains, he was "callit Archibald Grym be the Englismen, becaus of his terrible countenace in weirfair."

Besides the lordship in 1372, Archibald received in perpetual fee all the Crown lands in Galloway between the Nith and the Cree. He appointed a steward to collect his revenues and administer justice there, which is the origin of the name *Stewartry* of Kirkcudbright; while Galloway west of the Cree, remaining under the jurisdiction of the king's sheriff, has been known ever since as the *Shire*.[8] But by another and very remarkable transaction the earldom of Wigtown was added to Douglas's other honours and sources of emolument. Fleming, Earl of Wigtown, having got into uncomfortable relations with the Kennedys and other native families, and being, besides, in great need of money, sold to the Douglas not only all his property and rights in Wigtownshire, but also the earldom, resuming his ancient style and title as Thomas Fleming of Fulwood. That the title and right of the earl, as well as his possessions, were recognised as saleable commodities appears from the king's charter confirming the deed of sale, in which Fleming is termed "formerly Earl of Wigtown."[9] Thus was Galloway once more united under one lord, as it had not been since the death of Alan in 1234; and Archibald Douglas might be described in the words applied by Buchanan to Alan as "by far the most powerful Scotsman."

In gratitude for the benefits showered on him, Douglas built a hospital at the Monastery of Holywood, which he had already endowed with the lands of Crossmichael and Troqueer,

---

[8] Local usage has continued unaltered to this day. The Stewartry and the Shire are the recognised popular titles of the two divisions of Galloway.

[9] Registrum Magni Sigilli, p. 114, No. 5.

in the Stewartry. This Abbey of Holywood (Abbacia Sancti Nemoris) was one of Devorguila's foundations. Its ruins, sad to say, were pulled down in 1778, and the materials used for building a new parish church, by which heartless act Dumfriesshire was robbed of her only surviving ecclesiastical remains of the slightest beauty or importance. The abbey church is reported to have had a very fine roof and doorway. Two of the bells are still in use. Twelve large stones, of which eleven still remain, formed a circle a few hundred yards southwest of the church; and a mile to the east stood another circle of nine stones, which disappeared about the beginning of the century. These perhaps marked the site of the battle of Cludvein, or Cluden, as the stream which joins the Nith near this place is now called. This battle is recorded in the 'Book of Taliessin' as "kat glutvein gueith pen coet" (the battle at the head of the wood)—*i.e.*, the Holywood.

But Archibald the Grim's most enduring achievement in architecture was the erection of the Thrieve, the strongest fortalice in Galloway, on an island in the Dee, ten miles above the town of Kirkcudbright. This he made his chief residence, administering therefrom not only the affairs of his lordship but the wardenship of the Western Marches.

These two jurisdictions were administered under distinct codes. Galloway had retained from Pictish times special laws of her own, which often caused delays unduly favourable to turbulent subjects. They had, indeed, been modified by William the Lion; but that king had maintained a separate code for Galloway ("assisa mea de Galweia"), and separate judges for administering it. Some of their judgments, which are peculiar, have been preserved; for instance :—

"At Dumfries it was iugit be the iugis of Galloway, that gif ony Galloway man be convickyt, ouder be batal or be ony other way, of the kingis pece broken, the king sal haf of hym xii score ky and iii gatharions [horses?], or for ilk gatharion ix ky, the quhilk are in number xxx and vii.

"Na Galoway man aw to haf visnet, but gif[1] he refuse the law of Galoway and ask visnet.

"Item, thar the samyn day, be the samyn iuges, it was iugit that gif ony in the palice quhar that batal is wagit, quhair pece sulde be haldin, hapins for to spek outan thaim that ar to keip the palice, the king sal haf of hym x ky in forfalt. And gif ony man puttis his hand to, or makys a takyn[2] with his hand, he sal be in the kingis amerciament of lyf and lym."

These decisions, it will be understood, while maintaining the old Galloway custom of trial by battle, and providing against any interference with litigants preferring to decide their differences in that primitive way, did also confer on the king's subjects of Galloway the right of option to be tried under the feudal law of visnet (*voisinage*) or jury. This right was further recognised and confirmed by the Parliament of Robert I., held in Glasgow, June 13, 1324.

In the Parliament held at Holyrood in 1385, Archibald the Grim obtained power to suspend certain of these laws of Galloway, as they had been left in the reign of William the Lion; at the same time he made protest for maintaining the liberty of the code in other points. Thus the law of Galloway remained till 1426, when the province was brought under the general law of Scotland by Act of Parliament.

A truce for eight years, which had been concluded between England and Scotland in 1369, came to an end in 1377, and while negotiations were going on for its renewal the Earl of Douglas burnt the town of Penrith, raided the neighbourhood, and returned with much spoil to Dumfriesshire. To avenge this, Lord Talbot crossed the Esk and laid waste lower Annandale, but his force was surprised during the night

---

[1] Unless.   [2] Signal.

by a small body of Scots and routed with heavy slaughter. After this episode truce was renewed until Candlemas 1384. The English king, Richard II., still kept his grasp on Annandale and Teviotdale, but in January of that year, Archibald of Galloway and the Earl of Douglas, not so scrupulous as to wait for the actual close of the truce, swooped down and beleaguered Lochmaben Castle. This was a place of immense strength; but Fetherstonhaugh, commanding the English garrison, not being provisioned for a siege, and having besides but a small force in quarters, agreed to surrender if not relieved within eight days. It was a time of terrible tempest; the besiegers lay—

> "In wykkyd weddyr, as wind and rane,
> That thame dyd gret annoy and pane;"[3]

but on the ninth day, February 8, the castle was given up to them and utterly dismantled. Then, at last, were the Western Marches entirely rid of English rule. Poor Fetherstonhaugh was arrested at Carlisle and sent a prisoner to Windsor.[4]

The French king now found it suit his war policy with England to give assistance to the Scots. By the treaty of August 1383 he had bound himself to place a thousand men-at-arms, as many suits of armour, and 40,000 francs of gold at the disposal of King Robert. The engagement was more than redeemed when, in May 1385, Sir John de Vienne landed at Leith with 2000 men-at-arms, 1400 suits of armour, and 50,000 francs. Meanwhile, on March 12, the Lord of Galloway had concluded a local truce with the Earl of Northumberland at Salom Chapel on the Esk, to last till July 1. The English were in Scotland in 1384 under John of Gaunt, and again in 1385 under Richard II. in person. The Scots and

---

[3] Wyntoun, b. ix. c. v. l. 323.   [4] Bain, vol. iv. pp. 73, 77.

their French allies retired before the King of England, and left him to wreak his vengeance by burning Edinburgh, Melrose, Dryburgh, and Newbattle; but the return tide was led by James, the Earl of Douglas, Archibald the Grim, and their French allies, over the western Border. The Frenchmen were able to boast that in this foray they had burned in the bishoprics of Durham and Carlisle more than the value of all the towns in Scotland.

Again in the following year, 1386, it seems to have occurred to the Earl of Douglas that the country round Cockermouth had not been raided since the days of Robert the Bruce. So, accompanied by the Earl of Fife and Archibald the Grim, he set off to redress such a manifest oversight, and spent three days in that pleasant land to such good effect that it was said there was not one among the Scots so feeble that he was unable to fill his hands with good booty. Deeds of arms are never allowed to dwindle in narrative, and it is a good example of how little trust may be placed in statements made by mediæval historians of the numbers engaged on either side that Wyntoun, writing about thirty years after this foray, estimates the Scottish force at 30,000.

James, Earl of Douglas, was slain at Otterburn in 1388. By his wife Isabel, daughter of Robert II., he left no surviving issue, and the earldom devolved on Archibald the Grim, Lord of Galloway, by what Lord Hailes justly calls a "capricious entail." It is told of him that when Robert III. introduced the title of Duke into Scottish chivalry for the first time in 1398, by creating his son, David, Duke of Rothesay, and his brother, the Earl of Fife, Duke of Albany, he offered a like dignity to the Earl of Douglas. He proudly declined the honour, and when the heralds hailed him, "Sir Duke! Sir Duke!" he replied contemptuously, "Sir Drake! Sir Drake!"

Henry IV. invaded Scotland in 1400, and lay for some time at Leith; but Archibald the Grim was no longer, as heretofore, foremost in its defence, being, as is supposed, in his last illness. He died at the Thrieve on Christmas Eve 1400, and was buried at Bothwell, which, with extensive lands in the north, had come into his possession with his wife, Joanna Moray.[5] Lochmaben Castle and Annandale had fallen again under English dominion at this time, and Thomas Neville, Lord of Furnivalle, had been appointed their keeper for life by Henry IV.[6]

The dealings of Archibald the Grim with the Abbey and Nunnery of Lincluden have been the subject of much controversy. Whether, as has been alleged, the Sisters brought about their dispersal by the irregularity of their lives, or whether Douglas had other reasons for his conduct, the fact remains that he suppressed the convent, substituted a brotherhood of twelve canons and a provost, and changed the abbey into a college. A richly decorated church was built at this time, of which the ruins still remain—the expense of building and the endowment of the college being defrayed out of the forfeited lands of the abbey.

Before tracing further the annals of the lords of Galloway, mention must be made of a natural son of Archibald the Grim, named William, whose short career was of the essence of Border romance, and his exploits long the example of Border chivalry. He was a man of enormous strength, but is reported to have been as gentle among women and to his friends as he was terrible in combat with mace, sword, or lance. He stood so high in knightly renown that in 1387 Robert II., overlooking the slur of bastardy, gave him in marriage his younger daughter Egidia,

---

[5] The lands of Bothwell still remain in possession of the Earl of Home, as representing this branch of the Douglas.

[6] Bain, vol. iv. p. 111.

popularly called the Lady Gellis, and as a dowry the lordship of Nithsdale. The year after his marriage Sir William Douglas made a descent on the coast of Ireland with 500 men, in retaliation for raids made by Ulstermen in the Rhinns of Galloway during the expedition of Archibald the Grim into Cumberland. He burnt the town of Carlingford, captured the castle and fifteen ships in the harbour, and on his return voyage settled some old scores with the Manxmen by ravaging part of the Isle of Man. Sir William Douglas of Nithsdale was assassinated at Dantzic about the year 1392. He appears to have left a son, William, who inherited Nithsdale, on whose death, about 1408, the lordship passed to his sister Egidia, who married Henry, Earl of Orkney.

Archibald the Grim was succeeded in the lordship of Galloway by his son, the fourth earl of Douglas, Archibald "Tineman," so called because he "tined," or lost, more battles than he won. This was not from want of personal prowess, but the fortune of war was against him: notwithstanding which the influence of the house did not diminish in his hands; on the contrary, he added greatly to the Douglas territory, and took a foremost part in the affairs of the kingdom. These, indeed, absorbed his energies almost to the exclusion of personal rule in Galloway, and he only appears directly in connection with that district and Dumfriesshire shortly before his father's death. Elizabeth, daughter of George, Earl of March and Lord of Annandale,[7] had been betrothed to the Duke of Rothesay, heir to the throne, and a considerable dowry had been paid in advance. Archibald the Grim, taking advantage of the fact that the betrothal had not been sanctioned

[7] George Dunbar, Earl of March, was the nephew of Patrick, that earl who so long supported the English cause in Scotland, and finally came over to the side of David II. about 1334. The English lands of the earldom being thereby forfeited, he obtained from the King of Scots extensive lands in Ayrshire, Renfrewshire, Nithsdale, Annandale, and Galloway.

by the Three Estates, offered the king a larger dowry with his daughter Mary than March had paid; the king fell in with the proposal, and the new betrothals took place. March, not unnaturally incensed, demanded of the king that the original contract should be fulfilled, or, at least, that the dowry should be repaid, and failing to obtain satisfaction, withdrew in wrath to his English estates.[8] Upon this the "Tineman" not only seized March's Castle of Dunbar, and made it his residence, but also took possession of the lordship of Annandale and the lands of March. From that time forward March was openly in league with the English wardens, and made repeated forays across the Border. He led the English troops at the battle of Nisbet on June 22, 1402, and it was avowedly to avenge the Scottish defeat on that bloody field that Douglas devastated Northumberland as far south as Newcastle. But he was intercepted on his return near the village of Wooler by March and Hotspur Percy, and defeated at the battle of Homildon Hill on September 14. The suit of armour worn by Douglas is said to have taken three years to make, yet he was wounded in five places, including the loss of an eye, and taken prisoner. To follow his adventures during his nominal imprisonment of eleven years is a temptation to which it would be easy to yield, but it would lead us far from the Scottish Border.

In 1423 Douglas took an army of 10,000 men to France in the service of Charles VII. The French king made him lieutenant-general of his forces, and created him Duke of Touraine. The "Tineman's" last battle was fought and lost on August 17, 1424, at Verneuil, where he and his son Sir James Douglas perished with nearly the whole of their Scottish troops.

[8] King Henry's invasion of Scotland in 1400 was apparently prompted by March.

The title of Earl of Wigtoun, as has been explained above, had been surrendered to Archibald the Grim by Thomas Fleming when he parted with the superiority of Western Galloway, but it had lain in abeyance till the "Tineman's" eldest son, also named Archibald, adopted it. But his preference for this title did not imply his taking any active part in the administration of Galloway, for during his father's life the Earl of Wigtoun was incessantly employed in France, and on his accession as fifth Earl of Douglas the lordship of Galloway devolved by the "Tineman's" will, not upon him, but on his mother Margaret, Duchess of Touraine and sister of James I. She was a lady of considerable strength of character, who, having in 1426 appointed Andrew Agnew to be her constable of Lochnaw to administer her jurisdiction in Wigtownshire, took up her residence at the Thrieve, where she died about 1439, and was buried at Lincluden. Her beautiful tomb may still be seen in the abbey church, with an inscription in Latin to the following effect: "Here lies Lady Margaret, daughter of the King of Scotland, late Countess of Douglas, Lady of Galloway and Annandale." Judging from the absence of any records of disturbance, her rule of Galloway seems to have been a prosperous one, not only for herself but for her people, —for in those times happiest was the province which appeared most seldom in history.

William, sixth Earl of Douglas, a lad of fifteen, succeeded his grandmother as Lord of Galloway; but within a few months he and his brother David were arrested at a banquet by command of Chancellor Crichton, and after a mock trial, before the boy king, James II., they were summarily beheaded—an outrage which is denounced in a local ballad:—

> "Edinburgh Castle, town and tower,
> God grant thou sink for sin!
> And that e'en for the black dinner
> Earl Douglas got therein."

The earldom of Douglas, with Douglasdale and the entailed estates, now passed to the Earl of Avondale, son of Archibald the Grim; Galloway and Bothwell to Lady Margaret, sister of the murdered William, better known afterwards as the Fair Maid of Galloway; while Annandale lapsed to the Crown.

Thus dismembered, the house of Douglas seemed to have passed its zenith, for James the Gross of Avondale was an old man when he succeeded as seventh Earl of Douglas, and the influence of Crichton was supreme at Court and hostile to the Douglas interests. Nevertheless this great family was destined to attain to an eminence even prouder than it had yet occupied. James the Gross died in 1443, and was succeeded by his son William as eighth earl. He obtained a Papal dispensation to enable him to marry his second cousin, the Fair Maid of Galloway, and thus once more the enormous territory of the Douglas was reunited, Annandale only excepted.[9]

Previous to this he had persuaded the king to allow him to avenge the slaughter of his kinsman, the sixth earl, by waging war against Crichton, whose tower of Barnton he levelled with the ground. In 1445 Crichton, whom Douglas besieged in Edinburgh Castle, surrendered on terms, and the feud was at an end. In 1447 Douglas, turning his attention to the affairs of Galloway and the Western Marches, took up his residence at the Thrieve.

The town of Dumfries had not been fired by the English since 1415, but this unusually long immunity was now to come to an end. War broke out between England and

---

[9] It has been usually believed that, in order to make this marriage, Douglas had to divorce a wife whom he had already. Sir William Fraser maintains that the terms of the dispensation forbid that supposition. There was, however, nothing either in the character of the ambitious earl or in the morals of the Papal Court at that time to make it an improbable story.

Scotland in 1448. Lord Salisbury crossed the Western March in May and burnt Dumfries, while Lord Percy, on the east, did the same to Dunbar. Douglas retaliated a few weeks later by setting Alnwick and Warkworth in flames. But people were beginning to feel that the calamities of English farmers and burgesses afforded indifferent consolation to those in Scotland who were left houseless and bereft of every kind of movable goods. Accordingly in December of the same year, 1448, Douglas convened a meeting of freeholders and others at Lincluden Abbey (the castle of Dumfries having been dismantled by the English), and took evidence on oath from the oldest Borderers as to the laws of the Marches ordained by his grandfather, Archibald the Grim. These were written down and codified, and were ultimately printed in the appendix to the Scottish Acts of Parliament of the following year. The Scots had been taken at unawares by Lord Salisbury's sudden raid, so the whole system of signalling by bale-fires was overhauled at this conference. The Sheriffs of Nithsdale and Annandale were made responsible for employing watchmen to erect, maintain, and fire the beacons, and these were fixed at nine places in Nithsdale— Wardlaw, Tynron Doon, Barloch, Pittara, Malow, Corsincon, Corswel, Dowlback, and Watch Fell; and at eleven places in Annandale—Gallowhill, Kinnelknock, Blois, Brownmuirhill, Barr (near Hoddam), Dryfesdale, Quhitwoollen, Cowdens, Balehill, Pendicle Hill, and Trailtrow.[1]

It was not long before the new programme was put into effect. A truce of seven years which had been concluded after the burning of Alnwick was promptly broken by Percy raiding the royal lands of Annandale. Douglas was at hand this time, and drove the English back over the Border with the loss of all their booty. Waiting only to collect a larger force,

[1] See Note E, The Lochmaben Stone, p. 132.

he then pushed on into Cumberland, where he wrought such devastation as to be memorable for ferocity even among Border raids. The two kingdoms were once more in the vicious vortex of retaliatory invasion. It was probably early in 1449 [2] that the Earl of Northumberland entered the Debatable Land at the head of a strong army, estimated by some historians as high as 40,000 men, but in all probability not amounting to much more than an eighth part of that figure. He encamped on the banks of the Sark and sent out foraging parties. These were hastily recalled on the advance of Douglas's brother, the Earl of Ormond, from the north. A fierce encounter then took place, in which the English were badly worsted, young Percy being taken prisoner. A forward part was borne on this day by Herbert, first Lord Maxwell, head of a house which was soon to rise on the ashes of that of Douglas, and by Johnston of Lochwood, chief of a clan destined to become hereditary foes of the Maxwells.

In 1450 Douglas, who had been guilty of cruel oppression on some of his neighbours in Ayrshire, hanging Colville of Ochiltree at his own gate and maltreating the Ochiltree tenants, obtained a safe-conduct for three years to enable him to visit Rome, where the Papal jubilee was to be celebrated. His train was on the scale of royalty, consisting of six knights, fourteen gentlemen, and eighty men-at-arms.[3] But he had to return far sooner than he intended. His brother, John, Lord of Balvany, having been left to collect Douglas's rents and administer his estates, proceeded to do so with the utmost tyranny, and refused to come to Court to answer the charges made against him. James II. sent the

---

[2] The 'Auchinleck Chronicle' gives 23d October 1448 as the date of the battle.

[3] These numbers are confirmed by Henry VI.'s warrant to his Chancellor to give a safe-conduct to Douglas and his suite for "on hoole yere" (Bain, vol. iv. p. 250).

Chancellor, Orkney, to Galloway to redress matters; but as he was attended by but a small force, Balvany not only prevented his mission, but grossly insulted him.

On this the king himself marched into Galloway with a strong force and restored order, taking the castles of Douglas and Lochmaben, and causing the former to be razed. When the news of this reached the Earl of Douglas in Rome he hurried home, presented himself before the king at the Parliament of Edinburgh in June 1451, and was received back into favour. His whole territories were restored to him by charters, some of which contain the mysterious clause that the lands shall be enjoyed by Douglas as freely as by his predecessors, notwithstanding all statutes to the contrary, and notwithstanding all crimes committed by him or by his uncle the late Earl Archibald.

This leniency had no good effect on the earl's subsequent conduct, though there is much doubt regarding the separate incidents in his career. The hanging of Sir John Herries of Terregles for raiding in Annandale, and the beheading of Maclellan of Bomby, are traditions so firmly fixed in popular belief, and so closely associated with the gloomy Castle of Thrieve, that he would be a bold man that dared to declare they had no foundation in fact. But the first rests on the testimony of Boece, who, writing seventy years after the event, is a notoriously untrustworthy authority; and the second story, not given by Boece, is told by Lindsay of Pitscottie, who wrote not less than a hundred years after Douglas's death, to the effect that Bomby was beheaded in the courtyard of Douglas Castle, not the Thrieve, while his nephew, Sir Patrick Gray, who had been sent by the king to secure Maclellan's release, was seated at dinner with the savage earl. Heaven knows there is too much well-authenticated horror in the history of these times to tempt us to accept what has really little more weight than village gossip.[4] Even if Herries and Maclellan did not meet the ghastly doom of which Douglas is the reputed author, his power had excited enough alarm in the king's mind, not to justify, but to explain, the crowning tragedy. Summoned to attend the court at Stirling in February 1452, Douglas was graciously received, and bidden to the royal supper. After the banquet the king invited him to conference in a private chamber, the subject to be discussed being, it is believed, Douglas's secret treaty with the Earl of Crawford, which the king urged him to dissolve. Douglas declared nothing would induce him to break the confederacy, on which James exclaimed, "False traitor, if you will not, I shall!" and stabbed him twice in the neck and body. Sir Patrick Gray then rushed in and despatched Douglas with the blow of a pole-axe, while other attendants also plunged their weapons into his body, which received twenty-six wounds.

James II. was at this time only twenty-one: he had witnessed the murder of the sixth Earl of Douglas, and with his own hand taken the life of the eighth. Both victims had been lured to the slaughter-house by invitation to royal banquets, and it is not difficult to detect the same motive in each instance—namely, the instinct of self-preservation against the inordinate power of a subject.

An assembly of the Three Estates met on June 12 following, and passed an Act declaring the king innocent of murder on three grounds: first, because if the earl had a safe-conduct,

[4] Symson, in his 'Large Description of Galloway, 1684,' repeats this story without expressing any doubts about its authenticity, though in the same paragraph, when alluding to the legend of the forging of Mons Meg (*infra*, p. 139), he observes that "the common report goes in that countrey" that the gun was made on the spot, "but I am not bound to believe it upon their bare report."

he had renounced the benefit of it; second, because it was plainly proved that he had entered into a conspiracy with other nobles against the king; and third, that Douglas brought about his own death by obstinate resistance to the king's request for aid against rebellious subjects.

NOTE E.

THE LOCHMABEN STONE.

So much of Border history is associated with the Lochmaben Stone, and the significance of the name has hitherto been so obscure, that it deserves more than passing reference. It is a large boulder on the farm of Old Gretna, in Dumfriesshire, near the confluence of the Kirtle with the Solway. In the 'New Statistical Account' (published in 1845) it is stated that this boulder was once surrounded by a ring of large stones, enclosing about half an acre, which had not long before been removed in the course of agriculture. There is a careful drawing of the Lochmaben Stone in Mr Armstrong's excellent 'History of Liddesdale, Eskdale,' &c. (Edinburgh, 1883).

This stone is constantly mentioned in charters and other early writings as a trysting-place both for the assembly of troops to undertake or repel invasion, and for meetings between English and Scottish Wardens of the Marches to discuss matters concerning their jurisdiction, or to arrange the preliminaries of truce. Seeing that it is many miles distant from Lochmaben town and parish, and that there is no lake near it, the name of Lochmaben Stone has long been a puzzle to antiquaries, and it is only now that a satisfactory solution seems to have been arrived at.

In Rymer's 'Fœdera' (vol. iii. part 4, p. 152) it is recorded that in 1398 certain commissioners were appointed to carry out an agreement for the release of prisoners which had been entered into between the Dukes of Rothesay and Lancaster. These commissioners met on November 6 at Clockmabanstane, and decided that all prisoners on either side, captured since the truce of Lollynghame in 1389, should be released without ransom, and that those who had paid ransom should have it refunded. The important part of this incident, as regards the Lochmaben Stone, is the light shed on its original meaning by the form Clockmabanstane. Here it is obvious that the prefix is the well-known old Gaelic *cloch*, a stone (in modern Gaelic, *clach*). Anglian speech established itself at an early date in Dumfriesshire. The meaning of *cloch* having come to be forgotten, this notable stone received the Anglian suffix *stán*, and became Lochmaben Stane. Cloch Mabon, then the stone or burial-place of Mabon, was the original title, just as Cloriddrich, near Lochwinnoch, in Renfrewshire, commemorates Rydderch Hael, the Christian conqueror of Strathclyde.

The next thing is to ascertain if there was any notable individual called Mabon in early times, or if the name merely bore the signification it has in modern Welsh—a young hero : the sense, by the way, in which it is applied affectionately at this day by Welsh miners to Mr Abraham Thomas, M.P.

In the 'Black Book of Carmarthen,' a collection of Welsh poems, mostly attributable to the sixth century, the following occurs in No. xxxi. :—

> Line 11. "If Wythnaint were to go,
> The three would be unlucky :
> Mabon, the son of Mydron,
> The servant of Uthir Pendragon,
> Cysgaint, the son of Banon ;
> And Gwyn Godibrion.
>
> . . . . .
>
> Line 21. Did not Manawyd bring
> Shattered shields from Trywruid ?
> And Mabon, the son of Mellt,
> Spotted the grass with his blood."

Here are two individuals named Mabon, one of whom seems to have been killed in battle after the battle of Trywruid. Now, Mr Skene has identified Trywruid with Trathen Werid, the scene of Arthur's tenth battle, fought in 516. This poem, however, which is very obscure, gives no indication of the place where Mabon, son of Mellt, perished ; but Arthur's eleventh battle was fought in Mynyd Agned or Edinburgh, commemorated in the name Arthur's Seat, and this may have been the place of Mabon's death.

The following passage occurs in the important topographical poem of Taliessin, No. xi., which was written to celebrate the deeds of Gwallawg ap Lleenag, who has been identified with Galgacus, whom Tacitus describes as fighting against Agricola, A.D. 80, and with Galdus, of local Galloway tradition, mentioned by the untrustworthy Boece :—

> Line 26. "A battle in a wood of Beit at close of day,
> Thou didst not think of thy foes :
> A battle in the presence of Mabon."

"The wood of Beit" may be, as Mr Skene suggests, Beith in Ayrshire ; but it may just as probably be one of the many other places named from the birch, *beth*, such as Beoch in Wigtownshire, or Dalbeattie in Kirkcudbright. In the same poem two places are named as scenes of Gwallawg's battles : one in Wigtownshire,—"the marsh of Terra," where are the Standing-Stones of Glenterra, or Glentirrow ; and the other in Kirkcudbright—*pencoet Cledyfein*, or the woodhead of Cluden, near Lincluden. Moreover, Gwallawg or Galdus is supposed to be buried at Torhouse, near Wigtown, where there is a notable circle of stones called King Galdus's tomb.

But the most circumstantial reference to Mabon appears in the 'Book of Taliessin,' poem xviii., where the invasion of Strathclyde and the battles of Owen, the son of Urien, are described, as reported to the bard from Kelso (Calchvynyd) :—

Line 17.   "A battle, when Owen defends the cattle of his country,
           Will meet Mabon from another country,
           A battle at the ford of Alclud.

Line 23.   A battle on this side of Llachar,
           The trembling camp saw Mabon,
           A shield in hand, on the fair portion of Reidol.
           Against the kine of Reged they engaged,
           If they had wings they would have flown,
           Against Mabon without corpses they would not go.
           Meeting, they descend and commence a battle.
           The country of Mabon is pierced with destructive slaughter.

Line 43.   About the ford of the boundary, about the alders his battle-places.
           When was caused the battle of the king, sovereign, prince.
           Very wild will the kine be before Mabon.

Line 47.   The resting-place of the corpses of some was in Run.
           There was joy, there will be, for ravens.
           Loud the talk of men after the battle."

Here we have an account, in language fairly explicit for a bard, of a foray on the territory Alclud, which, of course, is the Cymric name for Dumbarton (*dûn Bretan*, the fort of the Britons or Cymri). A retaliatory invasion resulted in a defeat of Mabon at Reidol on this side of Llachar—that is, at Ruthwell on the east bank of Lochar. Reidol seems to be the Celtic rendering of Ruthwell, which in turn is the Anglo-Saxon *rod wæl*, the well of the rood or cross. There is still near the village a chalybeate well, which took its name from the celebrated Runic rood or cross now standing within the walls of the parish church, and afterwards gave the name to the parish. In lines 17, 24, and 45, "kine" and "cattle" are metaphorically used for "people." The "kine of Reged" are the people of the district between Dumbarton and Loch Lomond, which was known by that name. "The ford of the boundary about the alders" may either have been on the Lochar waters, or the pursuit may have been carried as far as the "ford of the boundary" on the Sark, so often used in the later days of Border warfare. Here we may imagine Mabon to have perished, and to have been laid under the boulder which bears his name. A circle of stones was afterwards added, according to that custom of interment which took the form of what are erroneously termed Druid circles.

As to the date of this event, Taliessin seems to be telling of something which has just happened. His own era may be pretty accurately fixed as early in the seventh century, for he speaks elsewhere of the Welsh leader Brochmail as being contemporary with himself; and we know from Bede ('Ecclesiastical History,' chap. ii.) that Brochmail was present at the battle of Chester in 607. So we may assume that there was at least one warrior of the name of Mabon, who gave his name both to the district of Lochmaben and also to the Lochmaben Stone, towards the close of the sixth or beginning of the seventh century.

A thousand years later it was the recognised place of muster for the royal levies of Dumfries and Galloway, and remained so until the union of the two kingdoms. In 'Pitcairn's Criminal Trials' it is recorded (vol. i. part i. p. 398) how on May 11, 1557, Roger Kirkpatrick of Closeburn, William Kirkpatrick of Kirkmichael, and Thomas Kirkpatrick of Friar's Carse got remission from the queen for abiding from the army ordered to assemble at Lochmabenstane on February 6, "to meet the Warden before sunrise, to pass fordwart with him to the day of Trew, for meiting of the Wardane of Ingland"; and three days later Alexander Stewart of Garlies, John Dunbar of Mochrum, John Gordon of Barskeoch, John M'Culloch of Torhouse, John Jardine of Applegirth, Robert Moffat, sen. and jun., of Grantown, Thomas Moffat of Knock, Robert Johnstone of Coittis, and John Crighton, tutor of Sanquhar, were ordered to underly the law at the next assize of Dumfries for the same offence.

The Lochmaben Stone is just one of those historical relics, of more than local interest, which ought to be placed without delay under the protection of the Ancient Monuments Act.

CHAPTER VI.

FROM THE FALL OF THE HOUSE OF DOUGLAS IN 1452 TO THE BATTLE OF FLODDEN IN 1513.

THE events following upon the slaughter of Douglas have been irremediably obscured by contradictory historians. James, brother of the murdered lord, who succeeded as ninth Earl of Douglas and Lord of Galloway, was not slow to take up the blood-feud. The king was at Lochmaben on March 2, but it was not till March 17 that Douglas made any overt move in rebellion. On that day, accompanied by his brother the Earl of Ormond and Lord Hamilton, he rode into Stirling with 600 men and caused twenty-four trumpeters to sound a flourish at the market-cross. He then proclaimed the king and his Council dishonourable covenant-breakers, and displayed the letter of safe-conduct with the royal seal attached. This was nailed to a board and dragged through the town at the tail of a horse, after which Stirling was sacked and burnt.

The Earl of Crawford was in arms in the north, but was defeated by the king's troops under the Earl of Huntly near Brechin on May 18. Shortly after this Douglas made overtures to Henry VI. of England, who appointed commissioners to receive his homage. Next, Douglas, Ormond, and Hamilton caused a formal renunciation of their allegiance to James to be affixed to the door of the Parliament Hall. It is said that James then marched an army to Selkirk, Peebles, and Dumfries, burning houses and corn, and slaying sundry spies. This must have been between July 9 and August 5, and it was followed by the submission of Douglas on August 28, and an obligation to renounce all leagues entered into by him against the king and to make no such league in future.

Then followed the strangest of all episodes. The king, whose very existence had been jeopardised by the immoderate power of the vassal he had destroyed, is now found actively occupied in bringing about the very thing best calculated to restore that power to the successor of his victim. He applied to the Pope for a dispensation to enable Douglas to marry his brother's widow, the Fair Maid of Galloway, and thus consolidate once more the Douglas estates. The marriage took place, and in 1453 the earl was appointed one of the king's three commissioners to proceed to Westminster to negotiate a new truce with England.

After this, the various narratives are even more conflicting and obscure. The king must have become convinced of some treasonable designs on the part of Douglas, for he suddenly laid siege to one of his castles, Inveravon, near Linlithgow, and demolished it. He then beleaguered Abercorn Castle, on the other side of Linlithgow. Douglas and Hamilton marched to its relief, but it is said that when Douglas came in sight of the royal array he refused to attack his sovereign. Hamilton remonstrated with him in vain, reproached him for his irresolution, and went over that night to the king. Next day the earl's troops, dismayed by the defection of Hamilton, and moved, according to Pitscottie, by the Primate, James Kennedy, himself a Galloway man, deserted their colours and dispersed. Douglas, seeing himself "all begylit," fled to England with four or five followers.

Meanwhile, Douglas's three brothers — Moray, Ormond, and John of Balvany—had summoned the men of Dumfriesshire and Galloway to support the cause of their chief; but there were many in the south-west who stood for the king. Agnew of Lochnaw, first hereditary Sheriff of Wigtown,[1] called out the barons of Western Galloway; Herries of Terregles, son of Sir John slain by the late Earl of Douglas, summoned those of the Stewartry; while Herbert, Lord Maxwell, assembled the Johnstones, Scotts, Carlyles, and other Border clans. The royalists, encamped at Arkenholme, where the waters of Ewes and Wauchope unite with the Esk, just where the town of Langholm now stands, were attacked by the Douglases on May 1, 1455, and gained a complete victory over them. Moray was slain, and his head was sent as a trophy to the king; Ormond was taken prisoner, tried, and executed; while Balvany escaped across the Border to join the earl in England, only to meet a rebel's doom eight years later, when he was taken by a band of Eskdale and Liddesdale men while endeavouring to foment a rising for the Douglas cause. A reward of 1200 merks had been set upon his head, and he was executed in Edinburgh in 1463.

Later in the year 1455 the final touches were given to the ruin of the most powerful house that ever owed allegiance

---

[1] The sheriffship of Wigtownshire had been in abeyance since the death of Archibald the Grim. But when James II. marched into Galloway in 1451 to repress the disloyal proceedings of Balvany, he appointed Andrew Agnew of Lochnaw hereditary sheriff, responsible to the Crown and independent of the house of Douglas. This appointment was renewed by charter in 1452, after the murder of Douglas; and, at the same time, to Herbert, first Lord Maxwell, Steward of Annandale, was committed the temporary stewardship of Kirkcudbright.

to the Scottish kings. The Douglas was attainted by Act of Parliament, and his honours and estates forfeited. Eskdale and Galloway were attached to the Crown; Annandale was granted by King James to his second son Alexander, Duke of Albany; and other lands were divided among the Maxwells, Johnstones, Scotts, Carlyles, and Beatties. Herries of Terregles was appointed Keeper of Lochmaben, and Agnew of Lochnaw received gifts in consideration of the death, in the king's service, of his father, the first sheriff, whom he now succeeded.

King James passed to Galloway in the autumn to receive the formal submission of the lieges, but the garrison of the Thrieve, which Douglas had made over to Henry VI., resisted his entrance. The whole story of the siege which followed rests entirely on local tradition, and is perhaps only worthy of repetition, however briefly, because it is deeply embedded in popular belief. It is said that King James's artillery was too weak to make any impression on the castle walls. The country people had gathered from far and near to witness the bombardment, and among them was one M'Min, a blacksmith, commonly called Brawny Kim, who undertook to make a piece strong enough for the work if he was supplied with plenty of iron bars. Assisted by his seven sons, he fashioned a cannon made as a cooper makes a cask with staves and hoops. His forge was at a place called Buchan Croft, near the Three Thorns of Carlingwark, and, while the work was in progress, another party was making balls of granite on the Bennan Hill. "The first charge of Kim's cannon is said to have consisted of a peck of powder and a stone ball the weight of a Carsphairn cow. The eminence from which this great gun was first discharged was from that circumstance called Knockcannon, and in the end of the Castle of Thrieve facing Knockcannon there is an aperture in the wall still called the Cannon Hole. . . . The first ball discharged from Kim's gun carried away the hand of the Fair Maid of Galloway, as she sat at table in the banqueting-room, and was about to raise the wine-cup to her lips. The destructive powers of this extraordinary weapon of war pleased the king so well that before leaving Galloway he erected the town of Kirkcudbright into a royal burgh, and granted the forfeited lands of Mollance to Brawny Kim." [2]

Train, who makes himself responsible for this story, goes on to say that the cannon was afterwards called Mollance Meg, in honour of Brawny Kim's wife, who had a very loud voice—a name which soon became corrupted into Mons Meg. Further, that when early in the present century Sir Alexander Gordon was clearing out the ruins for the reception of some French prisoners, a massive gold ring was found, inscribed "Margaret de Douglas," which of course was supposed to have been on the hand of the Fair Maid of Galloway when it was blown away.

There are several points in this story which render it less than probable. To make such a gun as that now mounted on the wall of Edinburgh Castle would have taken a much longer time than King James spent besieging the Thrieve. It is very unlikely that the Fair Maid of Galloway was in Scotland at the time. In June 1454 she received a safe-conduct to pass into England, and she is not known to have returned till 1459, when she separated from her husband. The finding of the ring is only less extraordinary than that such a priceless relic should have been allowed to disappear; yet no trace of it can now be found. The lands of Mollance belonged to the Abbey of Tungland, and there is no documentary evidence of any part of them being

[2] Mackenzie's History of Galloway, vol. i., Appendix M.

granted to M'Kim or M'Min.[3] Lastly, the name Knockcannon, which fits the narrative so nicely, certainly remains attached to the hill in question; but it may be reasonably explained in another way. In Gaelic, *ceann fhionn* (pronounced *canhon*) means literally white-headed, but it has also come to signify freckled or streaked. Knockcannon, therefore, like Carrigcannon, Drumcannon, Lettercannon, &c., in Ireland, would signify the same as Knockbrake (*cnoc breac*), the dappled or brindled hill.

It is true, however, that Kirkcudbright was made a royal burgh in 1455, having been until then a burgh of regality under the Douglas.[4] It was natural that the king, on the forfeiture of its superior, should confer a royal charter on the chief town in Eastern Galloway, and appoint as its first provost Maclellan of Bomby, whose house had been so deeply wronged by Douglas.

The Thrieve was now constituted a royal keep, and remained so till 1524, when, with Lochmaben Castle, the Crown lands of Duncow, and the stewardship of Kirkcudbright, it was vested in Robert, Lord Maxwell, and his sons, for nineteen years.

Of the six sons of James, seventh Earl of Douglas, one had died young, and four had met violent deaths; there remained alive only the ninth and last earl. He lived in high favour at the English Court, Edward IV. having made him a Knight of the Garter and given him an annuity of £500.[5] He

[3] William Makmyn, smith in Auchencairn, in the parish of Rerwick, adjacent to Tungland, who appeared in 1715 before the Earl of Nithsdale to lay a complaint of oppression against Robert Maxwell of Hazlefield, the earl's bailie of the barony of Dundrennan, was perhaps a descendant of Brawny Kim.

[4] In burghs of regality the jurisdiction was vested in barons or ecclesiastics, who held their own courts; while royal burghs, besides other privileges, were subject to the jurisdiction of the king and his judges.

[5] Bain, vol. iv. p. 269 *et passim*.

assisted Albany in his rebellion, and took part in the storming of Berwick in 1482. Two years later he again crossed the Border in July, in company with the Duke of Albany, at the head of 500 English horse, expecting that his ancient vassals would once more rally to his summons. But in this he was grievously mistaken. The party rode into Lochmaben on July 24, 1484. There was assembled a great number of country-people at the annual fair, many of whom had formerly owed feudal allegiance to Albany and Douglas. But for the most part they now turned a deaf ear to the command to ride with them. A fierce conflict began at noon and lasted till night, when the Scots being reinforced by king's troops under Charteris of Amisfield and Crichton of Sanquhar, the English force drew off to the south. John, Master of Maxwell and Steward of Annandale,[6] fell in with them on the banks of Kirtle, and inflicted heavy loss on them. But Maxwell, being sorely wounded, was leaning on his sword at the close of the engagement when a Scotsman named Gask stabbed him from behind, in revenge for the death of a cousin whom Maxwell, in administering justice, had caused to be hanged. Maxwell died on the spot, and a column surmounted by a cross fleury still stands on the farm of Woodhouse, in the parish of Kirkpatrick-Fleming, to commemorate his fall.

The Duke of Albany made good his escape, but Douglas was struck from his horse. No one seemed to recognise the old earl, but he, seeing a former retainer, Alexander Kirkpatrick, made himself known to him and surrendered himself his prisoner. Kirkpatrick was deeply moved at the sight of his old master, and offered to ride with him into England; but Douglas's spirit was broken at last, and he would make no effort to escape. He was taken before the king in Edinburgh. His life was spared, and he was ordered to live in

[6] Eldest son of Robert, second Lord Maxwell.

retirement in the Abbey of Lindores. Perhaps the sting of this sentence lay in the fact that Douglas had been trained in his youth for the Church. On hearing it, he simply said, "He that may no better be, must be a monk." He died in 1488.

There remains but to tell the fate of the Fair Maid of Galloway, and then the Douglas story is finished so far as concerns the south-west of Scotland.

Doubts have been thrown on the validity of her marriage with the ninth and last earl. He married again, when in England, Anne Holland, daughter of the Duke of Exeter and relict of two John Nevills, the second of whom was killed in 1461. In that year Margaret married King James's half-brother, the Earl of Athol; but she must have been dead or divorced before 1476, when Eleanor Sinclair is called the wife of Athol.[7]

Thus falls the curtain on the most powerful family that has helped to mould the destiny of Scotland. Undoubtedly a race of great physical and intellectual vigour, their rule over Galloway and parts of Dumfriesshire remains a striking illustration of the merits and defects of feudal government. The eighth earl, foremost peer of Scotland, hardly second to the king himself in resources and influence, might have proved an invincible barrier against English invasion had he kept clear of political intrigue and inordinate ambition; but the system of despotic government, whether vested in the monarch or delegated to the vassal, requires qualities in the ruler which are seldom found in human nature, and can never be reckoned on as hereditary.

There falls to be narrated here a picturesque incident of which Galloway was the scene, arising out of the reverses of Henry VI. in the Wars of the Roses. After the defeat of

[7] The Douglas Book, vol. i. p. 495.

the Lancastrian cause at Northampton in 1460, Queen Margaret and her boy, the Prince of Wales, sought asylum in Lincluden Abbey. Thither came the newly-made widow of James II. to welcome and confer with her. The Warden of the Marches, the Sheriffs of Wigtownshire, Dumfries, and Roxburgh, and the Steward of Kirkcudbright, were summoned to a conference in the hall of the college, where various questions touching the Borders were amicably discussed. No result followed upon this, for the English queen returned to England, only to encounter the crowning disaster to the cause of the Red Rose at Towton. Again she took refuge in Scotland: Henry VI., separated from her in her flight, crossed the Solway in an open boat with four men and a child and landed at Kirkcudbright in August 1461, whence he travelled to rejoin his queen at Linlithgow. The reward made for the hospitality shown to Henry in Scotland at this time was the surrender of Berwick.

Before proceeding with the narrative of the south-west, let us inquire how it had fared thus far with the people. When James I. returned in 1424 from his long imprisonment in England, he endeavoured to make his Parliament more truly representative by relieving the small barons from the duty of attending the sittings, and authorising each shire to send two representatives, elected by the freeholders. It was not a success, because the elected commissioners could not bear the expense of attending Parliament, and their constituents were reluctant to pay for representation from which they did not anticipate much advantage. So throughout his reign and that of James II. the General Council consisted of the clergy, barons, and commissars of burghs. But it is to the credit of an assembly so constituted that it should have passed sundry Acts "for the safetie and fauour of the puir peple that labouris the ground"—that is, the farmers, who enjoyed no direct representation. Thus one question which had long been occupying the attention of lawyers throughout Western Europe was set at rest, so far as Scottish farmers were concerned, by the Act of 1449, which secured every tenant in his holding to the end of his lease, even if the proprietor were to sell the land. Efficient culture was ensured under penalties. It was enacted that if a tenant put " gule " (corn-marigold, *Chrysanthemum segetum*) in the land he was liable to be punished as if he had led an enemy into the country—that is, apparently, by death; and a serf so offending was to pay the fine of a sheep. Some curious clauses were inserted in early leases, such as the stipulation that farmers were to wear decent clothes, as prescribed in the Act of 1429, which prohibited them from going about in rags.

It must not, however, be supposed that all the land was under lease by the close of the fifteenth century. The religious houses were foremost in disposing of their lands to tenants under agreement for a term of years, but both they and the barons continued to exercise feudal rights over the bondmen and neyfs. These are termed *vincinarii* in the charter of 1452 constituting Agnew Sheriff of Wigtownshire, and power is given him to raise them for the defence of the country.

Much the larger part of the rent paid by tenants was in kind, and remained so for long afterwards. It is true that in the days of Alexander II., when Scotland had begun to accumulate the wealth which was afterwards dissipated in the war of independence and the long struggle with England, the monarch himself had set the example of commuting rent in kind for money payment. He received from the royal lands of Nithsdale an annual tribute of cattle, part of which David I. had granted to the Abbey of Kelso; Alexander II. agreed to give them 100 shillings instead of the stipulated number of cattle.

In the thirteenth century the monks of this place in turn let 40 acres of land in Closeburn, with a brewhouse, for 2 merks yearly (26s. 8d.) For their lands in the parish of Dumfries they received a yearly rent of 12s. sterling.[8] But most rent was paid in the shape either of service or of the cumbrous *can*, a portion of the produce rendered by the occupier to the owner.

The chief wealth of the land over the greater extent of Galloway and the hilly part of Dumfriesshire must have consisted in flocks and herds; for although we know that plenty of good corn was found near Kirkcudbright by Edward I., and that he paid compensation to a Dumfriesshire proprietor for 80 acres of oats destroyed by his cavalry on their return march from Galloway on August 31, 1300, we also know that when King Alexander marched into Galloway in 1235 to put down an insurrection, he found it "full of marshes and goodly with grass."[9] It can only have been on exceptionally favourable spots where corn was grown previous to the invention of draining.

Except the towers of the barons and the monasteries, dwelling-houses of stone must have been almost unknown till the end of the fifteenth century. Wood was the staple material for buildings of the better class both in town and country, and if this conveys an impression of poverty or discomfort greater than actually existed, it must be remembered that in countries where wood is abundant, as it was still in Scotland at that time, it is always regarded as the natural material for architecture. In southern Europe the stately columns of the Parthenon represent the colonnade of tree-stems which supported the roof in other buildings

---

[8] The value of Scots and English money at this time was the same; the depreciation of the former did not take place till the fifteenth century.
[9] Fordun's Annals, c. xliii.

of an earlier age: in Norway, to this day, the walls and roofs of many houses of great pretensions are wholly built of timber. It was not till the reign of James III. that the lower storeys of houses came to be built of stone and lime, so lavishly used in the construction of castles with walls 10 or 12 feet thick. The projecting upper storeys were still made of wood. Hence the sinister power of the torch in Border warfare; and hence the apparent ease with which towns like Dumfries, repeatedly burnt down, were as often rebuilt,—for if wooden walls and thatched roofs were at the mercy of every band of raiders who could force the gates, there was plenty of material at hand for rebuilding them.

Farmhouses built of the same materials or of wattle and clay, thatched with heather, were enclosed in a garth of turf or stone, for the double purpose of defence, and for protection of the cattle at night. From this they got the name of "touns," from the Anglo-Saxon *tún*, a fence, which accounts for the innumerable names ending in "ton," such as Morton in Dumfriesshire, the moor-farm, and Powton in Wigtownshire, the stream-farm (from *pow*, a stream).[1] For, be it remembered, the country was then as devoid of fences as the Moor of Rannoch is now; a *tún* or fence was undertaken for special purposes only, and our use of the word "town," as equivalent to a city, may be traced to times when all cities were fenced, or protected by walls.

As one branch of the house of Douglas fell, the other rose into power. Archibald Douglas, fifth Earl of Angus, better known in later years as "Bell-the-Cat," had, while still a boy, succeeded his father in 1470. The part which he took in Scottish history is well known, and he was only incidentally connected with Dumfries and Galloway by his appointments

[1] The "farm-toun" is still spoken of occasionally in quiet parts of Galloway in the sense of the commoner and more modern term "steading."

as Justiciar south of the Forth, Steward of Kirkcudbright, and Keeper of the Thrieve. These offices he was called upon to resign on account of his treasonable alliance with the Duke of Albany, when, in 1483, a reconciliation took place between James III. and his rebellious brother. After the murder of King James, Angus enjoyed the favour of the new king, of whom he was appointed guardian; but in 1491 he was suddenly imprisoned at Tantallon because of treasonable transactions with the King of England, and the lordship of Liddesdale on the West Marches and Hermitage on the East was forfeited by him to the Crown.

There was good cause for this and even greater severity. The agreement between "Schir John Cheyney and Schir Thomas Tiler, knights, on the behalf of the king our soveraigne Lord [Henry VII.], on the oon part, and Archbalt Dowglas erle of Angwish on thother part," has been preserved, dated November 16, 1491. It provides for the delivery of the Castle of Hermitage to the English, and other treasonable matter.

Angus still retained Ewesdale and Eskdale, as well as Bothwell Castle, on the Clyde, which remains in the possession of his descendant, the Earl of Home, to this day. But with the loss of Hermitage and Liddesdale, which he never recovered, the power of the Douglas on the Border was broken. He regained favour with James IV., however, and in 1492 was appointed Chancellor of Scotland, an office which he held for five years.

Meanwhile another nobleman had risen into prominence on the Western Border. John, fourth Lord Maxwell and tenth Lord of Caerlaverock, was the son of the Master of Maxwell who fell in the affair of Kirtle Water. He had fought on the king's side at the fatal battle of Sauchieburn in 1488, though many Dumfriesshire and Galloway men were in the army of the insurgent nobles, and was now the king's Steward in Annandale. But Maxwell's power did not extend over Western Galloway, although already, in 1481, Edward, the son of Herbert, first Lord Maxwell, had been granted the lands of Monreith in Wigtownshire, which still remain in possession of his descendants. Another family, of Celtic descent, the Kennedys, had attained a preponderance on the western seaboard, which has been commemorated in local jingle:—

> "From Wigtown to the town of Ayr,
> Portpatrick to the Cruives o' Cree,
> Nae man need think for to bide there
> Unless he ride wi' Kennedy."

Besides the vassals on his own wide domains and the powerful cadets of his own house, Lord Kennedy held bonds of man-rent or feudal service from nearly every family in Carrick and Wigtownshire, as well as bonds of mutual defence with the neighbouring lords, Montgomery, Maxwell, Boyd, and Hamilton. Their chief residence in Wigtownshire was at the Inch, near Stranraer, between which place and Dunure in Ayrshire he divided his time. John, second Lord Kennedy, was in power at the close of the fifteenth century, and strengthened his position by a transaction which would scarcely be considered respectable in the present day. His eldest daughter, Janet, was betrothed to Archibald Bell-the-Cat, Earl of Angus, and matters went so far that Angus, in terms of great affection, actually made over to her the lands of Braidwood and Crawford-Lindsay. Notwithstanding this, Lady Janet received the addresses of that flower of chivalry and piety, James IV., and became his mistress. She bore a child to him, who became James, Earl of Moray, and she was splendidly endowed by the king with the lands and Castle of Darnaway. The least creditable part of the transaction remains to be told. King James quietly annexed the lands of Crawford-Lindsay, the gift of Bell-the-Cat to his betrothed, on the shabby plea that they had been conveyed without the royal licence, and when Angus presumed to claim the hand of his bride, he was promptly clapped into ward in Dunbarton Castle. But the house of Kennedy profited greatly by this left-handed alliance with royalty. David, Janet's brother, was created first Earl of Cassilis, and fell with his king on Flodden Field.

The first episode in the long connection of the house of Kennedy with Wigtownshire is told by the anonymous chronicler of that family in language so graphic and quaint that it would lose much of its salt if rendered into modern phrase. The subject of the story is the great-grandfather of the first earl, and how he bearded Archibald the Grim.

"Thair was ane broder of the House, quhilk was ather the fourt or fyft brother. The eldest, quha was laird, being deid, the freindis conwenit to tak ordour quha suld be Tutour; but this broder, albeit youngest, startt wp, and drawing his suord, said, 'I ame best and wordiest, and I wil be Tutour.' This broder wes callit Alschunder; and becaus he wor ane dagour, quhilk wes nocht comwne, he wes callit 'Alschunder Dalgour,' to ane to-name.

"This Alschunder, or Allexander, fell in mislyking with the Erll off Wigtone Douglasse, quha wes ane werry gritt manne, and had ane gritt forse in all the cuntry. This Douglas wes so far offendit at him, becaus it wes thocht that he vanne feid aganis him at Glaynnaip,[2] and ane wther agains Lindsay thane Laird of Craigy, at the watter of Done, bothe one ane day, that the Erll offeritt to many that wald bring this Allexanderis heid, 'thai suld haue the fourty-mark land of Stewarttoune in Cuninghame,' the quhilkis wordis cuming to Allexanderis

[2] Glenapp.

eiris, he conveynis to the number of ane hunder horse; and on the Yuill-day, in the morning, come to the toune of Wigtoune, about the time he knew the Erll to be at the morning Mess; and heffand all his rycht of the said xl-mark land put in forme, cumis in the kirk, and says, 'My Lord, ye haue hicht this xl-mark land to ony that wald bring yow my heid, and I knaw thair is nane so meitt as my selff! And thairfoir will desyr your lordship to keip to me, as ye bad[3] to ony wther.' The Erll perseivitt that, gif he refuissitt, the sam wald cost him his lyff; and thairfoir tuik the penne and subscryvit the samin. Alischunder thankeit his lordschip, and takand his horse, lap one, and cam his wayis. And he and his airis bruikis[4] the samin at this tyme, or at the least, to the (ane thowsande) sex hunder and tua yeir of God. . . . He gatt this in the fourth yeir of the ring of Robert the third, quhilk was about the yeir of God 1380. This Allexander, cuming hame to Donour[5] beganne to grow prowd, and it was feiritt that he suld haue disereist[6] his broder sone; and alse he beganne to be ane tirrane abuiff his frendis. Quhairupone thay, conveynand[7] in Donour, tuik him in his bed, kaist fedder bedis abuiff him, and smorrit[8] him, and thair he deit."

In spite of his somewhat frail morality, James IV. showed a strong desire to rule his kingdom well and diligently. An Act passed in his first Parliament ordained, "anent the furthputting of justice, throw all the Realme, that our Soverane Lord sal ride in proper persoune about to all his aieris" (assizes). Accordingly in 1504, the year after his marriage with Margaret, daughter of Henry VII. of England, the young king rode to Dumfries to hold a criminal court. The Lord Treasurer's accounts present a curiously minute picture of the royal proceedings, not only during his journeys upon judicial

[3] Must. [4] Enjoys. [5] Dunure.
[6] Disinherited. [7] Meeting. [8] Smothered.

business, but also on his frequent pilgrimages to the shrine of St Ninian at Whithorn. The following are a few extracts made from the accounts of expenditure incurred during James's first journey to Dumfries :—

"Aug. 13. *Item*, in Drumfreise, to Menstrales, to fe thaim horsis to Eskdale, and syne agane to Drumfreise . . . . . . xlij*s*.
,, 14. *Item*, to þe Pyparis of Drumfreise . . xiiij*s*.
,, 17. *Item*, to þe man hangit the Thevis at the Hullirbuss . . . . . xiiij*s*.
Item, for ane raip to hing thaim in . . viij*d*.
,, 18. *Item*, to ane gyde to pas with Sir Thomas Alane to Edinburghe for wyne to þe King in Eskdale . . . . . ix*s*.
,, 19. *Item*, to ane Ingliseman brocht ane deire to þe King fra Lord Dacre . . xxviij*s*.
Item, to þe Priour of Carliles tua men that brocht present and mavasy [Malvoisie, Malmsey wine] fra þe said Priour to þe King . . . lvj*s*.
Item, to tua wiffis [women] brocht aill to þe King, fra Sir Johne Musgrave . . . xxviij*s*.
,, 20. *Item*, to Sir Johne Musgrave's man that blew the hunting to þe King . . . . xiiij*s*.
,, 21. *Item*, to þe man that hangit the theves in Canonby, be the Kingis command . . . xiiij*s*.
Item, to tua Inglise wemen that sang in þe Kingis pailȝeoune [pavilion] . . . xxviij*s*.
,, 22. *Item*, for ane hors to þe cartair that hed his hors deid at the Hullirbuss, drawand þe pailȝeounis, be the Kingis command . . . iiij*l*.
,, 23. *Item*, in Lochmabane to þe King to play at þe Cartis with Lord Dacre . . . xlvj*s*. viij*d*.
,, 24. *Item*, the King come to Drumfreise furth of Eskdale, to the Justice and Lordis to the Justice Air thair, and remanit at þe said Air xxiij days, to þe Justices expenses ilk day xl*s*. . xlvj*l*.
,, 25. *Item*, to þe King at cartis with Lord Dakir . vij*l*.
Sept. 8. *Item*, to þe Freris of Drumfreise xiiij*s*., and of Wigtoune . . . . . xiiij*s*.
,, 11. *Item*, to þe piparis of Drumfreise . . xxviij*s*.

Sept. 12. *Item*, to þe Franche smyth to þe Kingis hors
shoing, sene þe King com fra Edinburgh xxviij*s*. vj*d*.
,, 13. *Item*, to Sir Richard Champley's Menstrales,
Inglise men, that playit to þe King . . lvj*s*.
Item, to William Cunnynghame's wif in Drumfreise, for þe Kingis bele chere [food and
drink]⁹ . . . . . . x*l*.
,, 14. *Item*, in Lochmabane to ane pur man that all
þe Court tuk his hay fra him, be the Kingis
command . . . . . x*s*."

The tenor of the gallant young king's life seems to be reflected in these silent records—capital punishment and cards with the English warden Lord Dacre, "bel-chere" from a buxom landlady and alms to the begging Friars, comedy and tragedy closely interwoven, as they were in his own progress from the mysterious murder of his father at Sauchieburn to his own soldierly death among his knights at Flodden.

At the assizes there was heavier business to dispose of than the judges are wont to find there nowadays. John Pattersoune, indeed, fined 5*l*. for fishing for salmon in the Annan during close time, is the sixteenth-century counterpart of many a sly fellow of our own times; but there fell also to be disposed of such weighty cases as the slaughter of the laird of Dinwoodie and the laird of Mouswald by some of their neighbours. The Jardines of Applegarth and Sibbald-besyde were put on trial for it, but managed to escape conviction.

In 1508 the feud that had long been smouldering between Lord Maxwell, Steward of Annandale, and Crichton, Lord Sanquhar, Sheriff of Nithsdale, broke out with violence. Sanquhar came to hold a court at Dumfries on July 30, accompanied by a considerable force, which, being drawn up on the Lower Sand-beds at the outskirts of the town, were attacked

⁹ William Cunnynghame is probably the same merchant to whom 42*l*. had been paid in June previous for 6 tuns of wine, sent by King James as a present to Lord Dacre, the English warden.

with great violence by Lord Maxwell and Sir William Douglas of Drumlanrig, who approached them along the Annan road. Sanquhar's men were put to flight, and Robert Crichton of Kirkpatrick, Hamilton laird of Dalzell, and Gordon laird of Craighlaw, with many others, were slain. Four years later Douglas and Fergusson of Craigdarroch were put upon their trial for this slaughter, before an assize of twenty-eight barons presided over by Angus and in the presence of the king; but there was evidently a preconcerted scheme for their acquittal, which was granted on the grounds that Robert Crichton happened to be an outlaw at the time, and those who were in arms with him were constructively rebels. Lord Maxwell did not even go through the form of trial, being probably too powerful to be interfered with.

This feudal civil war had its counterpart on a smaller scale in Galloway, where the hereditary sheriff, Agnew of Lochnaw, found his office no protection against his turbulent neighbour Sir David, son of Lord Kennedy.

Nothing is more remarkable than the light thrown on the social state of Scotland at this time by the justiciary records. By far the larger part of the criminals dealt with at the king's "justice aires" were men of good position, barons and landowners, burgesses or provosts of burghs. The humbler offenders were dealt with by the sheriff or at the baron's courts, and do not appear; but the following extracts from the records of the short reign of James IV., in which the culprits are all landowners, or members of their families, in Dumfriesshire or Galloway, illustrate the difficulty of maintaining order when the upper classes were so unruly :—

CRIMINAL RECORDS.

DUMFRIESSHIRE.

Year.	Name.	Charge.	Sentence.
1488	Cuthbert Murray of Cockpule	High treason . . .	Not recorded.
1498	Alexander Jardine, nephew and heir of Applegirth	Forethought felony to the dwellers in Dryfeholm	Pardoned.
1502	Robert Herries, yr. of Terrauchty	Houghing Sir James Crichton's horse	Respited for 40 days. No further proceedings recorded.
1504	Thomas Bell of Curre . .	Slaughter of the laird of Dinwoodie	Escaped trial.
	Robert Dinwoodie, son of the laird	Horse-stealing . .	To make restitution.
1505	John Lindsay of Wauchope	Slaughter of a messenger-at-arms	Death and forfeiture.
1512	William Douglas of Drumlanrig	Slaughter of Robert Crichton of Kirkpatrick	Acquitted, because the victim was an outlaw.

KIRKCUDBRIGHT.

Year.	Name.	Charge.	Sentence.
1507	John Gordon of Lochinvar .	Horse-stealing . .	Pardoned.
1508	Herbert Maxwell of Kirkconnel	Theft of wood, and taking part with Lord Maxwell in the affray with Lord Sanquhar	”
”	Ninian M'Culloch of Cardiness	Oppressing Elizabeth, Lady Cardiness, and stealing her goods	Bound in surety.
”	” ”	Taking and tearing the King's letters	” ”
”	John Gordon of Lochinvar .	Oppression of Mr Lennox of Cally	Acquitted.
”	” ”	Oppression of —— M'Adam	Bound in surety.
”	John Gordon of Crags . .	Poaching salmon in the Urr	Fined
”	John M'Ghie of Phumpton .	Oppressing the officer of the Abbot of Dundrennan, and throwing William Schankis, monk, from his horse	Fined vi merks, and bound in surety.
”	William Lennox, yr. of Cally	Besieging Thos. M'Ghie in the Kirk of Girtoun, poaching salmon in the Fleet, and burning the wood of Rusco	Compounded, and bound in surety.
”	David Kennedy of Craigneil .	Oppressing Sir David Kennedy of Cumston	Fined x merks, and to find surety.
”	William Maclellan of Bomby	Stealing two hogsheads of Gascony wine, &c.	Fined iij merks.
1509	Patrick Maclellan of Gelston	Cattle-stealing from the Sheriff of Wigtown	To be beheaded, but pardoned by the king.
1511	William Lennox of Cally .	Striking the Sheriff, and destroying the woods of Lochinvar	Bound in surety, and afterwards pardoned by the king.
1512	John Fergusson of Craigdarroch	Slaughter of Robert Crichton of Kirkpatrick	Acquitted because the victim was an outlaw.
1513	Patrick Maclellan of Gelston	Slaughter . . .	Forfeited bail and denounced a rebel.

WIGTOWNSHIRE.

Year.	Name.	Charge.	Sentence.
1498	John Dunbar, yr. of Mochrum	Theft of xliij*l*., a silver seal, and "uther small gere," in the possession of the Bishop of Galloway	Pardoned.
"	William Adair of Kilhilt	Forethought felony done on A. M'Dowall of Elrig	"
"	Sir Andrew M'Culloch of Myrtoun, and 29 others	Burning the houses of Dunskey and Ardwell	"
1502	John M'Kie of Merton, and 5 others	Burning the house of Dunskey	Respited for 19 years.
1506	Patrick Dunbar, yr. of Kilconquhar, and 2 others	Slaughter of Patrick M'Culloch, committed in Wigtown in 1496	Pardoned.
1509	Patrick Agnew of Lochnaw, Hereditary Sheriff	Taking a bribe to acquit a murderer	Fined v merks.
1513	" " "	Oppression of his tenants, and striking Thomas Kennedy in Wigtown	Compounded and found surety.
"	" " "	Forcibly preventing Sir David Kennedy holding a court in Leswalt	Fined x merks, and bound in surety.
"	" " "	Stealing four cows in Ayrshire	The laird of Orchardton became surety.
"	Patrick Vans of Ersock .	Stealing six silver cups from the Bishop of Galloway, houghing his cattle, and other crimes	The laird of Torhouse became surety.
"	Alexander Ahannay, brother of the laird of Sorby; Fergus M'Dowall, young laird of Dalreagle	Riotous assembly in burgh of Wigtown	Came in the king's will.
"	Ninian Edgar, young laird of Creechan; Thomas Vans, brother of the Prior of Whithorn; George M'Culloch, young laird of Durchdery (?); Patrick Murray, young laird of Broughton; the Laird of Killaser; Uthred M'Dowall of Mindork, and 20 others	Preventing Sir David Lindsay holding his court at Leswalt	" "
"	John Dunbar of Mochrum, and Patrick Hamilton of Boreland	For not appearing to answer for crimes imputed to them	Fined xl*l*. Scots each.
"	John M'Kie of Merton .	Stealing cattle, a horse, and other goods; also art and part in burning the Place of Dunskey	Compounded; Sir Gavin Kennedy to be surety.

But the bickerings of lairds and the raids of great feudal lords were to be hushed alike by a summons to arms on a national scale. James, devoted to the French queen, Anne of Brittany, espoused the quarrel of her nation with England, and on August 11, 1513, the Lyon King-at-arms delivered a declaration of war to Henry VIII. in his camp at Térouanne. The invasion of England which followed, ended within a month in the most disastrous defeat ever suffered by the Scottish arms. King James fell with almost all his chivalry round him. Among the slain, Dumfriesshire had to mourn for John Lord Maxwell and his four brothers; Robert Lord Herries and Andrew his brother; the Master of Angus and his brother; Sir William Douglas of Drumlanrig, Irving of Bonshaw, and many others; while among those who had marched from Galloway, never to return, were the Earl of Cassilis, Sir Alexander Gordon of Lochinvar, Sir Alexander Stewart of Garlies,[1] the MacDoualls lairds of Garthland, Logan and Freuch, M'Culloch of Myrtoun, Adair of Kilhilt, and Sir William Maclellan of Bomby. The Earl of Angus had marched with the king's army across the Border, but having expressed to the king disapproval of the strategy which preceded the battle, it is said that the king in extreme irritation told him that if he was afraid he might go home. Bell-the-Cat, not being of the stuff to brook such an insult from a young man, even though his sovereign, rode off the field and passed into Scotland with only six attendants. But eight days later he was present at the coronation of the baby king James V. at Stirling. In November he set out on a journey to repress disorders on the Border and in Galloway, but he died at Whithorn before the close of the year, and was buried there, though his heart was conveyed to St Bride's Chapel of Douglas.[2]

[1] Ancestor of the Earls of Galloway.
[2] In the course of exploring and putting in order the ruins of Whithorn Priory in 1886 and following years, a tomb richly carved in the style of the fifteenth century, on the north side of the church, was opened. It was found to contain a coffin, hewn out of solid stone, in which were two skeletons, one lying on the other. One of these was of gigantic proportions, and may perhaps have been that of Bell-the-Cat.

CHAPTER VII.

FROM THE BATTLE OF FLODDEN IN 1513 TO THE
TREATY OF NORHAM IN 1550.

ALTHOUGH the Earl of Surrey's victorious army had been disbanded after Flodden, the Scottish Border, shorn of the flower of its defenders, lay exposed to English raids. Numerous letters from the English Warden, Lord Dacre, the ancient opponent of James IV. at cards, attest how diligent he was to take advantage of such an opportunity, but it would be wearisome to follow all the incidents of this ferocious warfare. Two quotations may suffice to illustrate its character—not only as it was conducted at this time, but for a century before and after. On October 29, 1513, Lord Dacre writes to the Bishop of Durham :—

"On Tewsday at night last past, I sent diverse of my tennents of Gillislande to the nombre of lx personnes in Eskdalemoor upon the Middill Merches, and there brynt vii howses, tooke and brought awey xxxvj hede of cattell and much insight.[1] On Weddinsday at thre of the clok efter noon, my broder Sir Christopher assembled diverse of the kings subgjects beyng under my reull, and roode all that night into Scotland, and on Thurisday, in the mornynge, they began upon the said Middill Merchies and brynt the Stakeheugh

[1] Furnishing.

[the manor-place of Irewyn], with the hamletts belonging to them, down, Irewyn bwrne, being the chambrelain of Scotland owne lands and undre his reull, continewally birnyng from the breke of day to oone of the clok after noon, and there wan, tooke and brought awey cccc hede of cattell, ccc shepe, certain horses and verey miche insight, and slew two men, hurte and vounded diverse other persones and horses, and then entred Ingland grounde again at vij of the clok that night."

Of course the Scots retaliated, and Lord Dacre seems to have been rebuked by the English Government for not checking their raids. He defends himself against the imputation of want of vigilance by writing a letter to the council on May 17, 1514:—

"For oone cattell taken by the Scotts we have takyn, won and brought awey out of Scotland a hundreth; and for oone sheep, two hundreth of a surity. And has for townships and housis, burnt in any of the said Est, Middill and West Marches within my reull, fro the begynnyng of this warr unto this daye, . . . I assure your lordships for truthe that I have and hes caused to be burnt and distroyed sex tymes moo townys and howsys within the West and Middill Marches of Scotland, in the same season then is done to us, as I may be trusted, and as I shall evidently prove. For the watter of Liddall being xij myles of length, . . . whereupon was a hundreth pleughes; . . . the watter of Ewse being viij myles of length in the said Marches, whereupon was vii pleughes, . . . lyes all and every of them waist now, noo corne sawne upon none of the said grounds. . . . Upon the West Marches I have burnt and distroyed the townships of Annand," together with thirty-three others mentioned in detail, "and the Water of Esk from Stabulgorton down to Cannonby, being vi myles in lenth, whereas thare was in all tymes passed four hundreth ploughes and above, which er now clearely waisted and noo man duelling in any of them in this daye, save oonly in the towrys of Annand Stepel and Walghapp [Wauchope]."

The triple treaty of peace which was concluded in 1515 between England, Scotland, and France, made special and stringent provisions for the repression of Border raiding, but things went on much as before. The dalesmen had lost the habit of honest industry; they had also lost much in the endeavour to pursue it. Their only means of subsistence had come to be "lifting" from their neighbours.

It behoved all men in those troublous times to keep a watchful eye on politics. Angus had been up to now the representative of the monarchy: the Border barons had been under obligation to attend his musters and obey his orders as Chancellor of the realm. Suddenly, on July 9, 1528, without the slightest previous warning, out flies a royal proclamation from Edinburgh, declaring Angus and his two brothers rebels, forbidding all men to hold communication with them on pain of being dealt with as rebels also. James V. had at last shaken himself free from his powerful Minister, and a new order of things was set up. Gavin Dunbar, Archbishop of Glasgow, formerly Prior of Whithorn, was appointed Chancellor.

The young king, aged only seventeen, showed all the precocious energy of the Stuarts in assuming the direct rule of his kingdom. Angus having been declared by Parliament to be forfeited in life, lands, and goods, and having been driven to take refuge in England, James turned his attention to the Western and Middle Marches, which, to quote a letter written at the time, were "in grete ruyne and out of all good order."

The baronies of Kirkandrews, Bryntallone, and Morton,

lying between the Sark and the Esk as far up the latter as its junction with the Liddel, had remained since the days of Bruce neutral ground between the two kingdoms, and had come to be known as the "Batabel or threip lands" — the Debatable Lands. This district was conveniently situated for the resort of lawless men of both nations; in fact, it was peopled by men who, originally of good families in Dumfriesshire, had become demoralised by the incessant Border warfare into nothing better than banditti. It can easily be imagined that an honest living could hardly be made in Eskdale, Ewisdale, Wauchopedale, and Liddesdale, in times when, without warning, the growing crops or stackyards might be destroyed in a single night, and the whole live stock of an estate be driven over the English border; hence the people of these dales and of the Debatable Land, though not naturally worse than their fellow-countrymen, had been driven by force of circumstances into a mode of life which made their existence incompatible with the peace of the land. Foremost and most numerous among them were the Armstrongs, whom the Earl of Northumberland, writing to the king's treasurer in 1528, estimated, with their adherents, at 3000 horsemen. Then came the Elwands, Ellwoods, or Elliots, who extended into Teviotdale; the Nixons, who were more numerous in Cumberland than on Scottish soil; the Crosars in Upper Liddesdale, with their chief stronghold at Riccarton; and the Grahams, who owned five towers in the Debatable Land. Besides these clans there were families of Irvings, Olivers, Bells, Dicksons, Littles, and others associated with them.[1]

In 1501 the sheriffs on the Border were directed to summon the Armstrongs, to the number of seventy, to attend their trial at Selkirk for the slaughter of John Blackburn, &c.;

[1] See Note F, The Clans on the West Marches, p. 183.

and as they did not appear, the Earl of Bothwell, then Lord of Liddesdale, was directed to proceed against them, put them to death as the king's rebels, and seize their goods. This does not seem to have affected them much; neither did the justiciary visit of James IV. in 1504, with his minstrels, singing women, hunters and falconers, and gambling with Lord Dacre. After that attempts were made to conciliate the Armstrongs, Elliots, and others by repeated respites and remissions; but matters continued much the same as before. In 1525 representations were made by the English Government, who suffered as much as the Scottish by the lawlessness of their Border clans, that "the Armstrangs of Liddersdaill and the theiffs of Ewysdaill were joined with the rebels of Tyndaill, and were comyn untoe theym and kepet all company togedders." Angus, who was then Warden of the East and Middle Marches, swept down on the Armstrongs, captured twelve of them, burned many houses, and carried off 600 cattle, 3000 sheep, 500 goats, and many horses. This was a smart punishment, but scarcely judicial in character, nor of the sort to restore quiet in Liddesdale. The men who had lost their cattle could hardly be expected to sit down and starve; accordingly, no sooner had the warden turned his back, when 400 Scotsmen united with the English broken men of Tynedale in a raid upon Tarsett and Hesleyside.

There now appears on the scene an Armstrong to whose name there still clings the same kind of affectionate association as endears that of Robin Hood to Englishmen. Johnnie Armstrong's story has been romantically and pathetically woven into the ballad history of the time.

> "Sum speiks of lords, sum speiks of lairds,
>   And siklyke men of hie degrie;
> Of a gentleman I sing a sang,
>   Sumtime called Laird of Gilnockie." [2]

---

[2] Ballad of Johnnie Armstrong.

John Armstrong of Gilnockie was brother to the Laird of Mangerton, and early in the century had built himself a tower on the Esk, on the church lands of Canonbie. The Archbishop of Glasgow fulminated against Johnnie and his clan all the terrors of excommunication;[3] but Robert, Lord Maxwell, Warden of the West Marches, endeavoured to conciliate them by receiving Johnnie as his vassal for the lands of Stablegorton, Langholm, and others, and taking a bond of manrent from him.

In February 1527 the English warden, Lord Dacre, attempted to drive Gilnockie and his clan out of the Debatable Land, and attacked him with a force of 2000 men; but although he succeeded in burning Gilnockie Tower, he was driven back, and the Armstrongs retaliated by burning Netherby on the English side. Grievous complaints were made by Lord Dacre touching the countenance given by Robert, fifth Lord Maxwell, to the Armstrongs and their accomplices in this affair, as well as in numerous other raids and counter-raids which took place this year; in fact, the English Government threatened to put an end to the peace then existing between the two countries. The English were all the more incensed against Maxwell because of an agreement entered into by him in 1526 with the Earl of Cumberland, then the English warden, for the pacification of the Debatable Land.

At last young King James, impatient of the failure of his wardens to put an end to the murderous anarchy on the Border, and weary of the repeated assurance of improvement made by his lieutenants in these parts, resolved to take affairs into his own hands. He imprisoned the Lords Bothwell, Maxwell, and Home, Walter Scott of Buccleuch, and other Border lairds, because, in the words of Sir James Balfour,

[3] See Note G, Monition of Cursing against the Border Clans, p. 186.

"they had winked at the willanies" of the dalesmen. He then summoned all barons, gentlemen, landed and "substantious" men of the Lowlands, to meet him with their households, "boden in feir of weire," at Edinburgh on June 26, 1530, and those of Dumfriesshire and Galloway to meet him at Dumfries on June 30. Operations began by hunting on a great scale on the Meggat Water, when eighteen score of harts were pulled down by hounds, and all manner of small game killed by hawks.

On the king's arrival in Teviotdale it is said that royal proclamation was made that the lives of all broken men who would submit to the king's will should be spared. Relying on this, Gilnockie rode into the king's camp to make obeisance with his habitual following of twenty-four well-mounted men "verrie richlie apparelled." [4] It is difficult to reconcile what followed with any respect for kingly faith. It is true that James was acting in concert with the English Government in breaking up this clan of thieves and murderers, and it is also true that the Armstrongs and their accomplices having been excommunicated, all men were absolved from keeping faith with them. But it is sickening to think that a king, the fountain of honour, should have slipped through an ecclesiastical loophole in order to entrap his subjects, however rebellious. He had with him an army of 8000 men (according to Pitscottie, 12,000), and it would have protected his honour from a dark stain had he employed them, as a soldier, against the robbers of the dales. But the poisonous teaching of Machiavelli had filtered through the French Court into the understanding of the King of Scotland, and James, in thus dealing with these mosstroopers, was but carrying into effect the doctrine quoted some forty years later by the Duke of Alva in one of his letters to his master, Philip II. "A

[4] Pitscottie. Other accounts put Gilnockie's following at fifty.

monarch's promises," he wrote in 1573, "are not to be considered so sacred as those of humbler mortals. Not that the king should directly violate his word, but at the same time I have thought all my life, and I have learned it from the Emperor, your Majesty's father, that the negotiations of kings depend upon different principles from those of us private gentlemen who walk the world; and in this manner I always observed that your Majesty's father, who was so great a gentleman and so powerful a prince, conducted his affairs."

So Gilnockie came fearlessly before the king, who, pointing to the culprit's well-appointed suite, exclaimed angrily, "What wants yon knave that a king should have?" Gilnockie protested that he had never injured the king's lieges, but Englishmen only, and vowed to serve him with four-and-twenty men-at-arms, and to bring him any Englishman whom he chose to name, alive, or dead, within a given day. The rest of the interview, as given in the ballad, accords very closely with the grave accounts of Pitscottie and others:—

"'Grant me my lyfe, my liege, my king!
And a brave gift I'll gie to thee—
All between heir and Newcastle town
Sall pay their yeirly rent to thee.'

'Away, away, thou traytor strang!
Out o' my sicht thou mayest sune be.
I grantit nevir a traytor's lyfe,
And now I'll not begin with thee.'

'Ye lied, ye lied, now, king,' he says,
'Althocht a king and prince ye be!
For I lu'ed naithing in all my lyfe,
I daur weil say it, but honesty—

But a fat horse, and a fair woman,
Twa bonny dogs to kill a deir;
But Ingland suld haif found me meil and malt,
Gif I had lived this hundred yeir!

> She suld haif fund me meil and malt,
> And beif and mutton in all plentie;
> But neir a Scots wyfe could haif said
> That e'er I skaithed her a pure flie.
>
> To seik hot water beneth cauld ice,
> Surelie it is a great folie;
> I haif asked grace at a graceless face,
> And there is nane for my men and me.
>
> But had I ken'd or I cam frae hame
> How thou unkind wadst bene to me,
> I wad haif kept the Border syde,
> In spyte of all thy force and thee.'"

The king showed no mercy. Without any pretence of a trial Gilnockie and thirty-one others were hanged on trees at Carlanrig Chapel, about ten miles above Hawick on the Langholm road. In the words of Pitscottie:—

"The king hanged Johne Armstrang, Laird of Kilnokie, quhilk monie Scottis menne heavilie lamented, for he was ane doubtit [redoubtable] man, and als gude ane Christane as evir was vpoun the Borderis. And albeit he was ane lous leivand [loose-living] man, and sustained the number of xxiiij weill-horsed able gentlemen with him, yitt he nevir molested no Scottis man. Bot it is said from the Scottis border to New Castle of Ingland, thair was not ane of quhatsoever estate bot payed to this Johne Armstrang ane tribut, to be frie of his cumbir, he was so doubtit in England."

One Sandie Scot, a "prowd thieff," charged with having burnt a widow's house with some of her children, was burnt alive.

No sooner was Gilnockie disposed of than Lord Maxwell was set at liberty, and the forfeited lands of Gilnockie, with all the movable goods of the robber chief, bestowed on him. Probably he succeeded in persuading the king that though he had protected the Armstrongs, refusing to enforce their proclamation as rebels by Angus in 1528, and encouraged them to resist the English warden, his alliance with the Armstrongs was an act of policy, failing some better means of preventing their raids on Scottish lieges. At all events, in their subsequent feud with the Johnstones, the Maxwells received hearty support from the Armstrong clan.

During these transactions in Dumfriesshire, others of a kindred but more desultory character were going on in Galloway. The affray in 1527 on Prestwick Links between the forces of the Earl of Cassilis and Campbell of Loudon, the Sheriff of Ayr, in which Cassilis was slain, belongs to Ayrshire history, but it had reflex effects in Wigtownshire, where the Kennedys owned great possessions. The Earl of Arran was suspected of having abetted Campbell; so M'Douall of Freuch, son-in-law of the deceased earl, accompanied by M'Douall of Mindork, landed in Arran and burnt Brodick Castle to the ground. Public opinion seems to have been in favour of the M'Doualls, for although they were made to find caution to underly their trial at Wigtown, no further proceedings are recorded. Less lucky were Neilson of Craigcaffy and his cousins, who on January 15, 1529, were "put to the horn"—proclaimed rebels and outlaws—for communing with rebels in Carrick, Bute, and Arran, and for oppressing Dunbar of Mochrum by breaking up the doors and windows of the Place of Mochrum.

In 1532, Nevin Agnew of Croach had recourse to his kinsman the sheriff as surety for restitution of twelve cattle, two horses, and other goods "spulzeit and reft" from Dean Andrew Stevenson, sub-prior of Whithorn. Sometimes the scene of the misdeeds of Galloway lairds was the capital. In 1525 one Cornelius de Machitima, a Dutch nobleman, lost his life among others in a street brawl, which must have been a serious affair to judge from the remissions to gentlemen implicated in it, which amount to about 300. Among them are mentioned the following gentlemen—the Earl of Cassilis with two of his brothers and an uncle, Ahannay of Sorby, M'Kie of Myrtoun, MacDouall of Garthland, M'Douall of Freuch.

A few days later than this affair occurred another tragedy in which also the actors were gentlemen of Galloway. It is worth recording because of its romantic sequel. Gordon of Lochinvar, Sheriff Agnew of Galloway, Douglas of Drumlanrig, William Cairns younger of Orchardson, Gordon of Craighlaw, John Gordon of Whithorn, M'Culloch of Torhouse, and others, were parading down the High Street of Edinburgh with their followers when they encountered Sir Thomas Maclellan of Bomby with his men. Now there was a bloodfeud at this time between Bomby and Lochinvar; neither would yield the "croun o' the causeway" to the other; swords flashed out, and a furious affray took place, in which Bomby lost his life. Gordon and his partisans were "put to the horn" for this slaughter, but in these lawless times this was generally an empty threat against powerful lairds. The offenders remained at liberty for eleven years. By that time a softer influence had been imported into the quarrel. Young Maclellan of Bomby fell in love with the daughter of Lochinvar, his father's murderer; letters of remission were obtained for Gordon and his associates, and amicable relations were renewed with the music of marriage bells.

It is agreeable to turn from these records, alternately sanguinary and squalid, to one of sunnier aspect. In 1536 James V., who seems to have entertained a warm affection for Robert, fifth Lord Maxwell, set out in his company, disguised as a private gentleman, to look for a bride in France. The exploit miscarried, for the ship in which they sailed encountered a storm which drove them round Cape Wrath to Whithorn, where they landed.

Next year the king set out for France with a suitable retinue to bring home Marie, daughter of the Duc de Vendôme, with whom his marriage had been negotiated; but it so turned out that he fell in love with Madeleine, daughter of Francis I., and married her. He remained nine months in France, and having returned alone to Scotland, sent Lord Maxwell, "grete Admirall" and Warden of the West Marches, "for the sure convoying and accumpanying of his derrest fallow the Quene to this his realme." The young queen died within six weeks of landing at Leith.

Henry VIII., who had entertained hopes of winning the Scottish king to the cause of the Reformation, and had, it is said, offered him his daughter in marriage, had abstained for some years from the customary acts of invasion. James, however, though suspected of inclining at one time to the Reformed faith, was now confirmed in his adherence to Rome by the Pope conferring on him the title of Defender of the Faith, forfeited by Henry. Moreover, rejecting an alliance with his cousin the English princess, James married in 1539 the Catholic Marie of Guise; so Henry, after more than one futile attempt to gain his nephew by diplomacy, assembled an army in 1542 under Sir James Bowes, associated with whom were the exiled Angus and his brother, Sir George Douglas. The Earls of Huntly and Home succeeded in defeating this force at Hadden Rig on the East Marches. But if this fratricidal warfare had lacked any elements of bitterness in the past, these were now forthcoming by the importation of religious acrimony. The severity of the new laws against heresy was distasteful to some of the barons, especially to the king's favourite, Lord Maxwell. James marched his army as far as Fala on the Lammermoors, intending to oppose the invasion threatened by the Duke of Norfolk (the Surrey of Flodden). But here the dissension broke out into mutiny: the malcontent nobles refused to advance farther, and James was obliged to disband his forces. Another and smaller force having been mustered, the chief command was given to Oliver Sinclair, an officer of the king's household, an appointment which was a grievous slight on the great lords. Buchanan says that Maxwell offered to lead 10,000 men across the Esk to do the king's service; but James would not hear of it: he had resolved to mark his displeasure with the proud barons. He accompanied the army as far as Caerlaverock; perhaps if he had himself retained the command matters might have had a different sequel.

The peculiarity of the conditions of military service at this time must be borne in mind. There was no standing army. The monarch relied on the feudal following of the very men whom he wished to punish. The disaffected nobles themselves held the posts corresponding to divisional commanders, brigadiers, and colonels of battalions in a modern army; and these were now called on to serve under an obscure esquire, an ordinary gentleman of cloak and sword, suddenly elevated to the post of commander-in-chief. The result was as might have been foreseen. The Scottish army was led across the Sark, and, while crossing the Solway Moss in disarray, was attacked by a greatly inferior force. Hardly any show of resistance was made. Men who would fight to the last drop of blood for a leader to their liking, could hardly be got to swing a sword for the king's new favourite. The whole army fled. Pitscottie puts the numbers actually slain at only fifteen English and ten Scots, but many are supposed to have perished at nightfall in the morass. About 1000 prisoners were taken, of whom 200 were reckoned as gentlemen, including Oliver Sinclair and three of his brothers, Lord Maxwell and his brother John, the Lords Fleming, Somervile, Oliphant, and Gray, the Laird of Garlies, John Charteris brother of Amisfield, and David Gordon uncle of Lochinvar.

When the news was brought to King James at Caerlaverock he nearly went out of his mind with grief. It has never been explained why he stayed behind: it was contrary to all the traditions of his race to shrink from the danger of a battle-field, and equally irreconcilable with his own undoubted courage. He never recovered the shock of defeat, but died shortly after, apparently of a broken heart, at Falkland Palace, aged only thirty years. He left his crown to his infant daughter Mary, and his distracted kingdom to the evils of another regency.

The opposition of James V. having been removed by his death, Henry VIII. reverted to his scheme of winning over Scotland to the Protestant cause, and to that end enlisted the services of the prisoners of rank taken at Solway Moss. Maxwell and the others subscribed a bond, confirming it by knightly oath, binding them to acknowledge Henry as Lord Superior of the kingdom of Scotland, to do their utmost to put the Scottish strongholds in his hands, and to have the Princess Mary delivered to him. In the event of the Scottish Parliament refusing these terms, they were to assist Henry, with all the forces they could muster, in the conquest of Scotland. Each of them was to leave his eldest son or nearest relative as hostage for his fidelity, and on these humiliating terms they were allowed to return to Scotland in January 1542-43. A further condition exacted was that, in the event of failure, they were either to return to England or remain in Scotland, if so directed, to assist Henry in the war.[5] The exiled Earl of Angus returned with the prisoners, and was restored by the Regent

[5] Sadler's State Papers, vol. i. p. 97.

Arran to his forfeited honours and estates. Pressure was brought upon Maxwell by Arran and the Council to break his parole and join the Scottish army in opposing English invasion, but he replied, "I am the Kingis Majestyis prisoner, trustyng ye wyll not have me dysonneryd. But if I do go [back to England], what are you the wekar? . . . Are you not Governor? Do I not leve behynd me all my servauntes, al my tenauntes, my landes and my goodes; what nede you fere, whethur I go or tary?"[6]

Maxwell's first act on his return to Scotland was to give his daughter Margaret in marriage to the Earl of Angus. Besides the bride's dowry of 5000 merks, Angus received from his father-in-law a wedding present appropriate to the warlike character of the times—namely, five cannon, a brass falcon, a brass hagbut, and three sling-pieces, which remained on the walls of Douglas Castle till Oliver Cromwell carried them away.

Maxwell's second act was of wider national importance, being, in effect, the first overt step in the coming Scottish Reformation. On March 15, 1543, he introduced into Parliament, and carried, a bill making it lawful "to all our souirane Ladyis liegis to haif the Haly Writ, baith the New Testament and the Auld, in the vulgar toung in Inglis or Scottes,[7] of ane gude and trew translatioun, and that thai sal incur na crimes for the hefing or reding of the samin, prouiding alvayis that na Man despute or hold oppunzeonis [opinions], under the pains contenit in the Actis of Parliament." Cardinal Beaton happened to be in prison at the time this bill came up for discussion; but Gavin Dunbar, Archbishop of Glasgow, entered his strong dissent in name of the other prelates, constituting one of the Three Estates, and craved instruments. Notwithstanding this, on the rising of Parliament the Regent ordered proclamation to be made of the Acts

---

[6] Sadler's State Papers, vol. v. p. 428.   [7] English or Gaelic.

passed, "and in speciale the Act made for having the New Testament in the Vulgar Tongue."

In order to realise how great was the boon conferred by this Act on the people of Catholic Scotland, it is necessary to remember that the bloody edicts of Charles the Bold, condemning to the axe, the gallows, the flood, or the stake all who ventured to read the Scriptures in public or private, were at this moment in force throughout his vast dominions, representing the orthodox ecclesiastical law against heresy :—

"The Clargy hearto long repugned: butt in the end, convicted by reassonis and by multitud of votes in thar contrar, thei also condiscended. . . . Then mycht have bene sein the Byble lying almaist upoun euerie gentilmanis table. The New Testament was borne about in many manis handes. We grant that some (alace!) prophaned that blessed wourd; for some that, perchance, had never it maist common in thare hand; thei would chope thare familiares on the cheak with it and say, 'This hes lyne hyd under my bed-feitt these ten yeiris.' Otheris wold glorie, 'O! how oft have I bein in danger for this booke! How secreatlie have I stollen fra my wyff at mydnycht to reid upoun it!'"[8]

No progress, however, was made by Angus, Maxwell, and the rest of the English party in their secret mission. Sadler, the English ambassador at the Scottish Court, quotes Sir Adam Otterburn, on whom he had been urging the expediency of the union of the two kingdoms by marriage. "If you had the las," said Otterburn, "and we the lad, we coulde be well content with it; but I cannot beleve that your nacyon coulde agree to have a Scotte to be Kyng of England; and lykewise I assure you, that our nacyon, being a stout nacyon, will never agree to have an Englishman to be King of Scotland; and though the whole nobilite of the realme wolde consent unto

[8] Knox's History, vol. i. p. 100.

it, yet our comen people and the stones in the strete wolde ryse and rebelle agenst it." [9]

In December 1544 Lord Maxwell was appointed Warden of the West Marches. This, coupled with the failure of the secret negotiations, aroused the English king's suspicion of Maxwell's fidelity. Angus, moreover, had openly deserted the English party in Scotland and gone over to the French. So Lord Maxwell was recalled to his parole and imprisoned in the Tower of London.

Border hostilities were once more resumed. Sir Thomas Wharton marched through Annandale, took Dumfries without opposition, and wasted all the country round. His enterprise was made an easier one than usual, because the feud between the clans of Maxwell and Johnston, afterwards to become so disastrous, was just beginning to take definite shape. Some idea of the frightful waste entailed by this kind of warfare may be gathered from Sir Thomas Wharton's reports to his Government, preserved in the Harleian Miscellany (Collection B.M., No. 1757). The total, of which all the particulars of date and place are specified, from September 9, 1543, to June 29, 1544, is given as follows :—

"Townes, onsettz, graunges, and hamlettis spoyled and burnt	124
Oxen and kene brought awaye	3285
Horss and naggis brought awaye	332
Shepe and gete brought awaye	4710
Prisoners taken	408
Menne slayne	35

Grete quantite of insight brought awaye, over and besydes a grete quantite of corne and insight, and a greate nombre of all sortes of catail burned in the townes and howss, and is not nombred in the lettres, and menye menne also hurt."

[9] *Sadler's State Papers*, vol. ii. p. 559.

Again, under the heading, "Exploits doon uppon the Scottis," the following report summarises the results of raids from the beginning of July to the end of November 1544 :—

"Touns, towers, stedes, barnekyns, parysh churches, bastell-houses	192
Scotts slain	403
Prisoners taken	816
Nolt	10,386
Shepe	12,492
Nags and geldings	1,296
Gayt [goats]	200
Bolls of corn	850
Insight gear	..."

After passing his Act for the translation of Scripture, two years' further imprisonment, the latter part of which was endured at Carlisle, combined with despair of Scottish politics, undermined the resolution of Lord Maxwell, who had hitherto resisted all pressure put on him by the English Government to surrender his castles to them. He now sent orders to his second son, John (afterwards Lord Herries), to deliver Lochmaben Castle, of which he was keeper, to the English warden. Further, the eldest son, Robert, was to hand over Caerlaverock Castle as soon as his father was set at liberty. This was not at all to the mind of Robert, who with his uncle, Maxwell of Cowhill, promptly led a foray across the Border in the old style, and had the misfortune to be taken prisoner. Cowhill was then sent to John at Lochmaben with letters from his father, urging him to surrender his castle, and to come himself to Carlisle as a hostage for his father's good faith. Of this good faith Wharton expresses suspicions in a report to the Earl of Hertford, October 5, 1545, suggesting that Lord Maxwell is privy to the obstinacy of his sons—relying on regaining his liberty, and at the same time keeping his castles. However, in the end, Caerlaverock, which had been left in keeping of a priest related to the Maxwells, was given up to the English on October 28, 1545, and placed under command of Thomas Carleton. The cession of Lochmaben followed, but neither of these strongholds remained in English hands. The lairds of Johnstone, Drumlanrig, and Lochinvar promptly invested Caerlaverock with the levies of Nithsdale, Annandale, and Galloway, and took it, as we learn from a report made by Wharton to King Henry. Next year the Regent Arran collected an army to recapture the castle, but on arriving there found that the English had evacuated it. On November 21 Lochmaben was regained and siege was laid to the Thrieve, where, as it appears, Lord Maxwell had shut himself up. This place also was surrendered in two or three days, and Maxwell was put in ward as a traitor at Dumfries. Two Kirkcudbright lairds were then appointed keepers—Garlies of the Thrieve and Lochinvar of Lochmaben. Maxwell having made written declaration to the effect that he had made surrender of his castles under fear of death, and that he was and would ever remain a faithful subject of Queen Mary, was liberated after a short imprisonment, and on June 3, 1546, received appointment as Justiciar of Nithsdale, Annandale, and Galloway, as well as Warden of the West Marches. Lochmaben Castle was also restored to his keeping, but he died within a month of receiving his commission.

In 1547 Sir Thomas Carleton of Carleton in Cumberland, the same English officer who had been placed in command of Caerlaverock in 1545, coming by way of Teviotdale and Canonbie, seized the town of Dumfries, and issued a proclamation in the name of King Henry, calling on all men to come and make oath to the king's majesty. The majority of lairds seem to have submitted ; but let it be reckoned to the lasting honour of Kirkcudbright that, at a time when the whole of Dumfriesshire was thus under the English yoke, that gallant little burgh repelled the invader. Its magistrates offered defiance to Carleton's proclamation, wherefore that gentleman determined to burn down the town. Late one evening a brisk assault was delivered on the walls, minutely described in Carleton's despatches. Maclellan of Bomby, coming to the rescue, is reported to have been repulsed with the loss of three men slain; but, by Carleton's own admission, he succeeded in making the English raise the siege and turn to cattle-lifting. About 2000 sheep, 200 cattle, and 50 horses were collected; but a force of "Galloway folks from beyond the water of Dee" appeared on the scene, and the sheep had to be left behind. The horses and cattle, however, were driven into Dumfries.

Carleton's next exploit was the capture of Lochwood Tower, Johnstone's principal stronghold, by a clever stratagem. Having secured this important place, he was in a position to administer the government of Annandale and Nithsdale for the English, and make forays into Clydesdale. Sad to say, "Kircobree," seeing the whole country overrun with English, and no help at hand, at last surrendered at discretion.

A vigorous attempt was made by the Regent Arran in 1547 to deliver Dumfriesshire from the English grasp. He began operations by capturing Langholm Tower, but was then recalled to the east, where he suffered the crushing defeat of Pinkie at the hands of the Duke of Somerset, Protector of England. Among the dead on that fatal field lay Agnew, Sheriff of Galloway, Gordon of Lochinvar, MacDouall of Garthland, M'Douall of Freuch, and Vans of Barnbarroch.

Dumfriesshire and the Stewartry of Kirkcudbright were at this time as completely under English rule as in the days of Edward Longshanks. Wigtownshire, however, being under the strong grasp of the Earl of Cassilis, still held for Queen Mary. Lord Wharton, commander of the English forces in Scotland, has left a memorandum professing to give the names of those gentlemen who had sworn allegiance to young Edward VI., and the strength each could bring into the field. Even if, as is probable, many of them made submission under stress of circumstances, without any serious intention of remaining faithful to an oath exacted by force, the list is interesting as showing the distribution of territorial influence in the closing years of feudalism :—

DUMFRIESSHIRE.

	Men.
Lord Carlyle	101
John, Master of Maxwell	1000 and more.
Edward Maxwell of Tinwald	102
Robert Maxwell of Cowhills	91
John Maxwell of Brekinside, vicar of Caerlaverock	320
Johnstone of Cragburn	64
Johnstone of the Cotes	162
Johnstone of Craigieland	37
Johnstone of Dryfesdale	46
Johnstone of Malinshawe	65
Gavin Johnstone	31
William Johnstone, the laird's brother	110
Robin Johnstone of Lochmaben	67
Irvine of Bonshaw	102
Irvine of Robgill	34
Richard Irvine	142
Irvine of Sennersack	40
Wattie Irvine	20
Jeffrey Irvine	93
Jardine of Applegarth	242
Kirkpatrick of Closeburn	403
Grierson of Lagg	202
The Laird of Kirkmichael	122
Laird of Rosse	165
Charteris of Amisfield	163
Laird of Holmends	162

	Men.
The Captain of Crawford	110
Simon Carruthers	71
Laird of Wamphray	102
Laird of Dinwoodie	41
Laird of Newbie and Graitney	122
Laird of Criffell	27
Patrick Murray (Cockpule)	203
Laird of Gillsby	30
Moffats	24
Bell of Toftyetts	142
Bell of Tindells	112
Sir John Lawson	32
Sir Edward Crichton	10
Rome of Torduff	32
Batesons and Thomsons (Eskdale)	166
Armstrongs	300
Ellwoodes (Elliots)	74
Nixons	32
The Town of Dumfries	221
The Town of Annan	33
	5970

STEWARTRY OF KIRKCUDBRIGHT.

	Men.
The Laird of Tabatye or Dawbaylie (probably Dalbeattie)	41
The Laird of Orchardton	102
The Laird of Carlile	206
Gordon of Lochinvar	95
The Tutor of Bomby	150
The Town of Kirkcudbright	36
The Abbot of New Abbey	141
	771

It is not pleasant to read of the submission of so many local magnates to alien rule; but there is this consoling feature in it, that some of the best known names are absent from the list. In the Stewartry Maclellan is represented by a cadet of the family, called the Tutor of Bomby; while the M'Cullochs,

Ahannays, M'Kies, and Stewarts of Garlies are all conspicuous by their absence. Then, although there are many Maxwells and Johnstones, the chiefs of these great clans are not mentioned. The fact is, they were both in the hands of the English. The memorable feud between them had been smouldering for some years, though it had not yet reached its height. As long before as 1534 bitterness had arisen between them, by reason of Maxwell, at that time Lord Warden, having been obliged to do justice on certain of the name of Johnstone for the slaughter of "Rowe Armestrang, Red Dande son," which was committed close to the warden's castle, "in Caerlaverock mire." But when Lord Maxwell was taken prisoner at Solway Moss in 1542, Johnstone, who was in ward in Dunbarton Castle at the time of that battle, was released and made warden in Maxwell's room.

Wharton, however, the English warden, proved an overmatch for him. He sent forty light horsemen to burn the village of Wamphray, which was well within view of Johnstone's Castle of Lochwood, and placed 300 men in ambush, "thinkynge that the lard Johnstone wold come to the furst to vyew them, and so he dyd, and persued them sharplye to their ambushe." After a hard fight the warden was taken, though not till three spears had been broken on him and he had been severely wounded in the thigh. Upwards of 140 of his men were made prisoners: "there was viij Scotis slayne and many hurte. There ar four Englishemen hurt, never one slayne nor taken." Thus Wharton was able to report to the Duke of Somerset next day.

The enmity between the Johnstones and the Maxwells was habitually fomented by the English officials—being, indeed, a great source of weakness to the Scots in their defence of the Border. Wharton, having got Warden Johnstone within his power, employed every means, gentle and otherwise, to tempt him from his allegiance, and thought he had succeeded. "I trust yet," he wrote to Somerset, "to cause thos Johnstons be with others a scourge to the Maxwells and ther bands."

But Johnstone, if we may accept his own account, was proof against all Wharton's arts. In a petition to the Scottish Government for aid to pay his ransom he describes the rigours of his imprisonment successively in the castles of Carlisle, Lowther, Pontefract, Whartonhall, and Hartley. He tells how they "layit irnis and fettaris vpoun and trubillit me thairwith, in sic maner that I behuvit to ly on my bak with all my clathis on my body alswell be day as nycht. . . . Intending to haif gottin me secretlie distroyit thai gaif me evill and unhailsum metis and drinkis, and throu eting and drinking thairof I tuke havy seiknes, and lay therin be the space of six owkis[2] in parrell of my life;" in spite of which he refused to entertain the "mischewose purpose proponit" to him by the English warden "towart the hurt and destructioun of this realme." Johnstone's absence from the list of those making submission to the King of England is thus accounted for, and a similar cause prevented Lord Maxwell's fidelity to his monarch being tested at this time, for he had been taken prisoner by the English in Wauchopedale in 1545, and did not regain his liberty till 1549, one year sooner than Johnstone.

Luckily the Duke of Somerset was unable to follow up the victory of Pinkie, or Scottish history might have taken a very different course from that mapped out for it by destiny. Home politics called the duke back to London, and the Border chiefs gathered strength to resist Lord Wharton's rule. On March 24, 1550, was signed the treaty of Norham, which established a truce between England and Scotland for nearly ten years, and contained the singular scheme of neutralising the Debatable Land by depopulating it, thus rendering it a "buffer state" with-

[2] Weeks.

out inhabitants. This was found to be a policy too trenchant even for the statesmen of those heroic days, so in the following year the Bishop of Orkney, Robert Lord Maxwell, and two others, were appointed commissioners to negotiate a division of this contested territory between the two kingdoms. The result was that in September 1552 Sir James Douglas of Drumlanrig and Richard Maitland of Lethington met the English representatives, Sir Thomas Wharton and Sir Thomas Chaloner. Between them they managed to settle once for all that venerable bone of contention, the Debatable Land, by dividing it between the two countries—the more northerly parish of Canonbie being annexed to Dumfriesshire, and the more southerly one of Kirkandrews being added to Cumberland; and thus this long-contested boundary remains to this day. This settlement was ratified on December 15 by Maxwell of Herries, the warden, and the laird of Johnstone on the one side, and Sir Thomas Dacre and Sir Richard Musgrave on the other.

NOTE F.

THE CLANS ON THE WEST MARCHES.

'The Calendar of Border Papers,' of which vol. i. has lately been published (1894), at H.M. Register House, Edinburgh, is full of interesting reports and correspondence illustrating the condition of things on the West Marches. I am tempted to make the following extracts from a paper drawn up in 1583 by Thomas Musgrave for the information of Queen Elizabeth's chancellor, Lord Burghley, which describe the distribution of the different families on the West Marches, and the curious system of to-names used to distinguish men of the same surname. Musgrave writes :—

"Not takinge uppon me to doe anythinge as a good clarke, for that I have not applyed my mynd to so good an exersyes, but have bene traned in service, for defence of her Majesties poor people, that my father had the credyte and charge of, in which I have spente a great parte of my tyme, not without the losse of my bloode, and manye troublesome travels and dangers, but with the losse of my deare frendes and companyons which have bene cruelly murdered by the rebellyous Scottes. . . . I shall therefore sett downe the Ellottes of the head of Lyddell as my skyle will afforde, that your lordship maye knowe the better when their deedes shall come in question.

"*The Ellottes of Lyddisdall.*—Robin Ellot of the Reddhughe, cheife of the Ellottes; Wille Ellot of Harscarthe his brother; Gebbe Ellott his brother; Hobbe Ellot of the Hewghus; John Ellot his brother; Adam Ellot of the Shaws; Arche Ellot called Fyre the brayes; Gybbe Ellot of the Shaues; Gorth Simson; Martin Ellot called Rytchis Martyn. All theise are Robin Ellotes brethren, or his men that are daly at his comaundement. The grayne [branch] of the Ellotes called the Borneheedes : Joke Ellot called Joke of Ramsgill; Hob Ellot called Curst Hobbe; Addam Ellot called Condus; Arche Ellot called Arche of Hill; Joke Ellot of the Hill; Joke Ellot called Half loges. The grayne of the Ellotes of the Parke: Sims John Ellot of the Parke; Will Ellot, gray Wille; Hobbe Ellot called Scotes Hobbe; Jeme Ellot of the Parke; Jeme Ellot called gray Will's Jeme; Hobbe Ellot called Hobbs Hobbe. The grayne of Martyn Ellot of the Bradley hyghe in Lyddall : Martyn Ellot of the Bradley; Sime Ellot his sonne; Gowan Ellot called the clarke; Hobbe Ellot his brother; Arche Ellot his brother; Joke Ellot called Copshaws; John Ellot of

Thornesope; Will Ellot of the Steele; Dand Ellot of the Brandley; John Ellot of the same; Seme Ellot of Hardin. All theise Ellots and many more of them are at Robin Ellotes comaundment and dwell betwixt the Armytage [Hermitage] in Lyddisdall and Whethough towre—fewe of them marryed with Englishe women.

"*The Lord [Laird] of Mangerton* and his frendes.— . . . Seme Armestronge, lord of Mangerton; . . . Joke Armestronge called the Lordes Joke [Laird's Jock]; John Armestronge called the lordes John, . . . hathe two sonnes ryders in England. Joke his eldest sonne; . . . Thome Armestronge called the lordes Tome; . . . Runyon [Ninian] Armestronge called the lordes Runyon; Rowye Armestronge called the lordes Rowye dwelleth in Tarrasyde. Seme Armestronge called yonge Seme; . . . Thom Armestronge called Sims Thom dwelleth in the Demayn Holme by Lendall syde. Dik Armestronge of Dryup; . . . Joke Armestronge of the Caufeld; . . . Gorthe Armestronge of the Bygams. . . . All these are the Lorde of Morgertons unckles or unckles sonnes at the furthest.

"*The Armestronges of the Howse of Whetaughe Towre.*—Lance Armestronge the old lord [laird] of Whetaughe; Sime Armestronge the yonge lord his sonne; Andrewe Armestronge called the ladyes Andrew; Arche Armestronge his brother; John Armestronge called John of Whetaugh; Hobbe Armestronge his sonne; . . . Joke Armestronge his brother; Rynyon Armestronge called Gaudee; Rynyon Armstronge called Rynyon of Twedon; Hector Armestronge of the same; Joke Armestronge of the same. All theise, and more that I cannot call to remembraunce, are the lord of Whethaugh his sonnes and brothers sonnes.

"*Hector Armestronge of the Harlawe* and his frendes and allyes.—Hector Armestronge called old Hector; Hector his sonne called yonge Hector; . . . Wille Armestronge called Hector's Wille; Thome Armestronge called Hector's Tome; Andrewe Armestronge of the Harlawe; Patton Armestronge of the Harlaw; Alexander Armestronge called the Gatwarde.

"*The Armestronges of Melyonton quarter.*—Arche Armestronge called Rynyon's Arche; Gorthe Armestronge sonne to Rynyon; Sime Armestronge called Whetlesyde; . . . Aby Armestronge sonne to Rynyon; Will Armestronge called Will of Powterlampert; Gorthe Armestronge called yonge Gorthe of Arkyldon; . . . Rynyon Armestronge his brother; Martyn Armestronge his brother; Dave Armestronge of Whetlesyde; Andrew Armestronge of Kyrkton; Hector Armestronge of Chengles; Thome

Armestronge his brother; . . . Elle Armestronge his brother; . . . Eme Armestronge his brother; Arche Armestronge his brother; Riche Armestronge called Carhand ; Thome Armestronge called old Thome of Chengles ; Abye Armestronge called Thoms Abye ; Arche Armestronge his brother; Rynyon Armestronge his brother.

"*The Armestronges of the Langholme.*— . . . Creste Armestronge goodman of the Langholme castell ; . . . John Armestronge of the Hollus ; . . . Creste Armestronge of Borngles ; . . . Hector Armestronge of the Stobbam ; Rich Armestronge called Ekkes Riche.

"*The Armestronges that come of the off-spring of Ill Will's Sandy.*—Ebye Armestronge the goodman of Waddusles ; Wille Armestrong his eldest sonne dwelleth in England, and enjoyeth that land that King Henry the Eight gave old Sand Armestronge ; Dave Armestronge his brother; Sande Armestronge his brother; Creste Armestronge called Sandes Creste ; Creste Armestronge his sonne, and two other sonnes whose names I knowe not. Wille Armestronge called Kynmont ; . . . Joke Armestronge his sonne ; Gorthe Armestronge his brother; Frauncis Armestronge his brother; Thome Armestronge his brother; Rynyon Armestronge called Sandes Rynyon ; Thome Armestronge his sonne ; Arche Armestronge called Sandes Arche ; Forge Armestronge called Sandes Forge ; Joke Armestronge called Castills ; Joke Armestronge called Walls ; Dave Armestronge called Dave of Kannonby. . . . Wille Armestronge his brother ; Jeme his brother; John Armestronge called Skinabake ; Thome Armestronge of Rowenburn ; Gorthe Armestronge of the same.

"Thus I have come down Lyddell with the Ellotes and Armestronges along the Scottishe syde, and I will goe forward downe Eske syde so far as it is Scottishe, and I will goe on to Gratney to the sea, and then come back to the Englishe syde, and so goe down agayne, that your honor maye be the more parfyte howe they dwell one agaynst the other."

It is not, however, necessary to follow the writer further in his minute account of the clans on both sides of the Border, and their intermarriages, but the above extracts suffice to show the prevalence of particular surnames in different districts, and, when it became no longer prudent to bear a name of evil notoriety, how easy it was to find in the baptismal and nicknames material for the formation of patronymics now common in the district, such as Christison, Ellison, Thomson, Jamieson, Gibson, Davison, and Dickson.

NOTE G.

MONITION OF CURSING AGAINST THE BORDER CLANS.

THE following pastoral, issued by Gavin Dunbar, Archbishop of Glasgow, and directed to be read by the priests of Border parishes to their flocks, is no more than the ordinary form of the greater excommunication. But inasmuch as it was promulgated, contrary to the usual practice, in the vernacular, it is too fine an example of ecclesiastical execration uttered on the authority of a Wigtownshire man to be allowed to fall out of record :—

"GUDE FOLKS, heir at my Lord Archibischop of Glasgwis letters under his round sele, direct to me or any uther chapellane, makand mensioun, with greit regrait, how hevy he beris the pieteous, lamentabill and dolorous complaint that pass our all realme and cummis to his eris, be oppin voce and fame, how our soverane lordis trew liegis, men, wiffis and barnys, bocht and redemit be the precious blude of our Salviour Jhesu Crist, and levand in his lawis, ar saikleslie[1] part murdrist, part slane, brynt, heryit, spulzeit and reft, oppinly on day licht and under silens of the nicht, and thair takkis[2] and landis laid waist, and thair self banyst therfra, als wele kirklandis as utheris, be commoun tratouris, revaris,[3] theiffis, duelland in the south part of this realme, sic as Tevidale, Esdale, Liddisdale, Ewisdale, Nedisdale and Annanderdaill; quhilkis hes bene diverse ways persewit and punist be the temperale swerd and our Soverane Lordis auctorite, and dredis nocht the samyn.

"And thairfoir my said Lord Archibischop of Glasgw hes thocht expedient to strike thame with the terribill swerd of halykirk, quhilk thai may nocht lang endur and resist; and hes chargeit me, or any uther chapellane, to denounce, declair and proclame thaim oppinly and generalie cursit, at this market-croce, and all utheris public places.

"Heirfor throw the auctorite of Almichty God, the Fader of hevin, his Son, our Salviour, Jhesu Crist, and of the Halygaist; throw the auctorite of the Blissit Virgin Sanct Mary, Sanct Michael, Sanct Gabriell, and all the angellis; Sanct Johne the

---

[1] Innocently.   [2] Farms.   [3] Rievers, robbers.

Baptist, and all the haly patriarkis and prophets; Sanct Peter, Sanct Paull, Sanct Andro, and all haly appostillis; Sanct Stephin, Sanct Laurence, and all haly mertheris[4]; Sanct Gile, Sanct Martyn, and all haly confessouris; Sanct Anne, Sanct Katherin, and all haly virginis and matronis; and of all the sanctis and haly cumpany of hevin; be the auctorite of our Haly Fader the Paip and his cardinalis, and of my said Lord Archibischop of Glasgw, be the avise and assistance of my lordis, archibischop, bischopis, abbotis, priouris, and utheris prelatis and ministeris of halykirk, I DENOUNCE, PROCLAMIS, and DECLARIS all and sindry the committaris of the said saikles murthuris, slauchteris, birnyng, heirschippes, reiffis, thiftis and spulezeis, oppinly apon day licht and under silence of nicht, alswele within temporale landis as kirklandis; togither with thair part takaris, assistaris, supplearis, wittandlie resettaris of thair personis, the gudes reft and stollen be thaim, art or part therof, and thair counsalouris and defendouris, of thair evil dedis generalie cursit, waryit,[5] aggregeite, and re-aggregeite, with the greit cursing.

"I CURSE thair heid and all the haris of thair heid; I CURSE thair face, thair ene, thair mouth, thair neise, thair toung, thair teith, thair crag, thair schulderis, thair breist, thair hert, thair stomok, thair bak, thair wame, thair armes, thair leggis, thair handis, thair feit, and everilk part of thair body, fra the top of thair heid to the soill of thair feit, befoir and behind, within and without. I CURSE thaim gangand, and I CURSE thaim rydand; I CURSE thaim standand, and I CURSE thaim sittand; I CURSE thaim etand, I CURSE thaim drinkand; I CURSE thaim walkand,[6] I CURSE thaim slepand; I CURSE thaim rysand, I CURSE thaim lyand; I CURSE thaim at hame, I CURSE thaim fra hame; I CURSE thaim within the house, I CURSE thaim without the house; I CURSE thair wiffis, thair barnis, and thair servandis participand with thaim in thair deides. I WARY[7] thair cornys, thair catales, thair woll, thair scheip, thair horse, thair swyne, thair geise, thair hennys, and all thair quyk gude.[8] I WARY thair hallis, thair chalmeris, thair kechingis, thair stabillis, thair barnys, thair biris, thair bernyardis, thair cailyardis, thair plewis, thair harrowis, and the gudis and housis that is necessair for thair sustentatioun and weilfair. All the malesouns and waresouns[9] that ever gat warldlie creatur sen the begynnyng of the warlde to this hour mot licht apon thaim. The maledictioun of God, that lichtit apon

---

[4] Martyrs. [5] Execrated. [6] Waking.
[7] Execrate. [8] Live stock. [9] Curses and execrations.

Lucifer and all his fallowis, that strak thaim frae the hie hevin to the deip hell, mot licht apon thaim. The fire and the swerd that stoppit Adam fra the yettis of Paradise, mot stop thaim fra the gloir of Hevin, quhill thai forbere and mak amendis.[1] The malesoun that lichtit on cursit Cayein, quhen he slew his bruther just Abell saiklessly, mot licht on thaim for the saikles slauchter that thai commit dailie. The maledictioun that lichtit apon all the warlde, man and beist, and all that ever tuke life, quhen all wes drownit be the flude of Noye, except Noye and his ark, mot licht apon thame and droune thame, man and beist, and mak this realm cummirles[2] of thame for thair wicket synnys. The thunnour and fireflauchtis[3] that ȝet doun as rane apon the cities of Zodoma and Gomora, with all the landis about, and brynt thame for thair vile synnys, mot rane apon thame, and birne thame for oppin synnys. The malesoun and confusioun that lichtit on the Gigantis for thair oppressioun and pride, biggand the tour of Babiloun, mot confound thaim and all thair werkis, for thair oppin reiffs and oppressioun. All the plagis that fell apon Pharao and his pepill of Egipt, thair landis, corne and catail, mot fall apon thaim, thair takkis, rowmys[4] and stedingis, cornys and beistis. The watter of Tweid and utheris watteris quhair thai ride mot droun thaim, as the Reid Sey drownit King Pharao and the pepill of Egipt, persewing Godis pepill of Israell. The erd mot oppin, riffe and cleiff,[5] and swelly thaim quyk[6] to hell, as it swellyit cursit Dathan and Abiron, that ganestude Moeses and the command of God. The wyld fyre that brynt Thore and his fallowis to the nowmer of twa hundreth and fyfty, and utheris 14,000 and 700 at anys, usurpand aganis Moyses and Araon, servandis of God, mot suddanely birne and consume thaim, dailie ganestandand the commandis of God and halykirk. The maledictioun that lichtit suddanely upon fair Absolon, rydand contrair his fader, King David, servand of God, throw the wod, quhen the branchis of ane tre fred[7] him of his horse and hangit him be the hair, mot licht apon thaim, rydand agane trewe Scottis men, and hang thaim siclike that all the warld may se. The maledictioun that lichtit apon Oliefernus, lieutenent to Nabogodonoser, makand weir and heirschippis apon trew cristin [sic] men ; the maledictioun that lichtit apon Judas, Pylot, Herod, and the Jowis that crucifyit Our Lord, and all the plagis and trublis that lichtit on the citte of Jherusalem thairfor,

---

[1] As long as they forbear to make amends. [2] Disencumbered.
[3] Lightning.   [4] Places.   [5] May the earth open, split and cleave.
[6] Swallow them alive.   [7] Freed.

and upon Symon Magus for his symony, bludy Nero, cursit Ditius
Makcensius, Olibrius, Julianus, Apostita and the laiff of the cruell
tirrannis that slew and murthirit Cristis haly servandis, mot licht
apon thame for thair cruell tiranny and murthirdome of cristin
pepill. And all the vengeance that ever wes takin sen the warlde
began for oppin synnys, and all the plagis and pestilence that
ever fell on man or beist, mot fall on thaim for thair oppin reiff,
saiklesse slauchter and schedding of innocent blude. I DISSEVER
and PAIRTIS thaim fra the kirk of God, and deliveris thaim quyk
to the devill of hell, as the Apostill Sanct Paull deliverit Cor-
inthion. I INTERDITE the places thay cum in fra divine service,
ministracioun of the sacramentis of halykirk, except the sacrament
of baptissing allanerlie;[8] and forbiddis all kirkmen to schriffe or
absolve thaim of thaire synnys, quhill[9] thai be first absolyeit of
this cursing. I FORBID all cristin man or woman till have ony
cumpany with thame, etand, drynkand, spekand, prayand, lyand,
gangand, standand, or in any uther deid doand, under the paine
of deidly syn. I DISCHARGE all bandis, actis, contractis, aithis,
and obligatiounis made to thaim be ony persounis, outher of lawte,[1]
kyndenes or manrent, salang as thai susteine this cursing; sua
that na man be bundin to thaim, and that thai be bundin till all
men. I TAK fra thame and cryis doune all the gude dedis that
ever thai did or sall do, quhill thai ryse fra this cursing. I
DECLARE thaim partles[2] of all matynys, messis, evinsangis,
dirigeis or utheris prayeris, on buke or beid; of all pilgrimagis and
almouse dedis done or to be done in halykirk or be cristin pepill,
enduring this cursing.

"And, finaly, I CONDEMN thaim perpetualie to the deip pit of
hell, to remain with Luciфеir and all his fallowis, and thair bodeis
to the gallowis of the Burrow Mure, first to be hangit, syne revin
and ruggit with doggis, swyne and utheris wyld beistis, abhomin-
able to all the warld. And thir candillis gangis fra your sicht, as
mot[3] thair saulis gang fra the visage of God, and thair gude fame
fra the warld, quhill thai forbeir thair oppin synnys foirsaidis
and ryse fra this terribill cursing, and mak satisfactioun and
pennance."[4]

[8] Only. [9] Until. [1] Loyalty. [2] Without part in. [3] So may.
[4] Mr Armstrong has printed the above in his 'History of Liddesdale, &c.,'
from the 'State Papers of Henry VIII.,' vol. iv., note, pp. 417-419.

CHAPTER VIII.

FROM THE REFORMATION IN 1560 TO 1598.

WHEN Mary Stuart, the Catholic Queen of Scotland, returned to her kingdom in 1561, she found the Reformed religion established in her kingdom by Act of Parliament, and a great part of the people firmly attached to it. This was especially the case in Dumfriesshire and Galloway, where the influence of the Maxwells and the Johnstones, Douglas of Drumlanrig, Kirkpatrick of Closeburn, Stewarts of Dalswinton and Garlies, Charteris of Amisfield, and others, had been steadily in favour of the Reforming party. Perhaps it would be ungenerous to scrutinise too closely the motives of the great landowners in lending their countenance to the movement; but no doubt they were fully aware that the spoliation of Church lands had been followed in England by their partition among Protestant laymen.

No such sinister design, however, can have harboured in the mind of Alexander Gordon of Airds, whom Mr William M'Dowall has justly termed the pioneer of Reformation in the south-west.[1] This remarkable man, from whom is descended the present Sir William Gordon of Earlston, one of the heroes of Balaclava, being of immense size, was known in his youth as "Sannie Rough"; but, living to the great age of 101 in

[1] History of Dumfries, p. 251.

the same house as his son, grandchildren, and great-grandchildren, his title became changed to "the Patriarch." Long before Lord Maxwell's Act of 1543 had made it lawful for all men to read the Bible, Gordon, who had become penetrated with Wyclifite doctrine in England, had been in the practice of assembling his neighbours in a wood near his house, reading and discussing the Scriptures with him. It was then no question of pulling down the Church of Rome, or of setting up another in its place. The purging of manifold abuses among the clergy, liberty to worship and to read the Scriptures without interference, and to be allowed to believe according to conscience without fear of punishment — these were the utmost objects in view of these early Scottish reformers.

One of the most constant attendants at Gordon's sylvan assemblies was the eldest son of Stewart of Garlies. Garlies himself had been made prisoner at Solway Moss, and his son, having gone to England as a hostage in his place, had become thoroughly confirmed in his belief in the new teaching, and on his return from imprisonment about the year 1557 set about evangelist work in Dumfries.

Wigtownshire also had produced an evangelist in the person of one John M'Brair,[2] a canon of Glenluce, who had renounced his vows in 1548. Dury, Bishop of Galloway, who was also Abbot of Melrose, did not spend much time in his diocese, preferring the stir of the capital, and M'Brair profited by his absence to preach throughout Galloway. But Hamilton, Bishop of St Andrews, happening to be in Galloway, caused M'Brair to be apprehended and imprisoned in Hamilton Castle, whence, however, he was rescued by John Lockhart of Barr and conveyed in safety to England.

---

[2] The name of M'Brair contains in itself a reproach to a celibate order— *mac brathair* (braher), the friar's son.

While the minds of men were thus exercised in matters spiritual, it must not be supposed that they forgot their temporal amusements. The preamble of an Act passed in Queen Mary's fourth Parliament, 1551, is amusing reading, setting forth as it does that whereas, in spite of previous Acts, the lieges persist in "schutting with the halfehag, culverine and Pistolett at Deare, Rae, wild-beastes, or wilde-fowles, quhair-throw the Noble-men of the realme can get na pastime of halking and hunting, like as hes bene had in times by-past, bee reason that all sik wilde-beastes and wilde-fowles ar exiled and banished, be occasion foresaide." The enactment which follows is of appalling severity, bringing all persons who should shoot game with firearms under pain of death and confiscation: this, too, in the days when the barons had power of pit and gallows within their territories.

One of the most powerful of these barons in the south-west died in 1558. Kennedy, Earl of Cassilis, had been appointed to attend Queen Mary's marriage with the Dauphin in France, and was taken ill at Dieppe, from the effects, as was commonly reported, of poison. Just before his death he wrote an affecting little note to his friend Patrick Vaus, Lord Barnbarroch : [3]—

Fair ye weil, off Dieppe this vii of November. Item, ye sall wit my fevir is callit the cotedicene, and hes bene thir ix dayes paist, quharbe [whereby] I am grouing sa waik that I dow do na thing. —Youris, Caissaillis.[4]

This amiable and cultivated earl left his vast possessions to a son very different in character from himself, as will appear hereafter.

In 1562 John Knox visited Dumfries by instruction of the

[3] His title as a Lord of Session.
[4] Correspondence of Sir Patrick Vaus, p. 12.

General Assembly, in order to inaugurate a moderator for the congregations established in Dumfries and Galloway. Mr Robert Pont was elected to the office, and was charged with the appointment of parish ministers, visitation of kirks, superintendence of education, and, in general, all the duties that had hitherto devolved on the bishop. The following year Queen Mary was at Dumfries, and visited at Terregles the brother of Robert, sixth Lord Maxwell, Sir John Maxwell, afterwards better known as her devoted adherent Lord Herries.

It is hopeless to search the records of the sixteenth century for any signs of a tolerant spirit; people seemed unable to imagine the existence of one form of public worship unless all others were prohibited, and those who practised them were put to death. In Scotland, as on the Continent, the noble zeal for liberty of worship, which had animated Gordon of Airds and Stewart of Garlies, soon became clouded by the hateful tyranny which seeks to fetter conscience. This only may be urged in exculpation of the Presbyterians, that although a bloody example had been set them during the Catholic ascendancy by the burning of Wishart and other heretics, they proceeded only to the length of imprisoning and fining those who persisted in celebrating and attending Mass.

It affords a shrewd commentary on the stability of human judgment that, whereas in the Justiciary Records one may read how in 1559 men were condemned as criminals for preaching the doctrines of the Reformation, in 1562 a priest, Sir James Arthur,[5] was put on his trial for baptising children and marrying persons in "ye alde and abhominabill Papist

---

[5] The prefix "Sir" does not always imply knighthood: it was given by courtesy, as in this case, to curates, and to priests who had taken the degree of Bachelor of Arts.

maner."[6] In the following year Malcolm Fleming, Commendator[7] of Whithorn, and two priests, were arraigned for celebrating Mass.

But in the same year the law was set at defiance by the celebration of Mass in the royal chapel at Holyrood. Queen Mary was absent at Stirling: had she been present, no one could have objected, for, in assenting to the establishment of the Reformed religion, privilege had been reserved for the queen to hear Mass in her private chapel, an exception to which John Knox declared he would have preferred the invasion of 10,000 Frenchmen. Two Presbyterian divines, scandalised at this breach of the law, forced their way into the chapel and denounced the illegality of the proceedings, for which the queen ordered them to be put on trial for forethought felony. Thereupon Knox summoned the brethren to meet him in Edinburgh on October 24, to make common cause with the two ministers who were to be tried that day, and the letter by which he did so was pronounced treasonable. We have under Knox's own hand the relation how this led to a rupture between him and his intimate friend, the Master of Maxwell.[8] Maxwell gave the bold divine plainly to understand that he could not retain him as a friend unless he was ready to make amends for his offence to the queen's majesty. Knox maintained that in matters spiritual he owed no allegiance to an earthly monarch, and that, except in religion, he never

---

[6] Pitcairn's Trials, *ad ann.*

[7] The lay office of Commendator was created to supersede the Catholic ecclesiastical dignitaries in the administration of abbeys, priories, and Church lands.

[8] Sir John Maxwell of Terregles, second son of Robert, fifth Lord Maxwell, became fourth Lord Herries through marriage with Agnes, daughter and coheiress of the third Lord Herries. He was guardian to two nephews, who successively became seventh and eighth Lords Maxwell, and having thus management of the Maxwell estates, was commonly known as the Master of Maxwell.

had opposed or would oppose the royal authority. "Well," said Maxwell in conclusion, "you are wise enough, but you will not find that men will bear with you in times to come, as they have done in times by-past." He then withdrew in company with Gordon of Lochinvar, and the old familiarity between them was never renewed.

Two years after this, in 1565, Queen Mary married Lord Darnley, in consequence of which the Protestant lords summoned their forces and marched to Edinburgh. Thence they went to Lanark, and then to Hamilton, where they were joined by the Master of Maxwell and Douglas of Drumlanrig. Maxwell wrote to the queen to explain that he had advised his friends to disband their troops, that they were going to pass to Dumfries, there to consider their future course, and that her Majesty should be informed of their decision. Accordingly the Protestant host went to Dumfries, but Maxwell failed to prevail with his peers, and they remained in arms. Mary meanwhile had assembled 3000 men in Edinburgh, and marched, with the king, by way of Lanark and Clydesdale to Dumfries. On the approach of the royal army the malcontent lords retired to Carlisle, leaving behind them, however, Maxwell, Douglas of Drumlanrig, and Gordon of Lochinvar, whose loyalty prevailed over their love for the Reformed religion. After a short stay at Dumfries and a visit to Lochmaben, the king and queen returned to Edinburgh. Sir John Maxwell, Master of Maxwell, was now created Lord Herries, by which name he is known in the troublous times to come.

Mary had at this time another trusty servant in Galloway in the person of Gilbert, fourth Earl of Cassilis, in whose keeping the power of the Kennedys grew to such a height that he was known in the south-west as the King of Carrick.

On February 9, 1567, Darnley was murdered: on May 15 following, the public were horrified to hear that their queen had married the Earl of Bothwell, who, though he had gone through the form of trial for the assassination of Darnley and been acquitted in the absence of any witnesses for the prosecution, was firmly believed to be the real culprit. A month later and Mary was taken prisoner at Carberry by the Confederate lords under the Earl of Morton, and lodged in ward at Lochleven. There she signed her abdication in favour of her son, the Earl of Moray being appointed Regent of Scotland.

It is not surprising, considering the influence of Herries in Dumfriesshire—"for," as John Knox wrote, "he had the government of all that country"—and of Cassilis in western Galloway, that although this was the district where the Reformation had taken firmest hold, it was also here that Mary's cause was most popular. When a herald appeared at the market-cross of Dumfries to proclaim the regency of Moray, he was hustled off the steps before he could pronounce a sentence, and came nigh losing his life. When the queen escaped from Lochleven, nearly all the landowners of the district rallied to her cause. These included the Lords Herries and Maxwell, the Abbot of Dundrennan, Gordon of Lochinvar, Maclellan of Bomby, Douglas of Drumlanrig, Sheriff Agnew of Galloway, Bishop Gordon of Galloway, the commendators of Dundrennan, Soulseat, and Glenluce, the Kennedys, headed by the Earl of Cassilis, Vaus of Barnbarroch, the M'Cullochs, Gordon of Craighlaw, and Baillie of Dunragit, all of whom brought the best of the fighting men of their estates with them. Stewart of Garlies, the Dunbars and M'Kies, however, declared for the Regent. The issue was soon decided. On May 13, 1568, Mary Stuart's cause was shattered irrevocably at the battle of Langside. A fugitive from the field, she made her way, guided by Lord Herries, to the banks of the Kirkcudbrightshire Dee near Tungland Bridge, where there is shown the Queen's Well, at which she is said to have rested and drank. That night she lay at Corra, a house belonging to Herries, and next day rode to Terregles. On the 15th she moved to Dundrennan Abbey, of which Edward Maxwell, third son of Herries, was the commendator. It was the last night she ever passed in Scotland. Next morning she set sail with a handful of followers in a fishing-boat from a creek on the coast of Rerwick parish, since then known as Port Mary, and landed on the coast of Cumberland at a place now known as Maryport. Her intention was to throw herself on the mercy of her cousin Elizabeth of England; but how little she realised that she was leaving her kingdom for ever may be seen in a letter which she wrote at Carlisle on May 20 to the Earl of Cassilis :—

TRAIST CUSING,—Forsamekle as I for the salftie of my bodie findand na suir acces nor place within my realme to retire me at this tyme, as ye may knaw, I was constraignit to leve the samin and to pas in this cuntrey of Ingland, quhair I assuir yow I have bene Rycht weill Ressauit [received] and honorablie accompaigned and traicted. I have deliberit to pas fortherward in France to pray the King my gude broder to support and help me to delyuer and Releue my Realme of sic Rebelliouis troublis and oppressionis that now regnis within the samin, and to depart furth of this toun the xxiiij day of this Instant moneth. Thairfore I pray you effectuouslie, traist cusing, that ye in the menetyme hald yourself constant in my seruice and aduertiss your freinds and neighbouris to do the samin, and to be in readienes to serue me quhan the occatioun sall offer, as ye have done trewlie afoir this tyme, Speciallie at the last battall quhair (I am adwerteist) ye have done Rycht weill your deuoir, ye beand on your featis [on foot], quhilk sall nocht be forgit be me in tyme coming. With the help of God I houp to returne agane about the xv day of August nixt with gud company for the effect foresaid God willing. This I beleve ye will do as my traist is

and wes ay in you. And for to mak ane end of my bill I will commit you to the protectioun of the eternall God. At Carlell, the xx day of Maij 1568.
MARIE R.

I pray you my lord excuss this stamp because the quene hes na uthir at this tyme.

"To my lord ERLE OF CASSILIS."

Ever since the War of Independence it had been chiefly in the two Border-lands — the Highland Border and the English Marches — that broken men gathered and reaped their harvest whenever the central authority was weakened. Moray, who was a vigorous and well-meaning ruler, exerted himself to protect life and property in these dangerous districts, and showed himself especially anxious to repress disorder in the south-west, where Queen Mary's strength lay. There was plenty of occasion for it. Maitland of Lethington's picture of the state of matters was probably no exaggeration :—

> "Of Liddesdale the common thieves
> Sae pertly steals now and reaves,
>   That nane may keep
>   Horse, nolt or sheep
> For their mischieves.
>
> They plainly through the countrie rides,
> I trow the mickle De'il them guides,
>   Where they onset
>   Ay in their gait [9]
>   There is nae yett [1]
> Nor door them bides.
>
> Thae thieves that steals and turses [2] hame
> Ilk ane o' them has ane to-name,[3]
>   Will o' the Laws,
>   Hab o' the Shaws,
>   To mak bare wa's
> Thae think nae shame.

---

[9] Road.   [1] Gate.   [2] Carries.   [3] Nickname.

> They spulyie puir men o' their packs,
> They leave them nought on bed or balks,[4]
>   Baith hen and cock,
>   With reel and rock,
>   The Laird's Jock
> All with him taks.
>
> They leave not spendle, spoon nor spit,
> Bed, blanket, bolster, sark nor sheet,
>   John o' the Park [5]
>   Rypes kist and ark;
>   For all sic wark
> He is right meet.
>
> He is well-kenned—Jock o' the Syde—
> A greater thief did never ride;
>   He never tires
>   For to break byres;
>   O'er muir and mires
> Ower guid ane guide. . . .
>
> O' stouth [6] though now they come guid speed
> That nother of God nor man has dread,
>   Yet, or [7] I die,
>   Some shall them see
>   Hing on a tree
> While [8] they be dead."[9]

The Regent caused the prophecy in the last stanza to be fulfilled. On October 20, 1567, he swooped down from Dalkeith upon Hawick and seized thirty-four mosstroopers. Of these he hanged and drowned nineteen, took ten in chains to Edinburgh, and released five on caution. Next month the Privy Council passed an Act against black-mailing, and directing that " quhen ony companies of thieves or broken men comes ower the swires [1] within the in-country," the inhabitants shall "incontinent cry on hie, raise the fray and follow them, as weel in

---

[4] Rafters.
[5] Was afterwards killed by Lord Bothwell, whom he had wounded in a hand-to-hand fight.
[6] Robbery.　　　　　[7] Before.　　　　　[8] Till.
[9] Ancient Scottish Poems, 1786.　　　　　[1] Passes.

their in-passing as out-passing." Unfortunately this injunction proved a fresh source of blood-feuds, the standing curse of the Border-lands.

The Regent made yet another expedition to the Borders before his assassination. He occupied Dumfries in September 1569:—

> "To Liddesdale he did again resort.
> Through Ewesdale, Esdale and all the dales rade he,
> And also lay three nichts in Cannonbie,
> Where nae prince lay thir hunder years befoir.
> Nae thief daured stir, they did him fear sae sore;
> And, that they sud nae mair thair theft allege,
> Threescore and twelve he brocht of thaim in pledge,
> Syne warded thaim, whilk made the rest keep order;
> Than micht the rash buss keep kye on the Border." [2]

Moray also caused Kenmure Castle to be burnt down because of the resistance of its owner, Gordon of Lochinvar. But as regards Wigtownshire, he contented himself by issuing a proclamation to the lairds of that county, calling on them to appear before him at Ayr on March 20, to answer such things as might be laid to their charge, on pain of treason. These turbulent gentry, pending the return of their queen, had been trying to turn the disturbed state of the country to their own advantage. Alexander Vaus or Vans of Barnbarroch had been killed at the battle of Pinkie, leaving an infant daughter, Helen, as his heiress, in ward of his brother Patrick (afterwards a Lord of Session). Sir Alexander M'Kie of Myrtoun [3] was, like all of his name, a supporter of the regency, and the heiress of an adherent of Queen Mary was fair game. Patrick Vaus lived at Carscreuch near Glenluce, now a ruin. M'Kie, having taken Dunbar of Mochrum,

[2] Ane Trajedie in form of ane Diallog betwix Honour, Gude Fame, and the Authour hereof, 1570.

[3] There are two places of this name in Wigtownshire—Myrtoun-M'Culloch in Mochrum parish, now the property of the author, and Myrtoun-M'Kie near Newton Stewart, the property of Mr Boyd.

Stewart of Garlies, and Johnstone of Lochwood into his confidence, gathered his men and forcibly took possession of Carscreugh on the night of July 31, 1568. Vaus himself was absent on the queen's business, but his lady was at home, and she had to witness not only the abduction of the heiress, but the theft of 8000 merks in cash, and jewellery to the value of £3000 Scots. The fair Helen, who was only eleven years old, was taken to Annandale, to the Tower of Lochwood, where she was married to young M'Kie. The offenders were all put to the horn and denounced as rebels, but no further proceedings followed. The bridegroom made peace with Helen's guardian, and the marriage was formally acknowledged.

The temporalities of the old Church were also the cause of many lawless acts. Lord Fleming, Chamberlain of Scotland, had in 1567 been appointed Commendator of Whithorn, with possession of the lands of Cruggleton and others. But after the flight of Queen Mary the Regent forfeited Fleming and gave the office to his half-brother, Lord Robert Stewart (created Earl of Orkney in 1581). Fleming refused to give up his Castle of Cruggleton, whereupon Agnew, the Sheriff, drove off from the disputed land seventeen score of ewes and seventeen tups.

There does not seem to have been any bloodshed in this affair, but the disposal of the abbey lands of Glenluce had been already the cause of an atrocious crime, if the anonymous historian of the Kennedy family is to be credited.[4] Gilbert, Earl of Cassilis, the "traist cusing" of Queen Mary, was, according to the authority last quoted, "ane particuler manne and ane werry greidy manne, and cairitt nocht how he gatt land, sa that he culd cum be the samin." He was negotiating with the convent of Glenluce for a lease of the

[4] Historie of the Kennedyis. Edited by R. Pitcairn. Edinburgh, 1830.

abbey lands, when the proceedings were stopped by the abbot's death. Cassilis then employed a monk to forge the dead man's handwriting in a deed purporting to dispose of the lands in question to the Earl. Next, fearing that the monk might betray him, he hired a ruffian called Carnochan to murder him; and lastly, lest Carnochan should reveal his guilt, he got his kinsman Hew Kennedy of Bargany to accuse the wretch of theft and hang him in Crossraguel. "And sa," drily observes the chronicler, "the landis of Glenluse wes conqueist."[5]

The spring of 1570 brought an English raid of the old sort upon the oft-harried county of Dumfries. Lord Scrope encamped at Ecclefechan, whence he sent Simon Musgrave to burn Hoddam, Ruthwell, and many other places. John, eighth Lord Maxwell, nephew of Lord Herries, attacked Musgrave at Cockpool with his own men and the townsmen of Dumfries, but was repulsed with the loss of 100 prisoners. Maxwell having rallied his force, attacked Musgrave again at Locharwoods, this time with better effect, for Lord Scrope reported to his Government that the battle lasted three hours. Musgrave having caused his men to dismount, held out till Scrope, who was at Cummertrees, sent his brother Edward with reinforcements and drove the Scots off.

Worse was to follow. Scrope was joined by the Earl of Sussex with fresh troops from England. The town of Dumfries and the Maxwell estates were specially marked out for vengeance; and so, to quote again from Scrope's reports, he "took and cast down the castles of Caerlaverock, Hoddam, Dumfries, Tinwald, Cowhill, and sundry other gentlemen's houses, dependers on the house of Maxwell, and, having

---

[5] This was the same earl whose roasting of the Commendator of Crossraguel in order to force him to give up his lands is so famous in Ayrshire history.

burnt the town of Dumfries, returned with great spoil into England."

In the autumn of 1575 Regent Morton came to Dumfries and held a court there for the punishment of moss-trooping. But there was amusement for the virtuous as well as retribution on the unruly:—

"Many gentlemen of England came thither to behald the Regent's court, where there was great provocation made for the running of horses. By chance my Lord Hamilton had there a horse sae weel bridled and sae speedy, that although he was of a meaner stature than other horses that essayit their speed, he overran them all a great way upon Solway Sands, whereby he obtained great praise both of England and Scotland at that time."[6]

In 1598 a dispute arose between the burghs of Dumfries and Wigtown. Dumfries had been visited by the plague, and, according to the rule under similar visitations, was interdicted from all communication with other districts. This had serious effects upon the trade of the burgh, and brought great privation upon its inhabitants, who, in the words of the Privy Council Record, "were evil handlit for want of necessar sustentation." When the embargo was removed the town council sent two men to Wigtown to buy cattle. These men started to drive thirty-eight nolt back to Dumfries; but Patrick Ahannay, Provost of Wigtown, with two of his bailies and an armed party, overtook them at the ford of Cree at Monygaff, seized them, and took them with the cattle back to Wigtown. There they were detained eight days, the unfortunate cattle getting terribly lean for want of food, till, on payment of 100 merks, to satisfy some claim not specified, the drovers were allowed to proceed with them on their journey to Dumfries.

[6] Historie of King James the Sext.

CHAPTER IX.

FEUD BETWEEN THE MAXWELLS AND THE JOHNSTONES, FROM 1572 TO 1620.

ALLUSION having been made in a former chapter to the earlier stages of the last great blood-feud which marked the close of the clan system on the Borders—that, namely, between the Maxwells and the Johnstones—it is only necessary in this place to explain how matters stood in the year 1572, when James Douglas, nephew of the sixth Earl of Angus, was appointed Regent of Scotland.

Bickerings had been pretty constant for a long time between these two families, mutually jealous of the growing power of each other, the Johnstones having ascendancy in Annandale, the Maxwells in Nithsdale; but the strife was not more violent or enduring than that which often smouldered between country neighbours in those times.

When, however, Douglas assumed the earldom of Morton on the death of his father-in-law in 1542, Robert, sixth Lord Maxwell, put forward his claim as heir of one-third of the earldom in right of his wife, Lady Beatrix, second daughter of the deceased Lord Morton, and as having acquired another third by demission executed in his favour by Margaret, Duchess of Chatelherault, the eldest daughter. Earldoms in the sixteenth century were more than empty titles: that of Morton was a very desirable one, covering baronies and estates in all three Lothians, in the counties of Peebles, Perth, Lanark, Fife, and Berwick, besides the lands of Morton, Hutton-under-the-Moor, and Moffatdale in Dumfriesshire, and Preston Borgue and Buittle in the Stewartry of Kirkcudbright —truly a lordly heritage.

The claim was renewed by John, eighth Lord Maxwell, previous to 1576. Douglas, who had been appointed Regent in 1572 under the title of Earl of Morton, brought pressure on Maxwell to renounce his claim, but without success. Therefore in 1577 he deprived Maxwell of the wardenship of the West Marches, an office which had become almost hereditary in his house, and imprisoned him, first in Edinburgh Castle and then in Blackness; the Laird of Johnstone, Maxwell's principal rival, being made warden in his room.

The wardenship, besides being the most honourable appointment in the south-west, was also extremely lucrative, part of the fines and forfeits imposed in his courts going to the warden, and forage and rations being allowed him for his retinue. This degradation was endured by Maxwell without resistance, and nothing more was heard of the matter till after the execution of the Regent Morton in 1581, when the coveted earldom was at last bestowed upon him and he was received back into favour at Court.

Not for long, however; for though he supported the party of Lennox and Arran in the affair known as the Raid of Ruthven, and consequently was of the ruling party when the young king escaped from the Protestant nobles, he soon afterwards gave offence to the new Chancellor, Arran. That nobleman desired to negotiate with Maxwell for the sale or exchange of the lands of Pollok and Maxwellhaugh in Renfrewshire, which adjoined his own estates; but on Maxwell refusing to part with them on any terms, Arran resolved to clip his wings in Dumfriesshire. Maxwell of Newlaw, Lord Maxwell's uncle, being at that time Provost of Dumfries, Arran obtained a royal rescript directing the municipality to reject him at the election of 1584, and elect the Laird of Johnstone in his place. On the election day Lord Maxwell occupied all the approaches to the town, resisted the entry of Johnstone, and thus secured the re-election of the old provost. Johnstone was not slow to lay a complaint before the Chancellor, who, on the plea that Maxwell had maintained relations with the robber clan of Armstrong, pronounced sentence of outlawry upon him; Johnstone received the royal commission to apprehend him, and was furnished with troops for the purpose. The result of this was civil war involving the whole realm. Johnstone undertook his task with hearty goodwill, but his rival was too strong for him. Robert, natural brother of Lord Maxwell, attacked the Government forces in Nithsdale, thoroughly routed them, killed their commander Lammie, and took prisoner his lieutenant, Cranston. The clan war was carried on after the time-honoured fashion for some months after this: lands were wasted, crops destroyed, cattle driven off, houses burnt by both parties. At last Robert and David Maxwell attacked Lochwood, the principal castle of the Laird of Johnstone, and burnt it to the ground, "to give," as they said, "the Lady Johnstone light to set her hood."

The chief of the clan was not a laggard in the feud :—

"Upon Thursdaie laste the Earle of Morton [Maxwell] caused a gibett to be made and redye to be sett upp at Dunfreis, sherplye threateninge Johnston the late warden and all the rest of that surname of Johnstons, that unles they woulde yeilde and cause Loughmabell to be forthwith delivered upp unto him, they shuld all make their repentance fer the same at that piller, and be hanged thereon."[1]

The threat was successful: Lochmaben was surrendered to Maxwell; Johnstone, the warden, was made Maxwell's prisoner at Bonshaw, and died shortly after being liberated.

Lord Maxwell[2] was now proclaimed a rebel, and Arran, having obtained from the Estates a vote of £20,000, summoned the forces of all lands south of the Forth, and prepared to march into Dumfriesshire and crush the power of Maxwell. But the plague broke out in Edinburgh, causing the army to disperse.

Meanwhile Angus and other disaffected lords made a league against Arran, and it is not unnatural under the circumstances that they found a willing and powerful ally in Maxwell. With 2000 men they seized Stirling on November 2, 1585; Arran fled; his title and estates were forfeited, and an Act of indemnity was passed in favour of Lord Maxwell and about 1600 of his followers for all illegal acts done by them since 1569. Another Act extended the indemnity to the town of Dumfries, the inhabitants of which had, whether willingly or under pressure by Maxwell, resisted the authority of the warden, Johnstone.

But scarcely a month passed before Lord Maxwell was involved in fresh disgrace. The early inclination of his family to the reformed religion had yielded place to fervid attachment to the Church of Rome, and all the power of the Maxwells had latterly been exerted against the progress of the Reformation in the south-west. On Christmas Eve 1585

---

[1] Lord Scrope to Lord Walsingham, 21st August 1585. Border Papers, vol. i. p. 193.
[2] I continue to call the Earl of Morton by his better known title in order to avoid confusion.

Lord Maxwell assembled his followers at the Castle of Dumfries and marched in procession to the College of Lincluden, where mass was celebrated in the old form.[3] For this offence he was summoned before the king in Council and committed to ward, but was shortly afterwards liberated. However, during his incarceration, his brother Robert, with Drumlanrig, Amisfield, and Applegarth, made a furious raid on the Johnstone lands, "cominge about eighte of the clocke in the morninge neare unto the howse of Bonshawe, raysed a great fyre, and burned the Bonshawsyde and Todholes, with another towne [farmhouse] there called Dunberton, from whence turninge to the water of Milke, they also burned upon that water as much as appartayned to the Larde of Johnston. And passinge all alonge the water of Dryfe, comitted the lyke outeragies to all the frendes and tenantes of Johnston there. And in lyke manner uppon the water of Annon untill they came to the water of Podane, carryinge awaye with them a greate bootie, with the slaughter of two of the tenantes of Johnston onelie, withoute stoppe or hurte of any of their owne."[4]

Set a thief to catch a thief! It is hardly credible, but it is

[3] Lord Maxwell had given special cause for displeasure at this time by attending celebration of the Mass. "I have latelie receaved sondry brutes of the erectinge or usinge of the blasphemous ceremonye of the Masse heare in thes weste partes of Scotland—which reportes at the first I made daintie to credyte, . . . but nowe havinge a confirmacion by such as I dare well beleve, I have thought good to lett you understand for certen that the Erle of Morton [Maxwell], the Lorde Herris, with divers gentlemen and others of the countrey, to the number of 200 persons and above, weare assembled at a Masse in publique manner at the Colleidge aboute a myle from Drumfreis. . . . Moreover, yt is said that this infeccion spreadeth yt selfe into divers other places in Gallaway."—Lord Scrope to Lord Walsingham, January 13, 1585-86. The writer goes on to note that Maxwell retains a suite of 25 horse and 120 foot, that he is reconciled with Johnstone, but that a new outbreak between them is expected.

[4] Lord Scrope to Lord Walsingham, May 6, 1586. Border Papers, vol. i. p. 225.

nevertheless true, that, on the death of Johnstone in the same year, Lord Herries was appointed warden.

On February 8, 1587, Queen Mary was executed at Fotheringay. In April of that year James VI. appeared in Dumfries at the head of a strong force, to inquire into certain charges against Lord Herries for neglect of his duty as warden and attempting to restore the proscribed religion. In the same month Lord Maxwell, who, with the other Catholic nobles, Huntly, Errol, and Angus, was in active sympathy with the preparations being made by Philip II. of Spain to invade England, received the king's licence to go beyond the sea. This was a gentle sentence of exile, for he was forbidden to return without the royal permission. He bound himself under sureties not to attempt anything prejudicial to the reformed religion. This undertaking Maxwell did not scruple to disregard. He went straight to Spain, and concerted with the Spanish Government a plan of co-operation in the coming invasion. The Invincible Armada was being fitted out at the time. Maxwell advised that England should be attacked through Scotland, and in pursuance of this scheme he landed at Kirkcudbright in April 1588, and mustered his kinsmen and tenants so as to act in concert with the Armada on its arrival. Lord Herries, however, refused to join his cousin, and gave James VI. warning of what was on foot. Maxwell, summoned to appear before the king, defiantly replied by arming the royal castles of Lochmaben, Dumfries, Thrieve, and Langholm, and his own house of Caerlaverock. King James assembled some forces at Biggar, and advanced so swiftly upon Dumfries that Lord Maxwell was very nearly taken there. The castle had been so greatly dismantled by Lord Scrope in 1573 that it was in no condition to stand a siege. While, therefore, the royal troops were held at bay at the gate, the rebel lord, escaping by a postern, jumped on a horse and galloped to Kirkcudbright. There embarking in a small vessel, he was pursued by another ship commissioned by Sir William Stewart, brother of the quondam Arran, which overtook him on the coast of Carrick. Lord Maxwell landed in a small boat, but was taken at Crossraguel, and conveyed prisoner to Dumfries, thence to Edinburgh, where he was placed in ward. The garrisons of Langholm, Thrieve, and Caerlaverock then surrendered, but David Maxwell still held out stoutly in Lochmaben.

King James appeared before this castle and summoned David to submit. A defiant reply was returned, whereupon James, having borrowed siege artillery from the English warden, proceeded to bombard it so effectively that in two days the garrison capitulated on the faith of a written promise, purporting to be in the king's own hand, which guaranteed the lives of the captain and all his men. This document was conveyed to David Maxwell by Sir William Stewart, who had returned from his successful pursuit of Lord Maxwell, but was afterwards repudiated by the king, by whose orders David and five others were hanged before the castle gate on June 9, 1588. When Stewart returned to Edinburgh, Lord Maxwell was placed as a prisoner in his charge; but Stewart did not live long to enjoy his triumph. He got into a dispute with the Earl of Bothwell in the king's chamber, which led to an encounter in the High Street between the followers of the two gentlemen. Stewart killed one of Bothwell's servants, but in doing so lost his sword. He ran down Blackfriars Wynd, but Bothwell came up with him and "strake him in at the back and out at the belly," and so slew him.[5] But Stewart had forfeited all sympathy by his share in the affair at Lochmaben Castle, and Bothwell only kept in hiding for a few days, and then resumed his attend-

[5] Diary of Robert Birrel, 1532-1605.

ance at Court, "uncallit, unpursuit, unpunist." Indeed an anonymous contemporary chronicler declares that the slaughter of Stewart was "to the comfort of mony of the people, wha allegit that God did the same for his betraying of Mr David Maxwell and his company in Lochmaben, but specially the Lord Maxwell, wha was his prisoner in John Gourlay's house."[6]

The seventeen persons taken in the ship with Lord Maxwell were all condemned to the gallows. Barring the alleged treachery at Lochmaben, it cannot be said that all this severity was excessive, according to the code of the times, nor unmerited, seeing that David Maxwell was holding the king's own castle against his majesty in person; but it was in strange contrast to the leniency shown to the chief offender. Lord Maxwell not only was liberated in the following year, on the occasion of James's marriage with Anne of Denmark, but he was appointed one of the commissioners to assist Lord Hamilton as Lord Lieutenant during the king's absence in Norway.

It was now the turn of the Johnstones to fall into disfavour. Lord Maxwell was appointed Warden of the Western Marches and Justiciar of Dumfries and Galloway on July 28, 1592. An agreement of amity and co-operation was ratified between him and Sir James Johnstone as head of the Annandale clan. This seems to have been interpreted by the Johnstones as security against interference on the part of the warden, provided the lands and tenants of Maxwell were not molested. Accordingly next year a party of Johnstones raided the lands of Lord Crichton of Sanquhar.[7] William Johnstone of Wamphray, surnamed the Galliard, led the foray, and paid

---

[6] Chronicle of the Kings of Scotland. Maitland Club, 1830.
[7] This raid forms the subject of Scott's spirited ballad "The Lads of Wamphray" (Minstrelsy of the Scottish Border, vol. i. p. 308).

for it with his life; for although his party drove off the cattle and wrecked the farm, he had the bad luck to be taken prisoner, and was hanged by the Crichtons.

The Crichtons appealed to the warden for redress, and also to the king and Council in Edinburgh; but at first they met with little attention from either. Maxwell was probably indisposed to impair the newly formed friendship with Johnstone, and the Court was unwilling to stir afresh the ashes of the slumbering feud. But on July 23, 1593, a grisly procession paraded the streets of the capital. Fifteen widows of men slaughtered by the lads of Wamphray carried the bloody shirts of their husbands through the town, and excited such keen popular indignation that the Government were forced to action. They issued a Royal Commission directing Lord Maxwell to execute justice on the clan of Johnstone. In compliance with this, the warden, nothing loth, marched with 1500 men into Annandale. Johnstone, however, had received timely warning, and was prepared to meet him with 800, including Scotts from Eskdale and Teviotdale, and Elliots, Grahams, and others from the Debatable Lands, and some Englishmen. He awaited attack in a strong position on rising ground near the parish church of Dryfesdale. Maxwell, confident in superior numbers, crossed the Annan on December 6, 1593, in face of the enemy.[8] His advance party was attacked and outnumbered before the main body had forded the river. Thrown into confusion, they fell back on their comrades, and the disorder became general. There is probably truth in the story that the warden's men, having little stomach for the fray, deserted their leader. Anyhow, the whole force fled with scarce a show of resistance. Fore-

---

[8] Near the place where the Caledonian Railway bridge stands between Lochmaben and Lockerbie.

most in flight were the Lairds of Lag, Closeburn, and Drumlanrig, who are denounced thus in the old ballad, "Lord Maxwell's Good-night":—

> "Adieu, Drumlanrig, false wert aye,
>   And Closeburn in a band:
> The Laird o' Lag frae my father that fled
>   When the Johnstone struck off his hand.
>
> They were three brethren in a band,
>   Joy may they never see!
> Their treacherous art and cowardly heart
>   Has twined my love and me."

Maxwell had offered a ten-pound land to any one who should bring him the head or hand of Johnstone. To this Johnstone retaliated by offering land of half that value (for more he had not to bestow) for the head or hand of Maxwell. William Johnstone of Kirkhill earned the smaller reward, for he overtook the warden on the banks of Dryfe, about half a mile below the old churchyard, and struck him from his horse. Maxwell held out his hand for quarter, but Kirkhill struck it off, and rode away to claim his reward from his chief. According to a local tradition, the wife of James Johnstone of Kirkton, who had left her tower to attend to the wounded Johnstones, found the warden lying under a thorn-tree, and in response to his prayer for succour, smote out his brains with the castle key. There is no evidence to support this story, which, however, is just such a one as might take its rise in partisan bitterness, and there is nothing in the character of this ferocious warfare to make it improbable. Maxwell's head and right hand were taken, it is said, to Johnstone's castle of Lochwood, and nailed to the wall thereof.

Sir Walter Scott and others are responsible for the statement that upwards of 700 were slain on the Maxwell side at the battle of Dryfe Sands; but this is an exaggeration.[9] The loss, however, was probably considerable, though Johnstone, in his history of Scotland,[1] alleges that only five of Maxwell's company met their death. An authority, however, bearing the name of Johnstone, would naturally put the most favourable construction on the affair. The frightful nature of the wounds inflicted on head and face with Jeddart axes is said to have given rise to the expression "a Lockerbie lick."[2] Two aged thorn-trees stood at the place where Lord Maxwell is said to have perished; but these were carried away by a flood about fifty years ago. They have been replaced by two others, now enclosed in a railing and known as "Maxwell's thorns."

Such was the battle of Dryfe Sands, memorable as the last great encounter which took place between powerful feudal houses on the Border. But the feud was not laid to rest yet: there were still some dark episodes to be enacted in this long tragedy. Lord Maxwell's mutilated corpse was kept unburied as a token of vengeance to come, and it was nearly more than four years after the battle, in February 1597-98, that the king in Council decreed that the body should be laid in the ordinary place of sepulture within twenty days, under pain of rebellion.

In November of the preceding year, 1597, King James had made a vigorous personal effort to put down the normal brigandage of the Border. He held a court at Dumfries,

[9] Lord Scrope, writing from Carlisle to Lord Burghley the day after the battle, says: "The Larde Johnston having called together his frendes, did encounter with Lorde Maxwell, and haith not onlie kilde the sayd Lord Maxwell himself, but verie many of his company."

[1] MS., Advocates' Library; quoted by Chalmers.

[2] I possess at Monreith an immense two-handed sword, which was dug up on the battle-field about the year 1862. When I first saw it about two feet of the scabbard remained, but that had been lost before it came into my possession in 1878.

being "of resolution not to return therefra till that turn was effectuate."[3] In four weeks "he hangit fourteen or fifteen limmers and notorious thieves," and took thirty-six hostages from the Armstrongs, Johnstones, Bells, Batesons, Carlyles, and Irvings, who were charged the modest sum of 13s. 4d. a week for their keep, and were to be hanged if any further outrages took place. A Court of Redress was set up at Dumfries, consisting of "aucht special honest gentlemen of the country, least suspect, maist neutral and indifferent, and the best inclined to justice, with twa or three of his Majesty's council appointit to be present with them."[4]

Immediately after the battle Sir James Johnstone and his dependants were proclaimed rebels; but no active steps were taken against them by the Government, and a year later the offenders were respited for the space of five years.

On the death of Maxwell, Lord Herries was appointed warden, and having occasion in the discharge of his office in October 1595 to apprehend some malefactors in Lockerbie, his force of 300 men was attacked by a party of Johnstones, who slew about a score of them, put the others to flight, and rescued the prisoners. Among the slain was Sir John Maxwell of Pollok. The king and Council then took the extraordinary course of depriving Lord Herries of the wardenship in April 1596 and conferring it on the Laird of Johnstone. The experiment was not a happy one, for in November 1597 Lord Stewart of Ochiltree was appointed to this coveted post. In 1599 Lord Herries, Sir James Douglas of Drumlanrig, and Sir James Johnstone of Dunshellie, were apprehended and imprisoned in Edinburgh. Johnstone was liberated a year later, and again appointed Warden of the West Marches. The

[3] Memoirs of the Affairs of Scotland, 1577-1603. By David Moysie. Roxburgh Club, 1830.
[4] Privy Council Records.

secret of these otherwise inexplicable transactions seems to lie in the adherence of the house of Maxwell to the Church of Rome. In March 1601, John, ninth Lord Maxwell, son of the lord slain at Dryfe Sands, being about sixteen years old, was imprisoned in Edinburgh for Popish practices. He escaped in January 1602, perhaps finding the ministrations of Mr Henry Blyth, who was appointed by the General Assembly to attend upon him, more than he could endure.

Straightway he began active hostilities against the Johnstones by burning down the house of William Johnstone at Dalfebble, slaying its owner, who tried to escape, and burning James Johnstone alive in the house of Cuthbert Bratten. No punishment followed on this. On the contrary, Lord Maxwell is found in his seat in Parliament in 1606. In that year, however, he was once more imprisoned for Popery—for it seems that belief in auricular confession and the real presence was reckoned a far graver offence in a country gentleman than midnight murder and fire-raising. His captivity did not last long; but again, in August 1607, he was imprisoned in Edinburgh Castle, together with Sir Robert M'Connell or Macdonald and Robert Maxwell of Dinwoodie. These gentlemen laid their heads together and planned escape, which was effected in a spirited manner. Lord Maxwell gave an entertainment in his own room to the warders, "where he drinks them all fou."[5] Then, under pretence of acting a play, he induced them to give up their swords, and, having thus armed himself and his fellow-prisoners, he left the room, locking in the drunken warders. Overpowering the porter and his assistants, Lord Maxwell and M'Connell made their way to the west castle wall, managed to climb it, and got into the suburbs. Robert Maxwell, however, was not so lucky, being secured by some of the garrison. M'Connell also, who had

[5] Pitcairn's Criminal Trials, vol. iii. p. 47.

irons on him, was taken in the act of burying himself in a dunghill for concealment; but Lord Maxwell, having a horse ready for him, rode free.

The king was very angry, and a proclamation was issued that no one should "reset" Maxwell on pain of death.[6] Lord Scone was sent to Dumfries with the King's Guard to apprehend the fugitive, who remained in hiding on his own estates, occasionally, however, riding abroad with a strong escort. One of his hiding-places on Clawbelly Hill, in Kirkgunzeon parish, is still called Lord Maxwell's Cave. His condition being thus desperate, his best chance of deliverance lay in making friends with the Laird of Johnstone. He therefore engaged the good offices of Sir Robert Maxwell of Orchardtoun, whose wife was Johnstone's sister, to arrange a meeting between himself and his hereditary foe. Sir Robert, having exacted from his chief a solemn oath, with his hand "strekit" in his, that the tryst would not be violated by any treachery, arranged an interview to take place on April 6 beyond the house of Beal. Each of the parties was to have but one attendant, and Sir Robert was to act as mediator between them. What followed was minutely described in Sir R. Maxwell's subsequent deposition.

On the appointed day the Laird of Johnstone repaired to the tryst on "ane amling naig," which was less likely to attract attention than a war-horse. Sir Robert rode with him and William Johnstone of Lockerbie. When about a mile from the place of meeting, Sir Robert saw Lord Maxwell and his attendant riding towards them. He bade Johnstone and his friend to stay where they were, while he went forward to meet

---

[6] This was no empty threat. Five years later, in 1612, Ninian Armstrong, *alias* Ninian's Tom, and John Amulliekyn (O'Mulligan) in Cruiks, were tried for the "tressonabill resset, supplie, intercowmoning and accumpaneing of Johnne, sumtyme Lord Maxwall, his Maiesteis declairit traitour," convicted, and sentenced to be hanged.

the others. It was agreed that the Johnstones were not to move till Sir Robert signalled to them by raising a handkerchief on his riding-switch. Sir Robert then rode on to meet Lord Maxwell, and was distressed to find that his companion was Charles Maxwell, whose character was the reverse of pacific. He called on Lord Maxwell to repeat his oath of fidelity to the tryst and to be answerable for the behaviour of his companion. This having been done, Sir Robert rode back half-way towards the Johnstones, and gave the appointed signal for them to advance. He then took oaths of security from both Johnstone and his second, and the meeting took place.

Sir Robert was riding between Lord Maxwell and the Laird of Johnstone, when an altercation arose between the two seconds, who were following them.

"If I had known of this tryst," Charles Maxwell was saying, "the Lord Maxwell neither could nor should have brought me here."

"I hope in God, Charlie," answered Johnstone, "that you will not rue coming here. For these two noblemen have been long at variance, and I hope now they shall agree."

"The Laird of Johnstone," persisted Charles, "is not able to make amends for the great skaith and injury he has done."

"The laird will do all in his power to satisfy the lord and his friends," was Johnstone's conciliatory reply.

After more bitter words Charles Maxwell drew a pistol and shot William Johnstone through the cloak. Johnstone attempted to return the shot, but his piece missed fire, on which he cried, "Treason!" Lord Maxwell turned to ride to the combatants, when Sir Robert caught him by the cloak, saying—

"Fy! my lord. Make not yourself and me both traitors."

"I am witless" (innocent), answered Lord Maxwell.

The Laird of Johnstone rode off to succour his second, when Lord Maxwell broke away from Sir Robert, galloped after Johnstone, and shot him in the back. Johnstone kept his seat, but his palfrey became restive, the girths broke, and he fell to the ground. He rose to his feet, assisted by William Johnstone, but Charles Maxwell fired at them again. Then William Johnstone laid his chief on the ground, who exclaimed, "Lord have mercy on me! Christ have mercy on me! I am deceived;" and shortly expired.

"Come away!" cried Lord Maxwell to Charles.

"My lord!" remonstrated Charles, pointing to William Johnstone, "will you ride away and leave this bloody thief behind you?"

"What reck of him?" rejoined Lord Maxwell, "for the other has enough."

The two murderers then rode away together.

The horrible treachery of this crime, which it is difficult to believe was not premeditated, was too much even for the stomach of those times. Maxwell had alienated the sympathy of some of those who, deep though his guilt was, would have exerted themselves in protecting him from punishment; for he was at the time pressing an action of divorce against his wife, the sister of the powerful Marquis of Hamilton. He had, therefore, to reckon with the implacable enmity of the Hamiltons.

Nevertheless, he made good his escape to France, his departure being the subject of the well-known ballad, "Lord Maxwell's Good-night." After four years' exile he ventured to return to Scotland, though his lands had been forfeited and bestowed on others. But the pursuit was still hot; the young lord (he was but six-and-twenty) was broken in health; he was fain to trust to the offer of his relative, the Earl of Caithness, to shelter him till he could take ship to Sweden. But Caithness was a false friend. He caused Maxwell to be arrested at Thurso, whence he was taken to Edinburgh, tried, and suffered death on May 21, 1613.

The justice of the sentence none will dispute, but the conduct of Caithness in betraying Maxwell was made the more odious by reason that he himself had been guilty of murder, for which he had been lucky enough to obtain remission in 1585.

This was practically the closing scene in the great blood-feud which for so many years kept Dumfriesshire in anarchy. In the long struggle, each clan had lost two chieftains, many homes had been desolated, and hundreds of lives sacrificed. Men had abandoned industrial pursuits for the profession of banditti, so that, as Mr John Colville expressed it in a letter to Robert Bowes, "no man could safely go a mile from his own house." Robert, younger brother of the forfeited and executed Lord Maxwell, now became head of the clan. Letters patent granted in 1618, 1619, and 1620 restored him to the possessions, titles, and dignities of his predecessors; but inasmuch as Douglas had been restored to the earldom of Morton, which had been for two generations in the house of Maxwell, Robert's earldom was altered, without loss of precedence, to that of Nithsdale. Robert owed his restoration in no small degree to the influence of Villiers, Duke of Buckingham, whose cousin he had married. He proved himself well worthy of the favour shown him, and had, indeed, occasion to show much tact and forbearance in exercising the office of warden, lest old sores should be reopened. He acted with uniform discretion, and showed himself a man of very different temper from his brother.

Among those who assisted the Johnstones at the battle of Dryfe Sands were some 500 of the clan of Scott, hitherto connected rather with Teviotdale than with Dumfriesshire, but destined soon to rise into prominence in Nithsdale and Eskdale. Sir Walter Scott of Buccleuch was absent in France in 1593, but returning the following year, was reappointed keeper of Liddesdale—no sinecure, considering that it involved keeping in order the turbulent dalesmen. Among these, Willie Armstrong of Kinmont, better known as "Kinmont Willie," was one of the boldest and most dreaded. Willie had seven stark sons, who commanded a following of 300 horse, and were incessantly raiding over the English Border. A day of truce was held in 1596, on which a warden court was held at Dayholm of Kershope, where Thomas Salkeld, representing the English warden, Lord Scrope, met Robert Scott of Haining, deputy for Buccleuch. Willie Armstrong attended in the train of Scott, and, after the meeting had dispersed, was riding quietly home along the banks of Liddel with three or four attendants—for, despite the long score against him for his misdeeds, he considered himself safe from arrest during the truce. But he was pursued by a party of English, captured, and taken to prison at Carlisle.

> "They band his legs beneath the steed,
> They tied his hands behind his back,
> They guarded him fivesome on each side,
> And they brought him ower the Liddel-rack.[7]
>
> They led him through the Liddel-rack,
> And also through the Carlisle sands;
> They brought him to Carlisle castell,
> To be at my Lord Scroope's commands."[8]

Buccleuch was very angry at this violation of the truce and of the Border laws. He applied to Salkeld for redress; Salkeld referred him to Scrope, who declared that Willie

---

[7] *Rack*, a gravelly ford.   [8] Ballad of Kinmont Willie.

Armstrong was such a great malefactor he could not be released without express commands from Queen Elizabeth. King James then made application through his ambassador, but without result. Willie was too good a prize to be let slip.

Buccleuch resolved to undertake in person the liberation of Armstrong, and the exploit supplied one of the most stirring themes of Border minstrelsy:—

> " He has ta'en the table wi' his hand,
>   He gar'd the red wine spring on hie—
> ' Now a curse upon my head!' he cried,
> ' But avenged on Lord Scroope I'll be.
>
> . . . . . .
>
> And have they ta'en him, Kinmont Willie,
>   Against the truce of Border tide?
> And forgotten that the bauld Buccleuch
>   Is Keeper here on the Scottish side?
>
> And have they ta'en him, Kinmont Willie,
>   Withouten either dread or fear?
> And forgotten that the bauld Buccleuch
>   Can back a steed or shake a spear?' "

It was, in truth, chivalrously conceived and gallantly executed. Having previously employed spies to measure Carlisle walls, Buccleuch assembled a chosen band at Morton Tower, in the Debatable Land. Willie's seven sons were there, Sir Gilbert Elliot of Stobbs, and Scott of Harden, eighty horsemen in all. At nightfall they rode through the Esk, which was heavily flooded, and crossed the Eden two hours before daybreak.

> " Then on we held for Carlisle toun,
>   And at Staneshaw-bank the Eden we crossed;
> The water was great and meikle o' spait,
>   But the never a man or horse we lost.
>
> And when we reached the Staneshaw-bank
>   The wind was rising loud and hie,
> And there the laird gar'd us leave our naigs
>   For fear that they should stamp and nie."

An escalading party was then sent forward to the castle, but found that their ladders did not reach within several feet of the top of the wall. But such men were not easily daunted. They succeeded in forcing a breach through the masonry near a postern gate, through which Buccleuch himself was among the first to enter. The postern was then thrown open, the storming-party entered, and that part of the castle was secured. The main body remained between the postern and the town, making all possible noise with voice and trumpet so as to divert the attention of the garrison from what was going on inside the tower, and make them believe that a large force was before the walls. Lord Scrope was completely deceived, and, as he afterwards wrote to Burghley, thought that the castle was in possession of 500 Scots.

Meanwhile the storming-party were making their way to Willie Armstrong's cell, the position of which had been accurately explained to them.

"Wi' coulters and wi' forehammers
  We garr'd the bars bang merrilie,
Until we cam to the inner prison
  Where Willie o' Kinmont he did lie.

And when we cam to the lower prison
  Where Willie o' Kinmont he did lie—
'O sleep ye, wake ye, Kinmont Willie,
  Upon the morn that thou's to die?'

'O I sleep saft, and I wake aft,
  It's lang since sleeping was fley'd frae me;
Gie my service back to my wife and bairns,
  And a' guid fellows that spier[9] for me.'
  .   .   .   .
Then shoulder high, wi' shout and cry,
  We bore him down the ladder lang,
At every stride Red Rowan made
  I wot the Kinmont's airns played clang.

---

[9] *To spier*, to inquire.

> 'O mony a time,' quo' Kinmont Willie,
>   'I have ridden horse baith wild and wud,[1]
> But a rougher beast than Red Rowan,
>   I ween my legs have ne'er bestrode.'
>
> 'O mony a time,' quo' Kinmont Willie,
>   'I've pricked a horse out owre the furs;[2]
> But sin' the day I backed a steed,
>   I never wore sic cumbrous spurs.'"

Buccleuch now called his men together and started homeward with their prize. An attempt was made by the English to resist the passage of the Eden, but it was unsuccessful, and two hours after sunrise Kinmont Willie rode again on Scottish soil. He had complained of the weight of his fetters in swimming the flooded Eden, but Buccleuch would not allow time to strike them off till the party were over the Border again. Then, at a roadside cottage still standing between Longtown and Langholm, a blacksmith was found to knock off Willie's "cumbrous spurs."[3]

This affair led to long and heated controversy between the Courts of England and Scotland. Queen Elizabeth was furious at the infringement of the truce by the rescue of a prisoner; King James, on the other hand, protested that the original offence lay in the capture of Kinmont Willie during the truce. Finally, in 1597, when it looked as if the dispute would end in war, Elizabeth's ministers frightened James into compliance, and Buccleuch surrendered himself to the English warden at Berwick. The end was as much in accordance with the spirit of chivalry as every incident in this story had been. When he was brought before the English queen—

"How did you dare," she asked, "to commit such an offence?"

---

[1] *Wud*, mad.   [2] Furrows.
[3] Sir William Fraser's 'Scotts of Buccleuch,' vol. i. p. 186.

"Dare, madam!" replied Buccleuch, "what would a man not dare to do?"

Elizabeth was not insensible to this knightly sentiment. It is said she turned to those beside her and said—

"With ten thousand such men as this, our brother of Scotland might shake the firmest throne in Europe."

The honour of England having been satisfied by the surrender of Buccleuch, he was most leniently and even hospitably dealt with while a prisoner. The matter in dispute was allowed to drop, and Buccleuch received from Queen Elizabeth a safe-conduct to pass abroad for the benefit of his health.

Some years after John, Lord Maxwell, had paid the penalty of death for his misdeeds, the scaffold of Edinburgh flowed with the blood of an unworthy member of his clan. John Maxwell of Garrarie, a cadet of the house of Monreith, had induced another Wigtownshire laird, John M'Kie of Glassock, to mortgage in his favour all his land and goods, and M'Kie, being utterly destitute of means, became a dependant of Maxwell, and constantly lived with him in his house of Garrarie. Maxwell became weary of his presence; so one summer night in July 1618 he, his son George, and some servants seized the unfortunate Laird of Glassock, and, in the words of the ditty, "band baith his handis and feitt, and thaireftir, in maist crewell and mercieles maner, playing the pairt of hangmen and burriowis,[4] with ane hair tedder,[5] strangillit and wirreit him to deid; and haifing, be that violent and crewall meane, bereft him of his lyfe, thay thaireftir cayreit him to ane peit moss or burne, callit the Burne of Raniestoun,[6] within ane half myle to the said Hous of Garrarie, quhairin they flang him."

[4] French *bourreau*, an executioner.   [5] A horse-hair halter.
[6] Ravenstone.

Lord Maxwell acted as "prelocuteur in defence" for his vassal, with the Master of Maxwell, the Guidman of Hills, and Edward Forrester, Commissar of Kirkcudbright; while the "prelocuteurs in persute" were Lord Garlies and the Laird of Larg, M'Kie. The prisoner, John Maxwell, being "ane landit Gentilman, in the rank of ane Barroun, worth thre thowseand merkis of zeirlie rent and aboue," challenged various persons on the assize. Among others he objected to Edward Maxwell, tenant of Larroch under his kinsman of Monreith, because, *inter alia*, "thair is bluid and deidlie ffeid standing betuix the pannell and him vnreconceillit." Now Larroch is the land adjacent to Garrarie, so John cannot have been a very agreeable neighbour. Another objection taken seems more valid, according to modern ideas of justice—namely, that Edward Maxwell was one of the witnesses for the prosecution. This was defended on the following extraordinary grounds. "Becaus he hes alreddie deponit as ane Witnes, he may the mair cleirlie be admittit ane Assysour." However, "in respect thair was na penurie of Assysours," the justice ordered Edward to stand down. In the end John Maxwell and George, his son, were found guilty and beheaded, all their goods and land being forfeited to the Crown.[7]

[7] As Garrarie is now part of the estate of Monreith, the Laird of Monreith was probably allowed to obtain possession on easy terms.

CHAPTER X.

FROM 1598 TO THE BATTLE OF PHILIPHAUGH IN 1645.

IN 1603 was effected peaceably that which so many far-seeing statesmen had long laboured in vain to bring about—Scotland and England were united under one monarch. In England the supremacy of the Crown had been asserted by force of arms in the Wars of the Roses. Half, at least, of the English barons had then perished either on field of battle or on the scaffold; the rest had come to terms with their sovereign, and were content to live as his subjects, instead of allied or tributary princes. In Scotland the same end, long delayed, was brought about by different means, and the Crown for the first time became powerful enough to begin to exact obedience from the great feudal lords.

Yet the old system died hard in the south-west.

While Eastern Galloway or Kirkcudbright was involved in the hostilities between the Maxwells and Johnstones, Western Galloway or Wigtownshire was little disturbed on that account, owing to the predominance of the Kennedys in that quarter. But simultaneously with the warfare in Nithsdale and Annandale, a blood-feud, hardly less serious in extent and quite as ferocious in character, was raging between different branches of the Kennedy family. The scene of this lay chiefly in Ayrshire, but the Wigtownshire tenants of the Earl of Cassilis and other landowners of the clan had to share in the results of the evil deeds of their superiors.

Thus in 1598 Sir Thomas Kennedy of Culzean let the farm of Auchnotteroch, near Stranraer, to a farmer named M'Ewen. The Master of Cassilis, brother of the earl, had previously requested that Patrick Rickard, his foster-brother, should have the farm. The Master sent to M'Ewen warning him not to take the farm, "else he would make all his harness clatter." But M'Ewen "being ane proud carle, and having the Sheriff of Galloway [Sir Andrew Agnew] as well as Culzean to back him," replied that he would take any land the earl chose to give him. Hearing this, the Master rode to Auchnotteroch with Hugh Kennedy of Chappell and a servant, John Boyd, and slew the bold M'Ewen. "Whereat," says the chronicler, "my lord was far offendit."[1] Formal proceedings were taken against the Master of Cassilis, but, as was too commonly the case in dealing with powerful offenders, a remission was granted in 1601.

About this time the Earl of Cassilis came into conflict with his Wigtownshire vassals. His father had granted them very easy terms, which it was now proposed to raise. He obtained a decree against the Lairds of Garthland, Mertoun M'Kie, Kinhilt, Sir Andrew Agnew, and others, and rode to his house of Inch with forty horsemen to enforce payment. But the M'Doualls and M'Kies, encouraged and assisted by the sheriff, were not of such feeble fibre as to be overawed in this style. Cassilis proclaimed a court in Glenluce, to which he summoned his vassals. They were ready enough to attend it, but not in a way to please their feudal lord; for just as he

---

[1] Historie of the Kennedyis. "It is a curious coincidence," wrote the late Sir Andrew Agnew in his 'Hereditary Sheriffs of Galloway,' vol. i. p. 434, "that after the lapse of nearly three centuries a M'Ewen is still tenant of Auchnotteroch." This farm is now part of the Lochnaw estates.

was mounting at his castle door to ride to Glenluce with his escort of forty, he was informed that the gentlemen had passed before him with one hundred horsemen in geir. The earl did not consider it prudent to attend the court that day; but, trusting perhaps to the good liquor of Glenluce to have some effect on the array of his rebellious vassals, he waylaid them on their return. Howbeit, he was disappointed in his calculation of the strength either of the drink or of the heads of the troopers; for not only was his force put to flight, but he himself was closely besieged in his Castle of Inch. The earl was then at feud with Kennedy of Bargany, a baron nearly as powerful as himself; nevertheless, trusting to the adage that blood is thicker than water, he despatched his chaplain, the minister of Colmonell, to beg that gentleman to come to his rescue. Bargany responded gallantly, and early next day was at Craigcaffie, about six miles from Inch, with forty horsemen. There he received a deputation from the lairds, obtained from the earl a promise not to proceed further with his exactions, and accepted his (the earl's) invitation to stay and dine with him. But a few days later, when the earl was asked to set his hand to the agreement he had made, he declared that no promise was binding which was extorted by force. Bargany was very angry at this treachery. The feud between him and the earl became as bitter as ever; but the grievances of the Wigtownshire gentry were settled by arbitration. Bargany was not long afterwards killed in an encounter with the earl's forces near Maybole.

In contrast to the manner in which grave misdeeds, especially those committed by great men, were winked at, there appears an entry in the Criminal Records, in March 1600, against Uchtred M'Douall of Garthland, Alexander Hannay of Sorby, and Sir John Vans of Barnbarroch, who had incurred

penalties for boarding themselves and their households in
"oistlar housis"—hotels—which was an offence under an
Act of James VI.'s seventh Parliament. A similar difference
may be observed in the enforcement of Acts prohibiting the
maintenance of military forces by private individuals, and
those directing matters of religious belief. Every gentleman
vied with his neighbours in the equipment and efficiency of
as many soldiers, horse and foot, as he could afford. Every
tenant, as a matter of course, had to obey his landlord's
summons to the field, and the barons laughed at the statutes
against "raising bands of men of war on horse or foot, with
pistolets, spikes, spears, jaks, splents, steel bonnets, white
harness, or other munition, or making sound of trumpet or
talbrone, or using culvennes, with banners displayed, under
pain of death to the raisers, and also to those who rode with
them."[2] The spirit of these Acts was, indeed, scarcely compatible with others of the same reign, which enjoined the
sheriffs to see that every man in their jurisdictions was
"weaponed effeirand to his honour," and should display
his weapons twice in each year at wapinschaws appointed
by the sheriffs. To possess arms and not to use them at
the laird's bidding, but only when summoned to the royal
standard, was a nicety of distinction beyond rural intellects
in those days.

But Acts controlling spiritual observances were administered
far more energetically. Upon no part of the country did
the statute of 1581,[3] prohibiting the observance of saints'
days and suppressing pilgrimages, tell with more ruinous
effect than upon Wigtownshire. Whithorn, the Mecca of
the Scottish faithful down to the Reformation, had earned
large profits from royal and other visitors to St Ninian's shrine;

---

[2] Queen Mary's ninth Parliament, cap. 83.
[3] James VI.'s seventh Parliament, cap. 104.

and Exchequer accounts show how the rest of the county must have benefited by the expenditure incurred by trains of princes and knights as they passed to and fro. All that was now sternly put down.

But it is a strange commentary on human intelligence that the very legislators who were so earnest in suppressing the practices of the Roman Church on the ground of their idolatry and superstition, were indefatigable in framing Acts of horrible cruelty and iniquity against witchcraft. Sickening details have been preserved of proceedings during the reign of James VI. against unhappy women forced to confess to the most extravagant and impossible acts, and too often involving in their confession other innocent creatures. "Gentle King Jamie," as is well known, took the greatest interest in these proceedings, frequently attending in person when the accused were put to the torture. Fear is the parent of cruelty. James was physically a coward, which is quite enough to account for the extraordinary zeal he showed in carrying out to the letter the passages in Levit. xx. and Deut. xviii.

It seems, however, that this abominable and humiliating superstition did not take firm hold in Dumfriesshire and Galloway until the middle of the seventeenth century. Of the hundreds of hapless creatures who were put to death in the reign of James VI., often after enduring unspeakable torments, there is no record of any belonging to the south-western district. At the same time, it should be remembered that, as Pitcairn has pointed out,[4] while there remain on record the trials of those tried before the High Court of Justiciary, an immense number of reputed witches were dealt with in local courts by lords of regality, baron bailies, and royal commissioners, of whose proceedings no record has been

---

[4] Criminal Trials, vol. iii. p. 597.

preserved. But it was not till the authorities of the Presbyterian Church took up the trade of witch-hunting that such scenes were enacted in Dumfriesshire and Galloway as fill one with indignation.[5]

Of the topographical features of Scotland as it was at the close of the sixteenth and beginning of the seventeenth century a wonderfully faithful picture has been preserved in the great Atlas of Blaeu of Amsterdam. Timothy Pont, who surveyed Scotland and drew the maps, performed his labours between 1590 and 1600, when he became minister of Dunnett, in Caithness, but they were not engraved until sixty years later. The difficulties to be overcome in making such a minute survey of North Britain in its then social state, and when bridges and roads were few and far between, must indeed have been prodigious, and one is astonished at the accuracy with which natural features, towns, and houses are set forth. The descriptive letterpress accompanying the plates must be taken as referring to the country as it was half a century later than the labours of Pont.[6]

The year 1606 was a bad one for Border thieves. The Earl of Dunbar, Royal Commissioner on the Borders, caused hang 140 of them, and reported to his majesty that the district was now "satled, far by onything that has ever been done there before." Notwithstanding this boast, Dunbar had to return to Dumfries three years later in 1609, when he hanged many more. The Earl of Dunfermline, the Chancellor, wrote to the king this time, assuring him that Lord Dunbar " has had special care to repress . . . the insolence of all the proud bangsters, oppressors and

---

[5] Further reference to proceedings against witches will be found at p. 258 *et seq.*

[6] See Note H, Blaeu's Geography, p. 253.

nembroths [Nimrods], . . . has purgit the Borders of all the chiefest malefactors, robbers and brigands as were wont to reign and triumph there, as clean, and by as great wisdom and policy, as Hercules sometime is written to have purged Augeas, the King of Elide, his escuries; and by cutting off . . . the laird of Tynwald, Maxwell, sundry Douglases, Johnstons, Jardines, Armstrangs, Beatisons, and sic others, *magni nominis luces*, in that broken parts, has rendered all those ways and passages betwixt your majesty's kingdoms of Scotland and England as free and peaceable, as Phœbus in auld times made free and open the ways to his own oracle in Delphos, and to his Pythic plays and ceremonies, by the destruction of Phorbas and his Phlegians, all thieves, voleurs, bandsters and throat-cutters. These parts are now, I can assure your majesty, as lawful, as peaceable and as quiet, as any part in any civil kingdom of Christianity." [7]

Alas for the erudite Chancellor's confidence! It was not long before a new selection of classical parallels had to be hunted up, this time by the orderly people of the Border, to impress the mind of their pedantic king with the intolerable condition of affairs. They laid before him a memorial, crammed with Latin quotations, in which it was set forth that the thieves were like the beasts of the field, to use a metaphor of Cicero's in his oration for Cluentius, "quæ, fame dominante, ad eum locum ubi aliquando pastæ sunt, revertuntur. There is no more account made," the plaintive document continues, "of going to the horn than to the alehouse. . . . If diligent search were made . . . there would be found ane grit number of idle people, without any calling, industry or lawful means to live by, except it be upon the blood of the poorest and most obedient sort."

It must be confessed that those people who honestly

---

[7] Letters and State Papers of the Reign of James VI.

desired to make a living by legitimate means were sadly hampered by the spirit of seventeenth-century legislation. "Amang the mony abuses whilk the iniquity of the time and private respect of filthy lucre and gain has produced within the commonwealth," runs the preamble of an Act of the Privy Council in 1615, "there is of late discoverit a most unlawful and pernicious tred of transporting eggs furth of the kingdom. Certain avaritious and godless persons, void of modesty and discretion, preferring their awn private commodity to the commonweal, has gone and goes athort the country and buys the haill eggs that they can get, barrels the same, and transports them at their pleasure. . . . If this unlawful tred be sufferit to be of ony langer continuance, it will fall out that in a very short time there will no eggs nor poultry be funden within the country."

The export of eggs was therefore prohibited under heavy penalties. What room is there for wonder that many people, finding outlets for respectable industry closed against them by such an extraordinary inversion of protectionist policy, should be driven to brigandage as the only promising means of living!

The policy of prohibiting exports seems the more remarkable when it is remembered that, from time immemorial previous to the reign of James VI., Scotland had been distinguished among the nations of Europe as the only one which laid no duty upon imports, though of course the burghs levied their *parva costuma* on all produce, whether foreign or native, coming within their bounds. It was not till 1597 that an Act was passed imposing a duty upon imported cloth and other material. The object of this novel departure was not, as might be supposed, the patriotic one of protecting home industries, but the far less worthy one set forth in the preamble of the Act—namely, to enable King James, as the "free Prince of a soverane power," to acquire the means "for the enterteyning of his princely port." Allusion is made in the same preamble to the immemorial exemption from duty of all articles brought within the realm of Scotland, which is shown to be contrary to the practice of all other nations. Against this Act the Convention of Royal Burghs strenuously protested, as imposing "ane new and intollerabill custome."

The king, however, was more concerned about the establishment of Episcopacy in Scotland than about the protection of life and property or the fostering of native industry. To allay the alarm of his Presbyterian subjects at the threatened return to Popish observances, he encouraged the execution of the enactments against Papacy, and to this day we have reason to deplore some of the results of the energy with which these were enforced by Spottiswoode, Archbishop of Glasgow. Thus in 1609 this prelate went in person to New Abbey in the Stewartry of Kirkcudbright, and took possession of the house of Gilbert Brown, formerly abbot, who was suspected of Popish practices. It is stated in the Privy Council records how great a number of Popish books, pictures, images, vestments, and other articles were seized, taken to Dumfries, and there burnt in the High Street on market day, before a large assemblage. The old religion died hard in the neighbourhood of Devorguila's ancient church, and from time to time the same process had to be repeated. Nearly eighty years after Archbishop Spottiswoode's raid, the Presbyterians, in excess of rejoicing at the Revolution of 1688, "thought it someway belonged to them to go to all the Popish houses and destroy their monuments of idolatry, with their priests' robes, and put in prison themselves" (the priests). The houses of the Maxwells near Dumfries were then ransacked once more, and the spoil obtained was publicly burnt at the cross of Dumfries. Again, in 1704 the discovery of the intentions of the Jacobite party roused the fervour of the Presbyterians of Dumfriesshire, so that a fresh seizure and conflagration were made of books and vestments. It is sad to reflect on the inestimable value these books and relics would have possessed, had they been preserved to our days, and how greatly the country has suffered in beauty and interest by the defacement, under directions of the Government, of all the ancient places of worship.

Among the many malefactors who escaped from justice while the courts were occupied with the weightier matters of heresy-hunting and witch-finding, mention may be made of a young gentleman of Dumfriesshire, Alexander, son and heir of Sir Thomas Kirkpatrick of Closeburn. He was imprisoned in the Tolbooth of Edinburgh on a charge of murdering James Carmichael, younger of Spothe. Lady Amisfield, wife of Charteris, Laird of Amisfield, obtained leave for an interview with the accused in the gaoler's room. There she changed clothes with him, and Kirkpatrick escaped, nor is there any further mention of proceedings against him.

In 1617 James VI. yielded to what he called a "salmond-like instinct," and, after fourteen years' absence, revisited the land of his birth. Reaching Edinburgh in the middle of May, he made the return journey to England by the west coast, resting at Drumlanrig with Sir William Douglas on July 31. Sir William was the great-grandson of Sir James, mentioned above as one of the pioneers of Reformation in the west. He was afterwards created Earl of Queensberry, and built the present Castle of Drumlanrig. Lincluden College belonged at that time to Sir William, who acted as the king's host there on August 2. Next day the king and his suite, chief among whom was the favourite "Steenie," Duke of Buckingham, visited Dumfries, and were entertained at a banquet by the Provost and Town Council in the Painted

Chamber, a room in the town clerk's house. On this occasion the king presented the trades of Dumfries with a miniature piece of ordnance, now known as the Silver Gun, to be competed for at the wapinschaws. It was then mounted on a carriage, which has since disappeared, and during the present century a butt was fitted to the tube, which gives it the appearance of a small carbine, with a barrel about 10 inches long.[8]

These trades had a right to representation on the town council of Dumfries, each by its deacon. Their order of precedence was as follows: 1st, the gows[9] or smiths; 2d, the wrights and masons, including carpenters, painters, glaziers, and slaters; 3d, the weavers or websters; 4th, the tailors; 5th, the shoemakers; 6th, the skinners, furriers, and glovers; and 7th, the butchers or fleshers. In theory the rest of the town council were elected by the townspeople, but in effect the councillors chose persons to fill vacancies as they occurred. Four other trades were originally numbered in the corporation—namely, the lorimers or saddlers, the pewterers or tinsmiths, the litsters or dyers, and the bonnetmakers; but these had become extinct in the seventeenth century, though they were still represented by four votes in the election of magistrates, a provost, three bailies, a dean, and a treasurer. The council was composed of twelve merchant councillors, seven deacons of trades, with four "led votes" of the extinct trades, and six magistrates, to whom were added four new merchant councillors before the annual election of magistrates, making thirty-three in all. But as soon as the new bench was elected the four "led" votes became dormant till the next election,

---

[8] M'Dowall's 'History of Dumfries,' p. 350. But Chalmers was of opinion that the gift was made on the occasion of King James's visit to Dumfries in 1597 ('Domestic Annals of Scotland,' vol. i. p. 294).

[9] From the Gaelic *gobha* (gow), a smith.

and four merchant councillors ceased to hold office. This reduced the number of the council to twenty-five. Such was the local government of Dumfries until the Burgh Reform Act of 1833.

James's visit to Dumfries in 1617 was made the occasion of adding another to the list of royal burghs in Galloway. A charter was granted to Stranraer, formerly called St John's Chapel; but owing, it is said, to the jealousy of Wigtown, it was not enrolled as a royal burgh till many years later.

The commercial policy of the municipalities of Dumfries and other burghs was not such as modern political economists could approve of. It was strictly protective, of course, and besides, interfered to such an extent between buyer and seller as would seem fatal to all prosperous trade. Statutory prices were enforced for the sale of almost all goods, and heavy penalties were incurred by any one selling such goods by private bargain or elsewhere than in public market. No corn might be ground except in the burgh mills. This, indeed, was no more than the privilege exercised by every landowner, of whose revenues "multures" were always an important part. Private grinding, whether in town or country, was strictly prohibited—although the great number of querns or hand-mills which remain to this day suggests that there was much contraband practice in this matter. Thomas Irving, senior bailie of Dumfries, was more enlightened than his colleagues. In 1661 the council passed a resolution enacting that French wine should be sold for five groats a pint, under the penalty of 10 merks. Irving entered his protest against the folly of "setting pryce upon any forraine wair."

It will be shown later that the town councils of burghs took upon themselves duties far transcending these temporal affairs, and endeavoured to carry out Calvin's ideal of a Christian government, responsible to God for all the actions of the citizens.

The chief motive of James's progress through Scotland in 1617 is not obscure. It is well known that he ardently desired to effect the union of the Scottish and English Legislatures, and to assimilate the Protestantism of Scotland to the Episcopal Church system of England. He had begun filling up the Scottish sees three years before he became King of England, which resulted in the anomaly of the existence of bishops, with seats in Parliament, while the people were Presbyterian, and strongly opposed to Episcopacy. Gavin Hamilton was made Bishop of Galloway in 1603,[1] in which diocese there had been no bishop for twenty years. It was the richest bishopric in Scotland, being inferior in revenue only to the two primacies of St Andrews and Glasgow.[2]

The king's refusal to summon a General Assembly led to the meeting at Aberdeen in 1605 of the representatives of nine Presbyteries, who constituted themselves an Assembly of the Church of Christ. Their leader was John Welsh, a native of Nithsdale, minister of Kirkcudbright, and son-in-law of John Knox. He and five of his colleagues were sentenced to death for contumacy, but the penalty was commuted for transportation. Welsh went to France, where Louis XIII. gave him licence to preach. King James allowed him to return to England in 1622, but on no account to cross the Scottish Border, for he esteemed Welsh's power in the pulpit so highly that he said it would be fatal to Episcopacy in Scotland were he to resume his ministration there. Neither would the king allow him to preach in London till he was

[1] Some authorities give 1606 as the year of his appointment. Probably consecration was delayed till then. In 1610 Bishop Hamilton of Galloway was summoned to London to receive ordination from the Primate of England.

[2] In Chalmers's 'Caledonia' the net rental of the bishopric of Galloway at the Revolution, when Episcopacy in Scotland was suppressed, is given at £5634, 15s. *Scots*, besides the patronage of more than twenty churches, which, with the above revenue, was then vested in the Crown.

assured that Welsh was near his death. Then, permission having been given, Welsh preached once with great fervour. But the effort was too great for his strength, and he expired two hours afterwards.

In 1612 Parliament formally re-established Episcopacy in Scotland, and in 1614, on the death of Hamilton, William Cowper succeeded him and preached before the king in Dumfries in 1617. From this divine one of the hills near Glen Trool, the Cowper Cairn, is said to take its name, from the bishop's habit of retiring to the hills for meditation. He was a keen golfer, and when his duties as Dean of the Chapel Royal detained him in the capital, he used often to escape for a game on the links at Musselburgh. Perhaps it was this harmless relaxation that was alluded to in some of the numerous lampoons which were aimed at the Prelacy. One of the least ill-natured ran as follows :—

> "St Androes loves a cup of wine;
> Wine Glasgow, with an whoore;
> Rosse company; play Galloway;
> Brechin not to be poore."

But the bishops could afford for the nonce to laugh at their unpopularity. Their seats in Parliament enabled them to direct legislation in their own favour, which was not forgotten by the people when at length the day of reckoning came.

Bishop Cowper died in 1619. The acrimony with which Calderwood has described his character and career may be regarded as springing from that historian's hatred of Episcopacy. He charges him with extortion, simony, and even grosser crimes; nevertheless there is reason to believe that he was both pious and gentle, and not unworthy of the favour shown him by the king. Bishop Lamb of Brechin succeeded him in the see of Galloway.

When King James met the General Assembly in Edinburgh

in 1617, he made their position clear to the bishops, saying that they "must rule the ministers, and I rule both." Charles I. succeeded to his father's throne in 1625, and to a double share of his father's faith in right divine. He appointed the Earl of Nithsdale to hold a Convention of the Estates, and to obtain the acceptance of the English Liturgy by the General Assembly, and a renunciation of all the Church property which had been conferred on barons and other laymen since the Reformation. The barons, as might have been expected, refused to sacrifice their consciences and interests to further the king's project for strengthening the Prelacy, and resistance of all ranks to the Liturgy was so strong that it had to be abandoned.

In Dumfriesshire, notwithstanding the adherence of the Maxwells to the Church of Rome, popular resistance to Prelacy deepened as years went on. No one was more active in putting down Popery than Mr Thomas Ramsay, minister of Dumfries. It happened one day in 1625 that, as related in the Privy Council Records, he and some of his colleagues in the presbytery met, riding over the bridge, "ane mess priest by whom numbers of the country people were pervertit not only in their religion, but in their allegiance to the king's majesty." With the priest rode some proscribed Papists, who, when the minister tried to apprehend him, interfered and enabled him to escape. His horse and cloak-bag, however, fell into the hands of Mr Ramsay's party, and in the latter were found "a number of oisties,[3] superstitious pictures, priest's vestments, altar, chalice, &c." These, by direction of the Privy Council, were publicly burnt at the market-cross, except the silver articles, which were melted down for the poor.

The year 1627 was memorable on the shores of Solway

[3] A corruption of the Latin *hostia*, consecrated wafers.

by reason of an extraordinary high tide, which, driven before a furious gale, inundated the low-lying land of Caerlaverock and Ruthwell, drowned a great number of cattle, and seventeen poor salt-workers at Ruthwell. The moral effect of this disaster is described in somewhat ambiguous terms in Stevenson's 'History of the Church of Scotland.' "The ruin occasioned by it," writes the author of that work, quoting a contemporary chronicle, "had an agreeable influence on the surviving inhabitants, convincing them, more than ever, of what they owed to divine Providence."

In 1628 Grierson of Lag (a name to be indelibly associated with the suppression of Covenanting in later years) and Charteris of Amisfield were commissioned to make a raid on the Popish community of New Abbey. Herbert Maxwell of Kirkconnel, Barbara Maxwell, Lady Mabie, John Little, master of the household to Lord Nithsdale, and a number of people of less note, were apprehended, and ordered by the Council to be dealt with by the Commissioners at a court held in Dumfries.

Charles summoned a Parliament to meet him in Edinburgh in 1633, and, though he had been nearly ten years on the throne, went through the ceremony of coronation at the hands of the Archbishop of St Andrews. The Archbishop of Glasgow, disapproving of the Romish character of the ritual prescribed, fell into disfavour, and his place was taken by Bishop Maxwell of Ross, son of the Laird of Cavens, in the Stewartry of Kirkcudbright. Among those whom the king endeavoured to attach to his policy by the distribution of coronation honours, Sir John Gordon of Lochinvar was created Viscount Kenmure, Sir Robert M'Clellan Lord Kirkcudbright, Viscount Drumlanrig Earl of Queensberry; Sir James Johnstone became Lord Johnstone, and Viscount Sanquhar Earl of Dumfries.

A charter erecting the lands of Roddings, belonging to Lochinvar, into the royal burgh of New Galloway was ratified by Act of Parliament this year, notwithstanding the strenuous opposition of the burgh of Kirkcudbright. Lord Kenmure, however, died before his ambitious plan of building could be carried out, and New Galloway, though boasting the offices of provost, four bailies, dean of guild, treasurer, and twelve councillors, has never yet exceeded the dimensions of an upland village.

Before leaving Scotland, Charles, acting on the advice of Archbishop Laud, instituted the celebrated High Commission Court to inquire into the doctrines, religious practices, and morals of clergy and people. Further, warrants were issued for the establishment of a subsidiary court in each diocese. Bishop Sydserff now occupied the see of Galloway, and some of his lay colleagues on the Galloway inquisition found his method so little to their liking that they resigned their appointment. That was the course taken by the Lords Galloway and Kirkcudbright; but the effect was only to strengthen the power of the anti-Presbyterian commissioners, who deposed various ministers from their charges—among others, Samuel Rutherford of Anwoth, Dalgleish of Kirkmabreck, and Glendinning of Kirkcudbright. Glendinning was a venerable divine of seventy-nine, to whose ministrations the burgh magistrates of Kirkcudbright were greatly attached. As he refused to desist from preaching, and they persisted in attending his services, both he and they were lodged in Wigtown gaol for contumacy.

It is very difficult to follow the different lines of State interference in spiritual matters at this time. No sooner had the High Commission Court set to work, certainly not with any indulgent intention to Presbyterianism, than the Privy Council, on June 2, 1634, gave judgment in the case of several Dumfries Papists, and, *inter alia*, condemned Robert Rig to imprisonment during their pleasure for having married a woman according to the forbidden rites of Rome. Seven women also were sent to Edinburgh for imprisonment as recusant Papists, but after five days' durance they were remitted to the Archbishop of Glasgow, to be dealt with according to his pleasure.

In 1636 the king issued a proclamation by the hands of the Bishop of Ross, commanding the clergy and people to accept Laud's Book of Common Prayer, and enjoining the bishops and others in authority to enforce conformity. Sydserff, Bishop of Galloway, exceeded the other prelates in putting this decree in force, though scarcely any of the ministers in his diocese would accept the liturgies provided for their use. In the following year, after the king had refused to entertain the remonstrance of the people, Sydserff nearly paid the penalty of death for his zeal. He was beset by a mob in Edinburgh, and was only saved from their violence by the Earls of Wigtoun and Traquair, who first defended him with their armed followers, and then prevailed on some of the Presbyterian lords to speak to the people and induce them to disperse. A year later Sydserff met with similar treatment from the populace of Stirling.

After this the Presbyterian "Tables" were constituted; consisting of representatives of the four orders — nobility, gentry, ministers, and burgesses. This body drew up the Solemn League and Covenant, nominally for the purpose of establishing religious freedom, but really, as the event proved, for the defence of Presbyterianism and the suppression of every other doctrine or form of worship. The Covenant was inscribed on a sheet of parchment four feet long by three feet eight inches broad, and it was soon covered with signatures. Among the earliest to sign was the Marquis of Montrose, who was to end by forfeiting his life in resisting the principles which he had adhered to till they came in conflict with loyalty to his king. Mr John Livingston, appointed minister of Stranraer in 1638, was sent to London with several copies of the Covenant; but on arriving there he received a threat of imprisonment from the Marquis of Hamilton, on which he bought a horse and rode home again.

The long-smouldering fires, kindled by the creation of Episcopacy and the imposition of a liturgy, now broke forth. The General Assembly, in defiance of a writ of dissolution issued by Hamilton, continued to sit at Glasgow, and on November 21, 1638, and following days, abolished the Prelacy by excommunicating eight archbishops and bishops, deposing four and reducing two to the grade of pastor. To realise the scene it must be remembered that the bishops were members of the Assembly and voted on the question.

On the last day of the Assembly it was proposed that Mr Rutherford, minister of Anwoth, should be translated to the Chair of Divinity in the new college of Aberdeen. He, however, refused the honour, for, said he, "there is a woe unto me if I preach not the Gospel, and I know not who can go betwixt me and that woe."[4]

Before it separated this memorable Assembly made a fresh arrangement of the synods and presbyteries of Dumfries and Galloway. The Water of Urr was fixed as the division between the synods of Dumfries and Galloway. The eight parishes in the east of Wigtownshire, with Monygaff and Kirkmabreck in the Stewartry of Kirkcudbright, were formed into the Presbytery of Wigtown. The nine westerly parishes of Wigtownshire, with Colmonell and Ballantrae in Ayrshire, constituted the Presbytery of Stranraer; while the remaining

---

[4] This objection was overruled by the Assembly in August 1639, and Rutherford was ordained to go to St Andrews.

parishes of the Stewartry, west of Urr, made the Presbytery of Kirkcudbright. Although railways have greatly altered the considerations of transit which directed this arrangement, it continues unaltered to this day.

Presbyterianism had won the day in Scotland. But if it was civil tyranny in spiritual things that brought about the revolt, the spiritual tyranny thereby established was no whit less oppressive.

Preparations for war were begun as soon as the Assembly adjourned. Although the great territorial influence of the Maxwells was on the side of the king and bishops, the mass of the people in the south-west and many of the baronage had signed the Covenant, and were ready to fight for it. The Earls of Galloway, Cassilis, Wigtoun, and Dumfries[5] were members of the contumacious Assembly. Among the elders who attended it were Andrew Agnew of Lochnaw, young Charteris of Amisfield, Adair of Kinhilt, and Gordon of Earlston. Lord Johnstone took the field for the Covenant, and struck the first blow by attacking, though unsuccessfully, the castle of Caerlaverock. The Earl of Cassilis arrayed his forces in Galloway on the popular side, and Lord Kirkcudbright raised a regiment in Nithsdale. War committees were appointed in all the midland and southern counties of Scotland. The Kirkcudbright committee, of which the minute-book has been preserved at Cardiness,[6] sat at Dumfries, Kirkcudbright, Cullenoch, &c. The first entry, June 27, is a resolution to form a troop of eighty horse drawn from each parish in Galloway. Captains of infantry were ap-

[5] Lords Galloway, Dumfries, and Queensberry were known to be indisposed for active measures. When the king, in 1641, submitted to the Estates a list of those whom he had chosen for Privy Councillors, the names of Lords Galloway and Dumfries were struck out by Parliament.

[6] It has been printed and published by J. Nicholson, Kirkcudbright, 1855.

pointed, arrangements for enrolling foot-soldiers agreed to, and men of means were summoned before the committee to declare on oath what those means were, and were compelled to lend money in proportion. When the freewill offerings were exhausted recourse was had to forcible exaction from anti-Covenanters. The war committees were empowered by the Committee of Estates sitting in Edinburgh to exercise civil jurisdiction "in respect to the generall calamitie throw want of justice," but warlike preparation continued to be their chief business. Commissioners were appointed in each parish "to uplift the sogers, both the foote and horss, maintenance and armes; and to plunder any persone that shall happen no to mak thankfull peyment of the sogers' pay." Some of these commissioners, appointed to a duty for which they had not much stomach but not daring to decline it, were summoned before the Committee of Estates, "thair to ansuer for thair neglect for not outputting of the troupe and baggage horss." William Lindsay, commissioner for Colvend and Southwick parishes; John Charteris of Barncleuch, for Terregles; the Laird of Dalscairth and John Brown, for Troqueer; Robert Maxwell of Cavens, brother of the Bishop of Ross, for Loch Rutton; Hugh Maxwell in Torrorie, for Kirkbean; John Stewart of Shambellie, for New Abbey; and David Cannan, for Buittle, were among these defaulters.

King Charles was now at war with his Scottish subjects. On March 27, 1640, he wrote from Whitehall to Lord Nithsdale: "It is nou tyme for me to bidd you looke to your selfe, for longer than the 13 of the next month I will not warrant you, but that ye will heare of a breache betuixt me and my Couenanting Rebelles." Nithsdale thereupon convened all his friends, took them bound to obey the king, and set in defence his castles of Caerlaverock and Thrieve. There were thus two armies being recruited simultaneously in Dumfries and Galloway; those unhappy farmers and peasants who had no particular political or ecclesiastical convictions, but only wanted to till their lands in peace, must have been sorely puzzled sometimes which side it was wisest to please. All the silver and gold work in Scotland, "as weill to burgh and landwart, as weill noblemen, barrones, and burgess as uthers, of whatsomever degrie or qualitie they be," was to be handed to the Committee of Estates to be coined for the pay of the army; and security was to be given for repayment of the value—when?

"Lykeas, it is heirby declarit, that these quha hes any silver or gold worke quhich they crave raither to keip for thair ane use than delyver the samyn to be coinzed, shall have power to redeime the samyn at the prycess efter following—viz., fiftie sex schillinges [4s. 8d. sterling] for the unce of Scotts silver worke, fiftie aught schillings [4s. 10d.] for everie unce of Inglis silver worke, and xxxiiij lib. vjs viiid [about £2, 15s. sterling] for everie unce of gold."[7]

Poor John Charteris of Barncleuch, whose heart, as has been shown above, was in the Royalist camp, was "relieved of sex silver spoones, Scots work," weighing ten ounces. Marion M'Clellan, widow of James Ramsay deceased, was ordered to give up "her bairne's silver worke, and that notwithstanding of any reassones proponit in the contrair." Every plate-chest in Dumfries and Galloway to which the protection of Lord Nithsdale could not be extended seems to have been ransacked, and it makes sore the antiquary's heart to ponder on the loss to art of so much that, had it been preserved, would now be worth fifty times the value then realised.

The burgh of Dumfries, no longer amenable to its feudal

[7] Book of the Kirkcudbright War Committee, p. 22.

lord, declared for the Covenant. Nithsdale, therefore, had to rely on his own castle of Caerlaverock and on the Thrieve, of which he was keeper, to maintain the Royalist cause in the south-west. In Caerlaverock he had a garrison of 100 men, in Thrieve of 80. The local Covenanting troops were not yet to be relied on, so the Estates sent Colonel Home with a detachment from General Leslie's army to lay siege to both strongholds. After being invested for thirteen weeks, Nithsdale sent word to the king that he could hold out no longer unless he were relieved. To this the king replied that as it was impossible to send relief, the earl must capitulate on the best terms he could obtain. Accordingly, on September 26, 1640, both castles were surrendered to Colonel Home, the garrisons being allowed to march out with bag and baggage and all the honours of war. The furniture and other goods in Caerlaverock were exceedingly rich, and a full inventory of them was taken — the Estates holding themselves bound to make full restitution of all property belonging to Lord Nithsdale and his friends on condition that they should never again "tack arms in prejudice of this kingdom, nor shall have any intelligence with any prejudice thereof, upon their honour and credit."

Nithsdale being a man of considerable culture, and on this account popularly known as "The Philosopher," had collected a considerable library at Caerlaverock, at the cost, it was said, of £200 sterling, equivalent, according to present value, to about £1000. He had also built a fine range, forming the east and south sides of the courtyard, adopting the Renaissance style, and decorating the pediments of the windows with heraldic carving and representation of classical subjects. All this work now remains a melancholy monument to the vanity of human wishes. Since its surrender to Home in 1640 the castle has never been inhabited.

Lord Nithsdale interpreted taking arms "in prejudice of the kingdom" in a large sense. He threw himself heartily into the king's cause against the Covenant, and in consequence the Estates, as they were perfectly entitled to do, ordered the dismantling of Caerlaverock and the Thrieve. They remain to this day the most notable ruins of domestic and defensive architecture on the western border of Scotland.

Nithsdale justified his apparent breach of faith on the ground that Home had violated the conditions on which the castle had been surrendered, suffering damage to be done to it which, it was alleged, could not be repaired for less than £40,000.

As for the Thrieve, the war committee of Kirkcudbright committed the dismantling of it to the Laird of Balmaghie, and the materials were disposed of for the benefit of the war fund.

Notwithstanding the prevailing civil war, time was found in 1642 to establish postal communication between Great Britain and Ireland by way of Portpatrick, then known as Port Montgomerie. Postal service was also constituted between Portpatrick and Edinburgh and Portpatrick and Carlisle, and Robert Glencorse, merchant in Dumfries, was appointed in charge of the arrangements.

John Corsane of Meikleknox was Provost of Dumfries in the eventful year of 1640, and bestirred himself, as became a zealous Covenanter, to carry out the commission appointed to him in receiving from the collectors of Dumfries and Galloway the tenth and twentieth pennies levied by the Estates on all lands and heritages for the maintenance of the army of the Covenant. The South Regiment, as Lord Kirkcudbright's levy was called, had its headquarters at Dumfries, under the command of Colonel James Agnew of Auchrochar, brother of the hereditary sheriff. Keen Covenanter as was the Provost, blood is thicker than water: Corsane was not only a nephew of the Royalist Nithsdale, but, which touched him perhaps more nearly, his wife was a Maxwell, daughter and joint-heiress of Robert of Dinwoodie. He bestirred himself to bring about a reconciliation between the two parties; but all the reward he reaped for his pains was that in 1644 he was fined 10,000 merks by Parliament.

The Scottish Covenanters were now co-operating with the English Puritans under Cromwell, for the Solemn League and Covenant had been signed and ratified in 1643. The old order of things was passing swiftly away; feudal ties that had stood for centuries were falling apart; a new cleavage was developing, not on the lines of clan against clan, or nation against nation, as in the old Border times, but in the direction of class against class, creed against creed, Crown against people. There was less brutality than in the old warfare, but not less bitterness; less bloodshed and wanton destruction of property, but just as much desire to injure an opponent by legal confiscation.

The general drift of opinion, however, was not without occasional reaction. Such was the case in Dumfriesshire in 1644, when Sir James Maxwell, a zealous Royalist, was elected Provost of Dumfries. The South Regiment had been marched away to join Leslie's army, and the country was left exposed to the hereditary influence of local families. Montrose, accompanied by the Earls of Nithsdale, Hartfell,[8] and Annandale, and Sir John Charteris of Amisfield, crossed the Border with a small force of English troops, entered Dumfries on April 14, hauled down the blue banner of the Covenant, and hoisted the Royal Standard. Then he

---

[8] Johnstone, Earl of Hartfell, was son of the Johnstone chief slain by Nithsdale's elder brother. Hartfell, Annandale, and Charteris were all at this time members of the Covenanting war committee of Dumfries.

waited, but waited in vain, for the rising of Royalists which Hartfell and Annandale had promised should take place. Hearing that the Earl of Callendar, who was to have reinforced him, had gone over to the enemy and was advancing against him with 7000 men, he moved to Carlisle, bitterly inveighing against Hartfell and Annandale, whom he charged with treachery. These noblemen, it would seem, were playing a double game—one with which the student of Scottish history is only too familiar. They were trying to keep friends with both parties till one should prove decidedly stronger than the other.

The brief supremacy of Montrose, which followed on the series of his victories over the Covenanters culminating at Kilsyth, was overthrown by the crushing defeat at Philiphaugh on September 13, 1645. Of the men of Dumfries and Galloway engaged on that field the majority were on the winning side, including Lord Kirkcudbright's excellent South Regiment;[9] but some fought for the king under the Earl of Hartfell, who thus redeemed his fame from the slur of treachery imputed to it by Montrose.

[9] A bounty of 15,000 marks was voted by the Scottish Parliament to the South Regiment for their gallantry at Philiphaugh.

NOTE H.

BLAEU'S GEOGRAPHY.

OF this monumental work, executed by John Blaeu of Amsterdam, volume vi. contains a survey of the counties of Scotland. The survey of Scotland was carried out by Timothy Pont, appointed minister of Dunnett, in Caithness, in 1600, who died between 1610 and 1614. His maps and papers, containing a vast mass of topographic, historic, and antiquarian matter, passed into the hands of Sir Robert Gordon of Straloch, who was directed by Charles I. to use them in assisting John Blaeu in his Atlas of the World. But it was not till 1662 that the results of Pont's labours were made public. Sir John Scot of Scotstarvit had then received charge of the work; most of the explanatory articles are from the pen of Sir John Gordon, but the General Assembly directed the ministers to supply such further information as was wanted, and the descriptions are supplemented by extracts from Camden's 'Britannia.' The following extracts, translated from the Latin descriptions of Dumfries and Galloway, are such as refer to the appearance of the country and condition of the inhabitants in the early part of the seventeenth century. Genealogical references, which abound, have been omitted, as well as extracts from Camden :—

LIDDESDALE.

. . . In Liddesdale there are no crops; nothing but pasture and moor land, which we call *Venen*, the soil being most suitable for digging peats for fuel.

EWESDALE AND ESKDALE.

. . . The English wars prevent us treating more fully of these and certain other regions.

ANNANDALE.

. . . Lochmaben is famous for a fish unknown elsewhere, called by the country people Vandese or Gevandese [vendace].
. . . On the shores of Ruthwell, opposite England, they make excellent salt, by harrowing, heaping together, and boiling the sand. Also, which is both profitable and pleasant, the inhabitants

of that boundary watch for salmon entering the channels of the Solway, and when they see them ascending the flood, they enter the river on horseback and easily transfix and land them with spears of three prongs.

NITHSDALE.

. . . Dumfries is a pleasant, flourishing town, the capital of the whole county; celebrated for its bridge, supported on nine arches of squared stone, and of such width that it admits of two chariots being driven abreast. . . . At the second milestone from Dumfries lies that noble mine of peat, Lochar — ten miles long and three miles wide. The mossy sods dug thence, and dried in the sun, afford fuel to the whole of that district.

GALLOWAY, by Mr John Maclellan.

. . . All the rivers are celebrated for salmon-fisheries, but the Dee excels the others. The whole region is most healthy both in climate and soil. . . . The natives are strong and warlike. Assuredly in the battle of Newburn, on the Tyne in England, a handful of Galloway knights, under the leadership of Patrick M'Kie, whose son was killed in that action, gave a splendid example of their gallantry, for with their long spears they threw the dense body of the enemy into such confusion as to secure an easy victory for their comrades. Formerly this race was prone to maintaining feuds, but it has gradually learnt by more humane culture and civilised religion to lay aside its ferocity. The gentry, alike with hand and head, are quite equal to any in refinement of person and manners. The country-folk are of powerful build, and not deficient in understanding.

Those who live in the Moors—that is to say, in the wastes—make a living by rearing cattle, and have large flocks of sheep. The sheep there are of the best kind, both in respect of mutton and excellence of fleece. Large quantities of wool are carried hence to foreign parts by merchants, who derive no small profit thereby.

Those who live in the Machars—that is to say, the arable ground and plains—sustain life by agriculture; nor do they lack fertile pasture and flocks; oats of small but well-filled grain is grown there, from which they make the best of meal.

Galloway produces horses of but small size, but game and strong, which bring everywhere the highest price. . . . They call them Galloway nags; so that Englishmen call all good horses Galloways.

CHAPTER XI.

FROM THE SURRENDER OF CHARLES I. IN 1647 TO THE DEATH OF CHARLES II. IN 1685.

AFTER the surrender, in 1647, of Charles I. by the Scottish Covenanting army to the English commissioners, the captive king renewed negotiations with the Scottish Estates under the Marquis of Hamilton. He promised to ratify the Solemn League and Covenant by Act of Parliament, to establish Presbyterianism, provided the Covenant should not be forced on any one against his religious scruples. The moderate Covenanters, represented by Hamilton, who accepted these terms, became known as the Engagers. But their policy found no favour in the south-west. Headed by the Marquis of Argyll, the Westland Whigs prepared to resist by force; and in 1648, after Hamilton had been defeated by Cromwell at Preston, Lord Eglinton marched 6000 men to Edinburgh, and placed them at the disposal of Argyll. This was the famous "Whigamore Raid," and it was from these Westland Whigs of Ayrshire and Galloway that one of the great parties in the British Parliament afterwards derived its name. Argyll was now in a position to dictate the policy of the Estates. The Solemn League and Covenant was renewed, and an Act was passed removing all Engagers from offices of trust. Nevertheless, on the execution of Charles I., the Estates immediately proclaimed the Prince of Wales Charles II., which brought the country into war with Cromwell. The defeat of the Scottish Royalists under General David Leslie at Dunbar, and the extinction of the cause of Charles II. at Worcester, left the Protector and Commonwealth supreme in Scotland. In the army that fought for the king at Worcester, the three regiments of Kirkcudbright, Galloway, and Dumfries, as they are named in the Journals of Parliament, December 2, 1650, were under command of Robert Montgomerie, probably a cadet of the house of Eglinton.

Cromwell's task of subduing Scotland was made easy by the insane dissensions prevailing between the sterner Covenanters and Engagers. The Estates, at the instance of the General Assembly, were busy purging the army, not only of Engagers or Moderate Presbyterians, but of Popish Malignants. In this way, many of the king's stoutest and most influential supporters were compelled to inaction. But, when Cromwell's Ironsides rode to the gates of Edinburgh, it was time to throw aside such childish nonsense; and all, without distinction of creed or party, were admitted to serve in the army. Upon this, the more fanatical of the ministers, raising an outcry, led a new party into the field called the Protesters, and all was confusion once more.

Thus, in Galloway, where some new levies had been energetically brought together, Lord Kirkcudbright, Lord Cassilis, Gordon of Knockgray, and Macdowall of Garthland followed the popular preachers Rutherford, Livingstone, and Maclellan in declaring for the king and Estates against Cromwell, but only on condition of "the Protest": Sir Andrew Agnew, Sir Robert Adair of Kilhilt, and other lairds, bitterly denounced the Protesters, but stood for the king and Estates; while Sir Patrick Agnew (hereditary sheriff and father of Sir Andrew), Lord Galloway, and Lord Kenmure incurred the opprobrious name of Cavaliers, by declaring for the king independently of the Estates.

Cromwell ruled Scotland as a conquered kingdom. The constitution was suspended. English judges were appointed in place of the Lords of Session; and, in the rural districts, hereditary jurisdictions were replaced by the Protector's nominees. Colonel Matthew Alured was sent to Galloway as sheriff principal, superseding Sir Andrew Agnew and Lord Kirkcudbright. Heavy fines were exacted from those suspected of malignity. The Earl of Galloway was mulcted in 10,000 merks. Kenmure Castle was burnt to the ground, and so was M'Dowall's tower of Freuch. Mr John Livingstone, minister of Stranraer, a stout Protester, was required to wait on the Protector in London. "In the year 1654," he says, "I propounded to the Lord Protector in London that he would take off the heavy fines which he had laid on several in Scotland, which neither they were able to pay, and the payment would alienate their minds the more. He seemed to like the overture; but when he had spoken with his council, many of them being to have a share in these fines, they went on in their purpose."

Preaching before Cromwell and his generals during this visit, Livingstone is said to have prayed for King Charles. Some of his hearers were very angry, and desired that he should be arrested at once. "Let him alone," said Cromwell; "he is a good man, and what are we poor men to kings of England?"

Lord Kenmure, his fair house on Loch Ken being burnt to the ground, hoisted his "drum," a barrel of brandy on a pole, enlisted all the vagabonds and broken men he could find, and marched about the country robbing and making prisoners in the name of the king. Their chief haunt was the Highland border, but detachments scoured the Lowlands in all directions. One such band of brigands, under Captain Somerville of Drum, surprised Sir Andrew Agnew and Lady Agnes, his wife, in their house at Innermessan, and carried them off prisoners. But, finding the country much opposed to him, Somerville, having taken the ex-sheriff sixteen miles, released him on receiving as ransom a bond for 10,000 merks, and made his way back to the Highlands.

In 1656 M'Dowall of Garthland went to London to make formal submission to the Commonwealth on behalf of the barons of Galloway, in consideration of which Alured was recalled, and Sir Andrew Agnew was reinstated as sheriff.

It has been stated above that the activity of the Legislature in proceeding against witches was not manifested in Dumfriesshire and Galloway until a later period than in the rest of Scotland. From 1656 onwards, however, this devilish business was pressed with diligence by some of the Church courts.

A single instance, taken from each of the three counties, may suffice to show the terrible power which any malevolent or cowardly witness might exert against a fellow-creature. The acquittal of a person accused of witchcraft was exceedingly rare. In most instances torture sufficed to extort a confession, when the death sentence followed as a matter of course. Where no confession could be extracted, the result was the same; the jury, in terror of the consequences of suffering a witch to live, brought in a verdict of guilty, and the woman (for by far the greater number of accused were women) was sentenced either to be "wirreit" (strangled) first and burnt afterwards, or else to be burnt "quick" (alive).

On April 2, 1659, ten women were put on their trial as witches before two judges at Dumfries. Nine were convicted. Against the tenth the charge was found not proven; nevertheless she was required to find security to the extent of £50 for her good behaviour, and banished from the parish. Eight ministers were appointed by the presbytery to "attend the nine witches, and that they take their own convenient opportunity to confer with them; also that they be assisting to the brethren of Dumfries and Galloway the day of the execution." The victims were taken to the public place of execution in Dumfries, bound to stakes, strangled, and burnt to ashes. Such a scene, if enacted at the present day at the command of some Central African tyrant, would send a thrill of indignation through all our land, yet two centuries and a half have not elapsed since similar horrors took place in almost every market town of Scotland and England. Forty years more of civilisation, and we find a new generation carrying on the same odious persecution in Galloway. In 1698 Elspeth M'Ewen was charged before the kirk-session of Dalry with having a pin in her kipple-foot (the end of the rafters of her house), by means of which she could draw milk from the cows of her neighbours. She could also interfere with the poultry of others, to increase or diminish the supply of eggs. One of the most convincing parts of the evidence against the accused was, that the minister's horse, which was sent to bring her up for trial, trembled with fear when she mounted, and sweated drops of blood. On conviction, Elspeth was sent to prison at Kirkcudbright, where she was made to suffer such torments that she prayed to be put to death. There was no difficulty about that: she had only to make confession of witchcraft, and having done so, the helpless creature was mercilessly burnt to death.

The record is not so black in Wigtownshire. There is, indeed, no evidence of any witches having been put to death in that county, though one of the chief witnesses against Maggie Osborne, who was burnt as a witch in Ayr, was an elder of New Luce. This worthy deponed that, after Maggie had received the Holy Communion in the Moor Kirk of Luce, he saw her spit out the wafer at the church-door, and that the devil, in the shape of a toad, swallowed it. On this and many other charges of equal absurdity poor Maggie, who kept a hostelry at Ayr, was condemned to be burnt to death—which was done, as usual, in presence of many ministers of the message of peace and goodwill towards men.[1]

The marriage of the Honourable Janet Dalrymple, daughter of the first Lord Stair, to David Dunbar, younger of Baldoon, which took place in 1669, must be briefly referred to here, because it has formed the theme of one of the most celebrated romances—the 'Bride of Lammermoor.' Janet had plighted her troth to young Lord Rutherford, but her parents were opposed to their union, and favoured the rival suitor Dunbar. Rutherford pressed for an interview with his betrothed, which was granted, but in the presence of Lady Stair, who seems quite to have broken the girl's spirit. It ended in Janet giving him back her half of the coin which, according to custom, they had broken in plighting their troth; when Rutherford departed, declaring that she would be the world's wonder for the thing she had done.

The marriage with Dunbar took place, but on the wedding night terrible screams were heard in the bridal chamber. The

[1] In claiming for Wigtownshire a cleaner record than that of other counties in the persecution of witches, I do not wish to suggest that the belief in witchcraft was less prevalent there than elsewhere. It has, indeed, hardly died out at the present day. I was well acquainted with one Jean Tait, who gloried in the reputation of a witch. She died about twenty-five years ago; and an old man still living has told me many stories of the spells she cast on cattle, poultry, and even on human beings. One Sunday morning I went into this old woman's cottage to ask for a light. She was sitting reading, and when she rose to get me what I wanted, I had the curiosity to look at the book—for it would have been little in keeping with her reputation had the volume been, as I thought it was, the Holy Scriptures. It turned out, however, to be Lord Chesterfield's Letters to his Son!

wedding guests broke in, and found Dunbar fearfully wounded and the bride insane, shrieking to them to "take up their bonny bridegroom." Within three weeks she died raving mad, but young Baldoon recovered. It was never known who had attacked him—his bride or, as some said, the disappointed lover, who had hidden himself in order to take this revenge.[2]

On the restoration of Charles II. Scotland was placed under the government of Middleton, once a pikeman in the ranks of Colonel Hepburn's regiment, afterwards a soldier of fortune who led the Royalists against Monk in the Highlands, now created an earl. Under his presidency the Scottish Parliament of 1661 passed the Rescissory Act, whereby all Acts passed since 1640 were annulled, the Covenant was declared void, and all officials were compelled to renew their titles. Episcopacy was restored by the Act of 1662. Three hundred and fifty ministers stood firm for Presbyterianism, and were deprived of their livings. Among these were the incumbents of almost every parish in Galloway and Dumfriesshire. Only two ministers in the last-named county are reported to have conformed, and submitted to collation by the new bishops. Middleton, making a tour of inspection through the south-west in October 1662, found the whole mass of the people greatly exasperated against the oath of supremacy and the expulsion of their ministers. The landowners and civil office-bearers, though more pliant, were severely dealt with. Most of them, however, were reinstated on receiving what was inaccurately called the king's free pardon—a grace made conditional on payment of heavy

---

[2] Alexander Symson, minister of Kirkinner about 1663-1680, author of 'A Short Description of Galloway,' speaks highly of David Dunbar, and wrote his elegy when, in 1682, he was killed by a fall from his horse in Edinburgh.

fines by those who had made terms with the Commonwealth. These fines levied on landowners, merchants, and farmers amounted in Dumfriesshire to £164,200 Scots, in Kirkcudbright to £51,400, and in Wigtownshire to £45,560. It may be easily imagined how payment of this large amount, which was exacted within six months of notification, pressed with extraordinary hardship upon those who had already been taxed to the utmost by the Covenanting war committees, and in fact it brought about the ruin of many families.

The edicts against Nonconformity were little regarded by the Westland Whigs. The parish churches were neglected, and in 1663 Gabriel Semple, the ejected minister of Kirkpatrick-Durham, finding the house of Laird Neilson of Corsock insufficient to contain those who flocked to hear him, removed into the garden, whence, when it too was filled to overflowing, he went into a field. This, it is said, was the first of the field-conventicles which were to have such prominence in coming years.

The induction of curates, as the Episcopal incumbents of parishes were called, became the occasion of riots in several places. A commission, consisting of the Earls of Linlithgow, Galloway, and Annandale, Lord Drumlanrig, and Sir John Wauchope of Niddrie, was sent to inquire into one such disturbance at Kirkcudbright. In consequence of their finding, Lord Kirkcudbright, John Carson, ex-provost, and William Ewart, provost-elect, were sent prisoners to Edinburgh, as well as five men who went in place of their wives who had been arrested. It does not transpire what happened to the peer, but Carson was sentenced to pay a fine of 8000 merks, and Ewart to banishment from the kingdom for life. The other men were released, but their wives were condemned to stand for two hours on each of two market days at the cross of Kirkcudbright with papers on their faces setting forth their offence.

After disposing of the Kirkcudbright rioters, the commissioners held a sitting at Kirkpatrick-Irongray, where the induction of a curate had been the occasion of an uproar. William Arnot of Littlepark, who was found, on trial in Edinburgh, to have been the chief promoter of the riots here, was fined 5000 merks. The sentences on Carson, Ewart, and Arnot were subsequently mitigated on petition to the Privy Council.

In this year Middleton, who had incurred the enmity of Lauderdale, fell into disgrace and was removed from the office of viceroy. He was succeeded by Lauderdale. This nobleman, originally a keen Covenanter, showed little outward sympathy with Nonconformity, though supposed to be secretly in favour of tolerance. His position depended on his being able to act in harmony with Archbishop Sharpe and the other prelates, who were now once more Lords of Parliament. There was certainly no suspicion of leniency in their policy, though Sharpe had once been an ardent supporter of the Covenant.

By a Privy Council minute of February 24, 1663, twenty-five ministers of the Synod of Galloway were ordered to remove from their parishes before March 20, and to appear before the Council on March 24, "to answer for their former disobedience." The Parliament of that year greatly increased the stringency of the Acts against Nonconformity. It had already been made an offence to attend the ministrations of the suspended ministers; non-attendance at public worship was now made a crime, punishable by forfeiture of not more than one-fourth of the offender's property, and, in the case of merchants, loss of liberty to trade. Sir James Turner, another ex-Covenanter, was appointed to command the troops in Dumfriesshire, Galloway, and Ayrshire, and co-operated with Hamilton, the new Bishop of Galloway, in carrying out the Acts against Nonconformity. An irresponsible tribunal, consisting of nine prelates and thirty-five laymen, called the Court of High Commission, was instituted in 1664 to direct enforcement of these Acts. Fines were imposed on recusants, and relentlessly exacted. Resort was had to one specially odious kind of punishment, as shown by the following minute passed in a subsequent year by the packed town council of Dumfries :—

"September 5, 1670. The Counsall being informed that there is a company of foot and a partie of hors appoynted to quarter in this burgh, which is occasioned by several inhabitants who doe not frequent the ordinances, it is therefoir enacted that such as are able and have never yitt come to the churche of this burgh to hear the service of the minister, shall have sex foot soldiers quartered upon them, or two hors."

Where fines and oppressive billeting of soldiers in private houses failed to compel outward conformity, resort was had to banishing the more resolute Nonconformists. Gordon of Earlston was condemned in 1664 to perpetual exile on pain of death. Alexander Smith, minister of Colvend, was brought before the Court of High Commission, and on being interrogated by Archbishop Sharpe, he addressed him not as "my lord" but "sir." Lord Rothes asked Smith if he knew to whom he was speaking. "Yes, my lord," replied Smith, "I do. I speak to Mr James Sharpe, once a fellow-minister." Smith was punished by imprisonment in the Thieves' Hole, where he nearly died of hardship, and was afterwards banished to the Shetland Isles.

At this time many people of all ranks evaded transportation and the horrors of the plantations by taking refuge in Ulster. Those who remained had to endure the rigours of the repressive Acts, intensified in their severity by their enforcement at the hands of rough and dissipated dragoons. There were, of course, many cultivated and well-meaning gentlemen among the officers; but the very nature of the service demanded of the troops, required their employment in small detachments under sergeants and corporals not more gentle in manner or more scrupulous than themselves.

But the days of the Court of High Commission soon drew to a close. Some of its members sickened of the work. The Archbishop of Glasgow asked to be allowed to resign his see rather than continue to act on the court. It was dissolved in 1665. The oppression, however, within the limits of Turner's command, was not perceptibly relaxed. Treatment like this could have but one result among people of such stout mettle as the Covenanting Whigs. It drove them into rebellion against a tyrannical Government.

The attitude of the barons and chief landowners in the south-west has been greatly misrepresented, as if they had joined heartily in oppressing their tenants. Some of them, no doubt, as the Lords Galloway and Kenmure, were supporters of the Government and Episcopacy by conviction; others, like Nithsdale and most of the Maxwells, were in disgrace as Papists; but the majority of them, especially the better educated, though philosophically indifferent to theological and ecclesiastical controversy, yet sympathised with the people. Nevertheless, having had bitter experience of civil war, and having also a prudent eye to their own security, they supported the established Government to the best of their power. The time was at hand when every man had to cast his lot with one party or the other. On November 13, 1666, a party of Turner's troopers seized the patch of corn of an old man named Grier, in the Glenkens, and then tied lighted matches between his fingers, in order to extort from him a fine in which he had been condemned. Maclellan of Barscob, who had himself suffered for Nonconformity, accompanied by young John Maxwell of Monreith, Colonel Wallace, and one other, broke into the house and released the old man. The troopers drew their swords: Maclellan fired a pistol charged with a broken tobacco-pipe. A *mêlée* ensued, which ended in the flight of the troopers. Sir James Turner said Maclellan's shot landed in the belly of one of his corporals. There were more soldiers in the neighbouring village of Balmaclellan, so Maclellan, fearing a surprise, called for volunteers to capture them. Plenty of stout lads responded. They marched to Balmaclellan, making prisoners of a dozen troopers there, and the flame of civil war was kindled once more. On the 15th Maclellan made a masterly move on Dumfries, where he surprised Sir James Turner in his quarters at night and took him prisoner, with some of his men, of whom, as Turner himself says, there were only thirteen in the town at that time, the rest being on detachment duty in the country. He reported that one of his soldiers named Hamilton was killed because he would not take the Covenant. Next day the party returned in triumph to Dalry, where Mr Henderson, the expelled minister of Dumfries, gave Turner such a good dinner that the soldier confesses in his Memoirs, "Though he and I be of different persuasions, yet I will say he entertained me with real kindness."

It is natural that Turner's memory should be held in odium by the descendants of the people whom it was his duty to oppress. He went by the name of "Bite-the-sheep"; and, in fact, seems to have acted with such tyranny and cruelty as to bring discredit on his cause.

Colonel Wallace, a soldier of experience, was now placed in command of the insurgents, who numbered by this time some hundreds. They marched in very stormy weather through Clydesdale to Lanark, and are said to have numbered 2000 strong on leaving that town. But when the gates of Edinburgh were found to be closed against them many deserted the blue flag of the Covenant, and on November 28 the gallant band were dispersed at the battle of Rullion Green, on the Pentland Hills, by General Dalziel.

> "The trumpets blew, and the colours flew,
> And every man to his armour drew;
> The Whigs were never so much aghast,
> As to see their saddles toom sae fast.
>
> The cleverest men stood in the van,
> The Whigs they took to their heels and ran;
> But such a raking never was seen
> As the raking o' the Rullion Green." [3]

Here Sir James Turner, who had been kept a prisoner since his surprise at Dumfries, regained his liberty. Twenty of the insurgents were hanged in Edinburgh, and five-and-thirty in Clydesdale, Dumfries, and Galloway. Among the former were Major John M'Culloch of Barholm, Captain Andrew Arnot, and two brothers, John and Robert Gordon of Knockbrex, John Gordon from Irongray, and Neilson of Corsock. The heads of M'Culloch and the two Gordons of Knockbrex were sent to Kirkcudbright for exposure on the town gate, while the right arms of all the victims were consigned to Lanark, for exhibition in the place where they had been raised in swearing to the Covenant. Neilson was compelled to suffer the torture of the "boot" six days before his execution, in hopes of extracting from him information of an organised rebellion, but he confessed to no knowledge of anything premeditated.

Various families of the name of Gordon have left their mark on the page of Galloway history by reason of their

[3] Ballad of Rullion Green.

sufferings in the cause of religious liberty. William Gordon of Roberton was killed at Rullion Green, and his brother-in-law, John Gordon of Lagmore, died of his wounds a few days after the battle.

John Maxwell, flying from the field on a good grey horse, rode to his distant home in Galloway, and turning his steed into a field at Monreith, still known as Pentland, vowed that it should never look through a bridle again, as a reward for having saved his master's life. The proverb "As good as Pentland" is current in the district to this day. Maxwell was afterwards hotly pursued through various parts of the kingdom. On a subsequent occasion, to escape from some soldiers in Edinburgh, he darted down a close and into a change-house, where the landlady locked him into the meal-girnel. The soldiers came and hunted every corner of the house in vain. They vowed the fugitive had entered it; but baffled in their pursuit, they called for drink, and sat down to discuss it. One of them sat on the top of the meal-chest within which Maxwell lay hid. "I wadna say," cried he, "but yon bloody Whig is in this vera kist. Gudewife, gie's the key till we see for oorsells." The landlady was equal to the occasion. Going to the foot of the stairs she called up, "Jeanie, lass, rin awa' and ask the gudeman for the key o' the girnel, till we see if a Whig can lie in the meal and no gie a hoast[4] wi't." The soldiers laughed, finished their liquor, and went off. Maxwell eventually escaped to Ireland, where he died, and the lands of Monreith were resettled on his more wary younger brother, of whom the present proprietor is the direct descendant.

Among the prisoners taken at Rullion Green were John Grier in Fourmerkland, and William Welsh in Carsphairn. The court ordered these men to be taken to Dumfries and hanged there, and further charged the magistrates "to sie

[4] A cough.

their sentence for hanging the persounes, and affixing of the heides and right armes upon the eminenest pairts of this Burgh." The town council "condescendit that the bridgeport is the fittest place quhereupon that the heids and armes should be affixed; and therfoir appointed them to be affixed on that place."[5] Some time later information reached the council of a plot to take away these grisly trophies "under cloudes of nicht to the prejudice of this burgh," so they were removed to the top of the tolbooth.

The insurrection of Rullion Green having been quelled and avenged, strong representations were made to the Government by their staunchest supporters in Galloway—Lords Galloway and Kenmure and Sir Andrew Agnew—that the exactions of the soldiery, and specially the way in which they were enforced, were intolerable to the people. Upon this Lauderdale, who knew the danger and cruelty of the course forced on the Government by the prelates, appointed the Lords Nithsdale and Kenmure, and Ferguson of Craigdarroch, all undoubted king's men, to inquire into the allegations of embezzlement, oppression, and violence against Sir James Turner and Sir William Bannatyne in the exercise of their military commands in the south-west. They reported that these gentlemen had been guilty of various illegal acts and exactions, in consequence of which Turner was cashiered, Bannatyne was fined £300 and ordered to leave the kingdom, and officers were forbidden to billet their men in private houses.

Sir James Turner left behind him when he died a very remarkable memoir, and deserves to be heard in his own defence. He had served long as a soldier of fortune on the Continent—a pretty rough school, as he confesses: "I had swallowed without chewing, in Germanie, a very dangerous

[5] Town Council Minutes.

maxime which militarie men there too much follow: which was, that so we serve our master honnestlie, it is no great matter what master we serve."

In 1641, acting on this maxim, he joined Lord Kirkcudbright's regiment as major. But he cared little for Kirk and Covenant: "All this while I did not take the Nationall Covenant, not because I refused to do it, for I wold have no bones to take, sueare and sign it, and observe it too; for I had then principle, haveing not yet studied a better one, that I wronged not my conscience in doing any thing I was commanded to doe by those whom I served."

In fact, Turner was one of a school the world was becoming too squeamish to brook. He earned his living by the sword, and cared not a pint of wine for the justice of the cause which he served. Thus he remained a soldier of the Covenant till 1647, being with General Leslie when he slaughtered the garrison of Dunaverty in cold blood — 300 brave Highlanders; and afterwards changing sides, was sent back to Galloway, where he showed little tenderness for his old comrades: "In the month of March 1665 I was the second time commanded to that steuartrie, with a partie consisting of one hundreth and tuentie foot and threttie horse, to put the laws concerning Church ordinances in execution: the people haveing been extreamlie outragieous to their ministers, and disobedient to discipline. I stayd about two months in that countrey, and reduced it to ane indifferent good order, by cessing in some, and by both cessing and fineing others, and by faire meanes prevaileing with many. . . . From such as the ministers and I judged obstinate, I tooke some money, . . . as 20s. scots for everie Lord's day they had absented themselves from their parish churches."

Heaven help the folk who had such judges set over them in spiritual matters! One feels indignation, not at such instruments as rough, impatient Turner, but at the criminal folly of those who employed them.

Lauderdale, convinced of the impossibility of dragooning his resolute countrymen into conformity, set himself to devise conciliatory measures, and the Earl of Tweeddale proposed that an indulgence be granted to the more moderate among the ejected ministers. Unfortunately, at this juncture a fanatic preacher named Mitchell attempted, on July 7, 1668, to assassinate Archbishop Sharpe with a pistol. Missing the intended victim, the ball broke the arm of the Bishop of Orkney, who was entering the archbishop's carriage, and it may well be believed that the act reflected disgrace on the whole Presbyterian party. Nevertheless, a year later—in July 1669—the king empowered the Council to reinstate some of the ejected ministers in their churches.

This act—the Indulgence, as it was called—well as it was meant, proved to be but further cause of dissension. It pleased neither Episcopalians nor Presbyterians. The latter, indeed, were well pleased at first with what seemed a triumph of their cause, and was really a considerable concession to their principles. But those ministers who accepted the Indulgence, by devoting themselves to moral teaching and eschewing controversial and political topics, disappointed many of those who at first flocked to hear them. The sterner divines continued to hold field-conventicles, and denounced their brethren who had accepted the Indulgence as "Erastians," "king's curates," and "dumb dogs." This was more exciting doctrine than the calm exposition of Scriptural truth: the Covenanters had learnt to associate bitter party feeling with religion, and the parish churches were again emptied in favour of the field-meetings. These assemblies were proscribed by the Act of 1670, and the old and hateful order of things—resistance and repression—began again.

It is easy enough to blame the Government for resorting to a policy they had discarded because of its failure to restore order; but in truth much excuse is to be found for them in the dogged intolerance of the hill-folk, as the conventicle-men were called: the insults and injuries to which certain of them subjected the curates and indulged ministers formed some excuse for the authorities in their endeavour to put an end to fanaticism. For instance, the houses of Mr Rowe, minister of Balmaclellan, and Mr Lyon, minister of Urr, were broken into by these irreconcilables. Mr Rowe was dragged out of bed, beaten, and his goods stolen; Mrs Lyon, in the absence of her husband, was carried off to the hills. There must have been plenty who would have blamed the Government had they been slow to put an end to such disorder.

But the remedy was far worse than the disease. Field-preaching was made a capital offence, and field-preaching was interpreted to mean expounding Scripture in the open air to any beyond the members of the preacher's own household. Attendance at conventicles, and even knowledge that conventicles were to be held without making the same known, were construed into treason. To enforce this Act, Lauderdale directed the formation of a militia. Dumfriesshire was to furnish 700 foot and 77 horse, and, curiously enough, the ministers were called on to furnish lists of the fencible men [6] in each parish. The uniform decreed by the Commissioners at the cost of £24 Scots per man was a good blue cloth coat lined with white serge, stout shoes, stockings, a black hat, two shirts, two cravats, an "honest" pair of breeches, and a waistcoat. Of the infantry two-thirds were to be musketeers, the remainder pikemen.

Lauderdale, incensed, not unreasonably, at the rejection by

[6] Men fit for military service.

the Presbyterian leaders of a comprehensive scheme proposed by Archbishop Leighton of Glasgow for the incorporation of Episcopalians and Presbyterians in one Established Church, now showed himself resolved to enforce the penal Act of 1670.

The impending storm was a long time in brewing. The lords and lairds of Dumfries and Galloway, though mostly favouring the Covenanting cause, continued to discharge their duties as Commissioners, and the Acts against conventicles, if not allowed to slumber, were drowsily administered. Indeed, but for the bitterness between the two sects of Presbyterians—those who accepted the Indulgence and the Irreconcilables—matters would probably have continued to run their course until they settled down, either by the people becoming reconciled to Episcopacy, or by the gradual re-establishment of Presbyterian Church government. Unhappily the prelates proved incapable of the necessary forbearance. Field-preaching continued as popular as ever in the south-west, owing to the favourite preachers having refused the Indulgence, and the bishops, irritated by seeing the parish churches deserted for the hillsides, prevailed on the Council in 1678 to require the barons to come under signed obligation, binding themselves, their families and servants, to abstain from attending conventicles or harbouring such as did attend them. This brought matters to a crisis. Many of the western nobility and gentry were summoned to appear before the Privy Council to answer for their nonconformity, and, failing to obey, were declared outlaws. Others, again, were appointed as commissioners to enforce the Acts against conventicles, and were rewarded for doing so by receiving part of the fines levied on offenders. Not only the militia, but a large force of Highlanders, were marched into Galloway and Nithsdale.

The sheriffs and stewards of the district, being suspected of too much leniency in dealing with their people, were obliged to appoint deputies selected by the Privy Council. The Earl of Nithsdale, staunch Papist though he was, was called on to delegate his powers as steward of Kirkcudbright to Graham of Claverhouse and two others; so also was Sir Andrew Agnew as Sheriff of Wigtownshire.

John Graham of Claverhouse, who, by the sternness with which he subsequently administered the Acts against the Covenanters, earned the undying hatred of the Westland Whigs and their descendants, was appointed in December 1678 to command the forces in Dumfries and Galloway. His first act as Sheriff-Depute of Kirkcudbright, an office in which he was associated with the fierce Sir Robert Grierson of Lag, was the demolition of a large building on the west bank of the Nith, opposite Dumfries, which the non-indulgers used as a meeting-house. In his report of this action to the Privy Council there occurs a sentence which, being the keynote of all his subsequent conduct, should never be forgotten in forming a judgment upon his acts and character. It was, indeed, much the same as the principle professed by the less illustrious Turner: "I must acknowledge that till now, in any service that I have ever been in, I never inquired further into the laws than the orders of my superior officers."

Claverhouse was a soldier: with the policy of his masters he had no concern; he had undertaken to do their work, and he fulfilled the duty, however odious, faithfully. There is, however, a note of regret in the remark with which he concludes his report of the demolition of the meeting-house on Nithside: "So perished the charity of many ladies."

Having begun thus energetically his military administration

in Dumfries and Galloway, Claverhouse continued to carry out his orders with relentless zeal. He complained bitterly of the laxity shown by the "well-affected" magistrates of Dumfries in dealing with prisoners.[7] They even allowed a minister, who had been apprehended by Lord Nithsdale, to hold prayer-meetings in the prison, largely attended by the townspeople. The attitude of the Dumfries bailies is not difficult to understand. They desired to remain loyal subjects if from no loftier motive than fear of the consequences of disaffection, yet they could not bring themselves to deal harshly with their fellow-townsmen on account of their religious scruples. But the time had come when the action of the prelatic party was to bear bitter fruit. There was to be no more tender dealing with Nonconformists. The murder of Archbishop Sharpe on May 3, 1679, precipitated a collision. Claverhouse was summoned from Dumfries to suppress the Covenanters' rising in Lanarkshire. On June 7 he suffered a defeat at Drumclog at the hands of the insurgents, among whom were many gentlemen of Dumfries and Galloway. The immediate consequence of this was to bring into the field so many supporters of the Covenant as might have ensured the final success of the cause but for the irreconcilable difference between the two sects of Covenanters. Distracted by recrimination and conflicting counsels, their army was routed by the Duke of Monmouth[8] at Bothwell Brig on June 22. Gordon of Earlston, whose son fought on this disastrous field, was taken prisoner on his way to join the insurgent army, and put to death. M'Dowall of Freuch, having been driven from his house by the High-

[7] Letter to Earl of Linlithgow, April 21, 1679.
[8] The Duke of Monmouth, a natural son of Charles II. by Lucy Walters, was directly connected with Dumfriesshire by his marriage with the heiress of Buccleuch.

land Host, joined the insurgents. He was attainted as a rebel, his lands in Wigtownshire were forfeited and bestowed on Claverhouse.

Hitherto the Covenanters, though carrying arms against the Royal troops, had professed loyalty to Charles II. Now, however, driven to open rebellion by tyrannical interference with their consciences, they renounced their allegiance on the ground that the king had "altered and destroyed the Lord's established religion, overturned the fundamental laws of the kingdom, and changed the civil government of this land, which was by a king and free Parliament, into tyranny." This proclamation was made on June 22, 1681, at the market-cross of Sanquhar by Richard Cameron at the head of a score of armed horsemen. War was declared against Charles Stuart, as having forfeited "all right, title to, or interest in the Crown of Scotland. . . . Come what may, and hold silent who list, we must and will publish the truth of this cruel King, protest against his misdeeds, and proclaim in the face of Heaven that he has forfeited his claim to the throne and to our allegiance." Cameron and his followers, to the number of sixty-three, were attacked by Bruce of Earlshall at Airds Moss near Cumnock: Cameron himself and many others were slain, and the rest dispersed.

On January 19, 1682, Claverhouse was gazetted Sheriff of Galloway, superseding Sir Andrew Agnew, who had refused the Test, and he at once travelled thither in order to suppress the insurrection. He made Kenmure Castle his headquarters, whence he directed the rigorous measures against the Covenanters which have attached so much hatred to the memory of his name. Writing to Lord Queensberry on March 5 from Wigtown he says:—

"Here in this shire I find the lairds all following the example of a late great man and considerable heritor among them,[9] which is to live regularly themselves, but have their houses constant haunts of rebels and intercommuned persons, and have their children baptized by the same, and then lay the blame on their wives. But I am resolved this jest shall pass no longer here, for it [is] laughing and fooling the Government."

Another letter written at Stranraer on March 13 is interesting by reason of the mention of one M'Lurg, whose name recalls the protection given to Robert the Bruce by the widow of Loch Dee:[1]—

"I am just beginning to send out many parties, finding the rebels become secure, and the country so quiet in all appearance. I sent out a party with my brother Dave three nights ago. The first night he took Drumbui[2] and one M'Lellan, and that great villain M'Clorg, the smith at Minnigaff that made all the clikys,[3] and after whom the forces have trotted so often. It cost me both pains and money to know how to find him: I am resolved to hang him; for it is necessary I make some example of severity, lest rebellion be thought cheap here. There cannot be alive a more wicked fellow."[4]

By the month of March 1684 Graham and his fellow-commissioners, Queensberry and Drumlanrig, were able to report that the "haill gentry and heritors within the shyre [of Wigtown] have taken the Test except Kennedy, minister in Ireland, and Mr James Laurie; and that all the Commons in the said Shyre who have not taken the Test, hes now done

---

[9] Sir James Dalrymple of Stair, who in the month of October previous had been superseded as Lord President for refusing the Test.

[1] The name is still a common one in the district.

[2] M'Kie of Drumbuie, outlawed in 1679. He was tried for high treason in December 1682, with about a dozen other Galloway lairds, all of whom were condemned to be hanged. The sentence, however, was not executed.

[3] Cleiks, hooked knives on staves for cutting the cavalry bridles.

[4] M'Lurg seems to have escaped from ward, for in 1684 his name appears among the fugitive outlaws proclaimed by the Government.

the same, except six or seven, qhoo are now prisoners." The persons specially charged with the duty of administering the Test in Wigtownshire were David Graham, William Coltran, Provost of Wigtown, and Sir Godfrey M'Culloch of Myrton.

Though Cameron was dead and his followers dispersed, the sect he had founded had elected a new leader in the person of James Renwick, a native of Minnyhive, and had published a fresh manifesto, called the Apologetical Declaration. Subscribing to the Test was now declared by the Government an inadequate proof of loyalty, and in December 1684 a new device was resorted to in the form of the Abjuration Oath, by which all men were called on to declare their abhorrence of the Apologetical Declaration. Thus step by step were the people goaded into resistance and rebellion; the moorlands of Nithsdale and Galloway were resorted to by small bands of worshippers, and what has since been remembered as "the killing time" began. The Commissioners had hitherto conceived their duty to be fulfilled by transporting to the West Indies those refusing to take the Test or convicted of resetting rebels. It was a frightful penalty, involving not only exile and the miseries of a long sea voyage under most trying conditions, but being sold into *lifelong slavery in the plantations*. Among those whose fate had thus been sealed when Queensberry, Drumlanrig, and Claverhouse held their court at Wigtown on October 14, were Margaret Milligan, Margaret Gordon, and Margaret M'Lurg, who had confessed to the heinous offence of harbouring their husbands, who were rebels. Margaret Gordon was wife of Hay of Airieoland in Mochrum parish. She was of gentle blood, of the house of Craighlaw, and her crime was having conversed with her husband and sons.

But towards the end of 1684 the authorities began to realise that the bulk of the population of Galloway would have to be driven into exile before Nonconformity could be stamped out. The law was now enforced in all its terrible severity, with such lasting impression on the minds of the people that some of the details must be enumerated here.

James Graham, tailor in Crossmichael, was taken by a party of dragoons early in December, and, refusing to abjure the Apologetical Declaration, was taken to Edinburgh, tried, and executed.

On December 18 Claverhouse in person apprehended six men at Auchencloy in Girthon. Four of these — Robert Fergusson, John M'Michan, Robert Stewart, and John Grierson — were summarily shot. Their bodies were buried in Dalry by their friends, but the law required that the bodies of traitors should be exposed after execution, so Claverhouse ordered them to be exhumed for that purpose. It may readily be supposed how great was the horror aroused by this proceeding, interpreted by Wodrow and other writers as a piece of diabolical spite on the part of Claverhouse.[5] It was, however, like the other acts of that unflinching commander, merely literally carrying out the letter of the law of the day. The two other prisoners taken at Auchencloy — William Hunter and Robert Smith — were taken to Kirkcudbright for trial, hanged, and afterwards beheaded.[6]

John Hallume, aged eighteen, was captured in Tongland by Lieutenant Livingstone, and severely wounded in attempting to escape. Refusing to take the abjuration oath, he was hanged at Kirkcudbright, and a stone in the kirkyard there marks the resting-place of his remains. Even those who had conformed hated the very sight of a soldier, because of the

---

[5] A monument was erected in 1835 on the place of this execution.

[6] A gravestone, with a metrical inscription, marks the resting-place of these two martyrs in Kirkcudbright kirkyard.

cruelty executed upon their neighbours and relatives; but keeping out of the path of the military was sometimes interpreted as proof of guilt. Thus William Auchinleck, who, it is said, had taken the abjuration oath, riding in Buittle parish, made a detour to avoid a party of Douglas's infantry.[7] Stopping afterwards to drink a glass of beer at Carlingwark (now called Castle-Douglas), the soldiers overtook him and shot him on the spot. The report of their muskets frightened the horse of a lad in company with Auchinleck, so that it threw him in the street. He also was immediately shot.

Three men—Thomas Harkness, Andrew Clark, and Samuel M'Ewan—fugitives for a long time on account of having rescued some Covenanting prisoners who were being conveyed to Edinburgh, were at last caught asleep on a hill in Closeburn. They were taken to Edinburgh and executed, says Wodrow, on the day of their arrival there.

John Gibson, Robert Grierson, Robert Mitchell, James Bennoch, and John Edgar were hiding in a cave at Ingleston in Nithsdale. Andrew Watson betrayed their refuge to Colonel Douglas or one of his officers, and they were summarily shot. So was John Hunter at Corehead in Moffatdale, and Andrew Macquhan at New Galloway. Grierson of Lag put five men to death in Tongland parish on one day in 1685.

These are a few of the incidents in the "killing time"—the latter months of 1684 and the beginning of 1685. In all, it was estimated by Patrick Walker that eighty-two persons were summarily executed in this district, besides those taken to Edinburgh for trial. From Upper Nithsdale, across the moors

---

[7] Sir John Lauder of Fountainhall records in 1684 that Colonel Douglas was taking great pains with his regiment. He forbade his officers to sell drink to their men, insisted on all beards being trimmed uniformly, and made the men tie back their hair with ribbon "so it cannot blow in their eyes when they visy at their firing." Shabby cravats were replaced by new ones, paid for by stoppages from the men's pay.

of New Galloway, in secluded Glen Trool[8] and lonely Kirkcowan and New Luce, the traveller may trace the footsteps of purblind tyranny, marked by many a grey stone set up to mark the spot hallowed by the death of a martyr to conscience. Seeing that not only refusal to abjure, but intercommuning with nonjurors, was considered an act of rebellion and treated with such fearful severity, it is not surprising that our Westland Whigs were driven to deeds meriting the utmost penalty.

Mr Pierson, curate of Carsphairn, was detested in Galloway because of the activity he had shown in informing against Whigs. An attempt was made into intimidating him into desisting from persecution. A party of armed men went to his house and demanded an interview. Pierson, being a bold man, seized sword and pistol and prepared for defence, or, as the other side alleged, for offence, and was immediately shot dead. Other Episcopalian curates were made the object of insult and personal injury.[9]

Straggling soldiers were sometimes waylaid and murdered on the moors, and the sentry on Kirkcudbright Tolbooth was shot dead. Justification, therefore, for measures of great severity was not wanting.

Charles II. died in February 1685. That year will ever be memorable in the annals of Galloway, from a tragedy of peculiar horror which then took place on Wigtown sands. Margaret M'Lauchlan, sixty-three, widow of John Milligan

---

[8] A stone in Caldons Wood, at the foot of Loch Trool, marks the spot where James Dun and Robert Dun, Alexander M'Aulay, Thomas and John Stevenson, and John M'Leod were surprised and shot by Colonel Douglas's men, January 23, 1685.

[9] Andrew Symson, curate of Kirkinner at this time, mentions in the dedication to Lord Galloway of his 'Tripatriarchicon' how, "in the year 1679, when things were come to that hight, that the publick owning of us was almost look'd upon as a crime, and I for my own safety was necessitate to retire to a quiet lurking-place, his Lordship accidentally lighted on me, took me home with him to his house, and kindly entertained me there."

wright in Drumjargon, and two daughters of Gilbert Wilson, a farmer in Penninghame, were charged, on April 13, with nonconformity before Sheriff Graham, Grierson of Lag, Major Winram, and Captain Strachan. "They were indicted," runs the session record of the parish of Penninghame, "as being guilty of the Rebellion of Bothwell Bridge, Aird's Moss, 20 Field Conventicles, and 20 House Conventicles: the Assize did sit, and brought them in guilty, and the Judges sentenced them to be tied to palisadoes fixed in the sand, within the flood-mark of the sea, and there to stand till the flood o'erflowed them."

There has been bitter controversy whether this sentence was ever executed. That a reprieve was petitioned for and obtained is beyond all manner of doubt; for there is in existence the petition to the Privy Council of Margaret Lauchlison, containing her abjuration and the reprieve of the sentence, issued by the Lords on April 30, though the date to which the reprieve was to extend is left in blank. Nothing can be clearer than that. On the other hand, there are the statements of historians, who, however prejudiced, are confirmed by the records of the session-books of the parishes of Penninghame and Kirkinner. These were drawn up in 1710-11, twenty-five years after the trial, in accordance with "a general design through the nation to have a history of the late sufferings of the People of God; and every Session within this national Church being desired to get well attested informations of the godly's sufferings within their bounds."[1] The late Mr Mark Napier, who discovered the reprieve, disbelieved the whole story of the Wigtown martyrs, and attempted to bring it into derision in his 'Memorials of Viscount Dundee.' But the intemperance of his language imparts to his argument the

[1] Kirkinner Session-Book, January 15, 1710.

infirmity inseparable from partisan literature, and Mr Napier has been effectively answered by the late Dr Stewart, minister of Glasserton, in his 'History Vindicated.' The unquestioned existence of the letter of reprieve was triumphantly quoted by Napier as outweighing the entries in the kirk-session records, the testimony of the tombstones in Wigtown kirkyard, and the tenacity of popular tradition. But, on the whole, the evidence remains strong that the reprieve never had effect, that Margaret's abjuration was probably a pious figment of some well-wishing notary, and that the execution took place. The general belief was once well expressed in the words of an elder of Wigtown, addressed to one who was expressing historical doubts about the drowning. "Weel, weel!" he said, "they that doots the droonin' o' the women wad maybe doot the deein' o' Jesus Christ."

The cruel lingering death, the age of one victim and the youth of the others, the harshness of the law under which the spiritual predilections of weak women were construed into rebellion against a powerful monarchy, have combined to impress the imagination with the horror of this act. Sir Andrew Agnew relates how the descendants of the man on whose information the women were apprehended have been held in aversion by their neighbours; and how, not very long ago, one of them, getting into a dispute with another person, was taunted in these words: "I wadna like to hae a forebear that betrayed the martyrs. I wadna be come o' sic fowk."[2]

While admitting the justice of indignation against the Government for decreeing, and its officers for carrying out, such a horrible sentence, it ought not to be forgotten that there was nothing wanton or unusual in the manner of

[2] The Hereditary Sheriffs of Galloway, vol. ii. p. 143.

death. Drowning was one of the statutory modes of executing condemned women; and it may even have been in mercy that, instead of being flung headlong into the river, the victims were exposed to the aggravated terrors of the slowly rising tide, which might be expected to frighten them into taking the Test.

It fared as hardly with the Covenanters of Dumfries in these terrible times as with those who sought refuge among the hills and moors of Galloway. Bailie Muirhead, of Dumfries, died in prison at Leith; James Glover, who was wounded and taken in Tinwald woods, expired in Edinburgh Tolbooth; Andrew Hunter, an aged burgess, in that of Dumfries. Twenty-nine inhabitants of Dumfries and neighbourhood, men and women, were transferred in the summer of 1685 from Dumfries jail to the "Whigs' Vault" at Dunnottar, where several of them died while awaiting transportation.

The repressive measures were in full force when the Duke of York ascended the throne as James the Second of England and Seventh of Scotland, and the Nonconformists had not much cause to look for alleviation of their lot at the hands of that devoted Catholic. The Earl of Argyll perished on the scaffold in June 1685, and numbers of humbler victims suffered in the south and west. At this time the Privy Council had suspended the freedom of the royal burghs until the king's pleasure should be made known. No magistrates were permitted to be elected in Dumfries in 1686; and in 1687 John Maxwell of Barncleuch, a relative of the Catholic Earl of Nithsdale, was appointed provost by Act of the Privy Council. The following year Maxwell was re-appointed by the same authority, and a number of magistrates, councillors, and deacons known to have prelatic sympathies were named as his colleagues.

The adventures of two brothers, Gilbert and William Milroy

of Penninghame parish, are narrated by Wodrow, and perhaps exaggerated by that partisan writer, as accounts of other events are certainly known to be. Nevertheless the main facts seem to be beyond doubt. The Milroys had been in hiding for some time owing to their determination not to take the Test. When they ventured home a party of soldiers took them prisoners, destroyed their crops, and drove off a considerable number of cattle, sheep, and horses. After being submitted to examination before the Earl of Home at Monigaff, they were taken for trial to Edinburgh, and sentenced to banishment and the loss of their ears. John suffered this mutilation in common with a number of other prisoners, but Gilbert escaped it because he seemed to be on the point of death. The exiles, to the number of 190, were then put into the hold of a vessel at Newhaven for transportation. Thirty-two of them died from the horrors of the passage, which lasted upwards of three months. The survivors were sold as slaves in Jamaica; but Gilbert lived to be set free at the Revolution, returned to his wife, and became an elder of Kirkcowan parish. He was still alive in 1710.

James Renwick, the young champion of Nithsdale, had long eluded pursuit, though there was a large reward offered for his production, dead or alive. But ever when he preached on a hillside there was a fleet horse ready to his hand, on which he would spring at the first alarm and show a clean pair of heels to Claverhouse's dragoons. But in January 1688, having ventured into Edinburgh on business connected with the Indulgences, he was apprehended, tried, and condemned to death. On the scaffold he attempted to address the people, but drums were set beating to drown his voice, for the authorities feared a popular rising to rescue the hero. He died on February 17, 1688, at the age of twenty-six.

But at the moment when affairs were at their blackest signs

of relaxation appeared. No one suspected King James of tenderness to the Presbyterian conscience; but the failure of a repressive policy was too hopeless to be overlooked, and the king had other warnings of the necessity of conciliating as many of his subjects as possible. The penal laws against Nonconformity were repealed. Sir John Dalrymple, son of that old Covenanter Lord Stair, and a bitter enemy to Claverhouse, was appointed King's Advocate in room of Mackenzie, who still pressed for the former policy. For the first time during many centuries men were declared to be free to worship after what manner they pleased, though field-conventicles were still, in the interests of peace, prohibited. Sir John Dalrymple became Lord Justice-Clerk in January 1688. Nine months later, William of Orange landed at Torbay with 14,000 men, and among his personal following was Lord Stair, Sir John's father, who had been removed from his bench in 1682 because of his objection to the Test Act, and had since found Leyden a more convenient residence than his house of Carscreuch in Wigtownshire.

The revolution was quietly accomplished in Dumfries and Galloway. Provost Maxwell disappeared from Dumfries, where the mob indulged in anti-papal demonstrations on Christmas Day, and destroyed what vestments and images they could lay their hands on, which did not amount to much. Municipal freedom was restored to the burgh. In Galloway Sir Andrew Agnew was restored to his hereditary sheriffdom, superseding David Graham, who had been acting as sheriff-depute to his brother Claverhouse, and in March 1689 writs were issued in the name of the Prince of Orange for the election of a Convention of Estates. William and Mary were proclaimed king and queen on April 11, and the bad old times of tyranny were for ever past.

For a time, however, the new *régime* bore unpleasantly

close resemblance to the old. The Claim of Right made by the Estates in April 1689 declared that "the imprisoning of persons without expressing the reasons thereof, and delaying to put them to trial, is contrary to law." But revolutions, however beneficent, are not effected by abstract sentiments. Claverhouse, now Viscount Dundee, was still in arms for James VII. in the north, and the Government passed an Act for the securing of suspect persons. The prisons, lately filled with incorrigible Covenanters, were now stuffed full of known or suspected Papists and Jacobites. Sir Robert Grierson of Lag, pre-eminently hated in Dumfries and Galloway for his work as lieutenant of the "bloody Claver'se," was imprisoned at Kirkcudbright by Lord Kenmure, and was thence taken to Edinburgh Tolbooth. He was liberated, however, at the end of August, on finding security for good conduct. He died, a very old man, at Dumfries in 1733.

The Episcopal clergy had now to yield place to Presbyterians. The first meeting of the Synod of Galloway took place at Monigaff, May 14, 1689.[3] Fourteen ministers were present, and received presentation of calls from various parishes to clergy selected by the people. Many of the Episcopal curates suffered insults and contumely from their former parishioners, but it is not on record that the change was the cause of any violence.

John Gordon had been consecrated Bishop of Galloway in February 1688. He now retired from his see, and spent the rest of his life in France, the last of the long line of Whithorn prelates, beginning with Ninian in the fifth century.

One of the first acts of the new Government was the reorganisation of the postal service. The postmaster-generalship was put up to auction, and the rates authorised included 2s. Scots for each letter from Edinburgh to Dumfries, to Port-

[3] See Note I, Ecclesiastical Discipline, p. 289.

patrick 3s., to Kirkcudbright 4s. All letters entering Scotland from England or abroad were taken first to Edinburgh, and thence carried along the various lines of post.

In 1690 King William sailed for Ireland to reinforce the Duke of Schomberg in his operations against the late king, James VII. His fleet lay wind-bound at Kirkcudbright for many days, and afterwards put into Loch Ryan. This expedition was crowned by the victory over James at the Boyne on July 1.

The most notable of the Galloway landowners passed away in 1695. James Dalrymple, first Viscount Stair, lived long enough to see the establishment of those great principles of religious liberty, his adherence to which had been an impediment to his own career as a judge. His eldest son, Sir John, had at the time of his father's death resigned the office of Lord Advocate, owing to the odium incurred by his responsibility for the infamous massacre of Glencoe; but the second son, Sir Hew, was President of the Court of Session, and the third, Sir David Dalrymple of Hailes, afterwards became Lord Advocate. Truly, it was a great legal house.

NOTE I.

ECCLESIASTICAL DISCIPLINE.

IN 1697 the Synod of Galloway appointed a committee for visitation of churches in consequence of complaints made against various ministers. Some curious side-lights are reflected on social habits from certain of the statements of witnesses. Every opportunity was afforded for the repetition of scandalous gossip or trivial complaints against ministers. M'Cowan, minister of Kirkinner, Stewart of Mochrum, and Wilson of Sorbie, protested against the mode of inquiry as illegal and oppressive. This notwithstanding, the proceedings went on and censures were administered on offenders. The following evidence given against the minister of Mochrum is a fair example of much of the same kind :—

"Sir James Dunbar of Mochrum says he is not a hearer of the minister, for which he shall give his reasons.

"1. He accuses him of breach of the Sabbath by mending up the fallen stouks of barley and hounding of sheep with his dog, and adduces Andrew M'Guffock, witnesse. . . . Andrew M'Guffock compeared, aged 42 years. . . . Declared in Master Stewart's [the minister] presence, That upon a Sabbath-day after sermon he, lying at the hill-end of Drumskeoch, saw Mr James Stewart and his father among the fallen sheaves of barley, and saw Mr James Stewart lean one or two of the sheaves in to the stouk either with his hand or foot, and saw his father either tying or lengthening the threads with feathers which were put upon the stouks to fright away the fouls.

"The said Andrew M'Guffock upon his deposition declared that upon a Sabbath before sermon he saw Mr Stewart forsaid come out of the gate-door and a flecked dog with him, and seeing some sheep feeding before the gate he heard him say 'Hiss' to the dog, whereupon the dog pursued the sheep out of the deponent's sight by the Boghouse barn.

"2. Sir James Dunbar accuses Mr. Stewart forsaid that he did beat a boy called Coltran and wounded his head, . . . and further accuses Mr Stewart for beating of his servants frequently.

T

"Mr Stewart being interrogat answers that he acknowledgeth he strook when the boy with horse was abusing his corn, but knows not whether he strook the boy or not ; and denyes that it is his common practise to beat his servants, but confesses that sometymes he beats them when they prove stubborn and disobedient. . . .

"3. Sir James accuses him that he said to John Beatie his servant that his Lady was an enemy to the Gospell. Mr Stewart answers that he said to John Beatie that, in as far as Lady Mochrum was a hinderer of her servants to come to examination, she was ane enemy to the work of the Gospell. . . .

"Given in ane additional Lybell unsubscribed accusing the said Mr James Stewart as follows :—

"That the last year in the pulpit he said to us the people of this parish publickly, 'We were brave folk in this parish, our kilshes should be better ryped, for we had poacks of meal and clorts of butter under our beds-heads, and for witness (said he) take Drumskeoch and Glentriplock [two neighbouring farmers].

"Mr Stewart interrogat answers he confesseth that he mentioned Glentriplock and Drumskeoch ; as for Glentriplock, he had nothing to say against it, but being preaching against theft, he, alluding to Chorazin and Bethsaida, said that if they were well searched, some things would be found in their beds and beds-heads."—MS. Records of the Committee of the Synod of Galloway, 1697.

Further charges were brought of the same trivial character, which are hardly worth transcribing.

CHAPTER XII.

FROM THE REVOLUTION IN 1688 TO THE STUART RISING IN 1715.

HAVING brought the historical sketch of Dumfriesshire and Galloway to the close of the stormy era which, beginning with the disputed succession of Balliol and Bruce, witnessed the long struggle for national independence, the gradual decline of feudal institutions, the union of the Crowns, and the alternate ascendancy of Prelacy and Presbyterianism, we have now come to the threshold of the century which was to unfold such fruitful consequences to Scotland as the issue of her legislative union with England. It seems a fitting moment to review briefly the social condition of the inhabitants of the south-west and their material resources.[1]

In truth there was not much superfluous wealth remaining to any class of the community. Many of the landowners had been ruined by military expenditure incurred on behalf of one side or the other. Those who had taken the side of the Stuart dynasty, and ridden with Montrose and Claverhouse, now saw their last hopes of recouping themselves disappear; while of those who had thrown in their lot with the popular cause, many had already suffered so grievously

[1] See Note K, Condition of the South-western Counties in the Seventeenth Century, p. 313.

from fines and exactions that they were obliged to part with their lands, while others, still struggling on, had met their obligations by mortgages or "wadsets," many of which they were never able to redeem. In this way may be noted the disappearance from the list of heritors of many branches of the old Celtic families in Galloway, who had been settled in that province from times anterior to the Roman occupation. Maclellans,[2] Kennedys, M'Doualls, Hannays, M'Kies, M'Cullochs, were gradually displaced by families of later connection with the district. Many of the old names remain to this day among the landowners of Galloway, but they do not in every case betoken descent from the original barons. In the thirteenth and fourteenth centuries, when surnames were beginning to come into general use, vassals often assumed those of their feudal superiors. Some of these rose in the social scale and were ultimately able to take rank as lords of the soil. Perhaps of all the landowners of Dumfries and Galloway at the present time, the M'Doualls of Logan are the only family continuing to own any part of the lands possessed by their Pictish forefathers in the days of Malcolm Canmore.

The end of one of the old Celtic houses of Galloway came in a deplorable way. Sir Alexander M'Culloch of Myreton had formed, it seems, the design to possess himself of the estates of Gordon of Cardiness. In the old lawless days this might have been accomplished by force of arms, but this descendant of a race of freebooters availed himself to some extent of legal forms, and, according to the allegation

---

[2] The fifth Lord Kirkcudbright (Maclellan) died in 1730. He lived in the town of Kirkcudbright in such straitened circumstances that it is said he kept a small inn for his livelihood (Mackenzie's 'History of Galloway,' vol. ii. p. 322, note).

of William and Alexander Gordon, preserved in the Privy Council Record, "did buy several pleas, debts, comprisings, and factories of the estate, and used all means to get himself intruded thereinto." This went on for some years, till on August 19, 1664, Sir Alexander, with his two sons, Godfrey and John, Harry M'Culloch, younger of Barholm,[3] William M'Culloch, younger of Locharduie, John M'Culloch of Auchleach, Alexander Fergusson of Kilkerran,[4] and an armed force, came to Bussabiel, the residence of Lady Cardiness, the infirm widow of the late owner of that estate. They broke into the house, dragged Lady Cardiness out of bed, and beat her till she swooned. They also wounded her son William and wrecked the house. Next year, in October 1665, the same party attacked Bussabiel, and the widow suffered fresh ill-usage. Still she would not give up her property, which led these ruffians to commit a crowning outrage in March 1666. They wrecked the house afresh, and treated Lady Cardiness in such inhuman fashion that "she within a short time thereafter did burst forth her heart's blood and died."

Such is a summary of the charges laid by the Gordons against the M'Cullochs, containing many details of alleged revolting cruelty which are not repeated here, because the defence is not extant. Howbeit, the accused were condemned to fine and imprisonment—a judgment which was reversed next day, though in April 1669 Godfrey M'Culloch and Fergusson of Kilkerran were still under sentence of the court.

The last chapter in the M'Culloch tragedy opens thirty

---

[3] Barholm is still owned by the family of M'Culloch.

[4] Ancestor of the present owner of Kilkerran, in Ayrshire, the Right Hon. Sir James Fergusson, Bart., M.P.

years after these events. By this time old Sir Alexander had passed away, and his son, Sir Godfrey, was the head of the clan. He was desperately in debt, and though allowed 500 merks of aliment by the Court of Session, he was finally ejected by the sheriff from the mansion of Bardarroch. The feud with the Gordons was still alive. On October 2, 1690, Sir Godfrey went to Bussabiel, and sent in his servant to request William Gordon to speak to a gentleman on business. On Gordon appearing at the front door " with a bended gun, he [M'Culloch] did shoot him through the thigh, and brak the bane thereof to pieces," [5] of which Gordon died within a few hours. M'Culloch thereafter went abroad to escape justice, but returned after a few years. William Stewart of Castle Stewart, the husband of William Gordon's sister, offered to exert himself to get a remission in the murderer's favour on condition that he surrendered the title-deeds of Cardiness, over which M'Culloch, it is supposed, held a wadset, but the offer was not accepted. Doubtless Sir Godfrey trusted to the slowness of Scottish justice in dealing with criminals of rank. But in this he miscalculated; for, being in church in Edinburgh one Sunday, he was denounced as a murderer by a Galloway gentleman in the congregation, apprehended, tried, convicted, and executed on March 25, 1697.

A popular tradition, quoted by Sir Walter Scott in 'Minstrelsy of the Scottish Border,' gives a different ending to the story. The keep of Myrton stands, as may be seen at this day, on an ancient mote-hill. It is alleged that Sir Godfrey, in the early days of his possession, had occasion to cut a drain through this mound, when a little man in a green coat appeared and warned him that he was interfering with the fairies' abode therein. He promised that if Sir Godfrey would

[5] Justiciary Record.

desist, he (the gnome) would some day reward him by a signal service; but if not, the vengeance of the fairies would have to be reckoned with. Sir Godfrey obliged the little man by altering his plan, and the reward came on the day appointed for execution, when the gnome appeared on a white horse, took M'Culloch out of the cart, rode off with him, and neither of the twain was ever seen again.

The estate of Myrton passed into the possession of Sir William Maxwell of Monreith, whose mother was an aunt of M'Culloch, and continues to be owned by his lineal descendant. Cardiness also is now owned by another Sir William Maxwell, a descendant of the Maxwells of Calderwood.

Of the condition of the general rural population at the close of the seventeenth century it is not easy to obtain minute information. Mr Andrew Symson, the Episcopal curate of Kirkinner for more than twenty years previous to the Revolution of 1688, compiled a 'Large Description of Galloway'; but, albeit a man of wider sympathies and deeper culture than most of his order, he does not devote many observations to the lower orders. The natural features, the antiquities, agriculture, and industries of the province are touched on, and much attention is paid to the gentry and their houses; but of the habits of farmers and rural labourers just enough is told to make the reader wish for more. One singular passage, however, deserves to be repeated, because it seems to indicate a greater degree of refinement among the lower orders of Galloway than prevailed in other parts of Scotland :—

"Some of the countrey people here, in the night-time, sleep not except they pull off not only their cloaths, but their very shirts, and then wrap themselves in their blankets; yea, and I have known some of them who have so addicted themselves to this custome, that when they watch their cattell and sheep in the folds at night, (which they do constantly from the beginning of May, till the corne be taken off the ground, for fear they should breake the fold-dikes in the night-time, and do prejudice to themselves or their neighbours,) they ly on the ground with straw or fernes under them, and stripping themselves stark naked, be the night never so cold or stormie, they ly there, wrapping themselves in their blankets, having perhaps sometimes a few sticks placed cheveron-wise, and cover'd with truffs to keep their blankets from the raine."

People of such hardihood may have lived contented in cabins which in our day would be rightly condemned as unfit for human habitation; and with milk, cheese, corn, and poultry, the thrifty householders managed to keep extreme privation at bay. To one luxury, at least, they were greatly attached. "The common people," writes Symson, "are, for the most part, great chewers of tobacco, and are so greatly addicted to it that they will ask a peece thereof even from a stranger, as he is riding on the way; and therefore let not a traveller want an ounce or two of roll-tobacco in his pocket, and for an inch or two thereof he need not fear the want of a guide either by night or day."

One article of diet mentioned by Symson has completely gone out of use in Galloway—indeed it is held in general aversion. Eels, he said, used to be caught in large numbers about Martinmas, salted in barrels, and roasted in winter for food. In some respects the people of Wigtownshire seem to have been better off than those farther east, to which Symson attributes their indolence in fishing. "Our sea," he says, "is better stor'd with good fish, than our shoare is furnished with good fishers; for having such plenty of flesh on the shore, they take little paines to seek the sea for fish." The same may be said of Wigtownshire in the present day, for many of the best fishermen, both here and elsewhere in the Solway, are Englishmen, chiefly from Morecambe Bay.

Notwithstanding their hardihood, the stress of privation, a general low scale of diet, combined with imperfect house-shelter and disregard of all sanitary precautions, must have had its effect on the population. The rate of mortality, could we ascertain what it was, would surely prove to be higher than at present; weakly children and persons must have succumbed, and we have evidence from the earliest times of the presence of one disease, at least, which seems to have disappeared. Leprosy, unless it survive in the form of scrofula, is unknown in our rural population, though its dreaded presence is still commemorated in our place-names, and even our personal names. M'Clure is none other than *mac lobhair* (lour), the leper's son, though it is to be observed that the Gaelic *lobhar* (lour), in its strict sense a leper, came to be applied to any infirm or chronically diseased person.[6] Among Gaelic place-names from the same source may be mentioned Barlure in New Luce parish, and Ochtralure near Stranraer, respectively *barr* and *uachdarach lobhar*, the hill and upland of the lepers; while Liberland,[7] a desolate spot in Kirkcowan on the march of Ayrshire, denotes a place devoted of old to the isolation of sufferers from this loathsome disease.

Agriculture, as described by Symson, was in a lamentably backward condition. Wool was the chief surplus product of

---

[6] The English equivalent to M'Clure is found in the name Aikman, from the Anglo-Saxon *ace manne*, an infirm person.

[7] Written Liberlane on the Ordnance map, but pronounced Libberlan. In Pont's map it is called Eldricken Libberton, like Liberton in Mid-Lothian, the *toun* or homestead of the "libbers" or lepers. Bath is twice mentioned in the Anglo-Saxon Chronicle as Acemanne's-ceaster and Acemanne's-burh, the exact equivalent of Liberton.

the farmers, though some sheep were sent for sale in Edinburgh, and some cattle to England. The oats grown in Wigtownshire, he says, were bad compared with those of other districts, having long beards. Nevertheless "excellent and very hearty meal" was made therefrom, not ground so small as was usual in other counties. Oxen were commonly used for ploughing. "Some," says Symson, "till onely with eight oxen, but usualy they have ten, which ten oxen are not so expensive by far in keeping as four horses, which must be fed dayly with corne: besides, the oxen yield much more dung. As also when they grow old and unserviceable, they get a good price for them from the grasiers and drovers."

Corn was too valuable to spare for beasts of draught, seeing that the "ordinary encrease of corne is but three for one, which, for they sow much, will, except in years of great scarcitie, abundantly satisfy themselves, and furnish the moorlands plentifully with victuals; yea, and oftentimes they vend and transport much thereof to other countreys."

Nevertheless in parts of the Stewartry they ploughed with four horses abreast, led by a boy or woman walking backwards, while the ploughman drove.

The barley used to be very full of darnel, which strangers complained of as making the beer brewed from it very heady. Beer was the common drink, but in the moors they drank fermented whey "very sour and sharp." Hemp and flax, neither of which is now grown in these counties, were both grown on nearly every farm; homespun ropes were used in agriculture, and hides were tanned with green heather. The Gaelic word *lín* (leen), flax, survives in many place-names, such as Port Leen, in Kirkcolm parish, the port where flax was shipped or perhaps steeped; Ochteralinachan, in Leswalt, *uachdarach linachan*, the upland of the flax-field, &c.

In the towns the scale of comfort may be supposed to

have ranged somewhat higher than in the country, although they too betoken the general poverty to which the kingdom had been reduced. In 1695 Dumfries stood sixth among the sixty-six royal burghs assessed for taxation. Its relative importance to the others is thus given in the roll:—

		Scots.				Sterling.		
Edinburgh	rated at	£35	0	0	about	£3	0	0
Glasgow	"	15	0	0	"	1	5	0
Aberdeen	"	6	10	0	"	0	10	10
Dundee	"	5	6	8	"	0	8	6
Montrose	"	2	8	0	"	0	3	6
Dumfries	"	1	18	4	"	0	2	0

Of the other royal burghs in Dumfriesshire, Lochmaben paid 3s. Scots, Annan 2s., and Sanquhar 1s.

In 1692 the Convention of Royal Burghs caused a report to be drawn up on the trade and revenue of all the royal burghs in Scotland. Dumfries could boast a common good of the annual value of £2666, 13s. 4d. Scots, or about £222 sterling, against which had to be set a debt of 20,000 merks, or nearly £2100 sterling. The dues levied on Devorguila's ancient bridge were the chief source of revenue to the burgh, these amounting in 1692 to £122 sterling. The chief inland trade consisted of linen and sheep-skins; and complaint was uttered in the report of the prejudice done to the trade of Dumfries by the sale of staple commodities in "several regalities, baronies, kirk-towns" in the neighbourhood, notably the hamlet of Bridgend, which was afterwards, in 1810, erected into a burgh of barony under the name of Maxwelltown. The charges defrayed out of the common good, besides the interest on the debt, included a share of the minister's stipend, the salaries of a schoolmaster, doctor, precentor, and other public servants, the maintenance of the church, the bridge, the tolbooth, and the mills, and the expenses of commissioners attending Parliament.[8] As a seaport Dumfries was greatly at a disadvantage compared with its rival Ayr, owing to the difficult navigation of the Solway. In short, the report made to the commissioners of the Convention concluded dolefully enough to the effect that "the patrimonie [of the municipality] is exhausted and will necessarily endgadge them to contract debts; and by reasone of the inconvenience of the river, and the chairges of lighters, it's feared that trade will totally decay, even tho' there were peace." The fleet of the town, consisting of one large vessel of 140 tons and five smaller ones, was laid up and falling to decay, and only four vessels had discharged cargo in the port during the five years preceding the report.

But if the fortunes of Dumfries were at a low ebb in 1692, those of the other royal burghs were worse. Whithorn, once the favourite resort of royal pilgrims and an episcopal see, could only show a common good of about 12s. sterling, with a debt of £8. It had no "forraigne" trade, though possessing a sufficient harbour, and the inland trade is confined to a small retail of goods from Ayr or Dumfries. "Their wine, sack and brandie is so inconsiderable that they cannot condescend on it. . . . They have no ship, bark or boat belonging to them in regaird of the poverty of their inhabitants. . . . The rent of their houses are twixt fyfteen pound and twenty shillings Scots, many whereof are ruinous."

---

[8] The payment of members of Parliament, a practice which Mr Cosmo Innes traced to the closing years of the sixteenth century, immediately after the Reformation, had become general towards the end of the seventeenth, and was a considerable burden on the constituencies. It was fixed by Act of Parliament in 1661 at £5 Scots (about 5s. 3d.) per day during the session, and travelling expenses, besides, in some instances at least, the cost of foot mantle and horse-trappings for the ceremony of "riding the Parliament."

Wigtown admitted to a shade more of prosperity. Her common good amounted to nearly £40 sterling, with a debt of £100. House-rents varied from 24 lib. Scots to 20s.; but many houses were "either waist or ruinous." The only rival they complained of was Monigaff, which "prejudged them as to their weekly market." Symson says that the country-people used to make woollen cloth and sell it at Wigtown market.

The magistrates of Stranraer, with a common good of £7 sterling and a debt of 2500 merks, claimed to have a sufficient harbour "if they had any trade," but possess no vessels except four small boats employed in the herring-fishing. "They have only one burgh of baronie within precinct, called Portpatrick, which does no wayes prejudge them as having no trade."

Lastly, Kirkcudbright, with a yearly common good of £880 Scots (about £73 sterling), was represented as adding a debt of £300 each year in excess of the revenue. "They have a small boat of eight tunns, newly bought, for carrieing their coals, but she hath never as yet been imployed. . . . The most pairt of their houses are inhabited and possest by the respective heretors, and all the rest aither waist or ruinous, and that more than the half."

Making due allowance for the natural tendency of the town councils to underrate their resources in preparing information which was to be the basis of taxation, there can be little doubt that the affairs of the burghs in the south-west were at this time the reverse of flourishing. Commerce was at an even lower ebb than agriculture. Nevertheless a frugal, hardy population, living in a stormy, but generally mild, climate, had the means of preparing their own subsistence, and there does not seem to have been much abject poverty among them. The general scale of living, from the highest to the lowest, was humble, for the days had passed away when wealthy barons could afford to erect such beautiful and stately dwellings as Caerlaverock.

Taking the valuation as showing how things stood before the close of the old order of things, it is interesting to compare the estimated rental of the district at that time with a recent valuation, reducing the Scots money to approximate sterling value:—

	1692.	1894.
Wigtownshire	£5,634	£213,806
Kirkcudbright	9,549	337,373
Dumfriesshire	13,220	603,619
Total	£28,403	£1,154,798

The valuation of 1894, including railways, is upwards of forty times that of 1692.

The dawn of better times was at hand. Landowners began to devote attention to the improvement of the breed of cattle for the supply of the English markets, and to Lord Basil Hamilton, who had acquired the estate of Baldoon by his marriage with the heiress of Sir David Dunbar, may be given the credit of taking the initiative in developing what continued for nearly two centuries the principal source of the Galloway farmer's profit. He obtained special permission to import six score of cows from Ireland to improve the native breed. In concert with other lairds he moved the Privy Council in 1697 to appoint a commission "to make and mark a road and highway for droves from New Galloway to Dumfries, holding the high and accustomed travelling way betwixt the two said burghs." The necessity for this lay in the total absence of fences throughout the country. Affrays had become frequent between drovers and farmers whose crops were injured by travelling cattle. The commissioners speedily marked out the route, and ordered it to be fenced: other lines of communication were dealt with in a similar way, and the traveller in Galloway at this day is sometimes bewildered in contemplating the apparent perversity with which the highroad climbs steep and frequent hills, neglecting the level tracts on either hand, until he is reminded that at the time these routes were laid, the hollows being swampy and undrained, the engineers chose those parts of the ground which were hardest and driest.[9]

In the eighteenth century the convenience of fencing fields began to be generally recognised: proprietors carried it on vigorously — not, however, without encountering opposition from disciples of the old school. It interfered with the interests of rustics employed to herd and tend cattle and sheep on the pastures, as well as with the old and wasteful "runrig" system of cultivation and the rights of common pasturage. Bands of Levellers, as they called themselves, scoured the country at night, throwing down the fences and even houghing and maiming the cattle enclosed within them. The ringleader of these Levellers was the celebrated Billy Marshall, of the blood royal of the Gipsies, who deserted from the Royal Regiment of Dragoons (the Scots Greys) when serving under Marlborough in Flanders.

In addition to the grievance of loss of employment owing to discontinuance of herding cattle, was the discontent caused by throwing small crofts into larger farms in the ordinary process of land improvement. Probably the necessary evictions were not always carried out in a considerate way: bitter

---

[9] Many of our country roads preserve the lines of old pack-horse tracks. As late as the closing years of last century it is recorded that the author's great-grandfather, driving from Monreith in the family coach to meetings at Wigtown, a distance of ten miles, used to be obliged to halt five times each way while gaps were made in march dykes to allow the carriage to pass, and built up again.

feeling was engendered, and found expression in popular verse.

> "Against the poor the lairds prevail
>   With all their wicked works,
> Who will enclose both hill and dale,
>   And turn corn-field to parks.
> The lords and lairds they drive us out
>   From mailings where we dwell;
> The poor man cries, 'Where shall we go?'
>   The rich say, 'Go to hell!'"

Frequent riots ensued, and at Culquha in the Stewartry a serious encounter took place between the Levellers and Houghers and the soldiers acting under the sheriff's instructions. Some of the rioters were killed; 200 were taken prisoners, of whom some were imprisoned and others endured the horrible fate of banishment to the plantations.

Lord Basil Hamilton was drowned in 1701 when riding with his brother Lord Selkirk through the Nick o' the Balloch, a hill-pass between Galloway and Ayrshire. They came to the Minnock in full flood; Lord Basil's servant, riding forward to try the ford, was swept away, and his master was drowned in trying to save him. But the good work he had begun was energetically carried forward by other proprietors. Lime was imported from Ireland to lay on the pastures; herds were improved by selected blood from other districts; and the first systematic attempts to plant trees were made during the first fifteen years of the eighteenth century.

As early as 1669 the Privy Council had granted a warrant to the General Assembly to make a collection in all congregations south of the Forth to build a bridge over the Water of Luce. This bridge still stands, though it has been widened, and the older structure much concealed, in modern times. Similarly in 1692 the heritors of Dunscore got the Presbytery of Dumfries to certify that a bridge was required in the public interest over the Water of Cairn. The bridge over the Dee at Clattrinshaws was built after the year 1695 out of funds collected from house to house by order of the Synod of Galloway in consequence of the refusal of the Privy Council to undertake the work. The bridge between Monigaff and the town now called Newton-Stewart, over the Black Ford of Cree, was begun in 1703.

Evidence of the utter destruction of the old forest in the south-west may be found in the difficulty encountered by the Dumfries magistrates when, in 1703, they resolved to erect a council-house and steeple, the same which now stands in the principal street of the burgh. This building, though not on a large scale, is an interesting example of the architecture of Queen Anne's reign. It was built with a sum of 20,000 merks which accrued to the burgh from the sale to Mr Sharpe of Hoddam of their share of the tack of Scottish customs and excise. The architect was Mr Moffat of Liverpool, and the wrought-iron railing of the outer stair, designed by an Edinburgh tradesman called Sibbald, is of unusual elegance. The burgh minute-book remains to prove the extraordinary difficulty experienced in finding architects and builders in a district where formerly many stately structures had been reared. They made search for "a free Danish or Swedish bottom for fraughting for timber to Norway, and after diligent search, they found that there can be none gotten at an easy rate." So they had recourse to home-grown timber, and the nearest place it could be obtained was the wood of Garlies on the Cree.

A Dumfriesshire magnate, James, second Duke of Queensberry, was appointed by Queen Anne her Commissioner for settling the terms of the legislative Union between England and Scotland, but all his influence failed to commend the project to the people. The Presbyterian General Assembly detected danger in it to their establishment; the ministers easily alarmed their flocks by foretelling the reascendancy of Prelacy, and the Convention of Royal Burghs petitioned strenuously against the measure. The articles of Union were publicly burnt by tumultuous gatherings at Dumfries and Kirkcudbright. The only Galloway proprietor who at first was in favour of the Union was Viscount Stair; but so sagaciously and persuasively did he exert himself that the Earl of Galloway and the elected members for Wigtown and Kirkcudbright followed him in the division in favour of the first article of the Union, while the Earls of Selkirk and Wigtown, Fergusson of Isle, Sharpe of Hoddam, and Provost Johnston of Dumfries, voted against it. The bitterness of feeling was intensified when it came to be known afterwards that several of those who supported the bill had received English gold in consideration for their votes. William Stewart of Castle Stewart, member for Wigtownshire, pocketed £300, and Provost Coltran £25. In the final division, however, there was some cross-voting. Lord Galloway, Maxwell of Cardiness, and M'Kie of Balgown, who had supported Lord Stair in the earlier stages of the debate, now voted with the Duke of Athol as a protest against the surrender of Scottish independence.

Lord Stair did not live to see the fulfilment of the measure which he had promoted with so much energy. The 22d article of the Treaty of Union, whereby the representation of Scotland in the Imperial Parliament was fixed, gave rise to a warm debate on January 22, 1707. Stair spoke at length with great animation, retired much exhausted, and died during the night.

The Cameronian sect, representing the irreconcilable party of Presbyterians, exerted itself in resistance to the Union. Sanquhar was the headquarters of this body, which claimed the sounding title of the "Anti-Popish, Anti-Prelatic, Anti-Erastian, Anti-Sectarian, true Presbyterian Church of Scotland," and their leader was Mr John Macmillan, once chaplain to Murray of Broughton, subsequently minister of Balmaghie. In 1703 this worthy divine, with the ministers of Carsphairn and Buittle, had lodged a "statement of grievances" with the Presbytery of Kirkcudbright against the corruption and mismanagement of the Church of Scotland, and condemned the oath of allegiance to the monarch. The presbytery appointed a committee to consider the complaints, which reported that, "being desirous to be as condescending as they can, for peace' sake they do pass all bygone differences and misbehaviours of said John Macmillan." Seeing, however, that Macmillan continued to resist the authority of the synod and presbytery, he was deposed from his parish, which notwithstanding, he continued in possession of the kirk, manse, and glebe for fifteen years, and, with the physical and moral support of his devoted congregation, successfully resisted all attempts to eject him. This was the occasion of many scenes of disorder and violence. Fines were inflicted on the parishioners of Balmaghie for attending the ministrations of Macmillan. For instance, in 1707, Charles Livingstone, glover in Kirkcudbright, petitioned the Town Council to remit a fine of 500 merks (about £28), to which he had been condemned for being married by Macmillan. As reasons for pardon he submitted his excellent character, "the scarcitie of money," and many precedents for similar irregularity since the Revolution, and he was successful in obtaining remission. On May 26, 1712, Macmillan held a meeting of the "suffering remnant" at Auchensaugh, near Crawfordjohn, and renewed the Solemn League and Covenant. But beyond causing the Cameronians to become known to an unsympathetic public as Macmillanites, the movement had no effect beyond the bounds of Galloway and Nithsdale.[1] Macmillan died in 1753, ten years after he had founded the Reformed Presbytery.

The stimulus to Scottish commerce which was the immediate result of the Union had a reflex effect on smuggling, and it is to the years immediately following it that the rise may be traced of that contraband trade which was afterwards to assume such formidable dimensions in the Solway. But the death of Queen Anne in 1714 brought about such serious political disturbance as to throw minor matters into the shade. The cry went forth of "the auld Stuarts back again." The standard of James VIII. was unfurled on the Braes of Mar on August 26, 1715. The Earl of Nithsdale and Johnston of Wamphray declared for the Chevalier, and Viscount Kenmure was not backward. But the memory of Claverhouse and Lag was too fresh in the district to allow any popular enthusiasm for the Stuarts to find expression. Of all the Wigtownshire lairds, Hamilton of Baldoon alone mounted the white cockade; in Kirkcudbright, Gordon of Earlston, in Dumfriesshire the Marquis of Annandale, Kirkpatrick of Closeburn, and other county gentlemen, declared for King George. Many, no doubt, of all ranks held aloof; for the question was complicated by soreness at the recent Union, and by fear on the one hand of the re-establishment of Papacy by the Chevalier, and on the other of the renewal of Episcopacy which George I. was said to favour.

Times had undergone a change since the old "riding" days. The Maxwell gathering cry, "Bide Wardlaw!" to which the Nithsdale kinsmen and tenants used to rally so readily for a foray on English soil or against the neighbouring Johnstones, now fell on unheeding ears. Lord Nithsdale

---

[1] The Macmillan Free Church in Castle-Douglas is one of the buildings still set apart for the use of this section of Presbyterians.

had the mortification of seeing nearly all his dependants enrolled as volunteers in the cause of the house of Hanover. Most of Lord Kenmure's tenants, too, mustered in Dumfries with black cockades in their bonnets. But what was lacking in numbers was made up in minstrelsy. The Muses were all on the side of the Chevalier. Nithsdale being a Catholic, it was deemed politic to give the command of the slender force to the Protestant Viscount Kenmure, and their departure for the south is commemorated in the stirring stanzas beginning—

> "Kenmure's on and awa', Willie!
> Kenmure's on and awa';
> And Kenmure is the bravest lord
> That ever Galloway saw."

The Scottish lords, having joined forces with Lord Derwentwater and Mr Forster in Cumberland, marched on Preston, which they captured, but shortly afterwards were obliged to surrender at discretion to General Wills. This calamity, nearly coinciding with the disastrous defeat at Sheriffmuir on November 17, broke the Chevalier's cause and the movement collapsed.

Of the 1500 prisoners taken at Preston six were shot on the spot and many suffered banishment to the American plantations. Nithsdale and Kenmure, with Lord Derwentwater and the other lords and officers, were sent to London to be tried for high treason. On February 9, 1716, they were placed at the bar in Westminster Hall, and when they had pleaded guilty to the charges on which they were arraigned, the Lord High Steward pronounced sentence upon them according to the appalling formula usual in such cases:—

"And now, my Lords, nothing remains but that I pronounce upon you (and sorry I am that it falls to my lot to do it) that terrible sentence of the law, which must be the same that is usually given against the meanest offender in the like kind. The ignominious and painful parts of it are usually remitted by the grace of the Crown to persons of your quality; but the law in this case being deaf to all distinctions of persons, requires I should pronounce, and accordingly it is adjudged by this Court, that you, James Earl of Derwentwater, William Lord Widdrington, William Earl of Nithsdale, Robert Earl of Carnwath, William Viscount Kenmure, and William Lord Nairn, and every one of you, return to the prison of the Tower, from whence you came; from thence you must be drawn to the place of execution; when you come there you must be hanged by the neck, but not till you be dead, for you must be cut down alive, then your bowels must be taken out and burnt before your faces; then your heads must be severed from your bodies, and your bodies divided each into four quarters, and these must be at the King's disposal. And God Almighty be merciful to your souls!"

While Lord Nithsdale lay under sentence of death, some nameless bard composed the "Lament for Lord Maxwell," more remarkable for pathos than for poetry, of which the first and last stanzas run as follows:—

"Green Nithsdale, make moan, for thy leaf's in the fa',
 The lealest o' thy warriors are drappin' awa';
 The rose in thy bonnet, that flourished sae and shone,
 Has lost its white hue, and is faded and gone.
 . . . .
 And there I'll sit and moan, till I sink into the grave,
 For Nithsdale's bonny lord, the bravest o' the brave;
 O that I lay but wi' him in sorrow and in pine,
 And the steel that harms his gentle neck wad do as much for mine!" [2]

Great interest was made after the trial to obtain the royal

[2] Allan Cunningham's 'Songs of Scotland,' vol. iii. p. 186.

mercy for the condemned lords. The execution was fixed for February 24. A reprieve was actually resolved on for Lords Widdrington, Nithsdale, Carnwath, and Nairn, but of course this was not made known to the prisoners or their friends. Had it been so, one of the most romantic episodes in British history would never have taken place. Winifred, Countess of Nithsdale, a daughter of the Marquis of Powis, obtained leave to visit her husband in the Tower on the evening before what was believed to be the day of his execution. By the assistance of her faithful maid Evans, her landlady Mrs Mills, and a friend of Evans, Mrs Morgan, this brave lady succeeded in leading out her lord, disguised in Mrs Mills's clothes, under the very eyes of the guard and sentries. Dismissing the pretended Mrs Mills at the door of the prison with a message to another attendant, which she took care the soldiers should hear, Lady Nithsdale returned to the room where her husband had been confined, and talked as if he had really been present. Then leaving the chamber and pulling the string through the latch, so that it could only be opened from the inside, she left the Tower, telling the earl's servant not to carry candles to his master, as he desired to pray in solitude. Afterwards Lord Nithsdale, disguised as a livery servant of the Venetian ambassador, went on that dignitary's coach-and-six to Dover, and made good his escape to the Continent.

Lady Nithsdale had now to look after her own safety, for the king was greatly incensed against her, vowing that she had done him more injury than any woman in Christendom, and she was given to understand that the law of treason held a wife's head answerable for that of her husband. Notwithstanding the rigorous search made for her, and the disabling fact that she was within a short period of her confinement, this devoted lady rode all the way down to Scotland to save the title-deeds of her husband's estates, which she had buried at Terregles before leaving for London. On May 22 she wrote from Traquair to Major Maxwell at Terregles, asking him to sell her movables in order to provide funds, and to make certain arrangements for her journey to the coast :—

"If there could be gott an able strong horse that would cary double, and had an easy trote, if not a pace, and were capable to goe through, I would be glad to buy it; for I am affraid almost of rideing single for fear of the pomell, I am grown so big."

On July 19 she sailed from the Thames, intending to go to Bruges, but she suffered so terribly from sea-sickness that she was taken ashore at Helvoetsluys in a very dangerous condition. Two years later she joined her husband, for whom she had suffered so much, at Rome. There William, fifth and last Earl of Nithsdale, died in 1744, on the eve of a second Stuart rising, and his gallant countess survived him five years. Lord Kenmure and Lord Derwentwater suffered the penalty of death on the day after Lord Nithsdale's escape from the Tower.

The estates of the insurgents were forfeited to the Crown, and were sold to a London company; but this proved a poor speculation, and the representatives of the old proprietors managed to buy most of them back at moderate prices.

NOTE K.

CONDITION OF THE SOUTH-WESTERN COUNTIES IN THE SEVENTEENTH CENTURY.

It is interesting to read the comments of travellers in Scotland during the seventeenth century, and to note their impressions of the country as compared with wealthier England.

John Taylor, the Water-Poet, travelled on foot from London to Edinburgh in 1618, and thus describes his first experience of Scotland:—

"My first night's lodging in Scotland was at a place called Mophot [Moffat], which, they say, is thirty miles from Carlile, but I suppose them to be longer than forty of such miles as are betwixt London and Saint Albanes [1] (but indeed the Scots doe allow almost as large measure of their miles as they doe of their drinke, for an English gallon, either of ale or wine, is but their quart, and one Scottish mile, now and then, may well stand for a mile and a halfe, or two English); but howsoever, short or long, I found that dayes journey the weariest that ever I footed; and at night being come to the towne, I found good ordinary countrey entertainment; my fare and my lodging was sweet and good, and might have served a farre better man than my selfe, although my selfe have had many times better; but this is to be noted, that though it rained not all the day, yet it was my fortune to be well wet twise, for I waded over a great river called the Eske in the morning, somewhat more than four miles from Carlile in England, and at night, within two miles of my lodging, I was fain to wade over the river of Annan in Scotland. . . . And whilst I waded on foot, my man was mounted on horse-backe, like the George without the dragon."

In 1636 Sir William Brereton wrote an account of his travels in Scotland and Ireland. Leaving Culzean in Ayrshire on July 2, 1635—

"We came into Galloway about six miles from the chapel,[2] and

---

[1] The old Scots mile was the same as the Irish, 10 furlongs.
[2] St John's Chapel, the old name of Stranraer.

therein observed one of the widest, broadest, plainest moors that I have seen ; it is much moss, but now so dry, as it is good hauking. Coming off this moor, we observed an eminent stone and tried it with our knives, and it did ring and sound like metal. About eight hour we came to this long-desired chapel, the town is thence denominated and so called. This is situate upon a long loch four miles long, wherein the sea ebbs and flows. Here we found good accommodation (only wanted wheat bread) in Hughe Boyde's house ; ordinary 6d., good victuals, well-ordered, good wine and beer, lodging, and horse-meat. This house is seated four miles from the Port Patrick, whence it is to Carlingworke[3] 32 miles; best lodging there is Tho. Hutton ; thence to Don-Frise 28 miles ; best lodging is John Harstein ; thence to Carleil 24.

"*Julii* 4. We went from hence [Stranraer] to the Port Patrick, which is foul winter way over the mossy moors, and there we found only one boat, though yesternight there were fifteen boats here. We hired a boat of about ten ton for five horses of ours and for five Yorkshiremen and horses ; for this we paid £1, and conditioned that no more horses should come aboard, save only two or three of an Irish laird's. . . . Here we shipped our horses two hours before we went aboard. It is a most craggy, filthy passage, and very dangerous for horses to go in and out ; a horse may easily be lamed, spoiled, and thrust into the sea ; and when any horses land here, they are thrown into the sea, and swim out. Here was demanded of us by our host, Thomas Marchbanke, a custom of 2s. an horse, which I stumbled at, and answered that if he had authority to demand and receive it, I was bound to pay it, otherwise not ; and therefore I demanded to see his authority, otherwise I was free to pay or refuse ; herewith he was satisfied, and declined his further demand."

Sir Walter Scott edited Richard Franck's 'Northern Memoirs' in 1821. It is an ambitious production, and gives, in the form of a dialogue between Arnoldus (Franck himself) and Theophilus, his experience of a tour in Scotland in 1656 :—

"*Theophilus*. However in the mean while reflect on yourself, and give us a description of the town of Dumfreez.

"*Arnoldus*. I fancy ere long you will change your note, when you traverse these pleasant northern tracts. In the mean time I'll gratify you with a breviate of Dumfreez, where a provost, as

---

[3] Now called Castle-Douglas.

superintendent, supplies the place of a mayor, a magistrate almost as venerable as an English constable.

"*Theoph.* That's wittily applied; what comes next?

"*Arn.* Nay, hold a little, I have not done yet with the eminencies and the remarks of the town of Dumfreez; for you are to consider it was anciently a town girt about with a strong stone wall; but the late irruptions, or perhaps some state disagreement, has in a manner defaced that regular ornament, otherwise the cankrous teeth of time have gnawn out the impressions, as evidently appears by those ruinous heaps. Nor is the Arnotus [4] in all parts portable, notwithstanding her shores are so delightful.

"*Theoph.* What, is there more yet? pray, go on.

"*Arn.* In the midst of that town is their market-place, and in the centre of that stands their tolbooth, round about which the rabble sit, that nauseate the very air with their tainted breath, so perfumed with onions, that to an Englishman it is almost infectious. But the kirk [5] is comely, and situate southward furnished once a week with movable spectrums (you know what that means), yet the outside than the inside is more eminently imbellished, if sepulchres and tombstones can be said to be ornaments; and where death and time stand to guard the steeple, whose rings of bells seldom or rarely exceed the critical number of three.

"Here also you may observe a large and spacious bridge, that leads directly into the country of Galloway, where thrice in a week you shall rarely fail to see their maid-maukins dance corantos in tubs. So on every Sunday some as seldom miss to make their appearance on the stool of repentance.

"*Theoph.* Then it seems by your relation they keep time with their Comers,[6] that hazard their reputation for a country-custom (or the love of liquor) rather than omit a four hours' drinking.

"*Arn.* That's true enough; and it's an antient practice among the female sex, to covee together (about that time) as naturally as geese flock'd to the Capitol.

.   .   .   .

"*Theoph.* Zanker[7] stands situate on a flat or level, surrounded, as you see, with excellent cornfields: but more remote it's besieged with mountains that are rich in lead-mines. . . . And tho' the people hereabouts are destitute of ingenuity, and their fields for the most part impoverish'd for want of cultivation; yet are their rivers and

---

[4] The Nith.   [5] The old church of St Michael's, removed in 1744.
[6] *Cummers*, gossips.   [7] Sanquhar.

rivulets replenished with trout, because undisturb'd with the noisy net, which augments the angler's if not the artisan's entertainment. . . . Zanker is a town and a corporation too; tho' not bulky in buildings, yet there is a bailiff, master sometimes of a brew-house, whose entertainments (in my opinion) may easily be guest at, provided you reflect on our late accommodation.

"There is also a market-place, such an one as it is, and a kind of thing they call a tolbooth, which at first sight might be suspected a prison, because it's so like one; whose decays, by the law of antiquity, are such that every prisoner is threatened with death before his trial; and every casement, because bound about with iron bars, discovers the entertainment destined only to felony. Now the market-place is less worthy of a description than the Tolbooth; for no man would know it to be such, were he not told so.

"There is also a kirk, or something like it; but I might as reverently call it a barn; because so little to distinguish between them, and the whole town reads daily lectures of decays; so do her ports,[8] her avenues and entrances. . . . It's true I was not murdered nor was I kill'd outright, yet I narrowly escaped as eminent a danger, when almost worried to death with lice."

John Ray, the naturalist, visited Dumfries about 1662, and gave his impressions of that neighbourhood in his Itinerary.

"*August* 24*th*. We rode to Dumfreis (from Douglas), or as they spelled it, Dumfrese, 28 miles. . . . They have there two ministers, one a young man named Campbell, related (as we were told) to the Marquis of Argyle, the other, an elder man, by name Henderson, who has married his daughter to the younger. . . . Here, as also at Dunbar, and other places, we observed the manner of their burials, which is this: when any one dies, the sexton or bellman goeth about the streets, with a small bell in his hand, which he tinkleth all along as he goeth, and now and then he makes a stand, and proclaims who is dead, and invites the people to come to the funeral at such an hour. The people and ministers many times accompany the corpse to the grave at the time appointed, with the bell before them, where there is nothing said, but only the corpse laid in. . . . The people here frequent their churches much better than in England, and have their ministers in more esteem and veneration. They seem to perform their devotions with

---

[8] Gates.

much alacrity. There are few or no sectaries or opinionists amongst them; they are much addicted to their church government, excepting the gentry, who love liberty, and care not to be so strictly tied down. The country abounds with poor people and beggars."

James Brome, a clergyman of the Church of England, passed through Annandale in 1669, and makes the following observation :—

"We came to Anandale [Annan] at the mouth of the river Anan in the County of Anandale, bordering upon our own nation, which lost all its glory and beauty upon the war, which was raised in Edward the Sixth's days; in these two last-named counties have been bred a sort of warlike men, who have been infamous for robbery and depredations, for they dwell upon Solway Frith, a fordable arm of the sea at low water, through which frequently they have made many inroads into England to fetch home great booty's, and in which they were wont after a delightful manner on horseback, with spears to hunt salmons, of which there are in these parts a very great abundance."

CHAPTER XIII.

FROM THE JACOBITE COLLAPSE IN 1715 TO THE CLOSE OF THE CENTURY.

THE second Earl of Stair maintained the high reputation of his family in public affairs. He was Colonel of the Scots Greys, in which regiment many cadets of gentle families in Galloway held commissions, while many of the yeomanry and peasantry served in the ranks. Lord Stair was also Ambassador to the Court of France, and maintained the British Embassy at Paris with great magnificence. During his absence abroad he sustained a heavy loss in the destruction by fire in 1716 of his favourite residence of Castle Kennedy.[1] It has never been rebuilt, but remains a picturesque ruin in the splendid grounds where the present earl has built the new Castle of Lochinch.

Signs of peaceful industry now began to manifest themselves in the oft-wasted Borderland. Better houses were built in the towns, of less inflammable materials than heretofore. In 1723 the town council of Dumfries enacted that, to lessen the risk of fire, all houses in the High Street should be roofed with tiles or slates. The Lochar Moss had been

---

[1] It is supposed that the fire originated in a flash of lightning. The new parish church of Inch, a handsome Gothic building, about a mile from Castle Kennedy, was burnt to the ground from the same cause in 1894.

from time immemorial a valuable defence to the town against its "auld enemies of England." Easier access to the south was desired in the interests of trade, and Pennant, writing in 1770, records how funds had been forthcoming to effect this in 1724:—

"Over Lochar Moss is a road remarkable for its origin. A stranger, a great number of years ago, sold some goods to certain merchants in Dumfries upon credit: he disappeared, and neither he nor his heirs ever claimed the money. The merchants, in expectation of the demand, very honestly put out the sum to interest; and, after the lapse of more than fifty years, the town of Dumfries obtained a gift of it, and applied the same to the making of this useful road. Another is now in erection for the military, to facilitate the communication between North Britain and Ireland by way of Portpatrick." [2]

About 1725 William Hyland of Kirkcudbright laid the foundation of an important extension of agriculture by introducing the potato into Galloway. He used to carry his crop to Edinburgh on pack-horses and sell the tubers by the pound.

Even at the end of the first quarter of the eighteenth century Galloway was far behind other parts of Scotland in agricultural prosperity. Mr Maxwell of Munches, writing as a very old man in 1811, thus described his recollection of the condition of farmers and peasantry in his boyhood and youth:—

"The tenants in general lived very meanly on kail, groats,

[2] Tour in Scotland, vol. ii. p. 95. Of the excellence of the second and later road mentioned in this extract the author received good testimony a few years ago. A friend coming to visit him at Monreith travelled the whole way from London on a bicycle. The cyclist declared that the best piece of road in all the journey was that between Castle Douglas and Newton-Stewart.

milk, gradden grinded in querns turned by the hand and the grain dried in a pot, together with a crock ewe [a ewe past bearing] now and then about Martinmas. They were clothed very plainly, and their habitations were most uncomfortable. Their general wear was of cloth made of waulked plaiding, black and white wool mixed, very coarse, and the cloth rarely dyed. Their hose were made of white plaiding cloth, sewed together, with single-soled shoes, and a black or blue bonnet, none having hats but the lairds, who thought themselves very well dressed for going to church on Sunday with a black kelt coat of their wife's making. . . . The distresses and poverty felt in the country during these times . . . continued till about the year 1735. . . . There was, for the most, a great scarcity of food, bordering on famine; for, in the stewartry of Kirkcudbright and county of Dumfries, there was not as much victual produced as was necessary for supplying the inhabitants; and the chief part of what was required for that purpose was brought from the sand-beds of Esk in tumbling cars, on the Wednesdays to Dumfries;[3] and when the waters were high by reason of spates—there being no bridges—so that these cars could not come with the meal, I have seen the tradesmen's wives, in the streets of Dumfries, crying because there was none to be got. At that period there was only one baker in Dumfries, and he made bawbee baps of coarse flour, chiefly bran, which he occasionally carried in creels to the fairs of Urr and Kirkpatrick. The produce of the country generally was grey corn, and you might have travelled from Dumfries to Kirkcudbright, which is twenty-seven miles, without seeing any other grain, except in a gentleman's croft, which, in general, produced bear or *bigg* for one-third part, another third in white oats, and the remaining third in grey oats. At that period there was no

[3] Wednesday is still the weekly market in Dumfries.

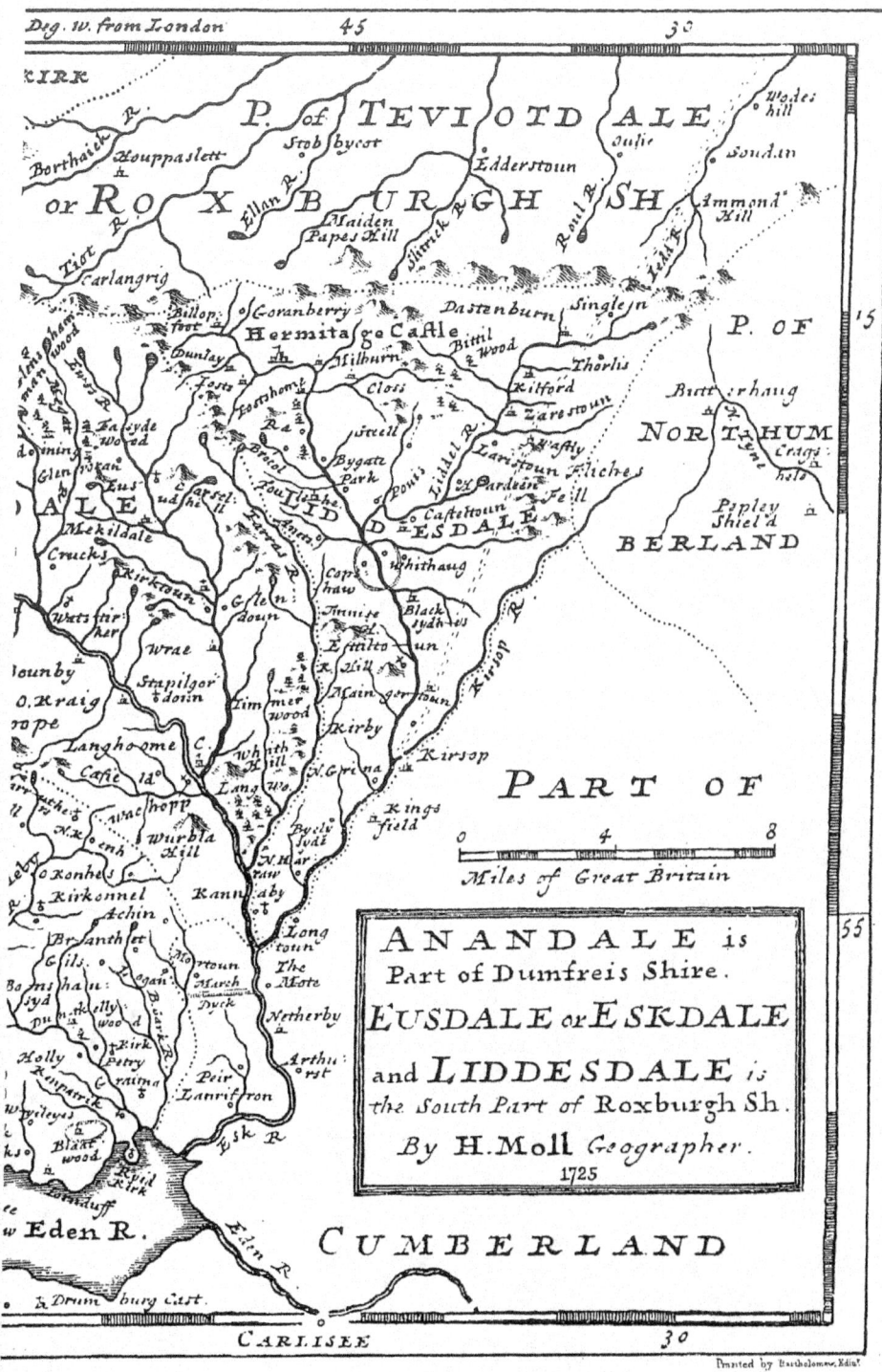

wheat raised in the country: what was used was brought from Teviot; and it was believed the soil would not produce wheat. . . . Cattle were very low. I remember being at the Bridge-end of Dumfries in 1736, when Anthony M'Kie of Netherlaw sold five score of five-year-old Galloway cattle in good condition to an Englishman at £2, 12s. 6d. each; and old Robert Halliday, who was tenant of a great part of the Preston estate, told me that he reckoned he could graze his cattle on his farm for 2s. 6d. a-head—that is to say, his rent corresponded to that sum."

While legitimate industry was thus pushing its way to prosperity, the contraband trade was also fast increasing in volume and activity. The nature and incidents of this traffic have lately been well described by a Galloway writer who has attained a high degree of popularity. In 'The Raiders' Mr S. R. Crockett has presented us with a story of which the smuggling adventures are probably no exaggeration of the reality. All along the Solway shore are numerous creeks and caves, of which the "fair traders" knew well how to avail themselves in running and storing their cargoes. The Excise were far too weak to cope with the smugglers, who had friends and allies in every rank. Many of the county and burgh magistrates thought it no dishonour to wink at what was going on, and even to accept the silent tribute of an anker of brandy, or a parcel of lace or tea for the ladies, left in a convenient place. Under many of the farmhouses extensive cellarage was constructed to store the goods till they could be safely removed inland by strings of pack-horses driven by armed men.

In the year 1894 the author had to lay out money in reconstructing a barn on the farm of Clone, Wigtownshire, the floor of which had given way and fallen into an old "brandy hole" underneath. On this farm there was formerly a concealed store-cellar of a very ingenious kind. Two subterranean chambers were constructed, one under the other. The excisemen were freely admitted to the upper one, and, not unnaturally, never thought of searching beneath it. But in the lower one, which was approached by a separate subterranean entrance, good store of contraband material was constantly kept. When this hiding-place was at length laid bare by the exertions of a new inspector-general in 1777, it was found to contain 80 chests of tea, 140 ankers of brandy, 200 bales of tobacco, and many other valuables. The value of the seizure may be estimated from the prize-money awarded, which was at the following rate: lieutenant, £269, 14s.; sergeant, £42, 16s. 10d.; corporal, £28, 14s. 4d.; private, £14, 5s. 8½d. The Preventive service men came in for much larger shares. Another *cache* at Drumtrodden, a farm in that neighbourhood, consisted of a fire-proof chamber constructed under a kiln. As often as the Excise officers were seen approaching the kiln fire was lighted on the top of the stone which covered the only access to the cellar.[4]

The gipsies were numerous in the Border counties in those days, and were among the most intrepid "riders" concerned in smuggling. There were many grades of them, from Big Will Baillie, the chief of one sept, who marauded on the romantic scale of Robin Hood, to the common "tinklers" or "cairds" who pitched their tents in Nithsdale and harboured among the Galloway hills. Sir Walter Scott, who never, so far as is known, was in Galloway, was able to make use of information given him by Joseph Train, an Excise officer in Castle Douglas, and to describe truthfully in 'Guy Mannering' the position held by gipsies in the social scale. Sir Walter's genius has been the means of making the whole civilised world familiar with the events in a domestic tragedy

---

[4] Agnew's Hereditary Sheriffs, vol. ii. p. 367.

which took its rise in the parish of Kirkpatrick-Irongray in 1738. The names of the various characters in the 'Heart of Mid-Lothian' are fictitious, and the scene has been transferred from the shores of Solway to those of Forth, but the main facts of the narrative are preserved in that romance as they happened in reality. Isabel Walker, sentenced to death at Dumfries for child-murder, was the original of Effie Deans; her sister, Helen, appears as Jeanie in the novel. Helen was given to understand that she could save her sister's life by declaring that Isabel had, at any time previous to the birth of the child, made known her condition to Helen. But trained as she had been as a strict Presbyterian, even this terrible trial could not induce her to tell a lie. She travelled on foot to London, obtained an interview with the Duke of Argyle, and gained a pardon for the condemned girl. Isabel afterwards married her seducer, and spent the rest of her life at Whitehaven. The heroic Helen remained single, a hard-working, thrifty country woman, and died in 1791. Over her grave in Kirkpatrick-Irongray Scott caused a stone to be erected, bearing an inscription in which Helen Walker is acknowledged to be the original of Jeanie Deans.

Notwithstanding the number of unruly and criminal characters frequenting the hill districts and coasts of Dumfries and Galloway, the general scale of life was being steadily raised, under the rule of the house of Hanover, to a higher level than it had touched since the death of Alexander III. But one more struggle was to be entered upon, one more blow struck for the old order of things, before it could be finally laid to rest, and the people apply their whole energy to the arts of peace. Charles Edward landed at Moidart on July 25, 1745. It is a far cry thence to Dumfries, and there were few explosive elements remaining in the south-west, so the authorities were slow to make preparations against a descent. Almost the only gentleman of note who mounted the white cockade this time was William Maxwell of Kirkconnell, who has left an interesting memoir of the rising, composed when he had fled to France after the battle of Culloden. Inaction prevailed in Dumfries and Galloway even after the Jacobite victory at Prestonpans on September 21, where John Stewart of Physgil fell beside Colonel Gardiner, and another Wigtownshire laird, Sir Thomas Hay of Park, lost an arm while serving in the Galloway militia against the Highlanders. But when the Prince's army marched south they had to encounter ill-feeling among the people. On November 6, 4000 Highlanders quartered themselves at Moffat. Passing on to Carlisle next day, they left some of their baggage, weakly guarded, at Ecclefechan, sixteen miles from Dumfries. An expedition having been hastily organised in the county town, a raid was made on the Jacobite depot, the guard was put to flight, and the baggage and arms carried off in triumph to Dumfries.

No more was seen of the Highland host till after the disastrous retreat from Derby. Then, on December 16, the news came to Dumfries that Prince Charles Edward's army was returning, and orders were issued to all the parishes of the presbytery to arm and intercept it. Volunteers were not wanting, and the Scottish bank of the Esk was strongly manned by descendants of the stout Borderers who had often withstood the English warden on the same ground. Men of the old names were there—Elliots, Irvings, Armstrongs, Maxwells, Johnstones; but where were the old feudal leaders? where the old stout spirit? Six thousand plaided Highlanders, under their Prince, Lord George Murray, Lord Tullibardine, Lord Elcho, and others, struck such terror into the souls of the men of Nithsdale and Annandale that before the first company entered the water at Longtown these gallant defenders of their country were in full flight, leaving only one

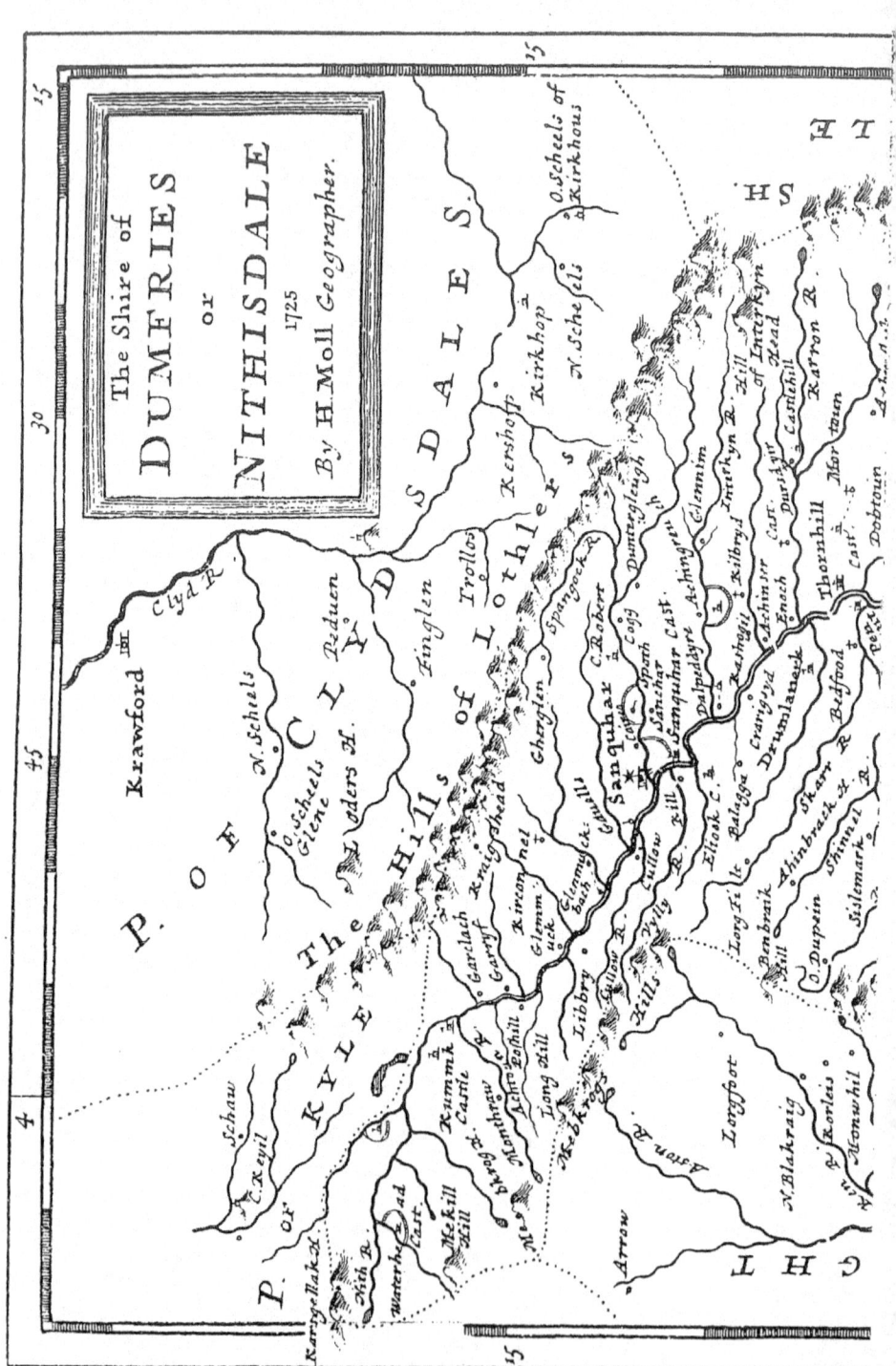

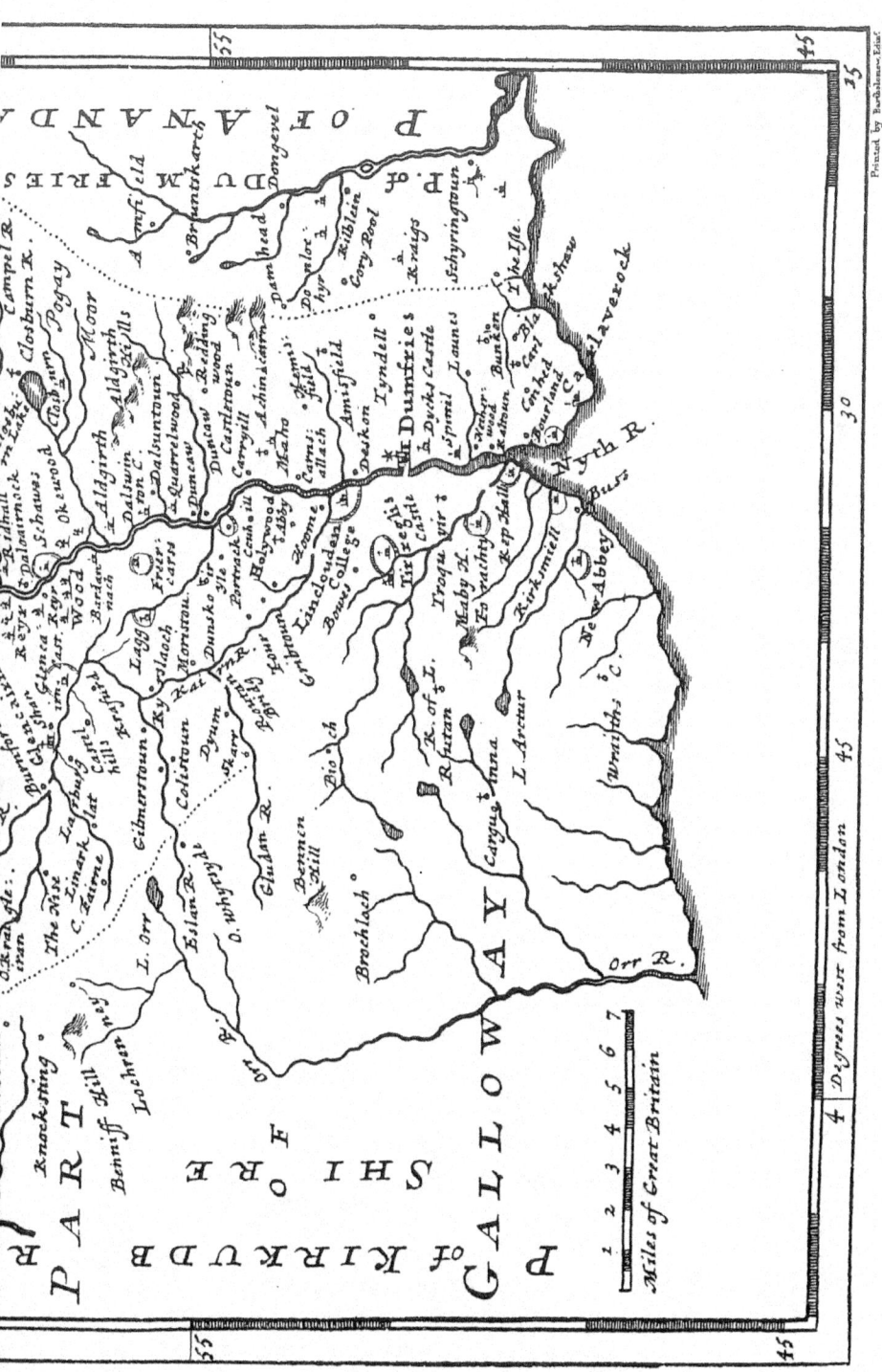

officer, afterwards minister of Middlebie, to fire a single defiant shot at the approaching troops. A hundred abreast the Highlanders forded the flooded Esk, which ran shoulder-high; then the pipes struck up, and they danced themselves dry on the wintry shore. Charles Edward slept that night in Annan; Lord Elcho rode forward with 500 men and took possession of Dumfries, where the Prince joined him next day, and took up his quarters at the Blue Bell, now called the Commercial Hotel. Mr Duncan, minister of Lochrutton, kept a journal of events at this time, and the following piteous entry occurs under Sabbath, December 22, 1745:—

"A melancholy day—the rebels in Drumfries—about 4000,[5] with the Pretender's son at their head, in great rage at the town for carrying off their baggage from Annandale, and for raising volunteers, and calling out the militia of the Country in defence of the Government—demanded £2000 sterling of contributions, . . . and that they convey their carts, with their carriages after them, to their headquarters. They were most rude in the town—pillaged some shops—pulled shoes off gentlemen's feet in the streets. In most of the churches for some miles about Drumfries no sermon. God be blessed! we[6] had public worship. I lectured 1 Sam. iv.; Mr John Scott, minister of Drumfries (there was no sermon there) preached. Much confusion in all the neighbouring parishes—rebels robbing people's stables—pillaging some houses. They came to the border of our parish, but, God be thanked! came no further, and we suffered no loose usage."

An exaction of £2000 and 1000 pairs of shoes was laid on the burgh, of which the Prince's officers, backed by 4000 claymores, succeeded in wringing from the unwarlike townsfolk

---

[5] Lord George Murray and Lord Tullibardine had marched northward from the Esk by way of Ecclefechan with 2000 men.

[6] In Lochrutton.

£1195 of the first and 255 pairs of the second. They also seized all arms within the town. But of goodwill Prince Charles got very little, except from a few ladies. Any man who secretly favoured the house of Stuart was too prudent to show his feelings, for it was already a broken cause. Mr Lowthian, proprietor of the house where the Prince lodged, was a staunch Jacobite. Equally afraid to offend his Prince by keeping out of his way, and his fellow-townsmen by frequenting the Pretender's Court, it is said that he deliberately and of prudent purpose became and remained so hopelessly drunk that his appearance in public was out of the question.

The Jacobite army left Dumfries hurriedly on the arrival of news that the king's troops, under the Duke of Cumberland, were advancing fast upon the town. The Sheriff of Galloway, Sir Andrew Agnew, commanded the Royal North British Fusiliers, forming part of Lord Sempill's brigade in the Duke's army. In leaving Dumfries, the insurgents carried off with them two hostages for payment of the balance of the exaction—namely, Provost Crosbie and Mr Walter Riddell of Newhouse. These two gentlemen were taken to Glasgow, and were released shortly after on the money being sent.[7] Thus ended the connection of Dumfriesshire with "the '45." Five years later the Treasury refunded to the provost and magistrates of Dumfries the sum of £2848, 5s. 11d. as indemnity for the losses sustained during the Jacobite occupation, and ordained the same to be paid out of the estates of Lord Elcho, which had been forfeited to the Crown.[8]

The suddenness with which the Jacobite lords and their

[7] 'Collection of Scottish Antiquities,' selected by Robert Riddell, Esq., of Friars Carse and Glenriddell, 1786, MS. in ten volumes, of which seven are in possession of the Society of Scottish Antiquaries, and three in that of Mr A. G. Reid of Auchterarder.

[8] See Note L, The Jacobite Rising of 1745, p. 360.

Highlanders had overrun Scotland, possessed themselves of Edinburgh, and, having thus secured a substantial base of operations, seriously threatened the capital of England, had convinced the Government of the necessity for bringing the counties into closer connection with the central authority. Heritable jurisdictions—the sheriffships, stewartries, regalities, and bailieries, administered by leading landowners in all the shires—had been expressly protected by a clause in the Act of Union, and the proposal to interfere with them was strongly opposed by Scottish members of Parliament as a breach of faith. Nevertheless it was held indispensable to the security of the realm that judicial functions, combined with military responsibility, should cease to be administered by men, without regard to their ability or character, simply because they were the sons of their fathers. On April 16, 1747, the bill abolishing heritable jurisdictions in Scotland was carried in the House of Commons by a majority of 131, and then passed the House of Lords under protest of the Scottish peers. Compensation was provided for persons thus deprived of hereditary office. The total amount claimed was £602,127, of which the judges appointed to award the compensation allowed £152,237. It is amusing to compare the amounts claimed by individuals with those received. Thus Sir Andrew Agnew asked for £7000 and received £4000. He was the only official who was able to prove continuous hereditary tenure of a sheriffship by his family since the days of James II. of Scotland, dating from 1451. The Marquis of Annandale claimed and received £5000 for loss of the stewartship of Kirkcudbright. The Earl of Galloway valued his regality of Whithorn and two minor offices at £6000; he was awarded £321, 6s. The Earl of Stair put in a claim of £3200 for the regality of Glenluce, &c., and had to be content with £450. Marmaduke Constable Maxwell, representing the attainted earldom of Nithsdale, estimated the loss of the regality of Terregles, the provostship of Lincluden, and four other offices, at £6600; he received £523, 4s. 1d. Hathorn of Castle Wigg valued the barony of Busby at £1000, but was awarded nothing.

No doubt this great social change was inevitable, but there can be equally little doubt that heritable jurisdictions had been, on the whole, faithfully and usefully discharged, and it was long before the people of Galloway ceased to speak regretfully of "gentlemen's law." The late Earl of Galloway used to repeat what was once said to him by one of his tenants who had lived under four generations of Stuarts, and complained of the dilatoriness of the new system in dealing with cattle-lifters or sheep-stealers. "Yerl John," he said, "was nae yerl, and Yerl Alexander was nae yerl ava'! Yerl James was the man! He'd hang them up juist at his ain word. Nane o' yer law!"[9]

Let it never be forgotten, to the credit of the old hereditary judges, that, but for their sympathy with the people, the "killing time" under the Test and Conventicle Acts would have been far more bloody, and the severity of the law far more rigorously carried out by officials appointed from Edinburgh. Galloway had a sample of this when Agnew was temporarily superseded as sheriff by Claverhouse.

The first Sheriff of Wigtownshire under the new system was Boswell of Auchinleck, father of Dr Johnson's panegyrist; and the first Steward of Kirkcudbright was Sir Thomas Miller, afterwards, as Lord Glenlee, President of the Court of Session.

By the Act of 1747 the old baron courts were deprived of criminal jurisdiction, part of their functions being transferred to the new sheriffs' courts, and part to the justices

[9] Agnew's Hereditary Sheriffs, vol. ii. p. 336.

of the peace, whose authority had been constituted in 1609. Nevertheless baron courts continued to be held for some years for the administration of the business of the estate. The agent or factor on large properties continued to be called the bailie, and under him was the barony officer, whose chief duty it was to summon the tenants to attend the courts. Close to the picturesque kirkyard of Old Penninghame may still be seen the barony officer's house of the Earls of Galloway bearing the fesse checquy and tressure of the Stuarts carved on a stone over the door. There are various places in Galloway named Officer's Croft; these represent former dwellings of officials. It does not appear that the barony officer received any salary in money from the laird; but, in addition to his enjoyment of a free croft, it was usual to bind each tenant to pay something towards his emolument.[1]

Farm-rents at this time, and for forty years later, continued to be paid partly in victual and service. Modern land-agents might be not a little perplexed if called on to collect the rents then exacted on Sir Andrew Agnew's estates in the parishes of Leswalt and Kirkcolm. Besides the silver rent, there was payable annually—

19 wethers.
48 lambs.
2 swine.
37 capons.
47 reek-hens.[2]
456 chickens.

3¾ stones of butter.
2½ stones of tallow.
120 eggs.
2000 oysters.
6 codfish.
105 bolls meal.
35 bolls barley.
3540 loads of peat.

---

[1] "Yearly to pay three stooks of Sergeant corn to the Barron officer."—Lease of Galdenoch, on Lochnaw estate, April 1762.

[2] *Reek-hens—i.e.*, a hen for every reek-house, for every house with a chimney. Before the Union the equivalent blench-duty for a reek-hen was reckoned at 4s. Scots (4d. sterling).

In addition the tenant was commonly bound to furnish so many days of farm labour, horse and man, in proportion to the size of his holding, — a trace of the old bond-service. Thus the laird got his larder supplied and his home farm worked in exchange for the use of his land, and the system answered fairly well in times when it was the general custom for proprietors to live with their families all the year round on their own lands. The tenant, too, must have found the "service" less onerous, though less exciting, than in the old riding days, when he was bound to leave wife and bairns at short notice and follow his feudal lord "boden in effeir of war," to take his share of hard knocks in some quarrel in which he felt no concern.

It is amusing to find reflected in the history of the municipality of Dumfries, as in almost every other elective government in all ages, the never-ending rivalry between privilege and popular rights. As Florence of the fifteenth century had its Ghibellines and Guelphs, and Holland in the sixteenth century its Hooks and Kabbeljaws, so Dumfries became divided in 1759 between the aristocratic Corbies (crows) and the plebeian Pyets (magpies). It is hardly worth while resuscitating this old squabble, except to record the fate of some unfortunate people who took leading parts in it. The Corbies were of the merchant class or capitalists, taking their name from Bailie James Corbet, whom they put in nomination and succeeded in electing as provost. The Pyets were the tradesmen or artisans, who, strange to say, ran a country gentleman as their candidate, John Graham of Kinharvie. The election of four new councillors gave rise to serious riots, for which twelve unlucky Pyets were put on their trial in Edinburgh. Deacon Smith of the weavers was sentenced to transportation for life, Deacon Smith of the tailors for fourteen years, and William Ewart, shoemaker, for seven. Two were outlawed for failing to appear, six were sentenced to various terms of imprisonment, and a Radical merchant who had thrown in his lot with the Pyets was fined 900 merks. It is horrible to think of kindly Scots folk undergoing the horrors of banishment to the plantations for no weightier offence than an election riot wherein no lives were lost.

Twelve years later more serious disturbance broke out in the burgh. Bread-stuffs were at famine prices in 1771, and the people rose to prevent flour and meal ground in the mills on Nithsdale being sent away for sale elsewhere. Two of the rioters were sentenced to transportation, and others to imprisonment.

In 1760 a Jacobite descent was made on the coast of Ireland. The young French admiral Thurot, whose real name was O'Farrel, son of an adherent of James II., appeared off Carrickfergus Castle with three ships of war. The castle surrendered, after which Thurot, having compelled the merchants of Belfast under threat of bombardment to furnish his flotilla with supplies, stood across the Channel and anchored in the Bay of Luce. There Commodore Elliot, who had been despatched with three ships in pursuit, came up with the French admiral, and a brisk engagement took place off the coast of Kirkmaiden. Thurot was killed and his ships taken, about 300 French sailors being slain.[3] Admiral Thurot's body was washed ashore near Monreith, and Sir William Maxwell invited the gentry and tenantry to the brave sailor's funeral, which took place in the quiet little burial-ground of Kirkmaiden-in-Fernes, on the opposite side of Luce Bay to Kirkmaiden-in-Rhindis.

[3] The Silurian beds near the Mull of Galloway contain large nodules of iron pyrites of a flattened globe shape. These, when washed out of the rock, are found lying on the beach, and the country-folk declare that they are cannon-balls fired during the conflict between Elliot and Thurot. The author received from an old fisherman at the Mull a long ballad describing the incidents of the combat, but it is hardly worth transcribing.

In 1772 many persons in Dumfriesshire and Galloway were ruined, and others suffered lamentable loss, by the collapse of Douglas, Heron, & Co.'s bank, a rashly speculative affair started only three years before, of which the shares had been freely taken up in the neighbourhood, owing to the confidence felt in the principal directors, the Hon. Archibald Douglas and Mr Patrick Heron. The headquarters of the bank were in Ayr, but one-fourth of the capital was subscribed in Dumfriesshire. The liability on each share amounted to £2600.

Smugglers became bolder as time went on, along the whole coast from Annanfoot to Glenluce. At the last-named locality a brisk encounter took place in 1771 between 200 men leading horses loaded with the cargo discharged from three vessels at the Crow's Nest in Luce Bay. The Excise had got notice of the landing. A party of sixteen soldiers under a sergeant had been placed in ambush to intercept the smugglers, and the coastguardsmen were posted so as to take them in rear when they had fallen into the trap. But the smugglers, too, had got notice of the ambuscade. When the soldiers fired a volley their intended victims charged, put the enemy to flight, and carried off their booty safely into the interior.

The contraband trade had become almost as common an investment for men of capital as any other business. Merchants fitted out well-found vessels for smuggling; lairds and ministers not only connived at it, but put their money into the venture. Mr Carson, minister of Anwoth, was deprived of his living in 1767 because he was proved to be deeply implicated in the " fair trade."

To the Stewartry of Kirkcudbright is due whatever degree of fame belongs to the birthplace of the celebrated privateer or pirate, Paul Jones. Son of the gardener at Arbigland, in

Kirkbean parish, his real name was John Paul. He was bound apprentice on board the Friendship of Whitehaven, belonging to Mr Younger, a merchant in the American trade. Mr Younger became bankrupt, and young Jones entered as third mate on board the King George of Whitehaven, a slave-ship. After three years' service in her he became first mate of the Two Friends of Jamaica, another slaver, and in a couple of years more returned at the age of twenty-one, taking a passage home in the John of Kirkcudbright. On the voyage both captain and mate died, John Paul took command, brought the John safe to port, and received the appointment of master from her owners. Two years later he took to the smuggling trade between Solway and Man, and in 1773 his elder brother died intestate in Virginia, said to have been possessed of considerable wealth. John Paul, or Paul Jones as he elected to be called, took charge of the estate on behalf of the family, but there is nothing to show that they ever profited by it. In 1775 he offered his services to the Americans in their war with England, and spent two years cruising against English commerce. He was then appointed by Congress to command the Ranger frigate of 26 guns, in which he once more made his appearance off the coast of Galloway, where his knowledge of the locality enabled him to do much damage. On April 18 he attempted to burn the shipping in Whitehaven, but nearly lost his own ship in a strong gale, which obliged him to sail for Belfast Lough. He returned to Whitehaven on the 22d, spiked the guns in the forts, burned the ships in the harbour, and bore up for Kirkcudbright Bay. Here the idea occurred to him of kidnapping the Earl of Selkirk, whom his boyish recollections doubtless caused him to regard as a political prize of the highest importance. Lord Selkirk, however, happened to be away from home; but Jones sent a party up to St Mary's

Isle, where Lady Selkirk was keeping house. They carried off considerable booty in the shape of plate and other valuables. This was restored to the earl by the freebooter after some years. With this incident his connection with Galloway ceases. His subsequent career is part of the world's naval history. He became commodore of a joint American and French squadron of five sail; sailed along the coasts of Scotland and Ireland, making several prizes; made a surprise descent on the Firth of Forth, and was only prevented doing a vast amount of mischief there by a heavy gale which drove him out to sea. In 1788 he entered the Russian navy with the rank of Rear-Admiral, served against the Turks, and died in 1792.

It may be asked, Why call this man by the harsh name of pirate, seeing that he was successively in the service of recognised Governments? He himself strenuously protested against being so classed. It is only necessary to quote a few extracts from the log of the Ranger, written by his own hand, to show how he carried into effect the teaching of the ruffianly school in which he had been reared. In the description of his voyage from Brest in 1778, on the expedition against Whitehaven, Belfast, and Kirkcudbright, the following significant passages occur:—

"Sailed from Brest April 10. My plan was extensive; I therefore did not at the beginning wish to encumber myself with prisoners. On the 14th I took a brigantine between Scilly and Cape Clear, with a cargo of flax-seed for Ireland, sunk her, and proceeded into St George's Channel. On the 17th I took the ship Lord Chatham, bound from London to Dublin; . . . this ship I manned and ordered for Brest. . . . On the 19th, off the Mull of Galloway, I found myself so near a Scotch coasting schooner, loaded with barley, that I could not avoid sinking her."

No prisoners! Paul Jones was a fine sailor, no doubt, but never was there a rogue should have swung more properly than he from a yard-arm.

It was in the spring of 1787 that Robert Burns, then in the early flush of fame, first visited Nithsdale, which was to form at once the birthplace and the scene of many of his finest poems. The previous year had been the most agitated in his existence, and the most momentous to his reputation as a bard. His wild oats were springing up into a crop of bewildering profusion. He had already one illegitimate daughter on his hands, without ready means of providing for her; Jean Armour of Mauchline was *enceinte*, and her father had taken out a warrant to compel Burns to give security for maintaining her offspring. Robert was joint tenant with his brother Gilbert of the farm of Mossgiel near Mauchline, but matters were not going well with that enterprise. Perplexed between pecuniary and amatory embarrassment, he decided to emigrate, and obtained an appointment as overseer on an estate in Jamaica at a salary of £30. But the passage-money was a difficulty, and it was to defray this expense that, acting under the advice of his staunch friend and admirer, Gavin Hamilton, writer in Mauchline, he took a collection of his poems to John Wilson, a printer in Kilmarnock. From the sale of this, his first publication,[4] Burns received £20,—enough to pay his passage to the West Indies. Within a month of publication 599 copies had been sold, leaving 15 only in the publisher's hands. Burns made over the copyright to his brother Gilbert, as trustee for his illegitimate daughter Elizabeth Paton, then a little more than a year old.

[4] 'Poems chiefly in the Scottish Dialect.' Kilmarnock, 1786. Copies of this edition, now of extreme rarity, have been sold of late years at prices varying from £80 to £100 each.

The poems proved so popular that their author wavered in his purpose of emigration — at least he postponed his departure. Blacklock, the blind poet, urged him to prepare a second edition, but the Kilmarnock printer refused to risk it unless Burns paid £27 in advance for the cost of paper. This was beyond his power. Mr Ballantyne of Ayr came to the rescue, and offered to advance the money, at the same time strongly advising Burns to put the work into the hands of an Edinburgh firm.

On September 3, Jean Armour gave birth to twin sons. Meanwhile her faithless lover had betrothed himself to Mary Campbell, daughter of a sailor near Dunoon, the "Highland Mary" of future poems. She died of fever in Greenock in October 1786, and shortly afterwards Burns borrowed a pony and rode to Edinburgh. There he found kind Ayrshire friends—Mrs Dunlop of Dunlop and Mr Dalrymple of Ayr—who soon brought him to the notice of influential people,[5] to such good purpose that when Creech issued the second edition in April 1787 there were 1500 subscribers for 2800 copies. This brought Burns the substantial sum of £500,[6] though it was not without prolonged anxiety and much trouble that he obtained payment.

Relieved from immediate pecuniary pressure, Burns had now, it seems, finally given up the idea of emigrating. His first care was to relieve the necessity of his brother Gilbert by a loan of £180, and then his thoughts reverted to his native industry of farming. He told Lord Buchan that he was resolved to "woo his rustic Muse at the plough-tail";

---

[5] Among those who most effectively befriended him was a lady from his own West Country, Jane, Duchess of Gordon, a daughter of Sir William Maxwell of Monreith.

[6] Burns said he received a little more than £400, but Creech declared he paid him £1100. The copyright was sold for £100, and the poet thus forfeited all rights in subsequent editions.

and in the course of a tour through the Border counties in May and June 1787, he visited the farm of Ellisland on the estate of Dalswinton, the tenancy of which was offered to him.

The factor on Dalswinton was the father of Allan Cunningham, Burns's future biographer, who observes that Burns looked at the farm with a poet's eye rather than a farmer's. Probably the charm of the scenery weighed at least as much in the decision he came to as the quality of the land. He became tenant of 110 acres under a lease for seventy-six years; the rent was to be £50 for the first three years, and then to rise to £70. Burns was to build house and steading and enclose the land, towards which the landlord paid £300.

During his stay in Edinburgh Burns had succumbed to a new passion. Mrs M'Lehose, whose husband had deserted her and gone abroad, became the Clarinda of his poems and correspondence, and had she been free, they would doubtless have been married. But Jean Armour was a second time *enceinte*, and before she gave birth to twin daughters Burns privately acknowledged her as his wife. Of this public profession was made in Mauchline Kirk on August 3, 1788. Poor Clarinda took this terribly to heart; it was not till three years later that their final parting came, of which Burns sang in one of his most beautiful lyrics, "Ae fond kiss and then we sever."

While the new house at Ellisland was being built Mrs Burns continued to live at Mauchline, which gave occasion to her husband to compose the well-known lines beginning "O' a' the airts the wind can blaw."[7] The verses beginning "O were I on Parnassus hill" also date from this summer, and contain allusion to some of the features in the scenery round Ellisland.

Allan Cunningham describes how, when the foundations of

---

[7] Mauchline lies about forty miles due north-west of Ellisland.

the house were being laid, the poet, bonnet in hand, offered up a prayer for blessing on his future home, and how carefully he watched every stage in the building. Cunningham asked an old mason who had been engaged in the work if Burns ever helped in it. "Ay! that he did," was the answer, "mony a time. If he saw us like to be beat wi' a big stane, he wad cry, 'Bide a wee,' and come rinnin'. We soon fand oot when he pit to his hand—he beat a' I ever met for a dour lift."

Burns brought home his wife after harvest. Cunningham describes the suspicious regard of some of his neighbours in Nithsdale at his settling among them. They did not relish the idea of their foibles being shown up in satirical verse. "An old farmer told me," writes Cunningham, "that at a penny-pay wedding, when one or two wild young fellows began to quarrel and threatened to fight, Burns rose up and said, 'Sit down and be damned to you! else I'll hing ye up like potato-bogles in sang to-morrow.' They ceased and sat down, said my informant, as if their noses had been bleeding."

The farm was not the only string to the poet's bow. During the spring of 1788 Burns had qualified as an exciseman, an appointment offered to him through the influence of Lord Glencairn. So when, after a few months' experience of Ellisland, the prospect of successful farming became faint, he met disappointment with the defiant philosophy breathed in the lines beginning "I hae a wife o' my ain."

His attempts to raise the intellectual activity of his neighbours were not more fruitful than those in agriculture; for although a small library in Dunscore, of which he undertook the management, started briskly enough, the attendance soon dwindled to nothing. So it was not long before he began to discharge the active duties of an exciseman.

"I do not know," wrote Burns to Ainslie, "if I have

informed you that I am now appointed to an excise division in the middle of which my farm and house lie. I know not how the word exciseman, or still more opprobrious gauger, will sound in your ears. I, too, have seen the day when my auditory nerves would have felt very delicately on the subject; but a wife and children have a wonderful power in blunting these kind of sensations. Fifty pounds a-year for life, and a provision for widows and orphans, you will allow, is no bad settlement for a *poet*."

The social relations that prevailed in Nithsdale at this time have no parallel in any rural neighbourhood of the present day. A farmer's life was as lowly as his craft was unpretending. One cannot but smile at Cunningham's description of the usual test of the readiness of the land to receive the seed. The farmer seated himself on the soil: if heat was imparted to his body, he began sowing; if, on the other hand, the soil drew heat from the cultivator, the operation was postponed. Yet the farmer was encouraged to meet on easy terms with the owners of the soil, many of whom had but one idea of spending their leisure—namely, in conviviality. Burns, with little natural inclination to austerity, was certainly not to learn abstemious habits in Nithsdale.

One of the orgies in which he took part has been immortalised in the poem entitled "The Whistle." Three neighbouring lairds—Captain Riddell of Friars Carse, Ferguson of Craigdarroch, and Sir Robert Lawrie—resolved to drink against each other, the prize being a whistle of ebony, which an ancestor of Lawrie's was recorded to have won by prodigious potation from a foreign toper of distinction. Robert Burns was invited to make a fourth and see fair play. So one afternoon the shutters were closed and the curtains drawn to shut out the fair summer sunshine, candles were lit, and the match began.

"They had already swallowed six bottles apiece and day was breaking when Ferguson, decanting a quart of wine, dismissed it at a draught. Upon this Glenriddell, recollecting that he was an elder and a ruling one in the Kirk, and feeling he was waging an ungodly strife, meekly withdrew from the contest. . . . Though Sir Robert could not well contend both with fate and quart bumpers, he fought to the last and fell not till the sun rose. Not so Ferguson, and not so Burns: the former sounded a note of triumph on his whistle. . . . It is said that the poet drank bottle for bottle in this arduous contest, and when daylight came, seemed much disposed to take up the conqueror."

It is said that Sir Robert Lawrie's health never recovered the severity of this bout. Another gathering at Friars Carse leaves less for the friendly veil of oblivion, and was even more fruitful of good poetry than the other. Francis Grose, the antiquary, having arrived as the guest of Captain Riddell, his advent was hailed by Burns in the stanzas beginning "Hear, Land o' Cakes and brither Scots." Burns asked him to make a drawing of Alloway Kirk, the burial-place of his family. Grose agreed on condition that Burns should write a poem on the place. The result was the immortal ballad of "Tam o' Shanter,"[8] composed, as the poet assured Lockhart, in a single day's walk beside the Nith.

Burns must have been a genius even more versatile than he was if, between poetic flights, bacchanalian descents, and long rides as an exciseman, he had reserved energy and time to make his farm pay. The summer of 1791 was not far spent when it became clear that if any of his capital was to be saved he must give up Ellisland. The lease was

---

[8] Shanter is a small farm on Lord Ailsa's property near Maybole. The name is Gaelic—*i.e.*, *sean* (shan) *tir*, old land or farm. Cf. Shambellie, Sanquhar, &c.

surrendered and a move was made to Dumfries. The Burnses lived first in the Wee Vennel (now Bank Street) from December 1791 till May 1793, and then moved into a house in Mill Vennel (now Burns Street). Before settling in Dumfries Burns paid a farewell visit to Edinburgh, where he bade adieu to Mrs M'Lehose.

Burns now drew £70 a-year as exciseman, but his acquaintance with the county lairds was a sad hindrance to the regular discharge of his duties. On the last day of 1792 he writes to Mrs Dunlop that though he has given up taverns, "hard-drinking is the devil to him." The excessive hospitality of Mr Walter Riddell of Woodley Park (now Goldielea), a brother of Captain Riddell of Friars Carse, was a mischievous snare to him, and it is melancholy to trace the rudderless course of this gifted mind.

About this time Burns earned a rebuke from his superiors for his advocacy of revolutionary politics. Hitherto he had professed a Platonic sympathy with the lost cause of the Jacobites. Lady Winifred Maxwell, daughter and heiress of the last Earl of Nithsdale, had wakened his song before he left Ellisland by the gift of a costly snuff-box with a portrait of Queen Mary on the lid. But now the course of events in France won his sympathy. "A Vision," composed in the ruins of Lincluden, was an ode to Liberty, very mild compared to certain of his writings at this time, of which some did not appear in print till nearly fifty years after his death. A little revolutionary club, presided over by his intimate friend Dr Maxwell, and frequented by John Syme, a distributer of stamps, became a favourite resort.

In February 1792 an armed smuggler got entangled in the shoals of Solway. Burns was posted to watch her while his superior officer rode to Dumfries for assistance. He employed his time in composing "The Deil's awa' wi' the

Exciseman"; but when the troops came up, he plunged foremost into the water and was first on board of the prize. Lockhart says that he purchased four of her brass guns for £3, and sent them as a present to the French Directory. Cunningham questions the truth of this story; but even if it be groundless, there was plenty of reason for the warning which he received from the authorities. His political tracts had already engaged serious attention, and in the October following the capture of the smuggler a scene took place in the theatre at Dumfries which could not be overlooked. "God save the King" was played at the close of the performance, the audience rising and uncovering. Burns alone remained hatted in his seat, and there were loud cries of "Turn him out!" and "Shame, Burns!" Cunningham[9] and his other biographers have censured the intolerance of the Government for taking notice of Burns's political opinions, and Burns hotly disclaimed any seditious intention, protesting that he stood by the constitution of 1688. But it should be remembered that, as a civil servant, he was transgressing the rules of the service by taking an active share in party politics, and there was no harshness in the warning he received. Burns took the hint given him, and in 1795 was anxiously expecting his promotion. But in truth it is only too likely that he was not fit for the office of supervisor, and he was passed over.

All this time he had been writing songs for publication by George Thomson and Andrew Erskine of Edinburgh. For these he obstinately refused payment, declaring that they were either above or below price. Neither would he take any remuneration for prose papers contributed to the 'Morning Chronicle.' Peter Stuart, editor of the 'Star,' offered him a salary equal to his salary as exciseman, but

[9] Allan Cunningham's 'Life of Burns,' vol. i. p. 279.

he would none of it. He said he would be damned if ever he wrote for money—a sentiment greatly at variance with that of Dr Johnson, who said that none but a blockhead ever wrote except for money. Burns was consistent in this to the last, for although he had insisted on payment for his volume published by Creech, those poems had not been written for gain, but for his own pleasure.

There is a curious story told by Currie about the composition of "Bruce's Address to his troops at Bannockburn"—the soul-stirring "Scots wha hae." On July 27, 1793, John Syme and Burns dined together at Parton, the seat of the Glendinnings.[1] The poet was greatly interested in viewing Airds, on the opposite side of the Dee, the dwelling-place of Lowe, author of "Mary's Dream."

The story of John Lowe had been a sad one. Son of the gardener at Kenmure Castle, he was born in 1750, and apprenticed at fourteen to a weaver in New Galloway. His taste for letters and lively manners engaged the attention of the Rev. J. Gillespie, minister of New Galloway, by whose interest and the assistance of some of the wealthier neighbours he was enabled to become a student in Edinburgh University when twenty-one years of age. Afterwards he was appointed tutor in the family of Mr M'Ghie of Airds, and became betrothed to one of the daughters of that house. Thereafter he emigrated to America, whence for two years he continued to send assurance of his constancy to Miss M'Ghie. Nevertheless he proved faithless; proposed to a Virginian lady, who refused him, and then, from a sentiment of gratitude, married her sister. His wife, it is said, proved unfaithful to him; Lowe took to drink, and died in 1789, aged thirty-nine.

After dinner, Burns and Syme rode on to Kenmure Castle to sup, where they stayed three days with the Gordons.

[1] Now the property of Mr Rigby Murray.

Thence they journeyed over the moors in a heavy thunderstorm to Gatehouse, where, being soaked to the skin, Burns insisted on both of them getting very drunk. Next day Burns produced the poem, having composed it during the ride from Kenmure to Gatehouse.

This account is not exactly consistent with what Burns told Thomson in sending him the poem in the month of September following, saying that it was "composed in my yesternight's evening walk." But it may be that he then put into their immortal form the stanzas which he had roughly outlined before.

This brilliant but troubled life was drawing to its close. The matchless voice was soon to fall silent for ever. Burns's irregular habits had told with fatal effect on his constitution. In June 1794 he complained of "a flying gout" to punish him for the follies of his youth. In October 1795 he was laid up till the following January. Convalescent, he took too much drink at the Globe Tavern, and fell asleep in the open air on his way home. This exposure brought on rheumatic fever, and he became a sheer wreck. On July 4 he went to Brow, on the Solway, for sea-bathing, leaving Mrs Burns at Dumfries, expecting her confinement. Worried about a few small debts, he was driven to borrow £15 from friends to pay them. On July 18 he was brought back to Dumfries, only to die on the 21st. On the day her husband was buried Mrs Burns bore a son, to be named Maxwell, after the doctor who had been so close a friend of Burns in his latter years and had attended him in his last illness.

One more figure in literature, though in a very different field thereof from the last, must be noticed before bringing the record of this century to a close.

Alexander Murray, son of a hill-shepherd at Kitterick on the Palnure, was born on October 22, 1775. From very early years he showed an extraordinary appetite and aptitude for learning, to satisfy which, as may be supposed, material was exceedingly scanty in the wild district where he was bred. He learnt his letters at home, and was then sent to school at New Galloway. His short sight disqualified him for the calling of his father and grandfather, and at twelve years of age he was already employed to teach the children of the neighbouring farmers. His local fame as a linguist attracted the attention of Mr Douglas of Orchardton, through whose assistance he entered Edinburgh University in 1794 as a divinity student. He had already some knowledge of Greek, Latin, French, German, Hebrew, and Arabic; while at the University he is said to have mastered most European languages. In 1806 he became assistant and successor to the Rev. Dr Muirhead of Urr, and in 1808 was appointed minister of that parish. In that quiet retreat he composed his 'History of the European Languages,' a work in which, notwithstanding the vast advance of comparative philology since that time, may be traced many of the sound principles, unformulated and even unsuspected until then, on which the science has since been constructed. The value of his researches was instantly recognised; in 1812 he was elected Professor of Oriental Languages in the University of Edinburgh, but he enjoyed the well-merited honour only a few months. He died April 15, 1813, in his thirty-seventh year. A noble obelisk of granite was erected on Dunkitterick in 1834 to mark the birthplace of Galloway's most learned son.

The ardour for land improvement in these and subsequent years in Galloway was the cause of the obliteration of many monuments of early times. Cairns, the burial-places of notable men among the primitive Picts, afforded convenient quarries for building field dykes, and most of these have long since disappeared. Sometimes there lingered in the neighbourhood of such ancient remains a feeling of reverence for their sanctity, which had survived all the destructive fervour of the Reformation and the Covenanters, and many stories might be collected tracing the punishment which followed on their disturbance. At Laggangarn,[2] for instance, a hill-farm in a wild moorland district on the borders of New Luce and Kirkcowan parishes, there are some very interesting remains. On the hillside to the east of Laggangarn is the site of the old chapel of Kilgallioch, which has been pulled down to build sheepfolds; but three wells, now known as the Wells of the Rees,[3] still remain. They are within a few yards of each other; each is covered with a massive dome of stones, built without mortar, with a niche above the aperture, either to receive the image of a saint, as a repository for offerings, or simply as a convenient resting-place for a pitcher. At the foot of this hill is the deserted farmhouse of Laggangarn, on the banks of the Tarf,[4] where the old pack-horse track crosses the water. Two standing-stones remain erect here, each bearing a large incised cross and five smaller crosses, representing the five wounds of God. There were formerly three such stones (some people say twelve), but one was taken to serve as a lintel for a new barn at Laggangarn. Some time after that, it is said, the tenant's sheep-dogs went mad and bit him. He also went mad, and in that solitary region no help was at hand, so his wife and daughters "took and smoored him atween twa cauf

[2] Laggangarn = *lagán carn*, hollow of the cairns. The cairns have disappeared, the material having been used for dyke and house building.
[3] Rees—*i.e.*, sheep-rees = sheepfolds.
[4] There are streams called Tarf in the counties of Perth, Inverness, Forfar, and Kirkcudbright, also the Tarth in Peeblesshire, all taking their name from the Gaelic *tarbh* (tarriv, tarve), a bull. But the fanciful explanation usually given, that the name was conferred because of the roaring of the stream, will not bear examination. The meaning is simply (*amhuinn*) *tarbh*, stream of the bulls—*i.e.*, a stream frequented by cattle, whether wild or domesticated.

beds,"[5] and buried him on the hillside, placing the broken stone over his grave. Thus, as I was informed by one who guided me to the place, was the sacrilege avenged.

Record remains of another act of utilitarian zeal, doubtless only one out of many which have been forgotten. In 1791 Sir Stair Agnew designed a new approach to his Castle of Lochnaw. The moat hill, where the baron's court used of old to assemble, afforded a convenient supply of material for road-making, so it was demolished without compunction.[6]

Better fortune has befriended a celebrated monument in Dumfriesshire, which long lay in sore peril of destruction. A richly sculptured cross, upwards of 17 feet high, dating from early Saxon days, stood beside the parish church of Ruthwell. It escaped the destructive fervour of the early Reformers, and remained uninjured until 1642, in which year the General Assembly, scandalised at the leniency shown to this monument of idolatry, decreed its destruction. Folk, however, had a kindly feeling for the old cross. It was cast down, indeed, and its beautiful shaft and nimbed head were broken into several pieces, but the fragments were laid within the kirk, where Pennant viewed them 130 years later. Subsequently even that degree of respect was withdrawn, and the cross was flung into the kirkyard, where wind, weather, and wanton mischief began to do their inevitable work. Then, by a happy disposition of lay patronage, Dr Duncan, the father of savings banks, was appointed minister of Ruthwell, when he pieced the fragments together and set them up in the manse garden. There the cross stood till, a few years ago, some local antiquaries concerned themselves to get it placed under shelter, and collected funds for this excellent purpose. Now, duly scheduled as an ancient

---

[5] Smothered him between two chaff mattresses.
[6] Agnew's Hereditary Sheriffs, vol. ii. p. 389.

monument under Act of Parliament, it stands within a small apse built to receive it in the parish church, where it suggests reflections on Scottish Church history almost as profound as those stirred by the recent restoration, in memory of Montrose, of a side-chapel in St Giles' Cathedral of Edinburgh.

Now this cross bears a long inscription in Runic characters. Early in the century an Icelandic scholar of renown, Thorleif Repp, undertook the translation of this inscription from a careful copy made by Dr Duncan. Inasmuch as all Runes known up to that time were in the Norse language, he proceeded on the assumption that the Ruthwell Runes were also Norse. He revealed a most interesting story, how "a vessel of Christ of eleven pounds weight, with ornaments, made by Therfusian fathers, was given in expiation for the devastation of Ashlafardhal—*i.e.*, the vale of Ashlafr. "As if to place the interpretation beyond doubt, there is," says the 'New Statistical Account,' "preserved along with the column an ornamental circular stone," no doubt "the vessel of Christ," or baptismal font, alluded to.

Complete satisfaction prevailed in antiquarian circles at the reading of the riddle by the erudite Repp. No one, it is true, had ever heard of the Therfusian fathers; but there were plenty of places in broad Scotland easily identified with Ashlafardhal—the only difficulty was to decide between them. Presently, however, comes Professor Finn Magnusson with a different rendering of the Runes. Still assuming the language to be Norse, he declares that it was not a "devastation" which was commemorated, but a marriage! Moreover, deceived by certain Latin characters inserted by Dr Duncan to fill up a blank in the inscription, he pronounced the "Therfusian fathers" to be a delusion, and interpreted these characters to mean "Ofa, the descendant of Toda, caused it [the stone] to be raised." This caused a stir, not altogether harmonious, among the wise men sitting at the feet of Thorleif Repp; but in the end Magnusson's explanation was accepted as orthodox.

But there are tiresome people who never know when to let well alone. In 1838 it occurred to Mr John Kemble, a student of Anglo-Saxon, who was spending the vacation in Dumfriesshire, that there was something curious in a stone bearing Saxon ornamentation, along with a Scandinavian inscription. Why, he asked, should the inscription not be Saxon also? Setting to work independently with this idea, Kemble made out that the cross was inscribed with a metrical soliloquy, supposed to be spoken by the cross itself. Forthwith there began a storm which raged for years between all the universities of Western Europe, and might be raging still but for a little incident that happened about forty years ago. Among some Anglo-Saxon homilies preserved at Vercelli, near Milan, there was found a hymn entitled the "Dream of the Holy Rood," since known as Cædmon's hymn. In this hymn the cross—the original cross of the crucifixion—is supposed to address the sleeping Cædmon. There are, in all, fifty-nine lines in the hymn; of these, seventeen were found to correspond word for word with the inscription on the Ruthwell cross, rendered into English by Mr Kemble as follows:—

> "Then the young hero prepared himself,
> That was Almighty God,
> Strong and firm of mood,
> He mounted the lofty cross
> Courageously in the sight of many.
>   .   .   .   .   .
> I raised the powerful King,
> The Lord of the heaven
> I dared not fall down.
>   .   .   .   .   .

> They reviled us both together,
> I was all stained with blood,
> Poured from the man's side.
>
> . . . .
>
> Christ was on the cross,
> Yet hither hastening
> Men came from afar
> Unto the noble one,
> I beheld that all
> With sorrow I was overwhelmed.
>
> . . . .
>
> I was all wounded with shafts;
> They laid him down limb-weary;
> They stood at the head of the corpse;
> They beheld the Lord of Heaven."

Thus, all learned controversy being set for ever at rest, the traveller may leave the train at Ruthwell station, and view this beautiful relic of the Anglo-Saxon church of Northumbria in the eighth or ninth century—by far the most important of the ecclesiastical remains of Dumfriesshire. He may quaff a cup from the chalybeate spring, now called the Brow Well, but formerly the Rood Well, softened into Ruthwell, and slurred in local dialect into Rivvel.

No notice of Dumfriesshire would be complete without reference to the new notoriety acquired in the eighteenth century by the once turbulent Debatable Land. According to the marriage law of Scotland, neither previous notice nor previous residence in the locality where the ceremony of marriage was gone through was necessary in order to constitute its legality. Hence it came to pass that at Gretna Green, close to the English Border, a number of self-constituted "parsons" sprang into existence, ready to tie the hymeneal knot for such persons as might find it inconvenient to submit to the dilatory forms of English law and ecclesiastical ritual. The name of Gretna became as familiar to anxious parents and guardians of youth as to readers of romance. But it is a popular mistake to suppose that the "parson" was a blacksmith. Joseph Paisley, it is true, who began to officiate about 1753, was commonly known as the Old Blacksmith; but though he started in life as a smuggler, a farmer, and a fisherman, and then became a tobacconist, he never was a blacksmith except in name. He used to wear some kind of canonical dress when officiating professionally, and was a notoriously hard drinker, weighing 25 stone when he died in 1811.

Paisley was succeeded by one Robert Elliot, son of a Northumbrian farmer, who married a couple on the day of Paisley's death. He was the author of a book entitled 'The Gretna Green Memoirs,' published in London in 1842. The business was so brisk in his time that he entered into partnership with Simon Lang, and used to state that between 1811 and 1839 he had transacted 3872 marriages, though no reliance can be placed on these figures.

John Murray, who used to officiate in Alison's Bank tollhouse, began business in 1827, and is said to have conducted on an average 400 marriages a-year up to 1856. In that year Lord Brougham's Act spoiled the trade, for it made illegal all such marriages unless one of the parties had resided twenty-one days in Scotland immediately before the ceremony. It is said, however, that the business is still carried on by a representative of the Langs—a family of which several members played the parson in their time—and that couples do occasionally present themselves.[7] But Gretna Green is but a ghost of its former self in the days when the trade was brisk enough to keep several rival "parsons" and a squadron of postboys. During the ten years previous to the passing of Lord Brougham's Act the

[7] See an interesting paper by Mr G. C. Boase, in 'Notes and Queries,' January 25, 1896.

yearly average of marriages is stated, on dubious authority, to have been over 700.

Perhaps the best known of the old postboys, who played so important a part in runaway matches, and had to be liberally propitiated, was William Graham, called "Carwinley," who died in 1864 at Carlisle.

One memorial of the old fame of Gretna Green is still conspicuous on the west side of the Glasgow and South-Western Railway — namely, the Sark Bar Inn. This was built by John Murray, who intended to extend his trade. But he had to build on English soil, because the landowner on the Scottish bank would not give him the necessary ground. Moreover, it has turned out a poor speculation on account of the fatal Act of 1856.

An attempt to carry this history beyond the close of the eighteenth century not only would have caused it to expand beyond the limits assigned to the author, but would have brought it within the period of which the records are plentiful, authentic, and easily accessible. The changes wrought by the invention of steam and telegraphy have been as marked in the south-west as in any other part of the country.

Agriculture remains at this day, as it has been from early time, the chief and almost the only important industry in these counties; for, except the small collieries at Canonbie and Sanquhar in Dumfriesshire, the red freestone quarries of Annandale and Nithsdale, and the granite quarries at Dalbeattie and Creetown, the soil affords no encouragement to mineral enterprise. Lead was worked till within a few years ago in the metamorphic beds round the base of

Cairnsmore of Fleet, but the mines are now abandoned.[8] The old phrase "Galloway for woo'" indicated the chief source of wealth to the province from the middle ages downwards, and this material is still the basis of a considerable industry in the mills of Dumfries, Minigaff, and Kirkcowan. But it is on the prosperity of agriculture that the rural population depend for their welfare, and not only they, but the townspeople also. We have seen the difficulties with which our farmers had to contend and the hazardous nature of their occupation in the centuries between the War of Independence and the legislative Union of the countries. These have been happily overcome long ago, and during the third quarter of the present century the steady and rapid rise in rents testified to the prosperity of agriculture. Vast sums were spent by landlords and tenants in reclaiming waste land, draining lakes and bogs, improving farmhouses and labourers' dwellings, and breeding stock of the best strains. Then there came a serious check: not now from rival factions in civil strife, nor from "our auld enemies of England," but by the keen competition of our own kinsmen in the colonies and the United States, who were enabled by the opening up of new means of transit and the invention of new scientific appliances to take full advantage of our free-trade fervour and pour their produce into British markets.

It is curious to trace, even amid the stress of modern conditions, survivals of the primitive superstition of old times. When a family removes at the term to another house, it is considered very unlucky to be the first to enter

---

[8] While these pages are being written, a rich deposit of plumbago and arsenic has been discovered near Dunkitterick, to the west of Cairnsmore. A company has been formed and works are in progress to develop what, at present, promises to be an important industry.

the new abode. Hence a cat is usually thrown in first at the open door, to act as scapegoat and appropriate the evil that may be incident to a new-comer. Careful dairymaids and housewives always throw a pinch of salt into the pail before beginning to churn, in which may be traced a custom originating in the days when salt was a dutiable and therefore a precious material, suitable for the propitiation of ill-natured spirits. Not seldom there may still be seen hung in the byre, or twisted into the tails of animals going to market, a spray of "wull-grown rowan"—that is, rowan or mountain-ash grown, not in a garden, but wild on the moor; for this was ever held a sovereign specific against witchcraft.

More objectionable, though not less rational, was the custom of sacrificing a beast to avert "muir ill," "blackleg," or other disease, from the rest of the herd. I myself can testify to a propitiatory calf having been buried alive on a low country farm within four miles of a railway station, to save the stock from "blackleg," and this within the last twenty years. The tenant of the farm was an elder of the Church, and his social position may be understood from the rent he paid—upwards of £300.

Incredible as belief in such folk-lore may seem, and discreditable to the intelligence of people engaged in practical business, it behoves us, before condemning it, to consider if our own eyes are quite free from beams. Are we all certain of the futility of setting the poker erect against the bars of the grate when the fire is first lighted? I have seen this done within the last few years by a housemaid in a large London hotel. Yet the original and forgotten meaning of it (for the physical effect, of course, is absolutely *nil*) was that the poker and the bars together formed the sign of the cross, which was believed to discourage the evil spirit that prevents the fire kindling readily.

The failure of the City of Glasgow Bank in 1878 was severely felt in the south-west, and coinciding as it did with the first serious pinch of foreign competition, marked the turning-point in the value of land for agricultural purposes. At the present time the depreciation in the annual letting value over these three counties amounts probably to not less than fifteen or twenty per cent on the gross rental of twenty years ago,[9] in addition to which must be reckoned the loss of capital by both landlords and tenants.

One satisfactory feature of this time of trial has been, that while the means of landlords and tenants have been so much reduced, the wages paid to farm-labourers have not been affected. Taking into account the unprecedented cheapness and abundance of every necessary of life, as well as of many luxuries, and the fact that education is gratuitously provided, it is certain that at no former period of the history of Dumfries and Galloway have the working classes enjoyed so much material comfort in their houses, clothing, and food as they do at the present day.

To realise the degree of improvement attained within the last hundred years, it is only necessary to examine the country on either side of the Glasgow and South-Western Railway between Dumfries and Carlisle, and to compare it with the following description given by a traveller in 1788:—

"The land between the Solway Sands and Annan is very poor, being chiefly a black gravel and bog, producing nothing but heath. . . . Immediately on crossing the Solway Firth, we found the children, and even many of the men and women, without either shoes or stockings. The cottages are miserable huts, made of mud, intermixed with round

[9] Royal Commission on Agriculture. Report on the Counties of Ayr, Wigtown, Kirkcudbright, and Dumfries. 1895.

stones, . . . and covered with turf. . . . On the road from Annan to Dumfries . . . the cottages are built of mud, and covered with turf or thatch, the poorest habitations that can be imagined, and extremely dirty. The inhabitants are turned yellow with the smoke of the turf, which is their only fuel. . . . Till you come within two miles of Dumfries the land is so exceedingly bad that it must baffle every effort towards cultivation. It seems to produce nothing but peat, which is cut here, and supplies all the country round. Dumfries is a pretty large town, and very clean. . . . The lands about it are tolerably well cultivated. . . . The adjacent country is very barren. The farmhouses are in general miserable huts, the people very poor, and the lower class of females exceedingly dirty. The old women, frightful enough of themselves, are rendered still more so by their dress, the outer garment being a long dirty cloak, reaching down to the ground, and the hood drawn over their heads, and most of them without shoes and stockings. Others among them wear what they call *huggers*—that is, stockings with the feet either worn away by long and hard service, or cut from them on purpose; so that the leg is covered by these uncouth integuments, while the foot, that bears the burden, and is exposed to brakes and stones, is left absolutely bare."[1]

Writing at the age of more than fourscore, the late Mr Samuel Robinson gave some interesting reminiscences of the condition of the rural population in Wigtownshire at the close of the eighteenth century.[2] He does not yield to the tendency to which old people are so proverbially prone, of describing the present as deplorably less happy and virtuous than the past.

[1] A Tour in England and Scotland in 1785. By an English Gentleman. London, 1788.
[2] Reminiscences of Wigtownshire. By Samuel Robinson. Hamilton, 1862.

"I have spoken," he says, "of the great advantages enjoyed by the people of the present day [1862] over those of a century ago, in respect of personal comfort, from the cheap and much improved quality of cleansing materials, and the equally improved quality of the food of the million, and I now beg the reader to have a little patience with me while I say a few words on the very uncomfortable condition of the agricultural portion of the natives in bygone times, and, by way of accounting for the indifference the farmers displayed regarding the hovels of their married servants, I will give a literal description of the first farmhouse I served in, and there were many to which the sketch would apply. The house referred to was connected with a farm of 400 acres; it stood or rather leant against a piece of rising ground from which the surface was dug away, and the floor underwent no further preparation, so that the one end of the erection stood perhaps 6 feet higher than the other—that is to say, they built on the incline as they found it.

"The first process in the erection was performed by the carpenter. A lot of oak trees of different diameters, which had been dug out of moss-bogs in the locality, were provided, and the roof bound by boring auger-holes in the different pieces, and bolting them together with oak-trennels of inch and a half diameter, leaving the projecting ends, no matter how long, uncut off. Eight uprights, of 8 feet in length, were cut out of the strongest trees, and set on end at the proper distances on each side, on which to rest the couples, four in number on a house of 50 feet in length, and firmly secured. The end of each couple, when set on the upright, was bolted to it with trennels through a coupling piece of wood, which made all firm, while strong poles were laid along the couples horizontally, and others of a lighter description from eave to roof-tree, to which the thatch was to be sewed by plaited ropes of straw. This was all done (except the thatch) before the mason was thought of. The stones were gathered promiscuously, a little mortar of lime, or oftener soil, and the mason proceeded by building two thick gables, with a flue in one of them, and filling up the spaces between the uprights, and the house was finished. No plasterer or joiner was needed in what is called finishing, but a huge *lum* of bramble and straw was stuck up to do duty in the kitchen end, and a small chimney in the other—the ridge having the same incline as the floor. But rough and uncouth as the structure seemed, when the floor was swept up and a bright fire blazing on the ground, there was a show of rude homely comfort about it, beyond what could be expected; and, notwithstanding its rude construction, it stood firm at the time of my sojourn; though it must have battled with the war of elements for at least one hundred years.

"Immediately in front, at right angles to the house, at a sufficient distance to allow a carriage to pass, stood a small house called the *chammer*, a kind of lumber-room, in which was a bed for the two indoor male servants.

"When the honest farmer was content with a fabric like this, it was not to be expected that his cottar was to have anything superior, or even equal; and so it was. . . . With the exception of the roof, the cottage was a facsimile of the other, but of more limited dimensions. It might be 25 feet by 15, in which space were sheltered the hind and his family, and, in very many cases, the cow and poultry; while the pig had a bedroom outside, but ate his meals in the kitchen, while the poultry dined on the crumbs he left."

Writing thirty-four years ago, Mr Robinson observed that, in the matter of housing the working classes, Wigtownshire had not kept abreast of other counties. But an immense deal has been accomplished in that direction since then; and it is satisfactory to know that the County Council is applying the spur at the present time where there is occasion for it.

But the blessings of plenty and cheapness are not confined to the working classes. They have greatly mitigated the difficulties of employers in struggling with the unremunerative markets of late years. The population as a whole is not exempt from the anxieties and risks inseparable from the cultivation of the soil; nevertheless the general diffusion of comfort and education among all classes is in agreeable contrast to the protracted poverty, lawlessness, and insecurity through which an attempt has been made in these pages to trace the progress of the people of Dumfriesshire and Galloway.

NOTE L.

THE JACOBITE RISING OF 1745.

IN the district of Dumfries and Galloway few people suffered for the rising of 1745. The following names of "rebels" are included in the list returned by the Supervisors of Excise on May 7, 1746, in obedience to orders :—

1. Gavin Brown of Bishoptoun : attended the Pretender's son at Dumfries with a white cockade, and gave him what assistance he could.
2. William Carruthers, servant to Maxwell of Kirkconnel : attended his master in the rebellion, but left them in England.
3. Erskine Douglas, surgeon, } brothers of Sir John Douglas
4. Francis Douglas, sailor, } of Hillhead : carried arms with the rebels from the time they left Edinburgh to their repassing the Forth. Reported lurking.
5. John Henderson of Castlemains : committed at Carlisle for drinking treasonable healths; set at liberty and made gaol-keeper by the rebels on their getting possession of that town. A prisoner in Carlisle. [Was afterwards tried and executed.]
6. James Leslie Johnstone of Knockhill, } carried arms with the
7. Andrew Johnstone, his son : } rebels from the time they left Edinburgh till they dispersed. Reported lurking.
8. James Irvine, yr. of Gribton : carried arms in the rebel service.
9. Edward Irvine of Wysbie : guided the rebels and their baggage from Ecclefechan to Gretna. Reported at home.
10. John Irvine of Whitehill : was active in pressing horses for the service of the rebels, and threatening the constables who would not assist. Reported at home.
11. William Johnstone of Lockerby : assisted the rebels in their march through Annandale to England. Reported at home.
12. William Irvine of Gribton : refused in a public company to drink his Majesty's health; forced his son into rebellion. Reported at home.
13. James Maxwell of Kirkconnel : served in the Pretender's Life Guards till the battle of Culloden. Whereabouts unknown.
14. William Maxwell of Carnichan : held a captain's commission

from the Pretender's son, and acted as chief engineer at Carlisle. Whereabouts unknown.
15. William Maxwell, son of Maxwell of Barncleugh : carried arms with the rebels. A prisoner.
16. William Maxwell, called Earl of Nithsdale : went to Edinburgh and attended the Pretender's son. At home.
17. Lady Katherine Maxwell : attended the Young Pretender in Edinburgh and Dumfries ; was most active in his interest, and presented a horse and chaise to the person commonly called the Duke of Perth. At home.
18. Sir William Maxwell of Springkell : entertained certain rebels and provided them with horses. At home.
19. William M'Ghie, glazier, Dumfries : served in the Young Pretender's army. A prisoner.

LIST OF BOOKS RELATING TO, OR PUBLISHED IN, DUMFRIESSHIRE AND GALLOWAY.

AGRICULTURE.

Biggar, James. The Agriculture of Kirkcudbrightshire and Wigtownshire. Castle-Douglas, 1876.

Blacklock, Ambrose. Description of Heathcoat's Steam Plough, with Illustrative Drawings. 8vo. Dumfries: John M'Kie, 1837.

Craig, Alexander. Two Letters on preparing Clay Ashes for Manure. Reprinted from the 'Dumfries Courier,' *c.* 1815.

Dumfries, Wigtown, and the Stewartry of Kirkcudbright, Transactions of the Society for the Encouragement of Agriculture in the Counties of. 2 parts, 8vo. Dumfries, 1776.

Galloway Herd-Book, The, containing the Pedigrees of Pure-bred Galloway Cattle. 15 vols. 8vo. Dumfries: 'Courier and Herald' Office, 1880-95.

Galloway, Rules, &c., of the Farmer's Society of the Rhins of. 8vo. Ayr, 1807.

Gillespie, Rev. John, Mouswald—
   Report on the Agriculture of Dumfriesshire. 8vo. Edinburgh, 1869.
   The Galloway Breed of Cattle. Trans. of H. and A. Soc. of Scot., 1878.

Husbandry of Gallowayshire—the Stewartry of Kirkcudbright and Shire of Galloway. Wight's Present State of Husbandry in Scotland, vol. iii. p. 34. 8vo. 1784.

Hutton, John. Practical Hints on improving Waste Land. 12mo. Kirkcudbright: Alexander Gordon, 1808.

AGRICULTURE—*continued.*
Johnston, the Rev. Bryce, D.D. Agricultural Survey of Dumfriesshire. 4to. 1794.
Levellers, The. The Opinion of Sir Thomas More concerning Inclosures, in answer to a Letter by some People in Galloway anent their Grievances through Inclosures. 12mo. Edinburgh, 1724.
MacLelland, Thomas, North Balfern. On the Agriculture of the Stewartry of Kirkcudbright and Wigtownshire. Trans. of H. and A. Soc. of Scot., vol. vii. p. 1. 1875.
Maxwell, J[ohn] H[unter]. Marks and Buists of Sheep in the Stewartry of Kirkcudbright. 12mo. Castle Douglas, 1880.
Miller, Patrick, of Dalswinton. Treatise on Fiorin Grass. Dumfries, 1810.
Singer, Dr. General View of the Agriculture in the County of Dumfries. 8vo. 1812.
Smith, Rev. Samuel, Minister of Borgue. General View of the Agriculture of Galloway. 8vo. 1810.

ARCHÆOLOGY.

Antiquaries of Scotland, Proceedings of the Society :—

DUMFRIESSHIRE.

Amisfield Castle, Notice of Carved Oak Bed-posts from. Vol. iv. p. 380. 1863.
Ardderyd (Arthuret), Notice of the Site of the Battle of. By W. F. Skene. Vol. vi. p. 91. 1868.
Auchentaggart, Notes on a Gold Lunette found at. By J. Gilchrist Clark. Vol. xiv. p. 222. 1880.
Bruce, Notice of the Family of. Vol. i. pp. 231, 239, 296. 1855.
Canonbie, Notice of Silver Ornaments, and Gold Ring with Sapphire, found at Woodhead, in the parish of. Vol. v. p. 216. 1865.
Cargen, Notice of St Queran's Well at. By Patrick Dudgeon. Vol. xxvi. p. 63. 1892.
Chisels or Punches of Bronze-like Metal from Sutherlandshire and Dumfriesshire, Notes on Two. By Joseph Anderson, LL.D. Vol. xxviii. p. 207. 1895.
Closeburn, Note respecting a Canoe found at. By John Adam. Vol. vi. p. 458. 1868.

ARCHÆOLOGY—*continued.*
> Coins found in Dumfriesshire, Notes of. By George Sim. Vol. vi. pp. 239, 457.
>
> Commissioners of Supply for Dumfriesshire, Donation of the Proceedings of the, from Jan. 3, 1692, to July 3, 1711, in manuscript. Vol. v. p. 241. 1865.
>
> Deil's Dyke, Notes of an Examination of the. By G. V. Irving. Vol. v. p. 189. 1865.
>
> Forts, Camps, and Motes of Dumfriesshire, A General View of the. By David Christison, M.D. Vol. xxv. p. 198. 1891.
>
> Friar's Carse, Notes of a Crannog at. By Robert Munro, M.D. Vol. xvi. p. 73. 1882.
>
> Hoddam, Notice of a Saxon Stone Cross found at. Vol. i. p. 11. 1855.
>
> Holywood, Notice of Bronze Figure of an Ecclesiastic found at. By Patrick Dudgeon. Vol. xvi. p. 417. 1882.
>
> Holywood, The Stone Circle at. By Fred. R. Coles. Vol. xxviii. p. 84. 1895.
>
> Local Museum at Dumfries, Report on the. By Joseph Anderson, LL.D. Vol. xxii. p. 417. 1888.
>
> Local Museum at Maxwelltown, Report on the. By Joseph Anderson, LL.D. Vol. xxii. p. 412.
>
> Local Museum at Thornhill, Report on the. By Joseph Anderson, LL.D. Vol. xxii. p. 373. 1888.
>
> Maxwell Inglis, Donation and Notice of the Manuscript Poems of Mrs Margaret. By the Rev. Charles Rogers, D.D. Vol. xvi. p. 403. 1882.
>
> Moffat, Notes on a Camp and Fort on the Garpel Burn, near. By R. H. Blyth. Vol. xx. p. 331. 1886.
>
> Mouswald and its Barons, The Barony of. A Page of Border History. By J. J. Reid. Vol. xxiii. p. 24. 1889.
>
> Old Town Hall of Dumfries, Notes on the. By W. R. M'Diarmid. Vol. xx. p. 186. 1886.
>
> Robert Riddell of Glenriddell, and of some of his Manuscripts and Books, Notice of. By James Irvine. Vol. vi. p. 451. 1868.
>
> Roman Inscribed Stones found in Dumfriesshire, Notice of. Vol. iii. p. 41. 1862.
>
> Roman Roads of Dumfriesshire, Notes on the. By James Macdonald, LL.D. Vol. xxviii. p. 298. 1895.
>
> Ruthwell Cross, Statement relative to the. By George Seton. Vol. xxi. p. 194. 1887.
>
> Skull of a large Bear found in a Moss, Notice of the. By J. A. Smith, M.D. Vol. xiii. p. 360. 1879.

ARCHÆOLOGY—*continued.*
  Solway Moss, List of Prisoners taken at the Battle of. Vol. ii. p. 239. 1859.
  Surnames in Dumfriesshire, A Note on Old. By Joseph Bain. Vol. xxv. p. 197. 1891.

DUMFRIESSHIRE AND GALLOWAY.

Church Communion Tokens, Description of 70, in lead and pewter, formerly used in Parish Churches in Dumfriesshire and Galloway. By the Rev. George Murray. Vol. v. p. 324. 1865.
Red-Deer in the South of Scotland, Notice of Remains of the. By J. Smith. Vol. xv. p. 37. 1881.

GALLOWAY.

Ancient Forest of Cree in Galloway, Remains of the. By Arthur Mitchell, M.D. Vol. v. p. 20. 1865.
Articles found in a Bronze Cauldron dredged up in Carlingwark Loch, Notice of. Vol. vii. p. 8. 1870.
Artificial Islets in the Loch of Dowalton, Notice of a Group of. By John Stuart. Vol. vi. p. 114. 1868.
Bos longifrons, Notes on the Remains of. Vol. ix. p. 624. 1873.
Bos primigenius, Notes on the Remains of. Vol. ix. p. 644. 1873.
Bronze Armlet found in a Turbary near Plunton Castle, Notice of a. Vol. iii. p. 236, 1862 ; vol. vii. p. 348, 1870.
Bronze Articles found at New Galloway, Notice of. Vol. iv. p. 294. 1863.
Bronze Articles found in the Stewartry of Kirkcudbright, Notice of. Vol. vii. p. 348. 1870.
Bronze Harness Ornament from Auchendolly, Notice of an Enamelled. By Sir Herbert Maxwell, Bart., M.P. Vol. xx. p. 396. 1886.
Bronze Ornament, with Horns, found at Torrs, Parish of Kelton, Notice of a remarkable. By J. A. Smith, M.D. Vol. vii. p. 334. 1870.
Bronze Ornament found in Dowalton Loch, Notice of a. By R. Vans Agnew. Vol. xv. p. 155. 1881.
Bronze Sword found in Carlinwark Loch, Notice of a. By John Stuart, LL.D. Vol. x. p. 286. 1875.

ARCHÆOLOGY—*continued.*
  Bronze Sword and small Bronze Ring found at Kelton, Notice of Fragments of a. By the Rev. C. J. Cowan. Vol. xix. p. 327. 1885.
  Burnt Cairn dug out in Culcaldie Moss, Note of a. By the Earl of Stair. Vol. x. p. 700. 1875.
  "Carles," or Wooden Candlesticks, of Wigtownshire, Notes on the. By Sir Herbert Maxwell, Bart., M.P. Vol. xxii. p. 113. 1888.
  Carsecreuch, in the Parish of Old Luce, Notes of two Stone Cists at. Vol. ix. p. 517. 1873.
  Carsphairn, Notes on Cairns, a Stone Circle, and an Incised Stone at. By W. R. M'Diarmid. Vol. xiv. p. 283. 1880.
  Cave containing Bones and Objects of Human Workmanship at Borness, On a. By W. B. Clarke. Vol. x. p. 476, 1875; vol. xii. p. 669, 1878.
  Claycrop, Parish of Kirkinner, Note of the Discovery of a Large Stone Hammer of peculiar form at. By R. Vans Agnew. Vol. xvi. p. 56. 1882.
  Craigcaffie Castle, Notes respecting. By John M'Lachlan. Vol. viii. p. 384. 1871.
  Crannogs and Lake-Dwellings of Wigtownshire, Notes on the. By the Rev. G. Wilson. Vol. ix. p. 368, 1873; vol. x. p. 737, 1875.
  Cup-shaped Urn, of a variety hitherto unknown in Scotland, Notice of the Discovery of a small. By F. R. Coles. Vol. xxviii. p. 204. 1895.
  Elk recently found in Wigtownshire, Notice of the Occurrence of the. By J. A. Smith, M.D. Vol. xvii. p. 325. 1883.
  Glenluce, Notes on a Collection of Implements and Ornaments of Stone, Bronze, &c., from. By the Rev. G. Wilson. Vol. xv. p. 263. 1881.
  Gold Ring found at Kirkpatrick-Durham, Notice of a massive. Vol. v. p. 214. 1865.
  Implements of Stone and Bronze, and other Antiquities, from Wigtownshire, Notice of a Collection of. By the Rev. G. Wilson. Vol. xiv. p. 127. 1880.
  Kirkmadrine, in the Parish of Stoneykirk, Inscribed Stones at. By Arthur Mitchell, M.D. Vol. ix. p. 569. 1872.
  Lignite Beads found in an Urn at Stranraer, Notice of. By the Rev. George Wilson. Vol. xii. p. 625. 1878.
  Local Museum at Kirkcudbright, Report on the. By Joseph Anderson, LL.D. Vol. xxii. p. 398. 1888.

ARCHÆOLOGY—*continued*.
> Motes, Forts, and Doons of the Stewartry of Kirkcudbright, The. By F. R. Coles. Vol. xxv. p. 352, 1891 ; vol. xxvi. p. 117, 1892 ; vol. xxvii. p. 84, 1894.
> Paul Jones, Note respecting an Autograph Letter and Medallion Portrait of. By Professor A. Campbell-Swinton. Vol. iii. pp. 389, 391. 1862.
> Primitive Implements, Weapons, Ornaments, and Utensils from Wigtownshire. By Sir Herbert Maxwell, Bart, M.P. Vol. xxiii. p. 200. 1889.
> Rhins of Galloway, Note on a Collection of Stone Implements from the. By the Rev. G. Wilson. Vol. xix. p. 62. 1885.
> Rock-sculpturings of Cups and Circles in the Stewartry of Kirkcudbright, Notices of. By George Hamilton. Vol. xxi. p. 151, 1887; vol. xxiii. p. 125, 1889.
> Standing-Stones at Laggangarn, &c., Notice of. By the Rev. G. Wilson. Vol. x. p. 56. 1875.
> St Ninian's Cave, Parish of Glasserton, Notice of the Excavation of. By Sir Herbert Maxwell, Bart., M.P. Vol. xx. p. 82, 1885 ; vol. xxi. p. 137, 1887.
> St Medan's Cave and Chapel, Kirkmaiden, Notes on the Excavation of. By Sir Herbert Maxwell, Bart., M.P. Vol. xx. p. 76. 1886.
> Urns found in Wigtownshire, Notice of. By the Rev. G. Wilson. Vol. xxi. p. 182, 1887; vol. xxii. p. 66, 1888.
>> *Note.*—Besides the above papers, the Proceedings contain numerous notices of objects of antiquities presented to or exhibited before the Society.

Ayrshire and Galloway, Archæological and Historical Collections relating to. 14 vols. 4to. Edinburgh, printed for the Ayrshire and Galloway Archæological Association, 1878-1895.

[Dudgeon, Patrick, of Cargen.] "Macs" in Galloway. 12mo. Dumfries : 'Courier and Herald' Office, 1887.
> Second edition. Edinburgh, 1888.

Duncan, Rev. Henry, D.D., Ruthwell—
> An Account of the tracks and footmarks of Animals found impressed on Sandstone in the Quarry of Corncockle Muir. Trans. of R. S. of E., vol. xi. p. 194. 1831.
> Account of the Remarkable Monument in the shape of a Cross . . . in the garden of Ruthwell Manse. 4to. Edinburgh, 1833.

Hamilton, George. Lecture on the origin of the word "Kirkcudbright." 8vo. Kirkcudbright : J. L. Grierson, 1885.

DUMFRIESSHIRE AND GALLOWAY.

ARCHÆOLOGY—*continued.*

Kemble, John M. Additional Observations on the Runic Obelisk at Ruthwell, the Poem of the Dream of the Holy Rood, &c. Archæologia of Soc. of Ant. of London, 1843, pp. 31-46.

Riddell, Robert. Account of a Brass Vessel found near Dumfries in Scotland, 1790. Archæologia of Soc. of Ant. of London, vol. xi. p. 105.

Ruthwell Cross, The. 8vo. Edinburgh, 1885.

Stephens, Professor George. The Ruthwell Cross, with its Runic Verses by Cædmon, &c.; with translation, comments, and facsimile plates. Folio. London and Copenhagen, 1866.

BIOGRAPHY.

Armstrong, William Kingo. Memoir of John Ross Coulthart of Ashton-under-Lyne [and afterwards of Greenlaw]. 8vo. Edinburgh, 1876.

Boyd, Mark. Reminiscences of Fifty Years. 8vo. London, 1871.

Carlyle, Thomas—
  Reminiscences by. Edited by James Anthony Froude. 2 vols. small 8vo. London, 1881.
  Letters and Memorials of Jane Welsh Carlyle, prepared by. Edited by James Anthony Froude. 3 vols. 8vo. London, 1883.
  The Correspondence of, and Ralph Waldo Emerson. Edited by Charles Eliot Norton. 2 vols. small 8vo. London, 1883.
  Correspondence between Goethe and Carlyle. Edited by Charles Eliot Norton. Sm. 8vo. London, 1887.
  Last Words of. London, 1892.

Catalogue of Portraits of Eminent Natives of Dumfriesshire and Galloway. Dumfries: J. Maxwell & Son. *N.d.*

Cowper, William, Bishop of Galloway. The Bischope of Galloway his Dikaiologie, contayning a iust Defence of his former Appologie against the uniust Imputations of Mr David Home. London, 1614.

Cowper, Mr William, Bishop of Galloway: The Life and Death of the Reverend Father and Faithful Servant of God, who departed this life at Edinburgh, 15th February 1619. 4to. London, 1619.

Cowper, William, Bishop of Galloway, Life of, written by himself, and prefixed to his works. Folio. London, 1629.

Crichton, Rev. Andrew—
  Memoirs of the Rev. John Blackader. Sm. 8vo. Edinburgh, 1823.

BIOGRAPHY—*continued.*

    The Life and Diary of Lieut.-Col. J. Blackader. Small 8vo. Edinburgh, 1824.

Currie, James, M.D., F.R.S., Memoir of the Life, Writings, and Correspondence of. Edited by his Son. 2 vols. 8vo. London, 1831.

Dalrymple, Sir James, of Stair, An Apology for. By himself. 4to. 1690.

    New edition, Bannatyne Club. 4to. Edinburgh, 1825.

Dodds, Rev. James. The Eminent Men of Dumfriesshire : A Lecture. 8vo. 1865.

Duncan, Rev. Geo. J. C. Memoir of the Rev. Henry Duncan, D.D., Minister of Ruthwell. Small 8vo. Edinburgh, 1848.

[Duncan, Rev. Henry, Ruthwell.] Some Interesting Particulars of the Life and Character of Maitland Smith, who was executed in Dumfries for the Crimes of Robbery and Murder. 8vo. Edinburgh, 1807.

Elliott, Robert. The Gretna Green Memoirs, with an Introduction and Appendix by the Rev. Caleb Brown. 12mo. London, 1842.

Fergusson, Lieut.-Col. A. The Laird of Lag : A Life Sketch. 8vo. Edinburgh, 1886.

Froude, James Anthony. Thomas Carlyle : A History of the first forty years of his Life. 2 vols. 8vo. London, 1882.

Gillespie, Rev. William. Brief Memoir of the Life of John Lowe. Appended to Cromek's Remains of Nithsdale and Galloway Song. 8vo. London, 1810.

Graham, John Murray. Annals and Correspondence of the Viscount and the First and Second Earls of Stair. 2 vols. 8vo. Edinburgh, 1875.

Henderson, Andrew. The Life of John, Earl of Stair. 12mo. London, 1748.

Hogg, Rev. David, Minister of Kirkmahoe—

    Life and Times of the Rev. John Wightman, D.D., late Minister of Kirkmahoe. Small 8vo. Dumfries : J. Anderson, 1873.

    Life of Allan Cunningham. Small 8vo. Dumfries : John Anderson, 1875.

Jones, Rev. T. S. The Life of Willielma (Maxwell) Viscountess Glenorchy. 8vo. Edinburgh, 1822.

[Kirkton, Rev. James.] The History of Mr John Welsh (Kirkcudbright). Edinburgh, 1703.

M'Crie, Thomas, D.D. Memoirs of the Life of Sir Andrew Agnew, Bart. 8vo. London, 1850.

BIOGRAPHY—*continued.*

[M'Diarmid, John.] The Widow of Burns : Her Death, Character, and Funeral. Dumfries : J. M'Diarmid & Co., 1834.

[M'Diarmid, William Ritchie.] Memoir of John M'Diarmid. 12mo. 1852.

M'Dowall, William. Burns in Dumfriesshire : A Sketch of the last eight years of the Poet's life. Small 8vo. Edinburgh, 1870.

M'Ilwraith, Rev. John. Life of Sir John Richardson. London, 1868.

Mackay, Æneas J. G. Memoir of Sir James Dalrymple, First Viscount Stair. 8vo. Edinburgh, 1873.

Mackenzie, J. C. Tribute to the Memory of Mr James Skelly, Ship-carpenter, Master Mariner, and Shipowner. Kirkcudbright : J. Nicholson, 1880.

Murray, Thomas—
Memoirs of Lord Kenmure. Prefixed to his Last and Heavenly Speeches. 12mo. Edinburgh, 1827.
The Life of Samuel Rutherford. 12mo. Edinburgh, 1828.

Oliphant, Mrs. The Life of Edward Irving, illustrated by his Journals and Correspondence. 2 vols. 8vo. London, 1862.

Patterson, John. Memoir of Joseph Train, F.S.A. Scot., the Antiquarian Correspondent of Sir Walter Scott. Small 8vo. Glasgow, 1857.

Paul Jones—
The Life of, from Original Documents in the possession of Henry Sherburne, Esq. London, 1825. [The preface to this work was one of the earliest literary essays of Benjamin Disraeli, Lord Beaconsfield.]
Rear-Admiral, Memoirs of : Now first compiled from his Original Journals and Correspondence. 2 vols. Edinburgh, 1830. Second edition, 1843.
The Life of. By Edward Hamilton. Aberdeen, 1848.
Rear-Admiral, Memoirs of. Illustrated. Chicago and New York. *N.d.* [*Circa* 1886.]
Life, Voyages, and Sea-Battles of the celebrated Pirate. (Chap-book.) *N.d.*

Reid, Rev. H. M. B., Balmaghie. A Cameronian Apostle, being some Account of John Macmillan of Balmaghie. Small 8vo. Paisley, 1896.

Roach, John, mariner, of Whitehaven. The Surprising Adventures of. 12mo. Dumfries : Robert Jackson, 1788.

Sharpe, Charles Kirkpatrick, Letters from and to. Edited by Alexander Allardyce, with a Memoir by the Rev. W. K. R. Bedford. 2 vols. 8vo. Edinburgh, 1888.

BIOGRAPHY—*continued*.

Shields, Rev. Alexander. The Life and Death of . . . Mr James Renwick. 12mo. Edinburgh, 1724.

Smith, J. Lockhart. Wigtownshire Agriculturists and Breeders. With Portraits. Small 4to. Stranraer: 'Free Press' Office, 1894.

Stair, John, Earl of, Memoirs of the Life, Family, and Character of. By an Impartial Hand. 1747.

Trotter, Memoirs of Robert, Esq., Surgeon, New Galloway. [By his Daughter.] 12mo. Dumfries: J. Swan, 1822.

Vauss of Barnbarroch. Royal Letters and other Original Documents addressed to the Lairds of Barnbarroch, 1559-1618. 4to. *N.d.*

Waus, Correspondence of Sir Patrick, of Barnbarroch, Knight, Parson of Wigtown, First Almoner to the Queen, Senator of the College of Justice, and Ambassador to Denmark, 1540-1597. Edited from the original documents by Robert Vans Agnew. 8vo. Edinburgh, 1882.

Welsh, Rev. D. Account of the Life and Writings of Thomas Brown, M.D., late Professor of Moral Philosophy in the University of Edinburgh. Edinburgh, 1825.

Wilson, William, a native of Dumfries, Life and Adventures of. Dumfries, 1837.

Young, Rev. James. Life of John Welsh (Kirkcudbright). 8vo. Edinburgh, 1866.

FICTION.

Armstrong, Andrew J.—
   Friend and Foe: A Tale of Galloway Seventy Years Ago. Dundee, 1885.
   Through the Shadows: A Story in Three Parts. Dumfries: J. Anderson & Son [1887].
   Robbie Rankine an' the County Council. Edinburgh. *N.d.*
   The Cobbler o' Kirkiebrae: A Romance of Galloway. Small 8vo. London, 1896.

Bell, Maria. The Country Minister's Love-Story. Crown 8vo. London: Hodder & Stoughton, 1896.

Buchan, John. Sir Quixote of the Moors. London, 1895.

Crockett, S. R.—
   The Raiders. 8vo. 1894.
   The Lilac Sunbonnet. 8vo. 1894.
   Mad Sir Uchtred of the Hills. London, 1894.
   The Men of the Moss Hags: A Story of the Covenanters. 8vo. London, 1895.

FICTION—*continued.*
> The Stickit Minister. 8vo. 1893. Tenth and illustrated edition, 1895.
>
> Bog-myrtle and Peat. Tales chiefly of Galloway. 8vo. London, 1895.

Cunningham, Allan. Paul Jones: A Romance. 3 vols. Edinburgh, 1826.

Hannay, David. Ned Allen; or, The Past Age. 2 vols. London, 1849.

Hogg, James. The Brownie of Bodsbeck and other Tales. 2 vols. small 8vo. Edinburgh, 1818.

[M'Clatchie, P. M.] Douglas; or, The Field of Otterburn: A Historical Romance. First edition, 4 vols. Dumfries, 1823. 8vo. Dumfries: Allan Anderson, 1858.

M'Keand, George—
> Lady Glenroy; or, The Mystery of the Moonlight. London. *N.d.*
>
> The Maid of Fleet: An Affecting Romance of Love of the Nineteenth Century. London. *N.d.*

Mackenzie, John. The Blakes of Listellick; or, Scenes from Irish Life. Castle-Douglas, 1881.

M'Vitie, William. Tales for the Ingle-Cheek. Second Series. Dumfries, 1824.

Maxwell, Sir Herbert, Bart., M.P. A Duke of Britain: A Romance of the Fourth Century. 8vo. Edinburgh, 1895.

Scott, Sir Walter—
> Guy Mannering.
> Redgauntlet.
> The Bride of Lammermoor.

Service, Rev. John. Lady Hetty. London: Daldy, Isbister, & Co., 1875. (First published in 'Good Words,' 1874, under the title 'Novantia.')

Trotter, Robert, M.D.—
> Lowran Castle; or, The Wild Boar of Curridoo: with other Tales. Small 8vo. Dumfries: J. Swan, 1822.
>
> Derwentwater; or, The Adherents of King James: A Tale of the first Rebellion. With an Appendix containing Genealogical Notices and Anecdotes of several Ancient and Honourable Families. Small 8vo. Edinburgh, 1825.
>
> Herbert Herries; or, The Days of Queen Mary: A Tale of Dundrennan Abbey. With Genealogical Notes. Small 8vo. Edinburgh, 1827.

Warburton, Eliot. Darien, or the Merchant Prince [William Paterson]: An Historical Romance. London, 1852.

HISTORY AND GENEALOGY.

Agnew, Sir Andrew, Bart. The Agnews of Lochnaw. A History of the Hereditary Sheriffs of Galloway. 8vo. Edinburgh, 1864.
    Second edition, with varying title, 2 vols. Edinburgh, 1893.
Annandale Peerage. Printed Documents connected with Action by Executors of the Marquis of Annandale against the Earl of Hopetoun, &c. 1796.
Armstrong, Robert Bruce. The History of Liddesdale, Eskdale, Ewesdale, Wauchopedale and the Debateable Land. Part I. from the Twelfth Century to 1530. Illustrated. 4to. Edinburgh, 1883.
Barbour, James, Glendarroch. Glenkens in Olden Times: A Paper read to the Dumfries and Galloway Antiquarian Society on 24th April 1896. 4to.
Brown, James, Burgh Assessor. The History of Sanquhar. To which is added the Flora and Fauna of the district, by Dr Anstruther Davidson. 8vo. Dumfries: W. Anderson & Son, 1891.
Bruce, M. E. Cumming. Family Records of the Bruces and the Cumyns, with an Historical Introduction and Appendix, from authentic public and private documents. 4to. Edinburgh, 1870.
Buccleuch, Account of the Noble Family of. Dumfries, 1827.
Carlaverock, The Siege of, in 1300. With the Arms of the Earls, Barons, and Knights who were present on the occasion. Edited by Nicholas Harris Nicolas. 4to. London, 1828.
    Another edition, edited by Thomas Wright. 4to. London, 1864.
Carlyle, T. J., Templehill, Waterbeck—
    The Debateable Land. 8vo. Dumfries: W. R. M'Diarmid & Co. 1868.
Fraser, Gordon. The Story of the Wigtown Martyrs. Wigtown, 1885.
Fraser, Rev. James. Scotland before and after the Reformation. Dumfries: J. Anderson & Son, 1861.
Fraser, Sir William, K.C.B.—
    The Book of Carlaverock: Memoirs of the Maxwells, Earls of Nithsdale, Lords Maxwell and Herries. 2 vols. 4to. Privately printed, Edinburgh, 1873.
    The Douglas Book. 4 vols. 4to. Privately printed. Edinburgh, 1885.
    The Annandale Family Book of the Johnstones, Earls and

HISTORY AND GENEALOGY—*continued.*
>   Marquises of Annandale. 2 vols. 4to. Privately printed. Edinburgh, 1894.

Glenkens. The Address of the Barons, Freeholders, Heritors, and others of the 4 Parishes of the Glenkenns, in the Stewartry of Kirkcudbright, conveened at St John's Clauchan of Dalray, the 19th of November 1706 years, Upon the great concern of the Union proposed and treated of in several Articles betwixt Scotland and England. Folio, pp. 3.

Hume, Master David, of Godscroft. The History of the Houses of Douglas and Angus. Small folio. Edinburgh, 1643-44.

Hutchinson, Peter Orlando. Chronicles of Gretna Green. 2 vols. 8vo. London, 1844.

Hutchison, Rev. Æneas B. Memorials of Dundrennan Abbey in Galloway. Illustrated. 4to. Exeter, 1857.

Irving, Joseph. The Drowned Women of Wigton. 8vo. Dumbarton, 1862.

Johnston, A. Genealogical Account of the Family of Johnston of that Ilk. Privately printed. Edinburgh, 1832.

Johnstone, C. L. Historical Families of Dumfriesshire and the Border Wars. 4to. Edinburgh and Glasgow, 1888.
>   Second edition. 8vo. *N.d.* [1889.]

Macdonald, A. Historical Account of the Family of Kennedy, Marquess of Ailsa and Earl of Cassillis. 4to. Privately printed. Edinburgh, 1849.

M'Dowall, William—
>   Chronicles of Lincluden as an Abbey and as a College, with Illustrations. 4to. Edinburgh, 1866.
>   History of the Burgh of Dumfries, with Notices of Nithsdale, Annandale, and the Western Border. 8vo. Edinburgh, 1867. Second edition. 8vo. Edinburgh, 1887.

[Mackenzie, Rev. William.] The History of Galloway, from the earliest period to the present time. 2 vols. 8vo. Kirkcudbright : J. Nicholson, 1841.

M'Kerlie, P. H.—
>   History of the Lands and their Owners in Galloway. Illustrated by Woodcuts of Notable Places and Objects, with Historical Sketches of the District. 5 vols. small 8vo. Edinburgh, 1870-79.
>   Galloway, Ancient and Modern. An Account of the Historic Celtic District. Crown 8vo. Edinburgh, 1891.

[Maidment, James.] The Glencairn Peerage. 8vo. *N.d.* [Before 1839.]

Marchbank, Agnes. The Covenanters of Annandale. Small 8vo. Paisley. *N.d.*

HISTORY AND GENEALOGY—*continued.*
Minute-Book of the War Committee of the Covenanters in the Stewartry of Kirkcudbright, in the years 1640 and 1641. 8vo. Kirkcudbright: J. Nicholson, 1855.
Monteith, Rev. John. The Parish of Glencairn. 12mo. Glasgow, 1876.
Murray, Thomas. The Literary History of Galloway. 8vo. Edinburgh, 1822. Second edition, Edinburgh, 1832.
Napier, Mark—
    The Case for the Crown *in re* the Wigtown Martyrs proved to be Myths. 8vo. Edinburgh, 1863.
    History rescued, in answer to History vindicated. 8vo. Edinburgh, 1870.
Neilson, George—
    Annandale under the Bruces. Sm. 8vo. Annan: W. Cuthbertson & Son, 1887.
    Old Annan: From the 12th Century until 1547. 8vo. Annan: W. Cuthbertson & Son, 1896.
Nithsdale, Letter from the Countess of, to her Sister, Lady Lucy Herbert. Containing a Circumstantial Account of the Escape of her Husband, William, fifth Earl of Nithsdale, from the Tower of London, 23d Feb. 1716; with Pedigree and Remarks by Sheffield Grace. Privately printed. London, 1827.
Parker, John. Lochmaben Five Hundred Years Ago. Selected from Papers collected by the late John Parker, Principal Extractor of the Court of Session. 8vo. Edinburgh, 1865.
Penninghame, Extracts from the Session Book of the Parish of. 8vo. Newton-Stewart: M'Nairn, 1826.
Pitcairn, Robert. Historical and Genealogical Account of the Principal Families of the Name of Kennedy. 4to. 1830.
Rae, Rev. Peter. The History of the Late Rebellion; Rais'd against His Majesty King George, by the Friends of the Popish Pretender. Small 4to. Drumfries: Robert Rae, 1718. Second edition. 8vo. London, 1746.
Ramage, C. T., LL.D. Drumlanrig Castle and the Douglases, with the Early History and Ancient Remains of Durisdeer, Closeburn, and Morton. Small 8vo. Dumfries: J. Anderson & Son, 1876.
Register of the Synod of Galloway, 1664-71. 8vo. Kirkcudbright: J. Nicholson, 1856.
Riddell, Robert, of Glenriddell. An Account of the Ancient Lordship of Galloway. 4to. 1787.
Simpson, Rev. Robert, D.D. History of Sanquhar. 12mo. Edinburgh, 1853. Second edition, 1865.

HISTORY AND GENEALOGY—*continued.*

Sinclair, Alexander—
 Heirs of the Royal House of Baliol. Privately printed. 8vo. *N.d.*
 Remarks on the Tables of the Heirs of the Royal House of Baliol. Privately printed. 8vo. *N.d.*

Smith, James—
 History of the Old Lodge of Dumfries. Cr. 8vo. Dumfries: J. Maxwell, 1892.
 History of St Michael's Lodge, Kilwinning No. 63 Dumfries. Cr. 8vo. Dumfries: J. Maxwell, 1895.

Stewart, Rev. Archibald, D.D., Minister of Glasserton. History Vindicated in the case of the Wigtown Martyrs. 8vo. Edinburgh, 1867. Second edition. Edinburgh, 1869.

[Stewart, Sir James, and Rev. James Stirling.] Naphtali; or, The Wrestlings of the Church of Scotland for the Kingdom of Christ, from the beginning of the Reformation of Religion until 1667, with a relation of the Sufferings and Death of Hew M'Kail, and some instances of the Sufferings of Galloway and Nithisdale. 12mo. *N.p.*, 1667.
 Many subsequent editions, including one with Introductory Remarks by the Rev. Henry Duncan, D.D., Ruthwell. 12mo. Kirkcudbright: J. Nicholson, 1845.

Stuart of Castlemilk. State of the Evidence for proving that Sir John Stuart of Castlemilk is the linear heir male and representative of Sir William Stuart of Castlemilk, who lived during part of the 14th and 15th Centuries. 4to. 1794.

Train, Joseph. The Buchanites from First to Last. 12mo. Edinburgh, 1846.

Turnbull, W. Robertson. History of Moffat. With frequent notices of Moffatdale and Annandale. 12mo. Edinburgh, 1871.

Vans, An Account of the Family of De Vaux, Vaux, Vaus, or Vans (Latine de Vallibus, of Barnbarroch). 8vo. Privately printed. *N.d.*

Weir, Rev. Robert W. A History of the Scottish Borderers Militia. 8vo. Dumfries: 'Herald' Office, 1877.

[Williams, Rev. E.]—
 A View of the Evidence for proving that the Earl of Galloway is the lineal heir male and lawful representative of Sir William Stuart of Jedworth. 4to. Privately printed, 1796.
 An Abstract of the Evidence adduced to prove that Sir William Stewart of Jedworth, the paternal ancestor of the Earl of Galloway, was the second son of Sir Alexander Stewart of Darnley. 4to. London, 1801.

MISCELLANEOUS.

Adam, A. Mercer, M.D. The Dumfries Album. Published by the Dumfries and Maxwelltown Mechanics' Institution. 4to. Dumfries, 1857.

Adoniazusæ of Theocritus, The ; or, The Syracusan Women at the Festival of Adonis. Translated by James Starke, Esq., Advocate. Dumfries : printed by W. R. M'Diarmid and Co., 1866.

[Aitken, James.] Tales of the Solway. By a Gallovidian. Dumfries : J. Martin, 1873.

[Barbour, John Gordon, in Bogue]—
    Queries connected with Christianity : " Is it Crime to Tell the Truth ? or, Hath Christianity been progressive in Europe for the last Seven Years ?" Small 8vo. Edinburgh, 1824.
    Lights and Shadows of Scottish Character and Scenery. By Cincinnatus Caledonius. Small 8vo. Edinburgh, 1824. The same, second series. Dumfries, 1825.
    Tributes to Scottish Genius, with the Life of the Rev. William Gillespie, late Minister of Kells. Small 8vo. 1827.
    Dialogues of the Dead, chiefly of the Moderns, by the author of ' Evenings in Greece.' Small 8vo. Edinburgh, 1836.
    Unique Traditions, chiefly of the West and South of Scotland. Small 8vo. Dumfries, 1833. Reprint, Glasgow, 1886.

Borland, Rev. R. Yarrow, its Poets and Poetry. Dalbeattie : T. Fraser, 1890.

[Broun, Sir Richard.] Memorabilia Curliana Mabenensia. 8vo. Dumfries : John Sinclair, 1830.

Brown, James. History of the Sanquhar Curling Society. 12mo. Dumfries : ' Courier' Office, 1874.

Browne, Dr W. A. F. Stories about Idiots. Small 8vo. Dumfries : ' Courier' Office, 1873.

Castle-Douglas Miscellany. Published in Castle-Douglas. Vol. 1, 1823-24 ; vol. 2, 1824-25 ; vol. 3, 1825 ; vol. 4, 1826-27.

Castle-Douglas Weekly Visitor and Literary Miscellany. Published in Castle-Douglas. Vol. 1, from 20th November 1829 to 12th November 1830. Vol. 2, from November 1830 to 1832.

Catalogue of Paintings, Statuary, Natural History, Antiquities, Relics of Burns, Models of Machinery, &c., in the Exhibition, Mechanics' Hall, Dumfries. 8vo. Dumfries: Joseph Dickson, 1865.

Clerke, Rev. J. T. The Wreck of the Orion off Portpatrick. 8vo. 1851.

Denniston, James—
    Legends of Galloway. 8vo. Edinburgh, 1825.
    The Ghost of Trool. Newton-Stewart, 1878.

MISCELLANEOUS—*continued*.

[Donaldson, Rev. John.] The Autobiography of Marcello, a Roman Patriot, A.D. 1786-1838. By MacIan. Dumfries: W. Anderson, 1891.

[Douglas, James, of Bombay.] Galloway, The Book of, 1745. 8vo. Newton-Stewart : 'Galloway Gazette' Office, 1882.

Dumfries, A Catalogue of the Books in the Library of the Presbytery of. 8vo. Dumfries : Robert Jackson, 1784.

Dumfries Monthly Magazine and Literary Compendium, The [containing a History of Dumfries by the Editor, William Bennet]. 3 vols. 8vo. Dumfries : J. M'Diarmid & Co., 1825-26.

Dumfries, Papers on the Burgh Politics of. 4to. Edinburgh, first edition, 1759. Second edition, 1760.

Dumfries, Report of the Trial by Jury, David Armstrong, writer in, against George Buchan Vair and Gideon Alston, for sending a challenge to fight a duel. With appendix and letters and other documents. 1839. [Refers to a breach of promise.]

Dumfries. Report of Trial of David M'Gill and John Anderson for alleged assault on Samuel Riddick. 8vo. Dumfries : D. Halliday, 1846.

Dumfries, Roll of Stent and Supply payable to the Crown within the Royalty of, for the year ending March 1829. 4to. Dumfries : W. Carson, 1829.

Dumfries. The Dumfries Mercury; containing an Account of the most Remarkable Occurrences . . . 4to. [A newspaper, probably between 1712 and 1718.]

Note.—Known apparently only through a fragment of the title of No. 12 in possession of Mr Macmath, Edinburgh.

Dumfries, Valuation Roll, Ancient and Modern, of the County of, with Appendix showing the alterations made in the Roll since 1671. Folio. Dumfries : W. Carson, 1827.

Dumfries, Valuation Roll of Sheriffdom of. Dumfries, 1787.

Dumfries Weekly Magazine, The. 8vo. Dumfries : R. Jackson & W. Boyd, 1773 and after.

Dumfriesshire and Galloway Monthly Magazine, The, 1821. 12mo. Dumfries : J. Swan.

Duncan, Rev. Henry, D.D., Minister of Ruthwell—

Scotch Cheap Repository, The. Containing Tales for the Instruction and Amusement of the Young. 12mo. Dumfries, 1808. Second edition, 1815.

Rules and Regulations of Dumfries Parish Bank Friendly Society for Savings for the Industrious. 12mo. Dumfries : 'Courier' Office, 1815.

The Cottage Fireside. 8vo. Edinburgh, 1815.

An Essay on the Nature and Advantages of Parish Banks, for

MISCELLANEOUS—*continued.*

 the Savings of the Industrious. Second edition, greatly enlarged, &c. Together with an Appendix containing a Copy of the Rules of the Dumfries Parish Bank, an Account of such Banks as differ from that of Dumfries, &c., &c. Edinburgh, 1816.

 Letter to John H. Forbes, Esq. 8vo. Dumfries, 1817.

 Letter to W. R. K. Douglas, Esq., M.P., on the Bill brought into Parliament for the protection and encouragement of Savings Banks. 8vo. Dumfries: 'Courier' Office, 1819.

Elliott, Robert. The Gretna Green Memoirs. With an Introduction and Appendix by the Rev. Caleb Brown. London, published by the Gretna Green Parson, 16 Leicester Square, 1842.

Fraser, Gordon—

 Wigtown and Whithorn : Historical and Descriptive Sketches, Stories and Anecdotes, illustrative of the Racy Wit and Pawky Humour of the District. 8vo. Wigtown, 1877.

 Lowland Lore ; or, the Wigtownshire of Long Ago. 8vo. Wigtown, 1880.

 Wigtown and Whithorn, Historical and Descriptive Sketches. 8vo. Wigtown, 1885.

 Davy Dumpytail ; or, The History of the Wigtown Crows. Wigtown : Gordon Fraser. *N.d.*

Galloway Register, The. 4to. 1827-37.

Gibson, J. Erskine. A Medical Sketch of Dumfriesshire. Dumfries : John Sinclair, 1827.

Gillespie, James. The Triumph of Philosophy ; or, The True System of the Universe. Dumfries, 1890.

Glass, Andrew—

 Tales and Traditions of Ayrshire and Galloway. 1873.

 Adventures and Traditions. Small 8vo. Glasgow : W. Rankin, 1884.

Glenkens Hunt Tales. 1870.

Goldie, Miss. Family Recollections and National Progress. Dumfries : Sinclair & M'Kie, 1841.

Gordon, Sir Alexander. An Address to the Inhabitants of the Stewartry of Kirkcudbright respecting the Laws relating to the Poor. 8vo. Edinburgh, 1820.

Historical and Traditional Tales in Prose and Verse, connected with the South of Scotland. Small 8vo. Kirkcudbright : John Nicholson, 1843.

Hutton, John. Selections from "Bloody Buoy," &c. Small 8vo. Dumfries : D. Halliday, 1847.

Johnstone, Walter. Letters descriptive of Prince Edward Island, in the Gulf of St Lawrence. 12mo. Dumfries : J. Swan, 1822.

MISCELLANEOUS—*continued*.

Kirkcudbright, Valuation Roll, Antient and Modern, of the Stewartry of, with an Appendix shewing the Alterations made in the Roll, from the commencement of the existing Records till 26th November 1819. Folio. Dumfries: 'Courier' Office, 1820.

Kirkcudbright, Valuation Roll of, in 1642 and 1777. Folio. Dumfries, 1778.

Kirkcudbright, Valuation Roll of the Stewartry of, as made up by the Commissioners of Land-Tax, 14th June 1799. Folio. Dumfries: R. Jackson, 1800.

Literary Gleaner, The: A Collection of Selected Literature. Dumfries : 1830.

Mackenzie, John Commelin—
Parliamentary Reform, Kirkcudbright. A pamphlet. Printed at the 'Stewartry Times' Office, 1860.
Statement of Facts as to the Writing, Printing, and Publishing of the History of Galloway. Castle-Douglas, 1882.

Macminn, Henry. Speeches on Various Public Occasions (chiefly in Dumfries). Small 8vo. Edinburgh : published for the Author, 1831.

M'Queen, James, of Crofts. Notes on a Trip to America, 1889. Castle-Douglas, 1890.

Mactaggart, John. The Scottish Gallovidian Encyclopædia ; or, The Original, Antiquated and Natural Curiosities of the South of Scotland. 8vo. London, 1824. Second edition. London, 1876. [A reprint.]

Maxwell, Jean, the Galloway Sorceress, The Remarkable Trial of, for pretending to exercise Witchcraft, Sorcery, Inchantment, Conjuration, &c. 12mo. Kirkcudbright : Alexander Gordon, 1805.

M[axwell], M. A. A Hallowe'en Guest ; or, Cottage Life in Scotland. 8vo. Dumfries : J. Maxwell. *N.d.*

Maxwell, The Hon. Marmaduke C. Religious Intolerance ; or, A Statement of Facts with reference to the Appointment of a Matron to the Crichton Royal Institution, Dumfries. 8vo. Edinburgh, 1859.

Maxwell, William, Esq., Younger of Cardoness, a Letter addressed to, as a Candidate for Parliament ; with some Remarks as to his fitness to serve the County of Kirkcudbright in the capacity of its Representative. Dedicated with feelings of much respect and affection to the Farmers resident therein by a devoted Friend to Non-intrusion. 1839.

Murray, J. A. H. Dialect of the Southern Counties of Scotland ; with Map. 8vo. London, 1873.

MISCELLANEOUS—*continued.*

Quin, Roger. Plain Truth; or, Error Exposed, &c. Dumfries: published and sold by the Author, 1869.

[Reid, Rev. H. M. B.] About Galloway Folk. By A Galloway Herd. 8vo. Edinburgh, 1889.

Reminiscences of a Quinquagenarian. Reprinted from the 'Dumfries and Galloway Courier,' 1867.

Robinson, Samuel. Reminiscences of Wigtownshire about the Close of Last Century, with Contrasts, and an Appendix of Odds and Ends in Rhyme. 12mo. Hamilton, 1862.

Rosebery, Lord. Robert Burns: Two Addresses delivered at Dumfries and Glasgow on the Centenary of the Poet's Death, 21st July 1896. Small 8vo. Edinburgh, 1896.

[Sharpe, Charles Kirkpatrick.] A Friendly Address to the Common People of Dumfriesshire. Signed Gracchus. Dumfries: R. Jackson [1803].

Simpson, Rev. Robert, D.D., of Sanquhar. Traditions of the Covenanters; or, Gleanings among the Mountains. 3 vols. Edinburgh [1842?]. Several subsequent editions.

Smith, William, banker, Moniaive. Notes of a Short American Tour. 12mo. Dumfries: M'Diarmid & Mitchell, 1873.

Solway Summer Annual. Dalbeattie: Ivie Callan, 1893.

Starke, J. G. H. County and Parish Government in Scotland. Small 8vo. Dumfries: J. Maxwell, 1882.

Stewart, W. Ross. Musings in Sweetheart Abbey and its Environs. Edinburgh, 1868.

Sulley, Philip. Robert Burns and Dumfries, 1796-1896. 8vo. Dumfries: Thos. Hunter & Co., 1896.

Tait, Thomas. Letter to the Magistrates and Town Council of the Royal Burgh of Lochmaben, pointing out the evils of their close system of Election. 8vo. Dumfries: William Burgess, 1853.

Traits and Stories of Scottish Life, and Pictures of Scenes and Character. 3 vols. crown 8vo. 1832.

> Most of the Tales relate to Galloway, and at end is a "Two Days' Tour in Annandale."

[Trotter, Robert.] Galloway Gossip Sixty Years Ago; being a Series of Articles illustrative of the Manners, Customs, and Peculiarities of the Aboriginal Picts of Galloway. Edited by Saxon. Small 8vo. Bedlington, 1878.

Watson, Thomas. Burns Centenary, 21st July 1896, Great Demonstration at Dumfries. Small 8vo. Dumfries: Thos. Hunter & Co., 'Standard' Office [1896].

Wood, John. 'Neath Southern Skies. Castle-Douglas, 1882.

NATURAL HISTORY.

Extraordinary Storms in Dumfriesshire and Galloway on 11th December 1883, and the 23d and 26th January 1894, as reported in the 'Dumfries and Galloway Standard'; with a brief notice of the Hurricane, 7th January 1839. Dumfries: 'Standard' Office. *N.d.*

Gray, Robert, and Thomas Anderson. On the Birds of Ayrshire and Wigtownshire. Proceedings of the Natural History Society of Glasgow.

Jameson, Professor Robert. A Mineralogical Description of the County of Dumfries. 8vo. Edinburgh, 1805.

Jardine, Sir William, Bart. Ichnology of Annandale, with Illustrations of Footmarks in the New Red Sandstone of Corncockle. Folio. Edinburgh, 1853.

M'Andrew, James—
    List of the Flowering Plants of Dumfriesshire and Kirkcudbrightshire. Compiled for the Dumfriesshire and Galloway Natural History and Antiquarian Society. 8vo. Dumfries: 'Herald' Office, 1882.
    A List of Wigtownshire Plants. New Galloway. 8vo. No place or date [1894].

Menteath, James Stuart. Geology of Dumfriesshire, with a coloured Geological Map. Transactions of the Highland Society, October 1844.

Sadler, John. Narrative of a Ramble among the Wild Flowers on the Moffat Hills in August 1857; with a List of Plants to be found in the District. Small 8vo. Moffat: William Muir, 1858.

Scott-Elliot, G. F., assisted by J. M'Andrew, J. T. Johnstone, Miss Hannay, and other Botanists. The Flora of Dumfriesshire, including Nithsdale and Kirkcudbrightshire. 8vo. Dumfries: J. Maxwell & Son, 1896.

Transactions of the Dumfriesshire and Galloway Natural History and Antiquarian Society. Dumfries: 'Courier,' 'Herald,' and 'Standard' Offices. 1862-96.

Williamson, Rev. D. S. Thoughts on the Present Scarcity of Salmon. 8vo. Stranraer, 1852.

POETRY.

Adamson, Robert. Musings in Leisure Hours. Dumfries, 1879.

Affleck, R. Poems. Dumfries, 1810.

Armstrong, A. J. Ingleside Musings and Tales in Rhyme. Illustrated. 8vo. Dalbeattie, 1890.

Armstrong, R. S., King's Dragoon Guards. Hours on Sentry. Dumfries, 1848.

Barbour, John. Life and Acts of the most victorious Conqueror, Robert Bruce, King of Scotland, and Blind Harry's Acts and Deeds of Sir William Wallace. 2 vols., with supplement. Dumfries, 1758.

Barbour, John Gordon—
Evenings in Greece, and Baronial Promenades. Edinburgh, 1829.
Helvetic Hours and Hebrew Melodies : A Series of Poetical Pieces, descriptive of the Sublime Scenery of Switzerland and the Simplon. By the Author of 'Evenings in Greece.' Edinburgh, 1831.

Bennoch [afterwards Bennet], William. The Sabbath, and other Poems. Small 8vo. Dumfries, 1822.

Buchanan, Robert. Poems on Several Occasions. *Contents:*—
(1) Earl William and Willie Hill, a True Tale in five cantos. (2) John Tamson's Sons, a True Tale in Two Parts in a letter to a Friend. (3) The Gallovidian Bard ; or, Pastorals, Songs, Elegies, &c., supposed to be sung by the Swains on the Banks of the Luce, Tarf, Bladnoch, Maylee, Cree, &c. (4) Detached Pieces.—Dedicated to John Hathorn, Esq. of Castlewigg, and to the Officers and Gentlemen who compose the Honourable and Patriotic Band, the Wigtownshire Volunteers. 12mo. Edinburgh : Printed for the Author, 1797. [An exceedingly rare book.]

Burney, William. Dumfries, a Poem. London, 1789.
Reprinted in the Dumfries Monthly Magazine, vol. iii. p. 167.

Cæsar, William. Poems in the Scottish Dialect, descriptive of the situation and feelings of Persons in humble Life. Dumfries : C. Munro & Co., 1817.

Carruthers, John. The Heroic Deeds of the Scots : A Poem, &c. Vol. I [all published]. Small 8vo. Dumfries: Robert Jackson, 1796.

Clerk, Alexander. Poems on Several Subjects. Dumfries, 1801.

Cromek, R. H. Remains of Nithsdale and Galloway Song ; with Historical and Traditional Notices relative to the Manners

POETRY—*continued.*

and Customs of the Peasantry. 8vo. London, 1810. Second edition (a reprint), 8vo. Paisley, 1880.

Cunningham, Allan. Sir Marmaduke Maxwell; a Dramatic Poem: The Mermaid of Galloway: and, The Legend of Richard Faulder. Small 8vo. London, 1822.

Davidson, David. Thoughts on the Seasons, &c., partly in the Scottish Dialect. 8vo. London, 1789.

[Davidson, John.] A Memorial of the Life and Death of two worthye Christians, Robert Campbel of the Kinyeancleugh, and his Wife Elizabeth Campbel. In English Meter. Edinburgh: Robert Waldegrave, 1595.

Denniston, Capt. The Battle of Craignilder, a very ancient Gallovidian Ballad; arranged for publication, with an Introduction and Notes. Small 8vo. Edinburgh, 1832.

> The antiquity of this ballad is wholly fictitious.

Dickson, A. S. The Siege of Dumfries, a Tragedy. Dumfries: Hunter, 1889.

Dunbar, David—
Poems and Songs. Small 8vo. Glasgow, 1859.
Poems of Home Life. Small 8vo. Edinburgh, 1873.

Edgar, Thomas. Poems on Various Subjects; but Chiefly Moral and Descriptive: with Songs and Copious Notes. Dumfries: J. M'Diarmid & Co., 1822.

Fisher, James—
Poems on Various Occasions. Dumfries: Printed by Robert Jackson for the Author, 1790.
Poems on Various Subjects. Dumfries, 1792.

Fisher, Robert. Poetical Sparks. 8vo. Dumfries: R. Fisher, 1881.

Fraser, Gordon. Poems. 8vo. Wigtown, 1885.

Fraser, Janet Douglas, Thornhill—
The Proverbs of Solomon in metre. Dumfries, 1835.
Poems on Religious Subjects. Dumfries. *N.d.*

Fullartoun, John, of Careltoun [Borgue]. The Turtle-Dove, under the Absence & Presence of her only Choise. By a Lover of the Celestiall Muses. 12mo. Edinburgh, 1664.

Galloway Hunt, The; or, Actæon in the Glenkens: an Epic Poem, in limping doggerel measure, dedicated to Willy, the Earth-stopper near Barmawhaple. Castle-Douglas: A. Davidson, 1820.

Gerrond, John. Poems on Several Occasions, chiefly in the Scottish Dialect. 12mo. Glasgow, 1802. Several subsequent publications, with varying titles and contents, including The New Poetical Works of Dumfries: Printed for the Author, 1818.

POETRY—*continued*.

Graham, W. Owl Cots, a Legendary Tale, and other Poems. Dumfries: 'Standard' Office, 1845.

Grierson, Sir Robert, of Lag. An Elegy in Memory of that Valiant Champion; or, The Prince of Darkness, his Lamentation for, and Commendation of, his trusty and well-beloved Friend, who died Dec. 23d, 1733.

Halliday, James. Musings on the River Nith. Small 8vo. Dumfries: W. Anderson, 1865.

Harper, Malcolm M'L. The Bards of Galloway: A Collection of Poems, Songs, Ballads, &c., by Natives of Galloway. With an Introduction and Notes. 8vo. Dalbeattie: T. Fraser, 1889. Large paper, with Illustrations by Faed and others.

Hawkins, Susannah. Poems and Song. 10 vols. 8vo. Dumfries: 'Courier' Office, 1832-67.

Hughan, Elizabeth Ewart. Estelle, and other Poems. Newton-Stewart, 1866.

Hutton, John, Manufacturer, Maxwellton, Poems by the Late. Selected by His Son. Dumfries, 1837.

H[utton], J[ohn], junior. The Seals, Trumpets, and Thunders of Revelation. 12mo. Dumfries: David Halliday, 1838.

Inglis, Henry. The Briar of Threave and the Lily of Barholm. A Metrical Romance. 8vo. London, 1855.

Irving, W. S. Fair Helen, a Tale of the Border. 8vo. Edinburgh, 1814.

Johnston, Hannah, Kirkmahoe. Poems on Religious Subjects. Small 8vo. Dumfries: D. Halliday, 1834.

Johnstone, John. Poems on Various Subjects, but chiefly Illustrations of the manners of Annandale. Dumfries, 1820. New edition, with Memoir by W. Johnstone, 1857.

Kelly, John Kelso. A Home of Heroes; or, A Lay of Galloway. To which is added a Prose Essay, "A Foray into Galloway Song-Land." 12mo. Edinburgh: The Darien Press, 1895.

Kennedy, Alexander W. M. Clark. Robert the Bruce: A Poem, Historical and Romantic. Illustrated by James Faed, jun. 8vo. London, 1884.

Kennedy, James—
Poems and Songs. Dumfries: M'Diarmid, 1843.
Poems and Prose Tales. Small 8vo. Dumfries: 'Standard' Office, 1849.

Kerr, Robert. Maggie o' the Moss, and other Poems. Edited by Malcolm M'L. Harper. Dalbeattie: T. Fraser, 1891.

Laing, William, Poems by, with Introductory Sketch by the Rev. Dr Simpson, Sanquhar. Sanquhar, 1859.

POETRY—*continued.*

Lewis, Stewart—
    Fair Helen of Kirkconnel, 8vo. Edinburgh, 1796. Fifth edition, Dumfries, 1818. Seventh edition, Annan, 1848.
    The African Slave, with other Poems. Second edition. 12mo. Dumfries: C. Munro & Co., 1818.

M'Culloch, J. M.—
    The Rivers of Galloway. 8vo. Kirkcudbright: J. Nicholson. *N.d.*
    The Rivers of Dumfriesshire. 8vo. Kirkcudbright: J. Nicholson. *N.d.*
    Fugitive Pieces. 8vo. [Kirkcudbright: J. Nicholson.] *N.d.*

M'Dowal, Henry. The Buchanites. 1792.

M'Dowall, Andrew. Will Wander of Benbarrone's Trip to New York, with other Poems. 8vo. Newton-Stewart: J. M'Nairn, 1832.

M'Dowall, William. Poems, chiefly in the Galloway Dialect. 8vo. Newton-Stewart: J. M'Nairn, 1828.

M'Dowall, William. The Man of the Woods, and other Poems. Small 8vo. Edinburgh, 1844. Second edition. Edinburgh, 1882.

[M'Millan, Rev. John, Balmaghie.] An Elegy upon the much lamented Death of that religious and virtuous Gentlewoman, Mrs Mary Gordon, daughter to the Honourable Sir Alexander Gordon of Earlstoun, and spouse, first to Edward Goldie of Craigmuie, and thereafter to the Reverend Mr John M'Millan, Minister of the Gospel at Balmaghie. 12mo. Edinburgh, 1723.

M'Vitie, William. The Battle of Dryfe Sands. Small 8vo. Dumfries: C. Munro & Co., 1818.

Macwhirter, David. A Ploughboy's Musings, being a selection of English and Humorous Scotch Poems. 8vo. Whithorn, 1883.

Mayne, John. The Siller Gun. Twelve stanzas, single sheet, 4to. Dumfries [1777?].

Miscellaneous Verses, A Collection of. By a Lady [W. Richardson]. Small 4to. Dumfries: J. Maxwell, 1864.

Moffat, A Souvenir of. The Gallowhill: A Poem. *Anon.* Moffat: Wm. Muir. *N.d.*

Montgomery, Capt. Alexander. The Cherrie and the Slae, with other Poems. With Notes and a Memoir of the Author's Life. 12mo. Kirkcudbright: John Nicholson [1842].

Morrison, John, Poems by. 12mo. Edinburgh, 1832.

POETRY—*continued.*

Murray, James—
    Minor Poems by. Dumfries, 1816.
    The Maid of Galloway : A Tale of Threave and Otterburn. Small 8vo. Edinburgh, 1849.

Murray, Rev. George—
    The Bridge : A Ballad. Castle-Douglas: 'Advertiser' Office, 1866.
    Sarah Rae, and other Poems. Small 8vo. Greenock, 1883.

Nicholson, William—
    Tales in Verse, and Miscellaneous Poems, Descriptive of Rural Life and Manners. 12mo. Edinburgh, 1814.
        Second edition (with Memoir by J. M'Diarmid). J. Johnston, Dumfries ; J. Nicholson, Kirkcudbright ; and J. M'Nairn, Newton-Stewart. Printed by N. M'L. Bruce, Dumfries, 1828.
    The Poetical Works of. With a Memoir by M. M'L. Harper, and Portrait by John Faed, R.S.A. Small 8vo. Castle-Douglas : Samuel Gordon. Kirkcudbright : James Nicholson, 1878.

Nithsdale Minstrel, The. Being Original Poetry chiefly by the Bards of Nithsdale. Dumfries : Preacher & Dunbar, 1815.

Palmer, John. Poems and Songs. (Printed for private circulation.) Annan, 1871.

Park, William, Eskdalemuir. The Vale of Esk, and other Poems. 12mo. Edinburgh, 1833.

Powhead, Bartholomew, Esq., Barrister at Law. The Clachan Fair : a Descriptive Poem. Fifth edition. Edinburgh, 1872. (Attributed to Dr James Trotter.)

Quin, Roger—
    The Death of Scottish Hospitality : A Poem in Five Cantos. Dumfries, 1848.
    The Heather Lintie ; being Poems, chiefly in the Scottish Dialect. Small 8vo. Dumfries : Johnstone, 1861. New edition. J. Maxwell, 1866.

Rae, David—
    The Political Contest ; or, O'Grady's Conquest ! A Musical Extravaganza. Castle-Douglas : John Welsh, 1880.
    Dundrennan Abbey : A Dramatic Poem in Three Acts. By D. R. Kirkcudbright : M. E. Maxwell. Dalbeattie : William Milligan. *N.d.*

Ramsay, Allan. The Gentle Shepherd. Small 8vo. Dumfries : David Halliday, 1839.

DUMFRIESSHIRE AND GALLOWAY.

POETRY—*continued*.

Reid, Robert "Wanlock." Moorland Rhymes. Dumfries: Anderson & Son, 1874.

Richardson, Mrs G. G., Dumfries. Poems. Small 8vo. Edinburgh, 1828.

[Riddell, Robert, of Glenriddell.] Legendary Fragments: The Bedesman of Nidsyde, Ye Mort o' Lauch, &c. 4to. London, 1790.

Scott, James K. Galloway Gleanings: Poems and Songs. Castle-Douglas, 1881.

[Sharpe, Charles Kirkpatrick.] The Wizard Peter. A Song of the Solway. 8vo. Edinburgh, 1834.

Shennan, Robert. Tales, Songs, and Miscellaneous Poems, chiefly in the Scottish Dialect. Fcap. 8vo. Dumfries: John M'Diarmid & Co., 1831.

Sproat, George G. B. The Rose o' Dalma Linn, and other Lays o' Gallowa'. Castle-Douglas, 1888.

[Symson, Rev. Andrew.] Elegies. 12mo. [Without title, and sometimes bound with Tripatriarchicon, 1705. Mostly on persons in Galloway. See 'The Bride of Lammermoor.' Scarce.]

Thom, R. W. Herbert and Rosana, a Tale, with other Poems. 12mo. Dumfries: John M'Diarmid, 1839.

Thomson, Margaret, The Poetical Epistles of, being a Series of Letters to her Son, a soldier in the 55th Regiment, with two other Poems. Small 8vo. Dumfries: C. Munro & Co., 1815.

Train, Joseph—
  Strains of the Mountain Muse. 8vo. Edinburgh, 1814.
  The Wild Scot of Galloway: A Poem. Small 8vo. Kirkcudbright: J. Nicholson. *N.d.* [1848.]

Turnbull, G., Comedian. Poems. Dumfries, 1794.

Walker, James Scott. Poems. Dumfries: Munro & Co., 1816.

[White, Thomas.] Saint Guerdun's Well: A Poem. 8vo. Dumfries: R. Jackson, 1795. Second edition. 4to. Dumfries [1797].

Whithorn Warblings. Whithorn: Belmont Hall Bazaar, 1888.

Williamson, Rev. D. S., Tongland—
  Metrical Paraphrase of the Book of Revelation. 8vo. Kirkcudbright: J. Nicholson [1838].
  The Rivers of Galloway: A Poem. In two Parts. Dumfries, 1840-41.

Wilson, William, Dumfries. A Collection of Poems on various subjects. 8vo. Edinburgh, 1803.

RELIGION AND ECCLESIASTICAL AFFAIRS.

A Collection of Psalm Tunes for the use of the Church of Scotland. Compos'd in four parts—viz., Trible, Contra, Tenor, Bassus. Engraven, printed, and sold by John Duncan, bookseller in Dumfries, MDCCXXIII. Oblong 12mo.

Anderson, Rev. J., Dornock. Speech on the Kirtle Case before the Synod of Dumfries, April 16, 1872. 12mo. Annan: W. Cuthbertson & Son.

An Essay upon the following questions: What Power has the Magistrate about Sacred Things? . . . By a Well-wisher of the Country's Peace. 4to. D*r*umfries: Robert Rae, 1715.

Bennet, Rev. Andrew, Closeburn. The Christian and the World: A Sermon. 8vo. Dumfries, 1848.

Beauties of Hugh Blair, D.D.; Beauties of John Wightman, D.D.; Extracts from the Sermons of Thomas Chalmers, D.D., &c. Dumfries: D. Halliday, 1848.

Bible, The. The Translator's Preface to the present authorised Translation of the Bible, and an Epitome of the History of the English Bible. 8vo. John Nicholson, Kirkcudbright, 1843.

Brown, Gilbert, Abbot of Sweetheart. Ane Answere to ane certane libell or writing sent by Mr John Welsche to ane Catholicke, as ane Answere to ane objection of the Roman Kirk, whereby they go about to deface the veritie of that only true religion whilk we professe. [1599?]

Bryden, William, D.D., Minister of Dalton. The Cause between Patronage and Popular Election, decided in the Presbytery of Friesburgh. 8vo. Edinburgh, 1769. [A squib on the appointment of Rev. Wm. Wright in New Abbey.]

Brydon, Rev. Robert, Dunscore—
 Remarks on Pestilence as a Divine Judgment. 12mo. Dumfries: John Anderson, 1833.
 Three Single Sermons. One of which, 8vo, Dumfries, 1853.

Brydon, Robert, Eskdalemuir. The Practical Bearings of the Doctrine of Christ's Headship over the Church. 12mo. Dumfries: D. Halliday, 1844.

Burnside, Rev. George M., Urr—
 Two Sermons. 8vo. Dumfries, 1829.
 Sermon on the Nature of Unbelief. 8vo. Dumfries, 1829.
 The Irongray Martyrs: A Sermon. 8vo. Dumfries, 1831.

RELIGION AND ECCLESIASTICAL AFFAIRS—*continued*.

Burnside, Rev. William, D.D. The Great Things God hath done for the British Nation : A Sermon. 8vo. Dumfries, 1798.

Coats, Rev. W. W. The Church of Scotland the People's Possession : A Sermon. Newton-Stewart : W. Anderson, 1887.

Collins, David. Lectures to all Nations. The Mystery of Iniquity, Glimpses of the Apostacy from the first Christian Church. 8vo. Dumfries : R. Johnstone, 1862.

Confession, The, of Faith used in the English Congregation at Geneva. Also John Knox's Confession of Faith. 12mo. Kirkcudbright : John Nicholson, 1843.

Cuthbert, J. M. Copy of Correspondence between the Rev. J. Mackie, Established Church, and J. M. Cuthbert, Dalbeattie, concerning the " Sleeping Rebuke." Dumfries, 1878.

Dow, Rev. W. Notes on a Sermon on Union to Christ. Castle-Douglas : A. Davidson, 1830.

Dumfries, Report of the Proceedings of the Presbytery and Synod of, following upon the Crown Presentation in favour of the Rev. W. W. Duncan to the Parish of Urr, 1835. Dumfries : J. M'Kinnel, 1836.

Dumfries, Report of the Speeches delivered at the Church Extension Meeting held in the New Church on Thursday the 16th February 1837. Dumfries : John Anderson and John M'Kie. *N.d.*

Duncan, Rev. Henry, D.D., Ruthwell—

A Series of Letters to his Parishioners, commenced during the progress of the Catholic Relief Bill. Small 8vo. Dumfries : J. M'Diarmid & Co., 1829.

A Series of Letters to the Rev. George Cook, D.D., on the late Enactment of the General Assembly relative to Patronage and Calls, &c. Small 8vo. Dumfries : J. M'Diarmid & Co., 1834.

Ewart, Rev. John, Minister of Troqueer. A Protestant Catechism, showing the Principal Errors of the Church of Rome. 12mo. Dumfries : Robert Jackson, 1778. Reprint, Edinburgh, 1813 ; also Kirkcudbright : John Nicholson. *N.d.*

Fergusson, Samuel. The Burnside Appointment to the Parish of Urr. 12mo. Dumfries : John M'Kinnell, 1836.

Fraser, Rev. James, Colvend. A Funeral Sermon preached in the Parish Church of Urr, on the death of the Rev. George M. Burnside. 8vo. Dumfries : John Anderson, 1855.

Gillespie, Rev. R. A. " How Long have I to live ? " a Funeral Sermon preached on the death of the late James Mackie of Bargaly, M.P. Castle-Douglas : S. Gordon. *N.d.* [1868.]

RELIGION AND ECCLESIASTICAL AFFAIRS—*continued.*
Gillespie, Rev. William, Kells—
  Mercy Recommended : A Sermon in St Michael's Church, Dumfries. Dumfries : R. Jackson, 1810.
  The Rebellion of Absolom : A Discourse preached at Kirkcudbright, 30th July 1820. 8vo. Dumfries, 1820.
Goold, Rev. James—
  The Repentance, Remission, Refreshing, and Restoration of the Gospel : A Sermon. Newton-Stewart, 1866.
  Glorifying God in Luther : A Sermon. Newton-Stewart, 1883.
Greig, Rev. George, Kirkpatrick-Durham. Sermon preached before the Synod of Dumfries. 8vo. Dumfries, 1848.
Grierson, Rev. Thomas, Kirkbean. Sermon in reference to the Revivals at Kilsyth. 8vo. Dumfries, 1839.
Guthrie, Rev. William. The Christian's Great Interest. 12mo. Dumfries : Robert M'Lachlan, 1785.
Halliday, Rev. Thomas. Lectures and Sermons. Dumfries : A. Halliday, 1833. Second edition, 1837.
Harrison, Thomas. Topica Sacra : Spiritual Logick. Some brief Hints and Helps to Faith, Meditation, Prayer, Comfort, and Holiness. Communicated at Christ Church, Dublin. Enlarged with Spiritual Pleadings in above xxx cases by Mr John Hunter, Minister of the Gospel at Ayre. 12mo. Kirkbride [Dumfriesshire] : Robert Rae, 1712.
Henderson, Rev. John. An Illustration of the Transfiguration on Mount Tabor. Dumfries, 1821.
Henry, Rev. Matthew. Sober-mindedness press'd upon Young People, in a Discourse on Titus ii. 6. D*r*umfries : Robert Rae, 1715.
Hepburn, Mr John, Minister at Orr in Galloway—
  Humble Pleadings for the Good Old Way. 12mo. 1713.
  True Copy of a Letter sent to the Rev. Will. Vetch, min. of Dumfries. 1719.
Hutton, John, Charterhouse, Troqueer—
  The Pictorial Illustrations of the Fulfilment of the Prophecies in the Book of Daniel. [Anonymous.] 12mo. Dumfries : David Halliday, 1839.
  Immanuel's Coming-on-the-Earth Church. 12mo. Dumfries : David Halliday, 1845.
Irving, Edward, Trial of, before the Presbytery of Annan. With Appendix of letters, notice of similar manifestations, &c. 12mo. Dumfries, 1833.
Johnston, Rev. Bryce, D.D., Holywood—
  The Lord's Call to bear the Rod, and Him who hath appointed it. Two Sermons. 8vo. Dumfries, 1795.

RELIGION AND ECCLESIASTICAL AFFAIRS—*continued*.
>   The Cause of God's Judgments on Great Britain, and the Way to remove them : considered in two Sermons. 8vo. Dumfries, 1801.
>   The Reason why the Enemies of Britain have so long threatened this Empire with Destruction, and the Way speedily to subdue those Enemies : considered in Two Sermons. 8vo. Dumfries, 1804.

Kae, Mr Adam, Minister of the Gospel at Borg. A Sermon preached from Canticles ii. 3, in the time of Scotland's purest Reformation, 1648. 12mo. Broad-wood, Carluke, 1735.

Kenmuir. The Last and Heavenly Speeches and Glorious Departure of John Viscount Kenmuir. [Attributed to Samuel Rutherford.] 4to. Edinburgh, 1649.

Keyden, Rev. William, Penpont. A Sermon preached on the Death of Charles, Duke of Queensberry and Dover. 8vo. Dumfries : Robert Jackson, 1778.

Lamont, Rev. David, D.D., Kirkpatrick-Durham—
>   A Sermon [preached at Kells] on 1 John iii. 7. 8vo. Dumfries : Robert Jackson, 1785.
>   A Sermon on Repentance, preached at Kirkpatrick-Durham. 8vo. Dumfries : Robert Jackson, 1798.
>   Charity Recommended : A Sermon. Dumfries : R. Jackson, 1808.

Lessons from the Bible for the use of Schools. Dumfries : Wood, 1816.

M'Ewan, David, weaver, Kirkcudbright. Three Essays on Infidelity, Hope, and Death. Dumfries : R. Palmer. Kirkcudbright : J. Nicholson, 1830.

M'Millan, Rev. James, Torthorwald. Sermon preached before the Dumfries Missionary Society. 8vo. Dumfries, 1798.

Macmillan, Rev. John, Balmaghie—
>   Pamphlets on the Controversy relating to him.
>   A True Narrative of the Proceedings of the Presbytery of Kirkcudbright against one of their Number. Small 8vo. *N.d.* [1704.] [By Macmillan himself.]
>   The Pamphlet entitled A True Narrative Examined and Found False, 1705. [By Cameron of Kirkcudbright.]
>   Answers to a Paper of Grievances, 1705. [Chiefly by Cameron and Ewart.]
>   An Account of the Deposition of Mr John M'Millan, 1706.
>   The Examination of the True Narrative Tryed and Found False. 4to. 1706. [By Macmillan.]
>   The Protestation, Declinature, and Appeal of Mr John Mac-

Religion and Ecclesiastical Affairs—*continued*.
>   millan . . . sent to the Commission of the Kirk at Edinburgh. 1708.
>   And other pamphlets.

M'Millan, Rev. John, Kirkcudbright. A Sermon preached on Opening of the New Church of Kirkcudbright on 21st of October 1838. Kirkcudbright : J. Nicholson, 1838.

Macwhir, Rev. John, Urr. A Doctrinal Catechism. . . . Some forms of family prayer. 12mo. Dumfries : C. Munro & Co., 1815.

Maitland, Rev. John, Garlies. A Sermon preached on 13th January 1814, being the day appointed for a National Thanksgiving. 8vo. Kirkcudbright : Alexander Gordon, 1814.

Marjoribanks, Rev. Thomas, Lochmaben. A few plain Remarks for plain men. 8vo. Dumfries, 1843.

Monteith, Rev. James, Minister of Borgue from 1693 to 1741. A Testimony to the Free Grace of God. With an answer to the question, "Am I a Christian?" by the Rev. Samuel Smith. 12mo. Kirkcudbright : John Nicholson, 1841.

Muter, Rev. Robert, D.D. Abounding Iniquity : A Sermon preached at Kirkcudbright in 1794. 8vo. Dumfries, 1794.

Mutter, Rev. Thomas. Sermon preached before the Governors of the Infirmary. 8vo. Dumfries, 1778.

Nine Letters on the subject of Church Patronage. Reprinted from the 'Dumfries Courier.' 12mo. Dumfries : J. M'Diarmid & Co., 1834.

Osborne, Rev. John. The Concern of Zion for the Cause of God. Preached at the Martyrs' Grave, Kirkconnel Moor, Galloway, September 11, 1831. Dumfries, 1831.

Pastoral Address on Public Baptism. Drawn up by a Committee of the Presbytery of Kirkcudbright, approved of by the Presbytery, and recommended to be read from all the Pulpits and circulated throughout all the Parishes within their bounds. Kirkcudbright : John Nicholson, 1840.

[Pollock, Rev. John, Glencairn.] An Answer to the First Part of Humble Pleadings, or a Vindication of the Church of Scotland from the unjust aspersions of Mr Hepburn and his Party. . . . By a Well-wisher of the Good-Old-Way. 4to. D*r*umfries : Robert Rae, 1717.

Purves, James. Eight Letters between the People called Buchanites and a Teacher near Edinburgh. 8vo. Edinburgh, 1785.

Reid, Rev. H. M. B.—
>   A Sermon preached in Balmaghie Church on the Queen's Jubilee, 1887. Castle-Douglas : 'Advertiser' Office, 1887.

RELIGION AND ECCLESIASTICAL AFFAIRS—*continued.*
  Union *versus* Disestablishment : A Sermon. Castle-Douglas : 'Advertiser' Office, 1892.
  The Progress of Church Service in Galloway : A Sermon. Small 8vo. Edinburgh, 1892.
  Revival in Dumfries, The. A Record of the Great Religious Awakening during the Visit of Mr E. P. Hammond to that Town in January and February 1861. Dumfries : 'Standard' Office, 1861.
Robesone, Rev. Alex., Tinwald—
  The Oath of Abjuration no ground of Separation. By a Lover of Truth and Peace. Small 8vo. Kirkbride [Dumfriesshire]: Robert Rae, 1713.
  Mene Tekel ; or, Separation weighed in the Balance of the Sanctuary and found wanting. 4to. D*r*umfries : Robert Rae, 1717.
Rutherford, Rev. Samuel.
  Joshua Redivivus, or, Mr Rutherford's Letters. 12mo. [Rotterdam], 1664.
  Many subsequent editions.
  Christ's Napkin ; or, A Sermon preached in Kirkcudbright at the Communion, May 12, 1633. By that Flower of the Church, famous, *famous* Mr Samuel Rutherford. Never before printed. 4to. *N.d.* Many subsequent editions.
  A Sermon preached in the Parish of Anwoth, on a Sacramental Occasion, 5th April 1637, with an Account of his Life. Small 8vo. Kirkcudbright : John Nicholson, 1842.
  A Communion Sermon, preached at Kirkcudbright. Kirkcudbright : J. Nicholson.
Scott, David. An Abstract of the Buchanites' large Book. Writ by Mr Hugh White, sometime a Relief Minister in Irvine. . . . 12mo. *N.d.*
Smith, Rev. Samuel. The Second Coming of Christ ; being the Substance of Two Discourses preached in the Free Church, Gatehouse, on 17th March 1844, after the funeral of the Rev. Robert Jeffrey, late Minister of Girthon. 8vo. Kirkcudbright : J. Nicholson. *N.d.*
Stark, Rev. William A. The Covenanters : A Contribution towards the Defence of the Church of Scotland. Castle-Douglas : Adam Rae. *N.d.*
Symington, Rev. William, Stranraer—
  Charges delivered at the Ordination of Rev. James M'Gill, Hightae, Dumfriesshire. Dumfries : D. Halliday, 1829.

RELIGION AND ECCLESIASTICAL AFFAIRS—*continued.*
   The Character and Claims of the Scottish Martyrs. 8vo. Dumfries : David Halliday, 1831.
Taylor, Rev. John, Wamphray. A Vindication of Mr John Taylor. [*Circa* 1718.]
Telfair, Rev. Alexander—
   A True relation of an Apparition, Expressions, and Actings of a Spirit which infested the House of Andrew Mackie in Ring-Croft of Stocking, in the Paroch of Rerrick, in the Stewartry of Kirkcudbright, in Scotland. By Mr Alexander Telfair, Minister of that Paroch, and attested by many other Persons, who were also Eye- and Ear-Witnesses. Small 4to. Edinburgh, 1696.
   A New Confutation of Sadducism, &c. Narrative of the Wonderful Expressions and Actions of a Spirit which infested the house of Andrew Mackie, of Ringcroft in Galloway, from February to May 1695. Small 4to. London, 1696.
Thomson, Rev. Andrew, D.D. Report of the Speech delivered by, at a Meeting of the Dumfriesshire Auxiliary Bible Society, 18th September 1826. 8vo. Dumfries : John Johnston, 1826.
Todd, William. Clerical History of Kirkmaiden. Glasgow, 1860.
Twisse, William, D.D. The Scriptures' Sufficiency to determine all matters of Faith. [Preface by James Reid.] 8vo. Dumfries : Robert Jackson, 1795.
Vetch [Veitch], Mr William, Minister of the Gospel at D*r*umfries—
   A Short History of Rome's Designs against the Protestant Interest in Britain, . . . with some information anent Mr Hepburn, and Advices to Dividers. 4to. D*r*umfries : Robert Rae, 1718.
   A Short Answer to a Letter pretendedly written by Mr John Hepburn, Division Maker, but really by Riddough and Hunter, and other Romish Emissaries, who are Defenders of his Faith, both Summer and Winter. 12mo. D*r*umfries : R. Rae, 1720.
Welsh, Rev. John, Kirkcudbright. A Reply against M. Gilbert Browne, priest. Wherein is handled many of the greatest and weightest points of controuversie between us and the papistes. . . . By M. John Welsche, preacher of Christ's Gospel. 4to. Edinburgh : Robert Waldegrave, 1602.
White, Rev. Hugh. The Divine Dictionary ; or, A Treatise indicted by Holy Inspiration, containing the Faith and Practice of that People (by this world) called Buchanites. 8vo. Dumfries : Robert Jackson, 1785.
[Wightman, Rev. David, Applegarth.] Mr Taylor's Case stated ;

RELIGION AND ECCLESIASTICAL AFFAIRS—*continued.*
    or, A just Reply to a book entitled A Vindication of Mr John
    Taylor, Minister of Wamfray. 4to. Dumfries, 1718.
Wightman, Rev. John, D.D., Kirkmahoe—
    The Question of Universal Concern : A Sermon preached in
        the New Church of Dumfries, May 7, 1812. 8vo. Dum-
        fries : Robert Jackson, 1812.
    Popular and Practical Observations on Contentment and
        Happiness : A Sermon preached in Kirkmahoe Church,
        December 14, 1828. 8vo. Dumfries : W. Carson, 1829.
    The Good Man and his Future Prospects : A Sermon preached
        on Jan. 22, 1837, after the Funeral of the Rev. David Lamont,
        D.D., Kirkpatrick-Durham. 8vo. Dumfries : J. Johnston,
        J. Anderson, and J. M'Kie, 1837.
    Ten other single Sermons. 8vo. Dumfries, 1812-1845.
Williamson, Rev. D. S.—
    A Funeral Sermon on the Death of Dr J. Somerville, Minister
        of Currie. Kirkcudbright : J. Nicholson.
    A Funeral Sermon on the Death of the Rev. James Hender-
        son, Minister of Balmaghie. Kirkcudbright : J. Nicholson.

TOPOGRAPHY.

A Run Round Galloway. Extracted from the 'Kilmarnock Weekly
    Post' of August 6, 1864. Kilmarnock : James M'Kie, 1864.
Allan, Miss E. The Beauties of the Border. Annan, 1846.
Armstrong, Andrew J. The Illustrated Visitor's Guide to Dum-
    fries and Vicinity. Dumfries : A. & T. Hunter, 1894.
Barbour, James, Glendarroch. Grand Coaching Tour from New
    Galloway Station to Carsphairn. Oblong 12mo. Dumfries :
    J. Maxwell & Son, 1896.
Complete Guide to Dumfries, Castle - Douglas, Kirkcudbright,
    Newton-Stewart, Gatehouse, Glenluce, Stranraer, Port Pat-
    rick, &c.: with Objects of Interest in their Several Localities.
    Dumfries : R. Johnstone, 1860.
Dumfries, Report by the Town Clerk on the Ecclesiastical Build-
    ings in. Dumfries, 1887.
Fyfe, William Wallace. Letters from the Wells : A Visit to Moffat,
    its Spas, and Neighbourhood. 12mo. Edinburgh, 1848.
Garnett, Dr Tho. Observations on Moffat and its Mineral Waters.
    Illustrated with 2 aqua-tinted Plates. 4to. London, 1800.
Grange, W. D'Oyly, M.D. Moffat and its Mineral Waters. 12mo.
    Moffat : Robert Knight, 1881.

TOPOGRAPHY—*continued*.

Gray, Peter. Dumfriesshire Illustrated. 1. Nithsdale, a series of descriptive and historical sketches of Stra'nith. With 32 Illustrations by J. Rutherford. Dumfries : J. Maxwell & Son, 1894.

Harper, Malcolm M'Lachlan. Rambles in Galloway, Topographical, Historical, Traditional, and Biographical. With Illustrations of the Scenery, Castles, Abbeys, and Objects of Antiquarian Interest, by Faed, Clark, Cowan, Moule, &c. 8vo. Edinburgh, 1876.

    Second edition. 8vo and (*édition de luxe*) 4to. Dalbeattie : Thomas Fraser, 1896.

Keddie, William. Moffat : Its Walks and Wells, with incidental Notices of its Botany and Geology. And Report on, and Chemical Analysis of, its Mineral Waters, by John Macadam. 12mo. Glasgow, 1854.

Lennox, James, F.S.A. Scot. A Road Guide to the Southern Scottish Counties. Dumfries, 1888.

Little, James. Annan, Ancient and Modern. Annan, 1843.

M'Diarmid, John—
    Sketches from Nature. Small 8vo. Edinburgh, 1830.
    Picture of Dumfries and its Environs, with Engravings by John Gellatly, from Drawings by A. S. Masson. 4to. Dumfries : J. Gellatly, 1832.
    A Guide to Moffat : Embracing Sketches of the Surrounding Scenery, &c. By a Visitor. 12mo. Dumfries : John M'Diarmid & Co. Moffat : Robert Burnie, 1833.
        New Edition, Dumfries, 1851.

M'Diarmid, W. R. Handbook of the United Parishes of Colvend and Southwick. 8vo. Dumfries, James Maxwell, 1873.

M'Dowall, William—
    Visitors' Guide to Dumfries and Vicinity. Second edition. Dumfries, 1871.
    Memorials of St Michael's Churchyard. 8vo. Edinburgh, 1876.

M'Ilwraith, William. The Visitor's Guide to Wigtownshire. 8vo. Dumfries : 'Courier' Office, 1877.

Mackaile, Dr Matthew—
    Fons Moffetensis. 12mo. Edinburgh, 1659.
    Moffat Well; or, A Topographico-Spagyricall description of the Mineral Wells at Moffat in Annandale. 12mo. Edinburgh, 1664.

[Mackenzie, John Commelin]—
    Scraps. Kirkcudbright Parish Church [&c.] By M'K. 12mo. Castle-Douglas [1881].
    Lochenbreck. By M'K. 12mo. [Castle-Douglas, 1881.]

TOPOGRAPHY—*continued*.

Maxwell, Sir Herbert, Bart., M.P. Studies in the Topography of Galloway, being a List of nearly 4000 Names of Places, with Remarks on their Origin and Meaning, and an Introductory Essay. 8vo. Edinburgh, 1887.

Maxwell, J. H. Tourist's Guide to the Stewartry of Kirkcudbright. Castle-Douglas, 1873. Sixth edition, 1896.

Moffat, Rides, Walks, and Drives about. Reprinted from 'The Moffat Register and Annandale Observer.' Moffat : William Muir, 1861.

[Muir, Thomas S.] The Lighthouse : A Sketch addressed to my Landlady in Limbus Patrum,—Mull of Galloway, October 18, 1864. 8vo. Privately printed.

Notes on the Established Churches of Dumfries and the Building of the Mid Steeple. *Anon.* 8vo. Dumfries : W. Anderson, 1865.

Paterson, James, R.S.W. Nithsdale : A Series of Reproductions in Photogravure from Water-Colour Drawings, by. With accompanying letterpress. Folio. Glasgow, 1893.

Queen of the South, A Visit to the. By Rev. Jos. Sk——. Carlisle, 1879.

Reid, Rev. H. M. B. The Kirk above Dee Water. 8vo. Illustrated. Castle-Douglas : Adam Rae, 1895.

Symson, Andrew, Minister of Kirkinner, MDCLXXXIV. A Large Description of Galloway, with an Appendix containing Original Papers from the Sibbald and Macfarlane MSS. [Edited by Thomas Maitland, Lord Dundrennan.] 8vo. Edinburgh, 1823.

Trip to the Isles of Fleet, A. *N.p.*, *N.d.*

[Waugh, Alexander]—

    Galloway Glimpses, Some. 8vo. Newton-Stewart : 'Galloway Gazette' Office, 1870.

    Newton-Stewart to Ravenshall. 8vo. Newton-Stewart : 'Galloway Gazette' Office, 1896.

Whithorn and Environs, Past and Present. Being a neat and concise Directory to all the Places and Objects of Interest in and around one of the most Ancient and Historical Burghs in Scotland. *Anon.* 8vo. Whithorn : J. Macdowall. *N.d.*

PRINCIPAL MAPS OF DUMFRIESSHIRE AND GALLOWAY.

Date.
1654. Blaeu's Great Atlas :—
    Map 9. Lidalia, vel Liddisdalia Regio. Liddisdail. *Auct. Tim. Pont.*
    „ 10. Evia et Escia, Scotis Eusdail et Eskdail. *Auct. Tim. Pont. I. Blaeu excud.*
    „ 11. Annandiæ Præfectura, vulgo The Stewartry of Annandail. *Auct. Tim. Pont. Excud Io. Blaeu.*
    „ 12. Nithia Vicecomitatus. The Sherifdome of Nidis-Dail. *Auct. Tim. Pont.*
    „ 13. Gallovidia, *vernacule* Galloway.[1] *Auct. Tim. Pont.*
    „ 14. Gallovidiæ Pars Occidentalior, *in qua* Vicecomitatus Victoniensis, *cum Regalitate Glenlucensi.* The Sherifdome of Wigtoun w^t the Regalitie of Glen-Luze, both in Galloway. *Auct. Timoth. Pont.*
    „ 15. Gallovidiæ Pars Media, *quæ Deam et Cream fluvios interjacet.* The middle-part of Galloway, *whiche lyeth betweene the rivers Dee and Cree. Auct. Tim. Pont.*
    „ 16. Præfectura Kircubriensis,*quæ Gallovidiæ maxime orientalis pars est.* The Steuartrie of Kircubright, *the most easterlie part of Galloway. Auct. Tim. Pont.*
1725. Moll's Atlas :—
    Galloway, contains the Shires of Wigton and Kirkcudbright. Her. Moll, Geographer.
    Wigton, the West Part of Galloway. Her. Moll, Geographer.

---

[1] A reproduction of this map accompanies the present volume.

MAPS OF DUMFRIESSHIRE AND GALLOWAY. 401

Date.
1725. Moll's Atlas :—
    Kirkcudbright (West Part), the Middle Part of Galloway. Her. Moll, Geographer.
    Galloway (East Part), being part of the shire of Kirkcudbright. Her. Moll, Geographer.
    Dumfries or Nithisdale.[1] By H. Moll, Geographer.
    Anandale, part of Dumfreis-Shire, Eusdale or Eskdale, South Part of Roxburgh-Shire.[1] By H. Moll, Geographer.
1782. Wigton, or Shire of Galloway. Surveyed and engraved by J. Ainslie. 4 sh.
1794. Dumfriesshire, Kirkcudbright, and Wigtown, in the Statistical Account of Scotland.
1796. A Topographical Map of the Stewartry of Kirkcudbright. Surveyed by John Ainslie. 4 sh.
1812. Dumfriesshire from an actual Survey by Wm. Crawford. Engraved by Kirkwood & Sons, Edinburgh. 4 sheets. Scale, 1 inch to 1 mile.
1832. Thomson's New General Atlas :—
    Map 6. Dumfries-shire, in 2 sheets—Northern and Southern. Surveyed by Crawford & Son. Scale, 1 inch to 1 mile.
    " 7. Kirkcudbrightshire, in 2 sheets — Northern and Southern. Scale, 1 inch to 1¾ mile.
    " 8. Wigton, or Shire of Galloway. Scale, 1 inch to 1½ mile.
1845. Dumfriesshire, Kirkcudbright, and Wigtown, in New Statistical Account of Scotland.
1856-64. Ordnance Survey, on scales of six inches and one inch to the mile.
1860-82. Philip's Handy Atlas of the Counties of Scotland.
1890. Bartholomew's Reduced Ordnance Survey, on scale of half an inch to the mile.
1895. Royal Scottish Geographical Atlas of Scotland. By J. G. Bartholomew. Where a full Bibliography of Atlases of Scotland is given, pp. 16-18.

[1] Reproductions of these maps accompany the present volume.

INDEX.

Aberdeen, the Presbyterian Assembly at, in 1605, 239.
Agricola in Britain, 1, 3, 12.
Agriculture, state of, in Scotland during the fifteenth century, 145 et seq.—backward condition of, in Galloway in seventeenth century, 297, 313 et seq.—the importance of, to Galloway, 352.
Alan, Lord of Galloway, 1199, does homage to King John, 58—present at the signing of Magna Charta at Runnymede, 59 — last "king" of Galloway, ib.
Alban, the four dominions of, in the seventh century, 35—unification of, by Kenneth MacAlpin, 40.
Alclut, the ancient kingdom of, 35.
Alexander III., prosperity of Scotland under, 67—conquest of the Isle of Man by, 68—death of, ib.
Alpin, invasion of Galloway by, 37—death of, ib.
Alured, Colonel Matthew, appointed by Cromwell as Sheriff of Galloway, 257—recall of, 258.
Angles, settlement of the, in Northumbria, 32.
Annandale, reference to, in Blaeu's Geography, 253.
Antonine, the wall of, 13.
Archibald the Grim, bearding of, by Alexander Kennedy, 150, 151.
Ardderyd, the decisive battle at, between Paganism and Christianity, 34.
Argyll, Marquis of, the champion of the Covenant, 255 — execution of, 284.
Arkenholme, the battle of, 138.
Armada, Spanish, complicity of Scottish Catholics in the, 209.
Armstrong, John, of Gilnockie, the Scottish Robin Hood, 162—retaliates against Lord Dacre, 163—execution of, 166.
Armstrong, Willie, of Kinmont, daring rescue of, by Scott of Buccleuch, 221 et seq.
Arran, Earl of, quarrel of, with Lord Maxwell, 205 — degradation of, 207.
Arthur, King, the exploits of, 33.
Atecotti, identification of the, with the Novantæ and Genonians, 23.
Auchinleck, William, execution of, 280.

Bailiie, Big Will, a gipsy chief, 323.
Bain, Mr Joseph, reference to the 'Calendar of Documents relating to Scotland' by, 56.
Balliol, Edward, crowned at Scone, 110—defeated at Annan, 111—victory at Halidon Hill, 112—a vassal of England, ib.—incompetency of, 113—final appearance in history, 115.
Balliol, John de, joint Lord of Galloway, 65—founds Balliol College, 67—claims the throne, 72—crowned at Scone, ib.—renounces allegiance and invades England, 73—abdication, 74.
Bannatyne, Sir William, fined for illegal extortion in Galloway, 269.
Barbour, John, quoted, 99, 106.
Beacons, the Border laws concerning, 127.
Bennoch, James, execution of, 280.
Bernicia, the ancient kingdom of, 35.
Birgham, the parliament of, 71.
Birrens, results of exploration of the Roman camp at, 10.

INDEX.

Blaeu of Amsterdam, the Atlas of, 232 —extracts from, 253 et seq.
Blind Harry an authority for the life of Wallace, 74, 75.
Border, account of some typical raids on the, in the beginning of the sixteenth century, 159, 160—the clans of the, 183 et seq.—form of excommunication issued in the vernacular against the clans of the, 186 et seq.—Maitland of Lethington's description of the mosstroopers on the, 198—vigorous proceedings by the Regent Moray on the, 199—James VI. and the mosstroopers of the, 233.
Boswell of Auchinleck, first Sheriff of Wigtownshire, 328.
Bothwell Brig, the battle of, 275.
Brereton, Sir William, quotation from, describing Scotland in 1635, 313.
Bride of Lammermoor, the story of the, 260 et seq.
Brigantes, the chief opponents of the Romans in Britain, 1, 12, 13.
Brome, James, extract from, describing Scotland in 1669, 317.
Bruce, Edward, defeats the English in Galloway, 99—death of, in Ireland, 100.
Bruce, Robert the, the "Competitor," sixth Lord of Annandale, a claimant for the throne, 69 et seq.—recognised as heir by Alexander II., 71.
Bruce, King Robert the, reputed presence at the battle of the Standard, 52—swears allegiance to Edward, 76—wavering attitude of, after the battle of Falkirk, 77 et seq.—compact with Comyn and Lamberton, 78—perfidious conduct of, 84, 85—how treated in history, ib.—further perjury of, 87—the murder of Comyn, ib. et seq.—coronation at Scone, 89 —sufferings of his relatives, ib.—a fugitive in Galloway, 91 et seq.—the story of the widow at Craigencallie, 94—success at Glen Trool, 96—pedigree of, 102—prosperity under his rule, 106—a conference with the English at Lochmaben, 108—death, 110.
Burns, Robert, first visit to Nithsdale, 335—in Edinburgh, 336—Clarinda, 337—Ellisland, 338 et seq.—Dumfries, 341—death, 344.

Caerlaverock Castle, siege of, by Edward I., 79—surrender of, to Bruce, 99—restored, 100—surrender and ruin of, 249.
Cages, imprisonment in, 89.
Cameron, Richard, proclaims war against Charles at Sanquhar, 276—death of, at Airds Moss, ib.
Cameronians, opposition of the, to the Union, 306.
Candlemas, Burnt, devastation of Scotland by Edward III., known as, 115.
Carleton, Sir Thomas, captures Dumfries, 176—repulsed by Bomby at Kirkcudbright, 177.
Carlisle, Bruce's unsuccessful siege of, the cause of future Border warfare, 106—storming of the castle by Scott of Buccleuch, 221 et seq.
Cassilis, the family of, 150, 192, 195.
Cassilis, Gilbert, fourth Earl of, known as the King of Carrick, 195—letter to, from Queen Mary, 197—the story of how he acquired the lands of Glenluce and Crossraguel, 201, 202.
Cave, St Ninian's, 26.
Charles I., attempts to force the liturgy on Scotland, 241—coronation in Scotland, 242—institutes a High Commission Court, 243—declaration of war, 246—surrendered by the Covenanters, 255.
Charles II., proclaimed King by the Scottish Estates, 256—cause ruined at Worcester, ib.—death, 281.
Christianity, the introduction of, into Britain, 23.
Church lands, lawlessness arising from the dispersion of the old, 201 et seq.
City of Glasgow Bank, effect of the failure of, on Galloway, 355.
Clans, enumeration of the chief Border, 183 et seq.
Clark, Andrew, execution of, 280.
Claudian, references to Britain by, 23.
Claverhouse, Sheriff of Galloway, 276 —in arms for James VII., 287.
Cockermouth, the raid of, by Douglas, 121.
Coel Hen, British King of Strathclyde, 32.
Commission Court, High, established by Charles I., 243.
Comyn, John, "The Red," first connection of the family with Galloway, 65—imprisonment, 76—guardian of Scotland, 78, 84—murdered by Bruce, 85 et seq.
Conventicles, the first of the, 262, 272.
Corsane, John, of Meikleknox, provost of Dumfries, 250.
Cowper, William, Bishop of Galloway, 240—character of, ib.
Craigencallie, the story of Bruce and the widow at, 94.

INDEX. 405

Crannogs, description of Scottish, 18 *et seq.*
Crichton, Chancellor, murder of two Douglases by, 125—surrenders Edinburgh Castle to Douglas, 126.
Crockett, S. R., novelist, 321.
Cromwell, the Scottish Covenanters co-operating with, 251—invades Scotland, 256—nature of his rule in Scotland, 257.

Dalgleish, minister of Kirkmabreck, deposition of, 243.
Dalriada, the ancient kingdom of, 35.
Dalrymple, James, Viscount Stair, a notable Galloway landowner, 288.
Dalrymple, Janet, the Bride of Lammermoor, story of, 260 *et seq.*
Dalrymple, Sir John, appointed Lord Justice-Clerk, 286—resignation, 288.
Dalziel, General, victory of, at Rullion Green, 267.
David I., education in England, 47—declares war against Stephen, 49—the battle of the Standard, 50, 51—death, 54.
David II., defeat at Neville's Cross, 113—negotiations for release of, 114—ransomed, 115 — power over all Scotland, 116—death, *ib.*
Deans, Jeanie, the original of, 323.
Debatable Lands, definition of, 161—reasons for the lawlessness in the, *ib.*—names of the chief clans, *ib.*—examples of the feuds, 162—a scheme to make them a "buffer state" by depopulation, 181—settlement of the question, 182.
Deil's Dyke, account of the, 14, 15.
Devorguila, wife of John Balliol, founds New or Sweetheart Abbey, 66—other foundations by, 67.
Discipline, examples of ecclesiastical, in end of seventeenth century, 289 *et seq.*
Douglas, Archibald, "the Grim," Lord of Galloway, 117—great power acquired by, *ib.*—succeeds to the earldom, 121—suppression of Lincluden Abbey, 122—death, *ib.*
Douglas, Archibald, "the Tineman," fourth Earl, 123—feud with the Earl of March, 124—defeat at Homildon Hill, *ib.*—death at Verneuil, *ib.*
Douglas, Archibald, fifth Earl of Angus, "Bell-the-Cat," Steward of Kirkcudbright, 148 — treasonable conduct against James IV., *ib.*—Chancellor of Scotland, *ib.*—robbed by James IV., 149, 150—quarrel of, with James before Flodden, 157—death of, at Whithorn, *ib.*

Douglas, James, ninth Earl of, submission of, to James II., 137—marriage to the Fair Maid of Galloway, *ib.*—defeated at Arkenholme, 138—attainted of treason, 139—favoured by Edward IV., 141—defeat at Lochmaben, 142—retirement to the Abbey of Lindores and death, 143—fate of his wife, *ib.*
Douglas, William, sixth Earl of, murder of, by Chancellor Crichton, 125.
Douglas, William, eighth Earl of, marriage of, to the Fair Maid of Galloway, 126—revenge on Crichton, *ib.*—institutes a code of Border Laws, 127—victory at Sark, 128—journey to Rome, *ib.*—rebellion of his brother, 129—reputed murders of Sir John Herries and Maclellan of Bomby, *ib.* —murdered by James II., 130.
Douglas, Sir William, of Nithsdale, account of the romantic career of, 122, 123.
Dowalton, lake-dwellings discovered at, 17.
Drumclog, the battle of, 275.
Dryfe Sands, the battle at, between the Maxwells and the Johnstones, 212 *et seq.*
Dumfries, origin of the name, 33—benefactions to, by Devorguila, 67—history of the castle, 101—visit of Queen Margaret of England, 144—details of James IV.'s visit, 152, 153—visits of Knox and Queen Mary, 193, 195 — visit of Regent Moray to suppress Border thieves, 200—burned by Scrope in 1570, 202—visit of Regent Morton, 203—a dispute with Wigtown, *ib.* —resumption of the feud between Maxwells and Johnstones due to the provostship, 206—visit of James VI., 209—castle stormed by James, *ib.* — a court of redress established by James VI., 215—James VI. presents a Silver Gun, 237—the local government for two centuries, *ib.*—commercial policy in seventeenth century, 238—Thomas Ramsay, minister, *ib.*—creation of an earldom, 242 — Lord Kirkcudbright's South Regiment, 250 — description in Blaeu's Geography, 254—a trial for witchcraft, 259—sixth town in Scotland, 299—erection of town-house, 305—taken possession of by Charles Edward, 325 — the battle between the Corbies and the Pyets, 330.
Dumfriesshire, havoc done by Border warfare, 107 *et seq.*—extracts from the criminal records in reign of James

INDEX.

IV., 155—losses sustained at Flodden, 157—the Armstrongs and the warfare in the Debatable Land, 161 et seq. — period of purely English dominion, 177 — list of gentry submitting to English rule, 178, 179—support given to the Reformation, 190—witchcraft, 231—antipathy to prelacy, 241—redistribution of the synods by the Assembly of 1638, 245—invaded by Montrose, 251—taxed by Charles II., 262—militia raised to suppress conventicles, 272 —persecutions, 284.
Dun, James, execution of, 281.
Dun, Robert, execution of, 281.
Dunbar, David, the husband of the Bride of Lammermoor, 260 et seq.
Dunbar, Gavin, Chancellor to James V., 160—exhaustive cursing of the Border clans, 186.
Duncan, Dr, of Ruthwell, the preserver of the Ruthwell Cross, 347.
Dundrennan Abbey built by Fergus of Galloway, 49.
Dunkitterick, discovery of plumbago and arsenic at, 353.
Dunnottar Castle, the Whig's vault at, 284.
Dwellings, description of lake-, in Scotland, 18 et seq.—Scottish, in the fifteenth century, 146, 147.
Dyke, the Deil's, account of, 14, 15.

Edgar, John, execution of, 280.
Edward I., scheme of, regarding the Maid of Norway, 69—arbitrator for the Scottish Crown, 72—war with Balliol, 73 — invasion of Dumfries and Galloway, 78 et seq.—compelled by Pope Boniface to leave Scotland, 82—vengeance on Bruce, 90—death of, 98.
Edward II., account of an early visit to Dumfries, 83—vacillation of, 98—abdication, 108.
Edward III., invades Scotland, 113—ravages Scotland after Balliol's resignation, 115—releases David, ib.
Edwin, King, 35.
Eglinton, Lord, the leader of the Whigamore Raid, 255.
Elizabeth, Queen, story of, and Scott of Buccleuch, 224.
Elliot, Commodore, victory of, over the French at Kirkmaiden, 331.
Engagers, the, 255, 256.
Episcopacy, re-establishment of, in Scotland, 240.
Eskdale, Ewesdale and, references to, in Blaeu's Geography, 253.

Ewesdale, Eskdale and, references to, in Blaeu's Geography, 253.
Excommunication, form of, issued in the vernacular against the Border clans, 186 et seq.
Exports, prohibition of, by James VI., 234.

Fair Maid of Galloway, marriage of, 137—subsequent history of, 143.
Fergus of Galloway, married a daughter of Henry I., 47—account of religious houses built by, 48, 49—introduction of the feudal system into the south-west of Scotland, 49 — revolt of, ib.—regains royal favour by a ruse, 53—defeat and death, 54.
Fergusson, Robert, execution of, 279.
Flodden, the losses of Galloway and Dumfries at, 157.
Fortrenn, the battle of, 40.
Franck's 'Northern Memoirs,' extracts from, describing Scotland in 1656, 314 et seq.
Friar's Vennel, an old street in Dumfries, 88.
Frisians, settlement of, in Britain, 32.
Froissart, quotation from, describing the Border troops in the time of Bruce, 109.

Galloway, origin of the name, 5, 39—the ancient topography of, 6 et seq. —Roman occupation of, 9 et seq.—Roman remains in, ib. — Roman roads, 11—the overlords of, 36—invaded by Alpin, 37 — recognised by David as a separate province, 48—invaded by Wymond of Man, 52, 53—how divided from Carrick, 56—close connection with English court, ib., 57—the last "king" of, 59—examples of the growth of surnames in, 60, 64—feudalism established, 62 et seq.—origin of the terms Shire and Stewartry, 117—specimens of the ancient laws in force till 1426, 119—losses sustained at Flodden, 157—troubles in the Debatable Land, 167 et seq.—support given to the Reformation, 190 — witchcraft, 231 — erection of the royal burgh of New Galloway, 243—redistribution of the synods and presbyteries by the Assembly of 1638, 245—described in Blaeu's Geography, 254 — the Engagers and Protesters, 256 — a witchcraft trial in 1698, 259 — the "killing time," 278 et seq.—the death of Margaret M'Lauchlan on Wigtown sands, 282 et seq.—Symson's account of the rural population of,

in end of seventeenth century, 295 et seq., 313 et seq.
Genunian sept, conjectures regarding the, 13.
Gibson, John, execution of, 280.
Gilla Aldan, Bishop of Whithorn, brave resistance of, to Wymond's invasion of Galloway, 53.
Gilnockie, bestowal of, on the Maxwells, 166.
Glasgow, abolition of Prelacy by the General Assembly at, 245.
Glen Trool, Bruce's success at, 96.
Glendinning, minister of Kirkcudbright, deposition of, 243.
Glenluce Abbey, founded by Roland, Lord of Galloway, 58—acquisition of the lands of, by Lord Cassilis, 201.
Gordon, Alexander, of Airds, a notable pioneer of the Reformation, 190.
* Gordon, John, last Bishop of Galloway, 287.
Gordon of Earlston, banishment of, 264.
Graham, James, a Covenanter martyr, 279.
Graham, William, "Carwinley," the Gretna Green postboy, 352.
Graham of Claverhouse, commander in Galloway and Dumfries, 274—character of, *ib.*—defeated at Drumclog, 275.
Gretna Green, account of, 350 *et seq.*
Grierson, John, execution of, 279.
Grierson, Robert, execution of, 280.
Grierson of Lag, Sir Robert, sheriff-depute of Kirkcudbright, 274—brutality of, 280—imprisonment, 287.

Hadrian, visit of, to Britain, 13.
Halidon Hill, Balliol victorious at, 112.
Hallume, John, execution of, 279.
Hamilton, Lord Basil, first breeder of Galloway cattle, 302—death of, 304.
Hamilton, Gavin, appointment of, to bishopric of Galloway, 239.
Hamilton, Marquis of, the leader of the "Engagers," 255—defeated by Cromwell, *ib.*
Harkness, Thomas, execution of, 280.
Harry the Minstrel, Blind, an authority for the life of Wallace, 74, 75.
Hatfield, formerly part of the Bruce estates, 78.
Henry IV. invades Scotland at the instigation of March, 122, 124.
Henry VI. seeks refuge in Scotland after Towton, 144.

Henry VIII., rupture with James V., 169—makes a compact with the captives from Solway Moss, 171.
Heritable jurisdiction, abolition of, 327.
Herries, Sir John, of Terregles, reputed murder of, by Douglas, 129.
Holywood, destruction of Devorguila's ancient abbey of, 118.
Homildon Hill, the battle of, 124.
Hunter, John, execution of, 280.
Hyland, William, of Kirkcudbright, introduction of potatoes into Galloway by, 319.

Imports, duty charged on, for the first time by James VI., 234.
Indulgence, The, ineffectiveness of, 271.

Jacobite rebellion, supporters of the '15 in Galloway, 308—hostility of Galloway to the '45, 324—list of Dumfries and Galloway rebels in the '45, 360, 361.
James I., parliamentary representation under, 144.
James II., present at the murder of Douglas, 125—murderer of the eighth Earl of Douglas, 130—acquitted by the Three Estates, *ib.*—parliamentary representation under, 144.
James IV., character as a sovereign, 151.
James V., coronation at Stirling, 157—precocity, 160—procedure against Johnnie Armstrong, 164—his treachery, 165—two visits to France and marriage, 168, 169—second marriage, *ib.*—rupture with Henry VIII., *ib.*—Solway Moss, 170—death at Falkland, 171.
James VI., siege of Lord Maxwell in Lochmaben Castle, 209, 210—establishes a Court of Redress at Dumfries, 215—action against the Border thieves, 233—pedantry of, *ib.*—imposes import duties and forbids exports, 234—encourages Presbyterian fanaticism, 235—revisits Scotland, and presents a Silver Gun to Dumfries, 237—restores bishops in Scotland, 239—at the General Assembly in Edinburgh, 240.
Jerome, St, reference to the Atecotti by, 23.
Johnstons, origin of the feud with the Maxwells and, 180—renewed fighting, 206—defeat, 207—a short-lived amity, 211—raid on the Crichtons, 212—victory over the Maxwells at Dryfe Sands, *ib. et seq.*—suffer

INDEX.

horrible treachery at the hands of John, ninth Lord Maxwell, 217 et seq.—end of the feud, 220.
Jones, Paul, account of, 333, 334.
Jurisdictions, abolition of heritable, 327.

Kemble, John, explanation of the Ruthwell Cross by, 349.
Kenmure, Viscount, supporter of the Chevalier, 309—trial and execution of, 310, 312.
Kennedy, the ascendancy of the family on the Western Border, 149 et seq.—examples of their feuds during the sixteenth century, 228, 229.
"Killing time," the, 278.
Kilmarnock edition of Burns, the value of, 335.
Kinmont Willie, the story of the rescue of, by Scott of Buccleuch, 221 et seq.
Kirkcudbright, origin of the name, 54—extracts from the criminal records in the reign of James IV., 155—gallant resistance to English invasion, 177—period of purely English dominion, ib.—list of gentry submitting to English rule, 179—support given to the Armada, 209—creation of M'Clellan as Lord Kirkcudbright, 242—rioting and severe penalties in connection with the induction of curates, 262—detention of King William's fleet at, 288.
Kirkmadrine, inscribed stones at, 28.
Kirkmaiden, naval encounter at, 331.
Kirkpatrick of Closeburn, Alexander, romantic escape of, from Edinburgh Tolbooth, 236.
Kirkpatrick, Sir Roger de, murder of, by Sir James Lindsay, 115.
Knox, John, visit of, to Dumfries, 193—rupture with Sir John Maxwell, 194.

Laggangarn, prehistoric remains at, 346.
Lake-dwellings, description of, 18 et seq., 146, 147.
Lamb, Bishop, appointed to the See of Galloway, 240.
Lamberton, William de, Bishop of St Andrews, secret treaty of, with Bruce, 78, 86.
Lammermoor, the Bride of, the story of, 260 et seq.
Lang, Simon, Gretna Green "parson," 351.
Lauderdale, appointed Governor of Scotland, 263—adopts conciliatory measures, 271—suppresses conventicles, 272.

Legislation, the inconsistencies of sixteenth century, 230 et seq.
Leprosy, existence of, in Scotland shown by place-names, 297.
Leslie, General, victory at Dunbar, 256.
Levellers, opposition of, to fencing fields, 303.
Liddesdale, description of, quoted from Blaeu's Geography, 253.
Lincluden Abbey, suppression of, by Archibald Douglas, 122 — Queen Margaret of Lancaster finds refuge in, 144.
Livingstone, John, minister of Stranraer, story of, before Cromwell in London, 257.
Lochmaben, important conference between Bruce and the English at, 108 — recapture of the castle from Richard II. by the Douglases, 120—description of the Stone, 132 et seq.—the battle of, 142—siege of the castle by James VI., 210.
Lollius Urbicus, campaign of, against the Brigantes, 13.
Lorn, John of, in pursuit of Bruce, 92.
Lowe, John, author of 'Mary's Dream,' tragic story of, 343.
Lucullus, the successor of Agricola, 12.

MacAlpin, Kenneth, crowned at Scone, 40—death, 41.
Macbeth, defeat of, by Malcolm Canmore, 43.
Macdonald, Dr, examination of supposed Romans roads in Dumfriesshire by, 11.
MacDouall, history of the clan, 81, 103.
Maclellan of Bomby, reputed murder of, by Douglas, 129.
Macmillan, John, leader of the Cameronians, 306.
Macquhan, Andrew, execution of, 280.
M'Brair, John, an early Scottish Reformer, 191.
M'Cullochs, brutality of the, to Lady Cardiness, 293 — end of their feud with the Gordons, 294 — tradition concerning the, ib.
M'Kie of Glassock, John, murder of, by a Maxwell, 225.
M'Lauchlan, Margaret, the drowning of, at Wigtown sands, 282 et seq.
Magnusson, Professor, explanation of the Ruthwell Cross by, 349.
Maid of Galloway, the Fair, 126.
Maid of Norway, the, 69, 71.
Maitland of Lethington, poem by, describing Border thieves, 198.

INDEX.   409

Malcolm Canmore, consolidation of the country under, 43—invasion of Northumbria, 45—death, *ib.*

Malcolm IV., incapacity of, 54—defeats Fergus of Galloway, *ib.*

March, George, Earl of, quarrel with Archibald "Tineman," 124 — joins cause with the English, *ib.*

Margaret, the Fair Maid of Galloway, 126.

Margaret, the Maid of Norway, 69, 71.

Marshall, Billy, gipsy and "leveller," 303.

Mary, Queen of Scots, visits Dumfries, 193, 195—celebrates Mass at Holyrood, 194 — marriage to Darnley, 195—escape from Lochleven, 196—letter to Cassilis, 197 — execution, 209.

Maxwell, Sir Eustace de, duplicity of, towards Bruce and Edward III., 111, 112.

Maxwell, John, fourth Lord, gradual ascendancy of, on the Western Border, 148—feud with Crichton, Lord Sanquhar, 153—death at Flodden, 157.

Maxwell, John, eighth Lord, claims the Earldom of Morton, 204 *et seq.* —imprisoned by the Regent Morton, 205—created Earl of Morton, *ib.*—a quarrel with Johnstone concerning the provostship of Dumfries, 206 — hostility to the Reformation, 207—complicity in the Spanish Armada, 209—capture and imprisonment, 210—Warden of the Western Marches, 211 — defeat at Dryfe Sands, 212—cruel death of, 213.

Maxwell, John, ninth Lord, imprisoned for Popery, 216—daring escape from Edinburgh Castle, *ib.* — outlawed, 217—treachery to Johnstone, *ib. et seq.*—escape to France, 219—execution, 220.

Maxwell, Sir John, Lord Herries, 193, 194, 195.

Maxwell, John, of Monreith, adventures of, after Rullion Green, 268.

Maxwell, Robert, fifth Lord, attempt to conciliate the Armstrongs, 163—receives the lands of Gilnockie, 166 —accompanies James V. to France, 168 — captured at Solway Moss, 171 —pioneer of the Reformation, 172—imprisoned in the Tower, 174—death, 176.

Maxwell of Garrarie, John, murder of M'Kie of Glassock by, 225.

Middleton, Lord, appointed Governor of Scotland, 261 — degradation of, 263.

Military forces, laws against the maintenance of private, 230.

Milroy, the adventures of Gilbert and William, 285.

Mitchell, a fanatic preacher, attempt of, to shoot Archbishop Sharpe, 271.

Monmouth, Duke of, victory of, at Bothwell Brig, 275—connection of, with Dumfries, *ib.*

Mons Meg, the legendary history of, 140.

Montgomerie, Robert, leader of the Royalist troops from Galloway, 256.

Montrose, invades Dumfries, 251—defeat at Philiphaugh, 252.

Moray, Regent, appointment of, 196 —vigorous action against the Border thieves, 199, 200.

Morton, Regent, visits Dumfries to suppress mosstroopers, 203—dispute with Maxwell concerning the earldom, 204 *et seq.*—degrades Maxwell, 205—death, *ib.*

Municipal government in the seventeenth century, 238.

Munro, Dr R., 17.

Murray, Alexander, a distinguished orientalist, account of, 344.

Murray, John, Gretna Green "parson," 351.

Nennius, the Chronicle of, 33.

Neville's Cross, King David captured at, 113.

Niduarii, Bæda's use of the name, 2.

Ninian, St, account of, converting the Galloway Picts, 24 *et seq.*—the cave of, 26.

Nisbet, the battle of, 124.

Nithsdale, Lord, trial of, 310—story of the escape of, 311.

Norham, the treaty of, 181.

Norsemen, settlement of, in Galloway, 39—end of dominion in Galloway, 44.

Northumbria, the formation of the province of, 34.

Norway, Margaret, the Maid of, 69, 71.

Novantæ, etymology of the name, 2—the ethnography of, 4—the religion of, 29.

Novios, Ptolemy's reference to the river, 2.

Olaf, a Galloway chief, wars by, 41.

Paisley, Joseph, the first Gretna Green "parson," 351.

Parliament, representation in, under James I., 144 *et seq.*—payment of members of the Scottish, 300.

2 D

INDEX.

Pausanias, chronicler of the Roman campaign against the Brigantes, 13.
Pennant's 'Tour in Scotland' quoted, 319.
Picts, the dominion of the, in the seventh century, 35.
Pierson, Mr, curate of Carsphairn, shot by Covenanters, 281.
Pinkie, the battle of, 177.
Pont, Timothy, a survey of Scotland in 1600 by, 232, 253.
Portpatrick, establishment of a postal service to Ireland viâ, 250.
Prelacy, abolition of, by the General Assembly at Glasgow, 245.
Protesters, the object of the sect of, 256.
Ptolemæus, Claudius, the geography of, 2, 5, 6, 7.

Queensberry, Earl of, creation of Viscount Drumlanrig as, 242.
Quenci, Roger de, joint lord of Galloway, 61.

Ray, John, naturalist, extract from, describing Scotland in 1662, 316.
Reformation, the first step taken by Lord Maxwell in carrying a bill for the translation of the Bible into the vulgar tongue, 172—attachment to, in Dumfriesshire and Galloway, 190—a Dumfriesshire pioneer of, *ib.*—intolerance characterising the, 193.
Renwick, James, leader of the Cameronians, 278—executed, 285.
Repp, Thorleif, explanation of the Ruthwell Cross by, 348.
Rescissory Act, the nature of the, 261.
Rhys, Professor J., 13.
Richard II., invasion of Scotland by, 121.
Robinson, Samuel, extracts from 'Reminiscences of Wigtownshire' by, 357, 358.
Roland, Lord of Galloway, Constable of Scotland, 58—founds Glenluce Abbey, *ib.*
Ronald the Dane, Duke of the Galwegians, 42.
Rosnat, the monastery of, 26, 46.
Rullion Green, Royalist victory at, 267.
Rutherford, Lord, story of, and the Bride of Lammermoor, 260 *et seq.*
Rutherford, Samuel, deposed from Anwoth, 243—elected to the chair at St Andrews, 245.
Ruthwell, the great flood of, 1627, 24.
Ruthwell Cross, account of the, 347 *et seq.*

Salisbury, the treaty of, concerning the Maid of Moray, 71.
Sanquhar, derivation of the word, 6.
Sark, victory of Douglas at the battle of, 128.
Saulseat, a religious house built by Fergus of Galloway, 48.
Scandinavian influence, traces of, in place-names, 44.
Scotland, account of the name, 40—first became a united realm, *ib.*—a survey of, in 1600, 232—re-establishment of Episcopacy in, 240—triumph of Presbyterianism, 246.
Scott, Sir Walter, of Buccleuch, rescue of Kinmont Willie and defiance of Elizabeth, 221 *et seq.*
Scrope, Lord, raid of, in 1570 upon Dumfries, 202—despatches to Lord Walsingham quoted, 207, 208—outwitted at Carlisle, 221 *et seq.*
Selgovæ, the etymology of the name, 2—the ethnography of, 4.
Semple, Gabriel, holder of the first field conventicle, 262.
Sharpe, Archbishop, severity of, against the Covenanters, 263—attack on, 271.
Shire, origin of the term as a division of Galloway, 117.
Sigurd the Stout, Lord of Galloway, 42.
Sir, the prefix, not always indicative of knighthood, 193.
Skene, W. F., references to 'Celtic Scotland' by, 3, 7, 8, 13.
Smith, Alexander, temerity of, before Archbishop Sharpe, 264.
Smuggling, prevalence of, in Galloway in last century, 321, 332.
Solway Moss, the battle of, 170.
Spottiswoode, Archbishop of Glasgow, excessive Presbyterian zeal of, 235.
Standard, the battle of the, 50, 51.
Stephen, King, war with David I., 50, 51.
Stewart, Sir William, capture of Lord Maxwell by, 210—treachery and death of, *ib.*, 211.
Stewartry, origin of the name as a division of Galloway, 117.
Stranraer, a charter granted to, in 1617 by James VI., 238.
Strathclyde, the ancient kingdom of, 35.
Surnames, examples of growth of, in Galloway, 60.
Sweetheart Abbey, founded by Devorguila, wife of John Balliol, 66.
Sydserff, Bishop of Galloway, 243, 244.
Symson, Andrew, quoted, 295.

INDEX.

"Tables," constitution of the Presbyterian, 244.
Tacitus, varying interpretations of statements by, 1, 3.
Taylor, John, the Water-Poet, quotation from, describing Scotland in 1618, 313.
Theodosius, campaign of, in Britain in 369 A.D., 22.
Thrieve, a fortalice built by Archibald the Grim, 118—besieged by King James, 139 et seq.—surrendered by Lord Nithsdale and subsequently dismantled, 249, 250.
Thurot, Admiral, defeat and death of, at Kirkmaiden, 331.
Trayle, the Priory of, built by Fergus of Galloway, 49, 53.
Tungland, a church on the Dee, built by Fergus of Galloway, 49.
Turner, Sir James, cruelty of, 266—captured by Maclellan, ib.—dismissed the service, 269—autobiography of, 270.

Uchtred, Lord of Galloway, 1161, founder of Lincluden Abbey, 54—death, 55.
Ulster, a favourite refuge for Covenanters, 265.
Union, opposition to the, in Galloway, 306.

Valentia, origin of the name, 32—the four races of, 33.
Vaus, Helen, of Barnbarroch, story of the marriage of, 201.
Verneuil, death of Douglas and his son at the battle of, 124.

Wales, the ancient extent of, 32, 33.
Walker, Helen, the original of Jeanie Deans, 323.
Wallace, Sir William, early exploits of, 74—victory at Stirling, 76—defeat at Falkirk, 77—deserted by Bruce, 85—execution, 86.
Wapinschaws, the holding of, a relic of feudalism, 230.
Welsh, John, minister of Kirkcudbright, leader of the Aberdeen Assembly in 1605, 239—banished, ib.—death, 240.
Whigamore Raid, the, 255.
Whithorn, mistaken etymology of, 7—history of the church at, 28 et seq.—the priory built by Fergus of Galloway, 48—a miracle at, 83—the Reformation and the revenues of, 230.
Wigtownshire, extracts from criminal records in reign of James IV., 156—turbulence during Moray's regency, 203—a dispute with Dumfries, 203—the feuds of the Kennedys, 228—the revenue diminished by the Reformation, 230—redistribution of synods and presbyteries by the Assembly of 1638, 245—rarity of witchcraft, 260—heavily taxed by Charles II., 262—drowning of Margaret M'Lauchlan and others, 282 et seq.—Boswell of Auchinleck, first sheriff, 328—described by Samuel Robinson, 357, 358.
William the Lion, invasion of England by, 55—pays homage to Henry II., 56.
Witchcraft, cowardice the cause of James VI.'s attitude to, 231—in Dumfriesshire and Galloway, ib.—account of certain trials at Dumfries in 1659, 259—instance of a trial in Galloway, 1698, ib.—a case at Ayr, ib.

PRINTED BY WILLIAM BLACKWOOD AND SONS.